Thailand

Christopher & Lindsey Evans

HUNTER

HUNTER PUBLISHING, INC,
130 Campus Drive, Edison, NJ 08818
☎ 732-225-1900; 800-255-0343; fax 732-417-1744
www.hunterpublishing.com

Ulysses Travel Publications
4176 Saint-Denis, Montréal, Québec
Canada H2W 2M5
☎ 514-843-9882, ext. 2232; fax 514-843-9448

Windsor Books
The Boundary, Wheatley Road, Garsington
Oxford, OX44 9EJ England
☎ 01865-361122; fax 01865-361133

ISBN 1-58843-518-0

Manufactured in the United States of America.

This and other Hunter travel guides are also available as e-books through Amazon.com, NetLibrary.com and other digital partners. For more information, e-mail us at comments@hunterpublishing.com.

Cover photo: *Hat Thram Phra Nang Beach, Krabi*,
©2006, SuperStock, Inc.
Back cover photo: *Lush gardens,* courtesy of Tohsang Khongjiam Resort
Spine: *Thailand's endless beaches and islands*

Photography courtesy of the authors
and the *Tourism Authority of Thailand* unless otherwise noted
Black-and-white line art by *Pu*

Maps by Four Seasons Info Media Co., Ltd.
Index by Wolff Index

4 3 2 1

About the Book

The tsunami that hurtled into Southeast Asia, including the southern coasts of Thailand, on December 26, 2004, was the worst natural disaster the world has known. It killed hundreds of thousands and affected the lives of millions (see *The Tsunami*, pages 1-29). We were in Phuket when the murderous waves struck, and were among the very fortunate who suffered no ill effects.

The exact number of deaths will never be known. In Thailand thousands of tourists and Thais died. The country is also home to thousands of illegal immigrants whose bodies were never claimed, and many more who would have been sucked to a watery grave, their families frightened to report them missing. Throughout Southeast Asia and beyond the total loss of life was in the hundreds of thousands. We witnessed the scenes of devastation and stood by helplessly, watching the grieving and agony of those trying to locate lost loved ones.

Throughout it all the Thais, a remarkably friendly and resilient people, retained an unbelievable dignity and desire to help others. They sought no pity. Instead we saw nothing but heroic acts of kindness and a determination to rebuild and return to a normal life.

Our work on this book was halfway complete when disaster struck. Days earlier we had visited resorts that now no longer exist. We had been on the Khao Lak strip and marveled at the luxury hotels that had been created. We returned to find the area flattened. Rubble of those fine buildings had become an early grave for hundreds. We had stood on the beaches of Phi Phi and saw some of Mother Nature's finest scenery. Now she had smashed the area from both sides and claimed hundreds of innocent lives.

Amazingly, just days after the disaster most of the southern Thai resorts were operating normally. But the world did not see that. Instead it saw the gruesome scenes of body bags and decomposed corpses. It saw the frantic faces of relatives searching for a loved one.

Through it all the Thais involved in the tourist industry took care of their personal problems and returned to work – if they were lucky enough to still have a place of employment – with a determined effort to make sure the remaining visitors enjoyed the pleasures that Thailand has to offer.

Understandably, the tourist numbers fell rapidly in the affected areas as people scurried home either hurt or horrified by what had happened. We stayed to continue our work and marveled at how quickly rubble and ruin were replaced with improved facilities. Not every area was able to recover so quickly; it is unlikely that Khao Lak will ever be the resort it was. But Phuket's hard-hit areas were soon to be ready for visitors once again.

When we began the work for this guide we had no inkling that it would be interrupted by such a catastrophe. We still intend to follow our initial plan, which was to create a book for those who seek luxury at an affordable price.

This book is one of an adventure series. But if you were expecting tough treks into the unknown at bargain prices you have bought the wrong book. While we much appreciate your purchase we suggest you close the volume now and gift wrap it as a surprise for someone else. To us, adventure means a gentle exploration or escapade, not a nightmare journey into uncharted jungles.

We believe that Thailand can provide a high degree of luxury at an affordable price. The words *mosquito net* appear now for the one and only time. We confess that we have never spent a night in Thailand without air conditioning, nor do we plan to do so. At home we do not travel on buses with chickens or goats so we don't do it when we are away. We are slightly more adventurous when it comes to food; in Thailand we try everything – well almost everything – once. And most times we come back for more. We are never far away from a television with news in the English language or a telephone that works. We enjoy getting lost as long as we are home in time for dinner and always sleep in something that resembles and feels like a bed.

To us luxury means lots of large, white fluffy towels in the bathroom. It means an ample supply of sweet-smelling lotions and soaps that are replenished daily. We relish not having not having to handle our baggage once we've lifted it from an airport carousel. We enjoy being whisked away in a limousine from the airport and not being kept waiting on a tour bus while Mrs. Brown argues about the scratches that have appeared on her brightly colored suitcases. Luxury to us is picking our favorite items from the menu and not having to flinch when the bill arrives.

At most Thai hotels you are greeted with genuine smiles. The necessary check-in formalities are conducted over a welcoming drink, while your luggage seems to find its own way to the room. These niceties, which seem to come automatically in Thailand whether you spend $50 a night or $500, are just one of the aspects that attract us, and millions of others, back to the shores of this magical kingdom. Thailand is a very foreign country with its own peculiar ways and culture. Respecting the different customs and lifestyle will make your stay here more enjoyable.

We hope that this book will give you ideas that will enhance your stay in this land of silk and smiles. If in some small way we can convert you to becoming a returning visitor then the words we have written have not been wasted.

About The Authors

Christopher Evans began his newspaper career as a copy boy in Fleet Street when it was home to the newspapers of the world. He learned from the bottom rung of the ladder how newspapers worked. His first income as a writer was as a junior reporter in northwest London, covering everything from births to burials. After three years he became news editor, the newspaper expanded, and his territory extended south of the River Thames.

At 21 he joined the London *Daily Mirror* as a sub-editor, the youngest person to hold such a position. In the middle of a bitter British winter he was lured away to the Bahamas to become editor of the country's morning newspaper, *The Nassau Guardian*.

He met Lindsey Hedger, who hailed from the same town in England, at a wedding reception in Nassau. Five months later they were married. Three children and three grandchildren later they are still together and split their time between southern Spain and Thailand.

In addition to writing travel articles and novels, Christopher was a pioneer in the cable-television industry in Florida, where he started the first pay-per-view cable channel. He owned and operated a printing company in Atlanta, Georgia which employed 150 people. And together they owned a travel agency in Atlanta, which heightened their desire to see more of the world.

Illustrations

MAPS

BLACK & WHITE DRAWINGS

Contents

The Tsunami

Force of Nature

At 9am on December 26, 2004 the western coastline of Phuket Island was battered by giant waves, resulting from an undersea earthquake near the island of Sumatra in Indonesia.

Within hours of the quake thousands of people had died. It was one of the world's biggest natural disasters. The tsunami's waves caused tremendous damage to a small part of Thailand and claimed several thousand lives but, as horrific as that was, it was minor compared to the havoc and death that occurred in other parts of Southeast Asia.

A Personal Account

We were on the island of Phuket when the tsunami hit. We had taken a couple of days off from working on this guidebook to enjoy the Christmas holidays with our three-year-old granddaughter and her mother, who were visiting us from Spain.

As we wound up our Christmas Day celebrations we had no idea of the devastation and disaster that was happening just a few hundred yards away from our rented home. We had decided not to visit the beach that morning, an incredibly lucky decision. Instead we planned to attend a Christmas pantomime that was to be staged at Phuket's English pub, The Green Man. (If you don't know about the Brits and their love of Christmas pantomimes, look in at the Simon Cabaret listing in the *Phuket* chapter, page 187.)

We were taking a leisurely breakfast at the nearby Orchid Coffee Garden when an English family arrived telling us that Nai Harn Beach had been washed away by a giant wave. They said there had been an earthquake. The girls operating the café look stunned, as did we. There was no radio or television nearby so we headed home and switched on the news. Yes, there had been an earthquake but at this point no mention of the tsunami. Then minutes later came word that giant waves had hit various coasts of the Indian Ocean.

We drove across the island and, as we reached a high point, saw hundreds of cars and motorcycles parked as their occupants looked down at Phang Nga Bay, where hundreds of boats sat safely in still water. Somehow the powerful tsunami had passed below them. As we drove down to the western beaches the first signs of the powerful battering began to appear. Outside The Boathouse the road was strewn with broken chairs, chunks of concrete and assorted debris.

Farther around Kata Beach, near the entrance to Club Med, a light pole lay across the road over a mountain of trash and rubble. A call went out that another wave was coming and people scurried to higher ground. The scores of motorcycles suddenly vanished into side streets and we turned inland and sped away. It had been a false alarm but few waited to find that out.

Hundreds of Burmese are thought to have died on boats just off Baan Nam Khem. They were moored close to shore since the Burmese thought it unlucky to be at sea when the moon was full, which is when the tsunami hit. Had they been at sea they would probably have survived.

At the Green Man the cheerfulness of Christmas had been replaced by somber faces watching a giant TV screen as, slowly, the dreadful drama unfolded. Contact with much of the island was lost and many feared the worst. The Boxing Day pantomime was replaced by TV pictures from CNN and BBC World, and everyone tried to contact friends to find out what was happening. Just hours after the tsunami hit nobody here had any idea of the magnitude of the disaster. It was just a normal hot Sunday afternoon. Children enjoyed the bounce house that had been inflated for the holiday. Their parents sipped mulled wine unaware that within a mile in any direction hundreds lay dead on the beaches or had been sucked out to sea by the vicious tsunami.

As new faces arrived an inkling of the gravity of the disaster began to unfold. The new arrivals told of escaping from hotels when water cascaded into their rooms. They had lost everything. The sound of police and ambulance sirens was heard over the children at play. We headed home feeling almost guilty that we were all safe and content relaxing in the swimming pool.

Many tourists who were offered alternative accommodation at other beachfront hotels refused it, opting to take shelter at the Phuket Provincial Hall.

Here at the southern end of Phuket nothing had changed and we sent e-mails to our nearest and dearest saying all was well. We telephoned as well. Never once did we lose contact with the outside world. Our power and water supplies remained constant and we slept uneasily, aware of the drama that was unfolding around us but miraculously leaving us safe and secure.

A gutsy waitress at a Kata resort not only pulled one of the beach chair attendants from the water, but she screamed at workers to evacuate the underground kitchens. She was one of the last to leave the resort before a mighty wave devastated the ground floor. She helped elder guests to higher ground and fortunately no employees or clients were hurt. She said later, "I was very lucky." So were the people she saved.

The Aftermath

It was not until New Year's Eve that we really learned the true severity of the damage to Thailand. It was then that rescue workers were able to reach Khao Lak, the coastal area just north of Phuket, to discover more than four thousand bodies. Just a few weeks earlier we had toured this area and marveled at the new resorts that were preparing for the Christmas onslaught of guests. For many of the resorts it would be the first Christmas of operation. And for many of them it would also be their last. Today the death toll stands at 4,510 (2,092 Thai, 2,230 foreigners and 188 of unknown nationality). A total of 9,849 were reported injured and 6,475 people are listed as missing. Officials warned that the fatality figures account only for bodies recovered. Actual number of deaths is far higher as many people would have been sucked out to sea by the undertow and it is unlikely their bodies will ever be recovered.

Our days between Christmas and the New Year were filled with sadness at the distress of others. Our own lives remained untouched. We kept a dental appointment at the Bangkok Phuket Hospital, which we had visited two days before the tsunami

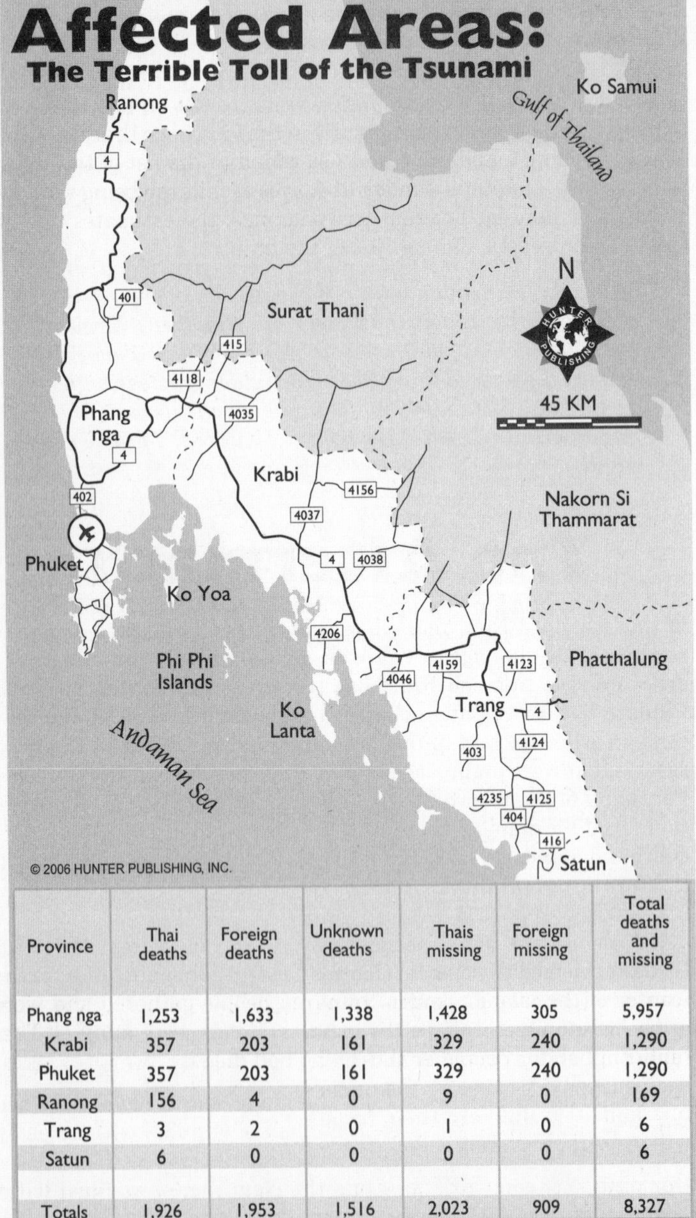

Province	Thai deaths	Foreign deaths	Unknown deaths	Thais missing	Foreign missing	Total deaths and missing
Phang nga	1,253	1,633	1,338	1,428	305	5,957
Krabi	357	203	161	329	240	1,290
Phuket	357	203	161	329	240	1,290
Ranong	156	4	0	9	0	169
Trang	3	2	0	1	0	6
Satun	6	0	0	0	0	6
Totals	1,926	1,953	1,516	2,023	909	8,327

struck. Then, we noted its spacious public areas and wide halls. Now those areas were filled with mattresses providing some comfort for the injured who lay dazed and bandaged. Saddest sight of all was in the entrance lobby where the walls were covered by photos and pictures of children from around the world. They had been placed there by parents and family in the vain hope that the young ones would be found alive and not added to the list of those lost. There were numerous wonderful stories of children being reunited with their families but far more sad ones; the estimates put the loss of children as high as 30% of the total.

> *Patong Mayor Pian Keesin had a lucky escape. He was standing in front of his hotel, the Patong Bay Garden Resort, when the first wave hit. He was carried some 200 meters before managing to hold onto a tree. He said some of the debris being washed away must have weighted as much as two tons. He hoped that one benefit from the disaster might be that redevelopment would be made strictly according to the town's planning codes. He also told of the difficulty convincing municipal workers that it was safe to begin the massive cleanup that Patong needed. He said he had offered as much as 10,000 Baht an hour to get road sweeping trucks into action but initially nobody wanted the work. A day later that changed and the massive cleanup began.*

New Year's Eve was not the lively event that Phuket is noted for. Several of the Patong bars had opened, though attendance was at a minimum, and those resorts that were still open attempted a fun evening for the guests who remained. Many had left the island before the festivities and sadly so many others were lost. Prime Minister Thaksin Shinawatra, who came to Phuket soon after the tsunami struck, had said he was not going to take part in any New Year celebrations and many of his countrymen followed his lead.

The most moving event of the day was a special memorial service held at the recently opened Central Festival Shopping Mall in the center of the island. Several hundred people gathered and were given white roses and yellow candles. Songs were sung in Thai and English to remember those who had died.

Since the devastating event, all the major stores have remained open as usual. There has been no lack of supplies and no panic buying. Prices at the stores and from street vendors have remained unchanged. The only price gouging we have heard of is from some small hotels in resort areas not affected by the tsunami that upped the rates for their few remaining rooms. Travel agents were quick to announce they were not going to act for those properties.

> *An Englishman living in Chalong returned home on Boxing Day night and told his family to put all their clothes and shoes in two piles. He then took one of the piles, together with half of the items in his kitchen and an assortment of toys to Khao Lak. "Lots of people there had nothing. At least we've still got 50%," he explained.*

There was looting initially along Patong Beach and police immediately arrested the culprits, who were jailed without bail as a deterrent to others. There were more Burmese arrested than Thais.

After the candlelight service at Central Festival Mall, we joined the New Year festivities at Mimmi's restaurant close to our home. Pleasant as it was, the aura of missing friends and grieving neighbors was apparent. At midnight just a few guests remained. They joined with the restaurant staff in a rare show of emotion wishing each other a safe 2005. Just a few fireworks could be seen the sky but all over the island Chinese firecrackers were set off in the belief they would dispel bad luck.

On New Year's Day we decided to visit other parts of the island to see first-hand what damage had been done. Our first stop was at The Boathouse on Kata Beach. Damage to the ground floor had been substantial but the cleanup was well underway and everyone was confident of reopening within two weeks. The accommodation on the second and third floors was ready for occupancy but the ground floor needed a lot of work. Best news, however, was that no member of staff or guest was killed or even injured.

The story was not so happy farther along the beach at the larger Kata Beach resorts, where several guests had been lost to the tsunami. Most of the resorts were open as were those farther north at Karon.

Our journey north became more depressing as we saw the beachfront at Patong. Despite the days of clean-up the area was still suffering under a mountain of debris. Trees that once provided shade for the beach were uprooted and dying. We understood now why so many people had been so badly injured. The large planks of wood and rubble would have been hurled at buildings where bodies hid or thrown at victims as they strived to beat the torturous currents. Like so many places on the island the damage only extended a f yards into the side streets.

Along the roads we spotted divers working in canals and searching for additional bodies, and everywhere there w eerie sense of thankfulness from those who had been spared unspoken condolences for those who mourned the missing.

> *A young Karon hairdresser and her neighbors put together 200 food parcels, collected all the money they could muster and split it between the boxes, added clothes, loaded the relief packages into pickups and cars and took them to the devastated victims in villages around Khao Lak.*

Worst hit along the stretch was Kamala Beach, where bungalows and cabins once faced the sea. They were gone as were many of their occupants. In one area the need for cleanup was minimal. The tsunami had done its own vacuuming. Farther along, soldiers in fatigues worked with military land-moving equipment to remove broken buildings and clear the roads.

Happily at Surin Beach, hardly touched by the tidal torrent, it was business as usual. Tourists stretched out on sun loungers while the Thai vendors along the beach edge continued their trades providing refreshment as the classic beach massages.

On Sunday, a week after the tsunami, we walked along Kata Beach. It was quiet and peaceful. The sea was shamefully calm and the beach incredibly clean and sparkling in the early morning sun. Seven days earlier, morning swimmers and sunbathers would have been tossed around like matchsticks in a whirlwind when the tsunami hit. A few survived with cuts and bruises, others had broken bones as they were thrown against the sea wall or onto the nearby road. Children unable to grip onto anything would have been sucked to a watery grave. Again we felt the pangs of guilt that we were safe enjoying the best that Mother Nature could afford and not a victim of her deadliest deed.

The news from elsewhere continued grim. On the Phi Phi islands 99 more bodies were found at a sewage farm. They were near a viewing platform where they had probably fled as the waves shattered the tiny island. Prime Minister Thaksin Shinawatra had visited the islands and said he felt they could recover despite the fact that so many resorts there had been destroyed. He said the infrastructure was sound. He wasn't so optimistic about Khao Lak, the coastal area to our north. There rescue work continued and bodies were still being found trapped in some of the resorts. The death toll in Khao Lak now totaled 3,854, over 2,000 of them tourists, mostly from Scandinavia. Sweden, Finland and Norway held an official day of mourning for the victims of the tsunamis. It was estimated that more than 1,000 Norwegians had died throughout Southeast Asia, making it the biggest loss of Norwegian lives in peacetime in history.

[illegible] government is considering plans for building a tsunami [illegible]ial, at a cost of two billion Baht. The proposal calls for a [illegible]h-tech dome showing the names of all those known to have died, to be built in the sea just off Bang Niang Beach in Khao Lak.

Recovery

Rescue and recovery work in Khao Lak was horrendous. The stench of week-old corpses in the tropical heat was sickening. Yet the workers toiled 'round the clock in the vain hope that someone might be found alive. Several thousand low-security prisoners were freed from jail to help with the massive cleanup. In return for their help the convicts were promised that their sentences would be cut.

In Phuket things were starting to return to normal. Inbound flights brought doctors to help at the hospitals. The major need was forensic experts who could help catalogue the corpses and take DNA samples. The government was providing endless cold storage containers so that bodies could be stored in the hope that relatives could reclaim them and provide funerals.

Consular offices from around the world set up help centers around the island to assist their respective countrymen. Twenty-one European countries reported lives lost or people missing. Altogether 41 countries were represented.

US Secretary of State Colin Powell flew in with Florida Governor Jeb Bush, the President's brother. Both pledged US support for the development of a tsunami warning system for the Indian Ocean, offered condolences to the victims and visited some of the stricken areas. Powell said, "I'd like to express our condolences to the Thai people, for the Thais who were lost, and also to the people of other nations who are here looking for their loved ones among those who are still missing." Bush praised the rescue teams and relief workers he said they were "true heroes, working 24 hours a day without asking for anything in return."

Volunteer divers with the help of local dive centers and Thailand's Department of Marine and Coastal Resources (DMCR) cleared debris away from coral beds off Patong, Kata and Karon beaches and also from islands in Krabi. They reported that although some coral had been damaged most was still in good condition. Ironically, the meeting point for divers undertaking the work off Patong was at the Seven Dolphins Memorial fountain, where the statue of dolphins had stood before the tsunami destroyed it.

Thailand's elephants, an important national symbol of strength having fought in ancient wars, were at work helping clear rubble and debris. An amazing story was told of a group of tourists taking an early morning elephant trek in Khao Lak. The elephant had sensed the impending tsunami and stampeded to higher ground. The riders were saved.

The true nature of the Thais and their desire to please others has been a shining light in a very gloomy period. Endless stories of kindness and caring are being told everywhere on the island and in the newspaper columns around the world.

> *After the second wave hit Kata Beach the water in the bay was rough and full of floating debris. Swimmers caught out in the sea were having a difficult time getting back to shore. Operators of personal watercraft along the beach immediately went to the rescue. Their bravery saved lives and we, normally critical of those waterborne craft, commend the operators for their heroic deeds.*

Two weeks after the disaster, bodies were still being discovered. British Foreign Secretary Jack Straw and a team of rescue workers from the UK visited the area of Khao Lak. They all commented that the scenes of devastation, destruction and death are like nothing they have seen before. And these are people who have worked in the aftermath of some horrendous events in Britain. Straw said that some 50 British were confirmed dead, but back in Britain the Foreign Office said there were still several thousand tourists in Southeast Asia who were not accounted for. Britons were told not to come to Thailand in search of family or friends. Bodies that were being discovered were unrecognizable and the only hope of identifying them was by taking DNA samples.

In the first phase of recovery, the economic impact started to show. Hotels not damaged in any way by the tsunami were reporting they had few guests. This is normally high season with occupancy rates between 80 and 90%. Today several major resorts admitted they were down to levels of occupancy as low as 5%. And every hotel we checked had lowered its prices to low-season rates in a futile attempt to attract more visitors.

At harbors and piers around Phang Nga hundreds of tourist boats lay idle. Normally they would be ferrying people to Phi Phi Island or making diving trips. Today nobody wanted to take a journey anywhere.

Air Asia, the no-frills air carrier, suspended its daily service linking Phuket with Singapore saying it had no idea when that service might be resumed. In recent days the airline had been operating with as few as three passengers.

Convoys continued from Phuket to Khao Lak taking supplies to some 400 families who had been rendered homeless. Now word was coming from Khao Lak that the resorts should never have been built in the first place. Thais complained that were bad spirits in the area and they would not want to work there again. Later those comments were forgotten. The Thais we spoke to later want the resorts rebuilt so that they could return to work.

Back in Phuket many of the local fishermen who had lost everything to the tsunami made vain attempts to get help from government offices to get their boats repaired. Some said they wanted to return to work. Others said they would never venture onto the water again. Government officials paid out more than 26 million Baht to help the facilities cope with the financial burden of treating victims. The fishermen complained that tourists were getting the attention and not the locals.

A Labor Department survey of Phuket showed 1,500 workplaces had suffered damage and 13,000 people were out of work.

> *As horrendous as the tsunami was, there were no dire financial consequences to Thailand's economy. The Bank of Thailand's Monetary Policy Committee reduced its economic growth forecast for 2005 by only 0.3% age points estimating growth would be between 5.25% and 6.75%. Its projections for 2006 were set at between 5.5% and 7%. According to the World Travel and Tourism Council (WTC), the tsunami cost Thailand $1.2 billion and the loss of 95,000 jobs.*

The football field at Phuket's Saphan Hin was the venue for a dramatic memorial service. The ceremony started with Islamic, Christian and Buddhist services, followed by condolence speeches. Most of the 10,000-strong audience was dressed in white, each holding a glass lantern containing a single candle. At sunset a light was passed from candle to candle until all the candles were lit and the stadium was filled with a yellow glow. Dozens of balloons were also released, as a traditional way of guiding the souls of the departed in the afterlife.

■ Spirit of Survival

Two weeks after the tsunami struck it was Children's Day in Thailand, a day when younger ones are showered with presents and treated to special trips. While so many youngsters in the nation beamed with joy there were hundreds who faced their first Children's Day without a mother, father or both. At the temporary camp set up north of Khao Lak some 300 youngsters orphaned by the disaster awoke to find games and toys that volunteers had provided in the hope of bringing some brightness to their dismal young lives. The really young seemed to enjoy themselves but the older ones lacked enthusiasm for fun. Many used the crayons and paper to draw depressing pictures of the huge waves that had left their little lives in a shambles. Other sat silently gazing into space not understanding what had happened.

Some cheering news from the World Tourism Organization (WTO) that announced the tsunami would have only limited impact on world tourism. Among the reasons given was that the destinations hit only represented 3% of world tourist arrivals, and that the afflicted had been confined to a few coastal resorts in each country. At the same time, the WTO announced it would hold an extraordinary session of the Executive Council of the organization in Phuket. In a statement the WTO said, "To everybody's pleasant surprise, Phuket, which has been severely affected by the recent unfortunate disaster in the Indian Ocean, is fast recovering from the damage caused by the tsunami. Things are returning to normalcy at an unbelievable pace. It is most heartening to note that a large number of tourists have insisted on staying on in Phuket to continue with their holidays, thus contributing to the early recovery of tourism on the island."

Many European tourists who are staying on are concerned about the holiday insurance. Many insurance companies do not honor claims when the home countries of the travelers issue travel advisory warnings. Such warnings were issued by the French Foreign Affairs department and the British Foreign and Commonwealth Office. The French lifted its warning with this notice about Phuket, "Daily life and the ordinary activities continue in a normal manner in most of the island. Many hotels, restaurants and dive centers are operating as usual. The situation is the same in Krabi. There are no more risks of appearance of infectious diseases. It is therefore completely possible to go into these areas safely."

It wasn't so simple for Britons. On its Website the Foreign Office advised against all but essential travel to affected resorts and towns along Thailand's west coast, in particular Phuket, Krabi and Khao Lak. "The infrastructure and public services are severely disrupted," the warning said. Later, during the visit of Foreign Minister Jack Straw, the wording was changed to say that Phuket was safe to visit. Then the original wording reappeared. Jack Straw was asked why the wording had been changed since he was in Phuket and could see for himself that things were operating normally. He said he would consult with Cabinet colleagues later. Meanwhile the British were left wondering if their holiday insurance was valid or not.

It was some weeks later before the US and Australian authorities modified their travel advisories, which had strongly warned against travel to the tsunami-hit areas.

Fifteen days after the tsunami hit, the authorities in Patong said that all the debris had been cleared from the streets of Patong and dumped in a disused tin mine. Chief Administration officer of Patong, Phunsak Naksena, said the town now had the opportunity to clear the illegal buildings along the beachfront, and he was waiting for the Tourism Authority of Thailand's plan for how the Patong of the future would look.

> *The FantaSea tourist attraction in Kamala closed for a week in January to undertake repairs caused by the tsunami. It reported a tremendous drop in visitors. Normally in high season it would have hosted over 3,000 people daily; instead, it was averaging just 15.*

It was almost a month after the tsunami hit that we ventured back to Khao Lak to see for ourselves what was left of the area. The scenes were incredible. Most of the area, where we had recently visited plush new resorts, was flattened. It was impossible to get our bearings. Where once streets and small shops had stood there was nothing but a sandy plateau. On higher knolls the elaborate entrances to swanky hotels still remained. Behind those just an occasional skeletal shell of a building stood like the victim of a bomb blast, with all its windows and interiors sucked away.

It seemed impossible but it only took moments to turn Thailand's up-and-coming Riviera into a massive graveyard. We exchanged no words but we both thought how horrible those moments would have been as families enjoying their Christmas holidays in the tropical sun suddenly perished. The tanned bodies would have been hurled to their deaths across the land before us or sucked into the Andaman Sea, now a placid stretch of water that cruelly had claimed so many lives.

And it wasn't only the tourists. The hotel workers, the Burmese gardeners, the pool attendants or the waiters serving breakfast coffee had no hope of surviving. Miraculously, some did, but there were precious few. Farther along the coast the tiny Thai villages that had just begun to benefit from the influx of tourism were devastated. Families had been split apart. Orphans were created. Homes had been destroyed and dreams of a better future gone for ever.

As we retreated from the scenes of disaster thousands of bodies were still waiting to be identified in makeshift mortuaries. Families still clung to the useless hope that a loved one would return. We learned today that Wachira, the artist who was helping us with maps for this guidebook was one of the missing. He had come to Khao Lak on Christmas Day to meet with a client. His car had been found. He had not. For weeks his colleagues in Phuket had been telling us that we were waiting for him to come back. We wrongly assumed he came here after the tsunami. It was only now, a month later, that we learned the horrible truth.

There were a couple of incidents that we felt were ill timed. The first involved a five-star resort in Phuket that had suffered no ill effects from the killer waves. The general manager offered a "special deal" to the travel trade of $170 for a three-night stay. He said he was offering this bargain to let travel agents see for themselves how much of Phuket was operating normally. He said he was concerned for those people who worked nearby the hotel, both the tuk-tuk and taxi drivers and the street traders. The fact is that most travel agents expect, and get, rooms for nothing or at large discounts. Also all hotels on the island, including his, had so many cancellations they would all have willingly matched or undercut his special.

The second incident occurred at Pattaya just a few hours after the tsunami hit. A hotel complex smugly announced that their operation was not affected, it was on high ground, and that they had plenty of rooms available and holidaymakers should come there. The announcement said the sun was shining at Pattaya. It was also shining on those devastated areas where thousands of dead bodies were lying.

Back in Phuket, the island, normally choked with tourists in high season, was quiet and subdued. The major hotels had predicted occupancy to exceed 80% before the tsunami. Now many of them were down to single-digit occupancy. Most hotels kept as many employees working as possible. Some used the time to give additional training. Salaries were way below what they would have been normally during this season since there were no service charges or tips to share. We were delighted to learn that many former hotel clients sent money to the hotels asking that it be shared by the employees. At the beginning of February a limited number of beach chairs were allowed on Patong Beach. The rental operators had fought for them to be returned, saying that they were a necessity for tourists. Unfortunately when we drove along the front only a few of the chairs were occupied. Initially the government had banned chairs completely, allowing only plastic mats and limiting the number of umbrellas to 2,000 (as opposed to the 7,000 that had been in use prior to the tsunami). New rules in effect state the chairs have to be plastic and not the heavy wooden ones that were, according to the government, responsible for many of the tsunami deaths, and there can only be a single row.

And it wasn't just those who gained their livelihood from working on the beach who were complaining. Plans to make Patong Beach a more attractive area included banning the rental car businesses from the beachfront road. This prompted a 300-vehicle protest rally by business owners opposed to the ban. The official response was that each beachfront business would be considered on its own merits. "The plan for a new Patong is flexible and can be adjusted," the protesters were told. "There is scope in it for small operators to have their businesses on the beach or nearby."

The protests were forgotten two nights later when the Phuket Provincial Administration Organization (OrBorJor) organized a very touching "Light up Patong" ceremony; over 100,000 candles were lit and placed along three kilometers of Patong Beach, in memory of the victims of the tsunami. OrBorJor plans to make the ceremony an annual event.

A special center for autistic children will be built in Phuket as a memorial to tsunami victim Bhumi Jensen, the 21-year-old grandson of King Bhumibol Adulyadej. The five-story building is expected to be in operation in 2007. Bhumi Jensen had been JetSkiing at Khao Lak when the tsunami hit. His body was recovered close to the resort when he had been staying with his mother, Princess Ubol Ratana Rajakanya. The Princess returned to the area in March and distributed gift bags to 200 students whose lives had been affected by the tsunami. She opened a memorial exhibition about her son's life at Loma Park in Patong. She told the young gathering that her visit was intended to inspire survivors and encourage them to make the region an even better place than it was before the disaster.

The World Tourism Organization (WTO) held an emergency session in Phuket in an effort to help tsunami-hit areas recover. Main thrust of the meeting attended by some 200 delegates was to convince travelers that the areas were safe to visit and everything was operating normally. Unfortunately, at the same time, Thai Airways announced cuts in its services to Phuket. Flights from Australia, Japan, Taipei and Hong Kong will fly direct to Bangkok and no longer stop at the island, and two early morning flights from Bangkok to Phuket, which connect with many overnight services from Europe, were cancelled. A spokesman said he hoped that the cuts were a temporary measure.

Offsetting that was news from **Tiger Airways**, the no-frills airline operating out of Singapore, that their special promotional fare, under 10 Singapore dollars (240 Baht), was attracting a lot of demand. The airline had put together packages with several Phuket hotels and only days after the special was announced it had 2,000 bookings. The airline offered 20,000 seats at the low fare. Another Singapore-based carrier, **SilkAir**, also offered packages for travelers to Phuket with deals starting at 2,400 Baht for three days and two nights. The price included airfare, accommodation, breakfast and airport transfers.

Prime Minister Thaksin Shinawatra promised that Thailand would have a tsunami early-warning system, based on seismic data alone, by mid-2005. He said the system would warn of any impending tsunami threat through radio networks and would serve as a stopgap measure while the planned international early-warning system was being developed. Mr. Thaksin said the international warning system would be more accurate, as it would operate automatically using data taken directly from the sea.

Deputy Prime Minister Suwat Liptapanlop visited Phuket and said that every year the government would invite tourists who lived through the tsunami, and relatives of the victims, to come to Phuket for a memorial ceremony. He said the government planned to open a tsunami museum to educate visitors about the dangers of the giant waves. Mr. Suwat, responsible for overseeing the recovery of tourism in the area, reported that only 13,000 of the island's 53,000 rooms had sustained damage.

Rebuilding

Our Day Of Giving

By the middle of February Phuket was full of volunteer aid workers falling over each other. The numbers were growing at such a rate that during the Chinese New Year festivities the immigration department insisted that charity workers should get work permits. Those who did not comply with the law would face large fines and even jail terms.

A trip was arranged, the brainchild of Jarinee Thongmool, front-office manager of Phuket's Boathouse Resort. She knew we were anxious to do something to help. Two guests from The Boathouse, Peter Lugg and Graham Lane, had arrived from Plymouth, England. They had brought money from customers and friends in England who wanted to place it in the right hands.

Jarinee knew there were villages in the Khao Lak area, north of Phuket, which had been totally destroyed. The survivors were existing in makeshift camps. They had shelter and food and more clothes and shoes than they would ever need. The one thing they didn't have was cash. We decided this was the opportunity we had been looking for. We sent e-mails to friends in the US, England and Spain telling them of our plan and within minutes the money was promised.

Early Friday morning six of us set out – Lindsey and I, the two men from Plymouth and Jarinee and her husband Sanit, a tour-car owner who was to be our driver for the day. Our first stop was at ATMs to gather as much cash as we could. As fast as deposits were made to our accounts in the US and UK we were withdrawing them. The wonder of the Internet, and Internet banking, meant that donations were made halfway across the world and just hours later the cash was in the hands of the deprived.

We passed the devastated resorts of Khao Lak and looked for the village of Bang Sak. It didn't exist any more. There were a few foundations standing but nothing to show that it was once a village. Roads, homes and shops were all gone. Many of those who had survived had moved to a temporary camp inland from the village. The turning for that was marked and that was our only clue that Bang Sak had ever existed.

The road to the camp passed through lush countryside and jungle; if you have to live in a temporary camp there are certainly worse places. The camp was home to 46 families, which meant that over 200 people were living here. They had lost not only their homes and all their possessions in the tsunami but 30 of their relatives or neighbors had perished. Their living quarters were huts on stilts that had been provided by the King's granddaughter, Princess Pa, in collaboration with the Thai Red Cross.

It was a pleasant but eerie welcome we got from the camp dwellers as they showed how they were attempting to make a pleasant place to live. Most were now out of work. Those who were fisherman had lost their boats. Those who tended the shrimp farms had lost the tanks. Farmers close to the coast had lost their crops. The hotels and resorts where many worked no longer existed and the shopkeepers no longer had shops. As we toured the tiny camp the men were busy making platforms that would serve as community meeting spots. Everywhere was incredibly neat and clean. There was no sign of litter and the cooking utensils and crockery we saw all sparkled in the bright sunlight. Good clean water was available in a stream and at the head of the camp a waterfall disgorged into a pool where several of the youngsters were swimming. Anyone expecting to find these villagers living in squalor would be mistaken. These people may have lost everything but they still had their dignity and they still maintained a high standard of hygiene and cleanliness.

The women were learning the art of weaving baskets. Lessons had only started the day before and so far only three baskets had been produced, which were offered to Lindsey. When she offered to buy all three the smiles on the group of women were memorable. The price asked was 50 Baht a basket, a little over $1, and for once there was no haggling about price. Lindsey gladly handed over 200 Baht, and there were further smiles when Lindsey said she didn't want any change.

These survivors were well organized. They had set up an office where the names and numbers of the families living in the camp were recorded. The families were summoned to the office and as each family name was called the head of the family came forward, gave the customary Thai wai, hands in prayer position and head bowed, and accepted the envelope. When all 46 envelopes had been handed out I was asked to speak. Another dreaded experience. There was silence as my words were translated. I said how sad it was to see their village destroyed and so many of its inhabitants lost. I explained where the money had come from and hoped that one day there would be a new village and a good life for all of them.

We had decided earlier to change our original plan of giving 300 Baht per family to 1,000 Baht. This is less than $25, but for people with nothing it was like a fortune. As the applause rang out I was desperate to leave. But instead we were shown around the area. So many people tried to say "thank you" in English, and the smiles of gratitude will always be treasured. We declined an offer of lunch and headed off to find the village of Ban Nam Khem and the school that survived the tsunami.

At the Ban Nam Khem school the headmaster explained how the village had been lost and with it so many lives. Fortunately the tsunami came on Sunday when the school was closed, and many of its pupils were in areas not affected by the waves.

He now had 400 pupils, and of those 100 were in great need of help. It was decided that we would have enough money to give each of the children 200 Baht, a little over $4, which he assured us would be taken to their foster homes. We had no reason to doubt it. There was certainly nowhere the children could spend the money. The remaining money we had was donated to the school meal fund. It would provide lunches for those without money for several weeks.

While he organized the children into the school hall we drove around the remains of the village. It was incredible just how much damage could be caused in such a short space of time. One large boat had been carried a good half-kilometer inland and had come to rest on someone's front porch. It was impressive to see how quickly new housing, basic as it was, was being constructed by the Thai Army. They had set up The Army Café where food was available free of charge to anyone, including us. Again we declined.

One hundred Thai children, resplendent in their school uniforms, sat on the floor in front of me. They were all smiling, silent and waiting for me to speak. Why they were all smiling is hard to know. These were children whose village, 32 days earlier, was wiped out by the tsunami. The vicious waves had claimed the lives of many of their parents, their school friends and neighbors – more than half of the 3,000 people who had lived here were now dead. Many of the victims were never found. Some may be among the hundreds that have yet to be identified, lying in makeshift morgues undergoing DNA testing.

Outside, the area between the school and the beach was flattened. Before the tsunami there had been homes where many of these youngsters once lived. Today there was nothing but rubble and the occasional tree. Dozens of fishing boats used by their fathers lay broken on the sands. Home for these children now was either with relatives whose homes farther inland had been spared or in one of the numerous temporary camps. Yet they were smiling and waiting for me to speak.

"*Sawadee krup*," I spluttered the two words of Thai greeting, about all I knew in the language. The greeting was returned loudly and proudly. Tears welled in my eyes. I reverted to English and with the aid of Jarinee, my friend and interpreter, I told that we had come to see their school and village. I explained that we had with us a present for each of them that had been given to us by friends in America and Europe. I made comments about coming back another day to see how their lives had improved and then the children all came up to us and proudly accepted the 200 Baht we gave each one.

This was the most distressing part of a difficult and dramatic day when we sought out families who were in many ways the forgotten victims of the tsunami. In many ways the tourists in the expensive resorts along the coast had been the focus of attention. The small villages dotted along the coast did not get much attention.

With the smiles of gratitude still fresh in our minds and the words of thanks still ringing in our ears, we drove the 200 kilometers back to Phuket, where we escaped into the luxury of our air conditioned hotel room. The people we had visited today felt lucky as they spent another tropical night cramped inside temporary housing in the jungle. But we were the lucky ones. We had experienced the satisfaction of being able to contribute something.

As we were making our rounds and putting cash into the hands of the survivors, Thai Prime Minister, **Thaksin Shinawatra**, and his ministers were holding meetings in Phuket and in Phang Nga province, the province we were currently in, trying to find a way to speed up getting aid to the homeless. We passed his motorcade during our journey.

At one stop Mr. Thaksin told ministers and governors to find a way through the red tape. He said, "Rules and regulations have to be relaxed if not adjusted. This is not a normal situation and we have to work it out with affected groups rather than go by the book." Later it in the day it was announced that payments to some fishermen who had lost their boats were to begin in about three weeks.

While we were visiting the camps and schools in Khao Lak, the Thai Royal Navy was holding a solemn ceremony eight kilometers out at sea. The aircraft carrier HTMS *Chakri Naruebeth* led a flotilla of nine other navy ships to float wreaths on the water in memory of those lost in the tsunami. Government officials and diplomats from many of the nations who had suffered losses were among those on board.

The Chinese New Year celebrations in Phuket are linked with the annual old Phuket festival. This year the festivities were held in early February. It was less than two months since the tsunami had struck but Phuket City managed to celebrate in fine style, with parades packed with colorfully attired youngsters and an elaborate series of Chinese cultural shows. Many of those taking part had suffered in some way. Some would have lost family and friends, possibly their homes, and almost certainly all would be suffering from lower incomes. But we saw no tears, just brave faces welcoming the year of the rooster.

Sirey Island

During the celebrations we visited Sirey Island, the islet just east of Phuket City. The tsunami had caused some damage but it was good to see that the local gypsy village was operating in its normal ramshackle fashion. There had been no loss of life, as the inhabitants claim they got a warning from nature. They say ants were scampering inland and that was an indication that something dire was about to happen. The villagers followed the tiny creatures to higher ground before the giant waves arrived. Some of their skimpy homes were destroyed and they lost several of their fishing boats. Today the fishermen were busy building new boats and repairing others. Damaged homes were being hammered back into shape with nails, wood and corrugated tin. It was good to see several volunteers, including some *farangs*, lending a hand.

> **AUTHOR'S NOTE:** *This is the first time we have used the word "farang" in the book, but it won't be the last. Originally it meant foreigners from France, but today it applies to any Westerner or non-Asian person.*

Farther around the island we were amazed to see how many new homes, some of them palatial, were under construction. Two local attractions, the abalone farm and the Island Hopper operation (see page 209), were still intact and operating as normal, except there were very few visitors at either spot. One pleasant plus was that the beaches around the island looked a great deal cleaner and the sea much clearer, thanks no doubt to the powerful tsunami.

Ko Khao

Two weeks after our visit to Khao Lak we made a trip to the island of Ko Khao, to distribute the donations we had received since our prior visit, when we handed out cash to those who had suffered so horribly. It was our first time on this island, which had been poised to enter the 21st century when the killer waves struck in the most devastating fashion. Not only were the coastal regions hit but the waves cut weird paths inland across grassy knolls, and sought out and flattened homes, leaving land close by untouched.

Until the resorts began to appearing on the island, the only industry was farming or fishing. The land is not as fertile as the mainland and its arid and sandy soil limited the farming to cashew nuts, coconuts, jack fruit and pineapples. Rubber trees grow at the base of the mountain. The island, 17 kilometers in length and three kilometers at its widest point, did have large green gardens that were wiped out by the tsunami. Its freshwater lakes are now contaminated with salt water, which will surely injure irrigation of the interior. The island, entirely Buddhist, was home to more than 300 families.

The incredible stories of the island and the tsunami began when we took the ferry across the narrow stretch of water from the village of Baan Nam Khem, south of Takuapa. The ferry itself had been mid-stream when the giant waves sped down between the island and the mainland. The ferry was washed rapidly north with a few passengers and motorcycles. When it returned after the waves had abated it was laden with survivors who had been washed away. The villagers say the ferry saved 200 lives.

Just as amazing was the story of the giant tree that graces the ferry arrival point. We admired its splendor, and learned that 100 islanders had scrambled up its trunk and had held onto its branches as the waves sucked away the surrounding buildings. Today a handmade ladder was attached to the tree, a recent addition, and put there in case of future problems.

As we moved across the island stories of survival were replaced by grim scenes of devastation and death. Little had been heard about the island since no foreigners died here. The few that were staying at the Andaman Princess Resort had been warned by a sister hotel in Phuket of the upcoming Tsunami and had fled to the island's tiny mountain. Many ran the long distance while others were piled into the back of pickup trucks.

Mongkol Inchaun is just one of millions whose lives were dramatically changed by the tsunami. Mongkol, a native of the island, had been in Phuket buying supplies for his soon-to-be-opened restaurant when news of the tsunami reached him. Communications to the island were downed and he sped back to find his home wrecked and his restaurant in ruins. A lone bathroom fitting and the remnants of a wall were all that remained of the restaurant. The walls of his home were still standing but all around the building dozens of lifeless bodies lay in pools of water that the tsunami had left. His mother was safe. When the first waves came she scrambled through the kitchen window and onto the roof of the house. There she found some neighbors who had swum their way from their homes closer to the beach. Together they watched the giant waves slam into the home below them, taking out windows, doors and all the contents and bringing with them the bodies of neighbors and friends who had been overpowered by the massive force of water.

Today the survivors of one of the island's five villages gathered in their camp as we arrived with desperately needed money. It was a much older group than we had encountered at other camps. Many would have been grandparents. Many had lost family members. All had lost their homes and everything that they contained. They sat quietly and heard how the money we had brought had been sent from farangs in foreign lands.

As each family member stepped forward to receive the welcome cash, everyone politely clapped. You could sense the feeling of gratitude. It was one step forward for everyone who had suffered so much. Later, as we looked at their temporary homes, everyone was anxious to talk. Our friends acted as translators as everyone told their version of the tsunami horror. Nobody complained. They just wanted us to know they were grateful for being spared, grateful for our visit, and sustained by their desire to rebuild their villages and their lives.

It is impossible to know just how many islanders were lost here. Best estimates put the total at over 300. There were numerous workers, construction crews and hotel staff, employed at the soon-to-be-opened Khao Lak Orchid Resort, who were not registered on the island; no one can say how many. Many bodies of villagers were recovered, many more were not. There is still a possibility that bodies are trapped below the new ponds the tsunami created.

The evening after the tsunami hit, the homeless spent the night in one of the island's two temples or crossed to the mainland to seek refuge with family or friends. Within days temporary homes were built by the army where now they're trying to rebuild their lives.

Mongkol, like many of his friends, had sought employment on the mainland. He had succeeded well in the better resorts on Phuket and saved money to return to his island and build the first true international restaurant there. We had met him years earlier when he was a receptionist at one of Phuket's premier hotels. Incredibly he remembered us and our names. He was preparing to open for business in 2005; at the same time the new resorts on the island would have been operating providing him with clientele. Now his dream lies in ruins and the resorts need to be rebuilt. The upmarket Orchid Resort had luxury bungalows built on the beach. All of those were washed away. The main hotel block was severely damaged and the lavish landscaping erased. The main buildings of the nearby Andaman Princess, with its still gleaming green tiled roofs, withstood the force of the water but the interior was ripped apart.

Mongkol still dreams of having his own restaurant on his native island. How he'll achieve his goal is still unknown. All of his savings were invested in the project. Today he hopes that the government will come to his aid. He had no insurance and all of his belongings were taken from him in the tsunami. He believes his home can be repaired, though it looks like an impossible job. But he, like everyone else we met on the island, believes that tourism and employment will return. They think it will happen quickly.

As we crossed back to the mainland we admired the optimism of the islanders. It took only minutes to destroy so much. Surely, it will take years to recover. The ferry terminal on the mainland offers little in the way of optimism. It is truly like a war zone. The area is jammed with debris and Thai army workers are everywhere clearing away broken buildings and constructing new ones to house the homeless. Signs everywhere offer free meals for anyone at The Army Café.

Back in Khao Lak

We get a brighter end to our day after the depressing island visit. On our return journey to Phuket we stopped off at the camp that we had visited two weeks earlier. There the village is amazingly vibrant. The basket-weaving group has grown in numbers and happy smiles tell us that sales of the work is going well. Hand-painting on batik is now being taught to add another item to the village's abilities.

On the community stage we saw being built, children are playing happily. Their laughter lightens the sadness we have carried with us from the island. Their smiles are contagious and suddenly our day has a happy ending.

The Thai government has made maps showing areas of the Andaman coast most likely to be hit by flooding resulting from any future tsunami. The maps, to be used by schoolchildren, will show escape routes from low-lying areas. The maps came as a result of the actions by 10-year-old British schoolgirl Tilly Smith during the tsunami. She saw the sea receding rapidly and recalled a geography lesson. Tilly warned her parents that a tsunami was approaching and everyone on the beach moved safely to higher ground.

VIPs from around the world made brief visits to the stricken areas. Former US presidents Bill Clinton and George Bush made Thailand their first stop on a four nation tour. They admired the way the rebuilding was going and stressed that international aid was vital but that the rebuilding had to be left in local hands. Clinton said, "It has got to be locally driven, with the rest of us just showing up to help. It is the lives of the people here, their future, their economy, and their children." Bush agreed. He said, "We should respect the local expertise and knowledge of the countries which are receiving assistance." Earlier King Carl Gustaf and Queen Silvia of Sweden flew over the stricken areas and thanked the Thai people for helping Swedes during the disaster. Almost a quarter of a million Swedes visit Thailand annually. It is thought that 700 people from that country perished in the tsunami.

Planning for the Future

Months after the tsunami the gruesome job of identifying the victims was still continuing. Bodies were still being stored in mortuaries while some 300 forensic experts from 32 countries tried to find matches for those still seeking news of their loved ones. Thousands who waited will never know exactly how their family members died. Their names will be recorded simply as missing.

After our visit to Khao Lak we learned that the Thai government had committed 10 billion Baht ($260 million) to rebuild the area. It also had set up special funds to encourage the international hotel chains to reinvest. Many are hesitant about rebuilding. There were more than 100 resorts in the area with over 7,000 rooms and a lot more under construction. Today there are less than 1,000 rooms and less than 30 hotels still able to operate. Certainly the Thai villagers will remain, perhaps not in their old villages, but in new housing developments that are already under construction.

Investors are nervous that tourists will not want to return to an area where so many people died. Also some local people don't want to work in an area that they feel is infected with unfriendly spirits.

The final grim toll for Thailand showed that over 8,000 people are known to have died as a result of the tsunami. More than 8,000 were recorded as injured, most of them Thais. Thousands more would not have reported their wounds. And there will be unknown thousands whose mental scars will never heal.

By Easter time, in late March, some of the areas hit by the tsunami were starting to recover. There were thousands out of work, and hundreds of businesses had been forced to close, but the major hotels were seeing their occupancy rates rise for the holiday period. For the first time in months shopkeepers began to start rebuilding their trade. Then Mother Nature struck again with an earthquake off the coast of Sumatra. This one sent out no tsunami but it caused major havoc with Thailand tourism. As soon as news of the earthquake reached Thailand the authorities, eager to show they were prepared for another tsunami, evacuated thousands from Phuket hotels and arranged accommodation on higher ground. Fortunately this time there was no tsunami but that did not appease those who had been moved. Within hours the airport was jammed with unhappy visitors anxious to return home. Vacations were curtailed and, sadly, many future bookings were canceled.

Despite so much pessimism there is optimism. This was the comment of Association of Thai Travel Agents president Suparerk Soorangura: "With government support in the form of interest-free loans and delayed payback of capital, investors who are wary of reinvesting are encouraged to rebuild. I'm optimistic the destination will be rebuilt sooner than people think – from six months to a year. And we're set to send a message to our overseas partners to come as soon as it's ready."

The Summer After

Phuket's slow, low summer season was expected to be slower and lower than usual in 2005, but the drop proved to be even more catastrophic than predicted. The Tourism Authority of Thailand (TAT) announced that the loss of tourism income was some $1.19 billion, far more than originally estimated. It was reported that a similar amount was being spent on rebuilding. Unemployment and closing of small businesses were inevitable. At least 19 hotels and guest houses went out of business, along with more than 50 operations in the recreation and leisure sector. The rise in oil prices caused an increase in the cost of living, hardly noticeable to the foreigner but a shattering burden for the low-paid Thai workers.

There was depressing news from all aspects of the tourist industry. Flight arrivals at Phuket International Airport plummeted from a normal 200 flights a week in the low season to a mere 66.

Even cutting landing fees by as much as 50% had not brought back the airlines.

And it was not only the tsunami-hit areas that suffered. In the Deep South, the continued conflict between the government and separatists spread into tourist areas, and the Tourism Authority suspended all its promotional activities in the provinces of Pattani, Narathiwat and Yala.

But through the gloom and depression there were several bright spots to keep hopes alive that tourism would recover.

Several airlines announced new services. Orient Thai resumed its daily Phuket-Hong Kong service and has announced that it would operate twice-weekly charter flights between Phuket and the South Korean cities of Inchon and Busan. Dragonair, which had closed its Phuket office and canceled its direct Phuket-Hong Kong service, announced it had made a deal with six Hong Kong travel agencies to fly charters. In August, Thai Airways International began operating two more flights a week between Phuket and Inchon, and in the same month China's Xiamen Airlines launched a charter service to Phuket. In November, Austrian Airlines began direct flights between Phuket and Vienna. Initially the flights were once a week but plans were to increase to twice weekly during the high season. The airline is expected to bring at least 14,000 people a year to Phuket. The Boeing 767-300ER aircraft is capable of carrying 239 passengers, 36 in business and 203 in economy, on its 12-hour flight. Tiger Airways, the Singapore-based low-cost airline, began scheduled flights to Krabi in October. The airline uses the Airbus 320 and operates four times weekly, on Mondays, Wednesday, Fridays and Sundays. Since Singapore's Changi Airport is used by 60 of the world's airlines the hope is that tourists would come not only from Singapore but all parts of the globe.

The Tourism Authority of Thailand began a new campaign to entice the tourists back by focusing on the 60th anniversary of King Bhumibol's accession to the throne, celebrated in 2006. A wide range of events were planned throughout the country but particularly in those areas hit by the tsunami. In addition to the foreign tourists the authority is putting special focus on those Thais who now live abroad. A TAT spokesman said, "These overseas Thais who we sometimes forget are significant in numbers and in potential tourism expenditure."

And the damaged hotels reopened. Le Meridien Phuket Beach Resort reopened with a special $95-per-night rate. The hotel was completely refurbished and boasts a new lobby and reception area, new swimming pools and several different restaurants. Public areas of the hotel have a contemporary Thai style with the use of fabrics and silks from the Mae Fah Luang Foundation, the organization established by the royal family to promote hill-tribe products. The Amari Coral Beach Resort at Patong Beach in Phuket reopened with all its rooms completely renovated. There was a new look in the lobby bar and a redesigned La Gritta Italian restaurant.

The greatest boost for Khao Lak came when its premier resort, the **Le Meridien Khao Lak Beach & Spa Resort** (see page 253), reopened in October. The resort's owner, Vitya Chakrabandhu, who lost a daughter in the tsunami, said that removing the sand from the area – much of it was 1.5 meters deep – had been one of the most difficult tasks in the rebuilding process. With Le Meridien open, the number of guest rooms available in Khao Lak is 1,700, compared with 7,000 before the tsunami.

In Ko Lanta (see page 266) the Royal Thai Navy handed over 60 homes it has built for tsunami victims. The Navy builders, some 400 sailors, then moved on to the island of Ko Khao to build a further 28 houses. This is the island we visited shortly after the tsunami (see page 21).

Elsewhere in Thailand new hotels were still being planned despite the tourism downturn. Marriott International said it would introduce its Renaissance and Courtyard brands to Thailand. The existing 78-unit Buriraya Resort & Spa in Ko Samui would become the Renaissance Ko Samui Resort & Spa, and a new 316-room Courtyard by Marriott Bangkok would open in 2007. The Ko Samui resort (more information on that in *Beyond Phuket*) will be renovated before it becomes the Renaissance. The Courtyard by Marriott Bangkok will be on Soi Mahadlekluang, in the embassy and business district. The Manatee Resort & Spa, a four-star boutique resort, is scheduled to open in late 2006 on Ko Mook, an island off the coast of the southern province of Trang. The resort will have 55 rooms, 11 pool villas and two two-bedroom villas and is costing close to $4 million to construct.

Best Western Hotels is expanding its presence in the kingdom with new contracts for hotels in Pattaya and Chiang Rai. In Pattaya, the group has signed a management contract for the new four-star Best Western Premier Silver Lake Estate, which is still in the planning stages. The resort, expected to have 200 rooms, will cost $10-million-plus. The property will be situated amid vineyards on lakefront land with an ocean view of southern Pattaya. In Chiang Rai the Golden Pine Resort & Spa, an 80-bungalow resort set amid rice paddies, was upgraded to meet Best Western brand standards. And in Khao Lak, The Best Western

Palm Galleria Khao Lak, badly damaged in the tsunami, reopened after $2.5 million was spent on structural repairs and new landscaping.

Despite the setbacks, hoteliers remained confident that the crowds would be back in force for the high season, when visitors would see some side benefits from the tsunami – cleaner beaches and more attractive coastal strips, particularly in Patong. Travel experts were confident that Phuket and Krabi would not have long-term problems. The Phi Phi Islands were expected to recover more slowly, however, and the long-term future of Khao Lak was still an unknown factor.

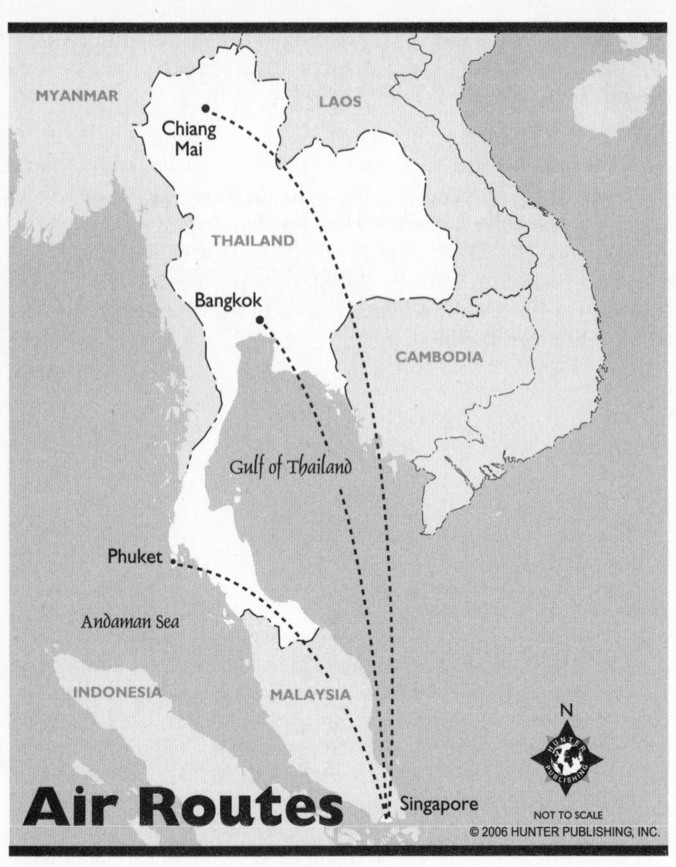

AIRLINES

Phuket Airport	☎ 07632 7230
Air Lanka	☎ 07621 2892
Bangkok Airways	☎ 07622 5033
China Airlines	☎ 07632 7099
Emirates Air	☎ 07621 2892
Malaysia Airlines	☎ 07621 6675
Silk Air	☎ 07621 6675
Thai Airways	☎ 07621 1195, 07621 2946, 07621 2499
Tiger Airlines	☎ 001800 656752

Thailand

Introduction

Introduction

It only takes a few days in Thailand to understand why this incredible place is the number-one tourist destination in Southeast Asia. As you soak up the complex culture, sample the exquisite cuisine and explore mystic temples or unspoiled islands you cannot fail to experience a dramatic rise in your feel-good factor.

IN THIS CHAPTER

It happens to us every time. This is our seventh visit and the anticipation is as great now as it was the first time we arrived in Bangkok, the nation's capital. On this trip we plan to explore destinations away from the normal tourist areas. And there is added excitement since we are hoping to buy a home and spend even more time here.

Our first trip six years ago was the ideal combination for first-time visitors. We spent four days in the capital and then flew south to the beaches and resorts of Phuket Island. It was this sample that gave us an enormous appetite to see and learn more.

The anticipation of any adventure can be as appealing as the adventure itself. We get tremendous enjoyment from planning and thinking about what lies ahead and fortunately our expectations of a trip to Thailand have always been exceeded by the reality.

A couple of facts before we get started: The country covers 514,000 square kilometers – about twice the size of Wyoming. The population is 62 million, compared to 500,000 people who live in the state of Wyoming. The country is 95% Buddhist, which explains why you will see so many monks in saffron-colored robes. Something you don't see in Wyoming.

The Buddhism they practice here is Theravada Buddhism, an offspring of the ancient Dvarati Buddhism, and it plays a major role in all aspects of Thai life.

Facts & Figures

Exchange Rates

With exchange rates fluctuating every day it is difficult to give costs in currencies other than the Thai Baht. Throughout the guide we have given most of the prices in the currency of Thailand. In our price guides for hotels, however, we have priced accommodation in US dollars since many of the major hotels quote prices on their Websites in US dollars. In June 2005 one US dollar was worth 38 Baht, one euro bought 53 Baht and the UK pound 75 Baht. We find it best to create a simple worksheet giving the various currencies. Once you've established the formulas it is easy to update every few weeks. You may also check current rates at www.exchangerates.com.

Geography

The country has the Andaman Sea on one side and the Gulf of Thailand on the other. It borders on Myanmar, Cambodia, Laos and Malaysia. Border skirmishes are not unknown but normally only last a few days. Less than 4% of the population is Muslim; most of that group lives in the south of the country and there have been problems with demonstrations over neglect and lack of understanding by the Bangkok-based government. The problems are not new. There has been unrest for over 40 years. To date, the fighting has only affected tourism in the far south and the situation is being closely monitored by foreign governments.

Tourism

Modern-day tourism got a shot in the arm back in 1974 when part of the James Bond movie *The Man with the Golden Gun* was filmed on an island named Ko Ping Kan. The scene featured Roger Moore and Christopher Lee. Today, tourists swarm to be photographed on the spot where the two men faced each other. The island has been renamed James Bond Island and now boasts 52 souvenir shops. More recently, another island was used for the movie *The Beach,* starring Leonardo DiCaprio. Local conservationists are delighted that access to that island is very difficult and as a result tourist vessels stay away.

Thailand's Prime Minister, Thaksin Shinawatra, says Thailand should attract 20 million foreign tourists a year to Thailand by 2008. To achieve this he is preparing to spend 40 billion Baht ($1 billion) on promotion.

Climate

If you don't like it hot you have made the wrong decision by coming this far from home. Snow gear is as much use here as an ashtray on a Harley Davidson. Without doubt, the best time to visit the resorts of southern Thailand is between November and March – and this is the most expensive time too – but do not be put off by the rainy season. Climate does vary from north to south (you will find more details about local climate in the destination chapters). Obviously nobody wants to suffer through a typhoon, and fortunately typhoons are very much a rarity in Thailand, but we have spent weeks when it has rained a little every day. Most times we were on the beach and just enjoyed the natural shower. Minutes later we dried off in the sun.

Prices

Where else in the world can two people dine well and walk away with change from $5? And low prices abound everywhere. Obviously, the copies of brand-name products are extremely inexpensive. But everywhere you will find excellent value for money. We do not know of another country that has so many truly luxurious hotels and, here, the finest hotels with their impressive service cost a fraction of what you would pay in other countries. The business hotels in Bangkok and throughout the kingdom are second to none and we know of nowhere in the US or Europe that has the quality of tourist resorts and spas that you will find here. You'll find that the word "wellness" has crept into the dictionary here. Not to content to tack the words "and spa" onto their names, the resorts now have wellness centers and wellness menus.

Public Holidays

Holidays listed without dates are *Theravada* Buddhist holidays; the date changes from year to year based on the lunar calendar.

January 1 ....New Year's Day (*Wan Khun Pee Mai)*
February ....*Makha Bucha*
April 6 ....*Chakri* Memorial Day
April 13-15 ....Thai New Year (*Songkran*)
May ....*Visakha Bucha*
May 1 ....Labor Day (bank holiday only)
May 5...............................Coronation Day
July ....*Khao Phansa*
August 12........Mothers' Day/Queen's Birthday (*Wan Mae)*
October 23 ....Chulalongkorn Day (*Wan Piyamharat)*
December 5.........Fathers' Day/King's Birthday (*Wan Pot)*
December 10 ....Constitution Day
December 31...............New Year's Eve (*Wan Sin Pee)*

Practicalities

Visas & Immigration Laws

On arrival you will be granted a visa for 30 days. On one trip we planned to stay longer and we explained that to the immigration officer. He smiled and said yes, as is the custom for those not speaking much English, and we assumed all was well. It was not. On departure we were fined for each day we had stayed over the one-month limit. We were not alone; there was a line of offenders waiting when we went to pay for our error. And to aid those, like us, who had let their supply of Thai Baht dwindle, there was an ATM close by. On subsequent extended stays we resolved the problem by making a visit to the local immigration office and having additional time granted. You can also leave the country and re-enter, whereupon you'll get an additional 30-day visa; on one occasion we made a trip to Singapore, which gave us an extension. If you are planning a longer-than-30-day visit it is worth checking with a Thai embassy for details about various visas that are available. The regulations do change.

The Embassies of Thailand

In the US

Royal Thai Embassy, 1024 Wisconsin Avenue NW, Washington, DC 20007, ☎ 202-944-3600.

Royal Thai Consulate General, 35 East Wacker Drive, Suite 1834, Chicago, IL 60601, ☎ 312-236-2447.

Royal Thai Consulate General, 801 North LaBrea Avenue, Los Angeles, CA 90038, ☎ 213-937-1894.

Royal Thai Consulate General, 351 East 52nd Street, New York, NY 10022, ☎ 212-754-1770.

In Canada

Royal Thai Embassy, 180 Island Park Drive, Ottawa, ON K1Y 0A2, ☎ 613-722-4444.

Royal Thai Consulate, Campus Tower Building, 8625-112 Street, Edmonton, AB T6G 1K8, ☎ 403-432-1387.

Royal Thai Consulate, 1155 René-Levesque West, Suite 2500, Montreal, QC H3B 2K4, ☎ 514-871-1271.

Royal Thai Consulate, Scotia Plaza, 40 King Street, West, 44th Floor, Toronto, ON M5H 3Y4, ☎ 416-367-6750.

Royal Thai Consulate, 736 Granville Street, Suite 106, Vancouver, BC V6Z 1G3, ☎ 604-687-4434.

In the United Kingdom

Royal Thai Embassy, 1-3 Yorkshire House, Grosvenor Crescent, London. SWIX7EBP, ☎ (0171) 259 5051, fax (0171) 235 9808.

In Europe & Elsewhere

The following listings are locations of the **Royal Thai Embassy**:

Australia, 111 Empire Circuit Yarralumla, A.C.T., 2600, Canberra, ☎ (06) 273 1149, fax (06) 273 1518.

Belgium, 2 Square du Val de la Cambre, Brussels, ☎ (322) 640 6810, fax (322) 648 3066.

Denmark, Norgesmindevej 18, 2900 Hellerup Copenhagen, ☎ (45) 3962-5010, fax (45) 3962-5059.

France, 12 Rue Lord Byron 75008, Paris, ☎ (0147) 046892, fax (0147) 556713.

Germany, Ubierstasse 65, 53173 Bonn, ☎ (49) 228 956 860, fax (49) 228 363 702.

Italy, Via Nomentana, 132, 00162 Rome, ☎ (396) 8620 4381, fax (396) 8620 8399.

The Netherlands, Buitenrustweg, 2517 KD, The Hague, ☎ (3170) 345 0632, fax (3170) 345 1929.

New Zealand, 2 Cook Street, Karori, POBox 17226, Wellington, ☎ (644) 476 8618, fax (644) 476 3677.

Norway, Munkedamsveien 59B, 0270 Oslo, ☎ (22) 832 517, fax (22) 830 384.

Portugal, Rua de Alcolena, 12, Restelo, 1400 Lisbon, ☎ (3511) 301 4848, fax (3511) 301 8181.

South Africa, 840 Church Street, Eastwood, Areadia 0083, Pretoria, ☎ (2712) 342 5470, fax (2712) 342 4805.

Spain, Joquin Costa 29, 28002 Madrid, ☎ (34) 91563 2903, fax (34) 91564 0033.

Sweden, Eloragatan3, 11431, Stockholm, Box 26220 100 40, ☎ (46-08) 791 7340, fax (46-08) 791 7351.

Switzerland, Srd Fl., 60 Eigerstrasse (5th Fl.), 3007 Bern, ☎ (4131) 372 2281, fax (4131) 372 0757.

Safety & Crime Prevention

Crime can be a problem, but a little forward-thinking can help avoid difficulties during your trip. Here are some suggestions:

- Beware of unauthorized people who offer their services as guides.

- Use common sense when it comes to personal safety. Walking alone through quiet or deserted areas is not recommended. Be sure that all your valuables – passports, money, jewelry, and airline tickets – are properly protected. Most hotel rooms have personal safes; if yours does not, the hotel will most likely have a safe at reception. The tourist police (see below) do a superb job and are there to assist you. In each destination chapter we will give a phone number where they can be contacted.

- Do not get involved with drugs. Penalties for drug offences are very severe in Thailand, and range from life imprisonment to death. Checks are made when you enter and leave the country that you are not carrying illegal drugs. If you are carrying legitimate medicines be sure they are correctly identified.

Tourist Police

Should a problem arise, the government, through the Tourism Authority of Thailand (TAT), has bi-lingual tourist police stationed throughout the country. Their sole job is to assist tourists who run into problems. They have a 24-hour emergency number – simply dial 1155 – or look them up at www.tourist.police.go.th.

Medical Attention

We have been very impressed with medical care in Thailand. Should you become ill while visiting you will find excellent facilities in all the major cities and towns. We have found charges to be extremely low and the cost of prescription drugs significantly lower than in the US. Doctors we have visited all spoke impeccable English and were extremely efficient. Many people come to Thailand for medical care, be it a simple health check-up or major surgery. We have devoted a chapter to *The Medical Vacation*; see page 407.

Money

This is one thing we all need while visiting Thailand. There are exchange bureaus in all the major towns, which readily change US dollars, pounds and euros. Most will cash travelers' checks and some will give advances on major US credit cards. We have found it better to use ATMs, or cash machines, which are everywhere. Most major stores and hotels accept credit cards but you will not be able to use them at the street markets or smaller restaurants. We have found that, when using a US credit card, the exchange rate applied when the charge reached the US was extremely good. The same holds true for the rate we have obtained by using cash/ATM machines.

Telephone Service

Keeping in touch with home or the rest of the world is not a problem today. The telephone system in major towns is greatly improved and you can make direct calls to the rest of the world from most hotel rooms. In September of 2004 the Communications Authority of Thailand (CAT) cut its rates to six Baht a minute for international calls to 30 countries including the US, the UK, Canada, Australia and South Africa. To take advantage of the low rates callers have to purchase a CAT PhoneNet card. These are available at some supermarkets and convenience stores. We didn't keep track of the time we spent using these cards. The first one we bought for 500 Baht allowed us to make us numerous calls to the US, UK and Spain. It was certainly a lot cheaper than using international direct dialing (IDD) from hotels.

The Royal Family

There are two delicate subjects that visitors to Thailand should be aware of – the Royal family and religion. The Thai people hold a deep reverence for the King and Queen and their children, and they expect visitors to show respect. King Bhumibol is an elderly man in his late 70s but he still plays a major role in Thai life. His lengthy unscripted speeches are listened to by almost everyone, and his word is important. He keeps a watchful eye on national affairs and is often critical of the prime minister and the government. In his 77th-birthday speech he covered a range of topics, from the dangers of smoking to his concern for young people's music and the damage it can cause to their hearing. His greatest attribute is that, despite his royal position, he is very much a man of the people and enjoys simple pleasures. After this latest speech he drove himself home in a Honda Civic. His birthday, on December 5, is celebrated as a national holiday. We have attended celebrations for his birthday; at exactly 7:27pm the nation maintains a one-minute silence in tribute to him, and many people do this while holding an illuminated candle.

Religion

If you did not see monks and temples within a couple of hours of your arrival in Thailand, something went amiss – either you got stuck in a lengthy line at the airport immigration desk or you wore blinkers on the ride to the hotel.

Monks and temples abound in this land of silk, smiles and saffron-colored robes. At any one time there are over a quarter of a million monks spread through the country. There are not so many temples, something you might doubt after a few days of sightseeing. In fact the nation has a total of 30,678 temples and monasteries. In addition to the monks, there are 90,000 novices and over 120,000 temple boys, who are usually students from poorer homes who help at temples by cleaning and running errands in return for free board and lodging.

Who are the monks and where do they come from? Any male in Thailand can become a monk. Kings have been monks, so have paupers and pimps. The wealthy, the wise, scholars and even criminals have entered into the temple with one intention: to better understand the teachings of Buddha and to improve not only their own lives but the lives of others within the community. And there are some temples that will accept farangs into their midst.

Buddhism and Society

All the kings of Thailand have been Buddhist – and have to be by law. Most have spent periods as monks. All the temples and the land they stand on are owned by the state. Government officials are encouraged to spend up to four months at some point in their careers in a monastery. They receive full pay during their absence from normal work.

The monks and temples play a major role in isolated rural areas, where the temple is very much the focal point for education, medication, meditation and even the postal service. As a result many of the rural people contribute a bigger percentage of their small incomes to their local temple than do city dwellers, where there are other resources, and religion is not as strong as it was. Nonetheless, there is still a tradition of earning merit and the fact that so many men return to the temples for short periods, particularly during the Buddhist Lent period, proves that Buddhism, now over 2,500 years old, is thriving and still playing a major part of life in Thailand.

■ The Life Of A Monk

Years ago most young men joined a temple and became a monk for a period of time. It was not compulsory but something that most young men did as part of growing up. In recent years the numbers have dwindled due in no small part to the social and cultural changes that have occurred in the kingdom. Much of the drop can be blamed on the westernization of the country. Financial and family commitments have changed so it is now not so easy as it was for a man to give up everything and devote time, no matter how short, to the non-paying community service.

The number of men becoming monks is still as high as 60% of the male population, which is incredible by Western standards where, in most modern countries, involvement with the church is dwindling.

A man entering the temple knows he has nothing to gain financially but everything to lose. The first thing that goes is his hair. The chief monk or abbot (*jao-awaht*) makes a symbolic gesture by removing the first locks, and then another monk totally shaves the head and eyebrows. The event normally takes place at the temple nearest the man's home. It is generally preceded by a party where the family celebrates the man's decision to enter the temple. Once inaugurated into the temple the man's life becomes a strict regime of study and prayer. His day will begin at 4am with a morning bath and then private prayers. When the sun appears the monks leave in groups to tour the community in search of food.

AUTHOR'S NOTE: *In Western eyes this gathering of alms would be considered begging but not so in Buddhist Thailand. It is considered an honor to give, and one makes merit, an important part of Buddhism, by giving to the monks.*

The monks' alms bowls are typically made out of strips of steel with brass tops. All the hand-made ones are produced in Bangkok in an area known as Baan Baat, a run-down neighborhood between Chinatown and the Golden Mount. A handful of families have produced these items for generations and they make unusual souvenirs. You'll find them on sale at monk supply stores, which are in every town and village in Thailand. You can expect to pay 1,500 Baht for a good-quality bowl.

After breakfast at the temple the monks enter the main sanctuary at 8am for morning prayers, and new arrivals receive special instruction from the abbot before taking their main meal of the day. This has to be completed before noon since monks are not allowed to eat from noon until breakfast the following day.

The afternoons are normally spent around the community before returning to the temple for a second bath at 5pm. The rest of the day is spent on religious instruction before the monks retire. And that is the routine that starts again the next morning with the 4am bell.

■ Visiting the Temples

Visitors to religious sites are expected to dress modestly. Always wear a top with sleeves. It is acceptable to wear shoes when walking around the compound of a Buddhist temple, but not inside the chapel where the principal Buddha image is kept. Shorts or miniskirts should not be worn in the temple. Every image of Buddha is regarded as a sacred object. Never climb onto one to take a photograph or do anything that might indicate a lack of respect. Buddhist monks are forbidden to touch or be touched by a woman, or to accept anything from the hand of one. If a woman has to give anything to a monk, she first hands it to a man, who then presents it.

To avoid embarrassment, here are some other tips: Thais regard the head as the highest part of the body, literally and figuratively. Avoid touching people on the head and try not to point your feet at people or an object. It is considered very rude. Shoes should be removed when entering a private Thai home. Public displays of affection between men and women are not considered correct, so do your kissing and cuddling in private.

Culture & Society

National Temperament

What is the magnet that pulls us back? It has nothing to do with James Bond. First it has to be the people. Thais are friendly and proud of their heritage. Thailand has never been colonized by a foreign power, unlike neighboring countries. Obviously there have to be a few parasites in paradise but as a nation the folk are friendly, and smiles offered to foreigners are genuine. During our travels around the kingdom we have been trying to discover what makes the majority of Thais such a smiling and happy group of people. We came up with several answers. The best answer centers on the old adage that a hungry man is an angry man. Thai people don't go hungry. They are blessed with a fertile country that produces the finest fruit and vegetables, and the waters that surround the nation are teeming with the full gamut of seafood. Nobody goes hungry. Not even the poorest farmer or the large family of the low-paid laborer goes without meals.

Another plus is the fact that the country has no unemployment. The country presently has one million people from adjoining countries doing a lot of jobs that Thais do not want. They are known as the neighbor laborers.

And the final factor has to be their following of Buddhism, which teaches one to be content with what one has. You rarely see a Thai lose his cool. It is considered loss of face, or demeaning, to do so. Envy does not appear to be in the Thai dictionary. Nobody we have met would understand the expression about "keeping up with the Joneses."

Food

Then there is the cuisine. It is pungent and spicy, seasoned with lashings of garlic and chilies complemented with lime juice, lemon grass and fresh coriander. Other items that make those mouth-watering meals include galangal root, basil, ground peanuts, coconut milk and tamarind juice. But Thai cooking is not just a matter of using lemon grass and tiny red bits of fiery pepper; it's a whole attitude of making eating a memorable experience. We originally thought that we would tire of eating Thai food during our extended stays. It never happened. The abundance of fresh seafood and garden-fresh vegetables gave us ample variety. There are wonderful soups and curries that vary in strength and sweetness. We learned two very important phrases early on. *Ped* means spicy and *mai ped* means not spicy. In the section on Thai cuisine we will also deal with buying food from the street vendors, a great experience (see page 379, in *Living in Thailand*).

We do confess to visiting a couple of KFC outlets and were greatly impressed with the quality and service. Labor is inexpensive in Thailand; as a result there are always ample hands to help. After we had placed our order there was someone to find us a seat, someone to bring the food and someone else to clear up. You don't find that in Wyoming!

We ordered the non-spicy meals and found them quite peppery. We never ventured to the full-spicy for fear that someone in the kitchen may be heavy handed with those fiery little red bits.

Recreation

The range of things to do outdoors is endless, thanks to the varied terrain in Thailand. There is golf – a very popular Thai pastime with over 200 fine courses across the nation; hiking; great deep-sea fishing; scuba diving, and when the weather turns sour there is surfing. For the more adventurous there is bungee-jumping or parasailing, elephant trekking (something we have never found comfortable), or the silent beauty of sea-canoeing inside eerie caves. For the really energetic the locals have improved on volleyball with a game called takraw that allows only feet and head to contact the ball.

We will give you more details of the activities available as you visit the various destination chapters.

Shopping

You will never tire of the vast selection of goodies that are available. You can haggle over prices of local handicrafts from a small boat in a floating market or ogle exotic jewelry in exclusive boutiques in Bangkok. You watch gems being assembled in a giant factory in Phuket or Pattaya. Silk is a must-buy item, be it a simple scarf or tie or a classic designer gown or jacket. Our advice: Come light – leave heavy! And to carry your purchases home you'll find someone selling luggage – be it the real thing or a clever copy – on most streetcorners.

If it is bargains you seek then the endless street markets and stalls that spring up in every part of every town are the places to start. Here the copies of designer clothes, look-alike Rolex watches, CDs and DVDs change hands for little money. Many of the items may not be on display since there is a continuing battle to rid the streets of the fakes. Chances are they are hidden behind shirts and swim suits that don't bear the polo player on horseback or the alligator logo.

These are the places to haggle. The vendors expect it and enjoy it. That hurt expression that you have cut the price too far will quickly vanish once cash changes hands. But don't go overboard. We once watched a woman barter away for a good 20 minutes. Her husband stood at her side with a calculator. When the purchase of some silk squares was completed he announced that his wife had managed to save them 32 US cents. He wondered how much the taxi that was waiting for them had charged for the time spent bartering. Normally you can expect to get between 10 and 40% off the asking price.

Tailor shops flourish in all the tourist areas. In some places it is hard to take 50 steps without being asked, "Where you from?" and being offered a made-to-measure suit for the price of a silk tie. Buyers beware. Once you enter these shop-fronts – many of them are just façades stuffed with mannequins and rolls of fabric that are solely for effect, not sewing – the prices soar and the quality may not be as good as the sample you are shown. Again, you can bargain, but like most things you will get what you pay for. Many of the shops may look different and have wonderful designer names but on closer examination you'll find they are all owned by the same person or a co-op that operates sweat-shops behind the town, where underpaid and overworked Indians sew garments together in a rush to meet absurd deadlines.

If you want quality work, get a recommendation from someone who has found a reputable tailor, or check with your hotel. Many of the larger hotels have tailor shops on the premises, and that normally guarantees good quality and value for money.

In each chapter you will find descriptions of specialty items for the area you are visiting. Just to give you an idea of what is available, here are some of the weird items we carried home on our last visit. First there were two gigantic fans, the kind you wave, not plug in. Will the vibrant hand-painted colors that we saw in the open-air market be as vivid hanging on a wall at home? At a supermarket we bought a Thai broom, a short stick – Thais are short people – with a bushy base of sticks that works wonders here. Will it work as well for us as it does in Thai hands?

Then there are clothes. Among the items we bought are dozens of shirts and shorts, blouses and scarves. It wasn't that we needed them but the prices were just too attractive. Fortunately we did not get stuck with an excess baggage charge, which would have negated the saving. We may well have to buy additional furniture to house this lot or make a generous donation to Goodwill Industries.

There are the two hand-carved tables that I bought on the beach. I have been adamant about not buying from beach vendors. I feel that bargains are better negotiated in the market rather than from the comfort of a beach chair. However, one day a young man appeared with a small table. It came in two parts. The top, circular, was neatly carved from a wood he claimed was teak. The legs were carved from a single piece of wood and splayed out to form a tripod base. He said he had made this and it had taken endless hours of toil and whittling. He showed me injuries to his hand, which I wrongly assumed were from his woodworking. (He probably hurt himself after overdosing on those tiny fiery red bits that Thais insist on putting in their food.) We bargained and I parted with 1,000 Baht, believing that I had a unique Thai table. Three days passed and another vendor appeared bearing an identical table. I was greatly depressed and offered him 350 Baht – he accepted. Thanks to the law of averaging I do not feel totally unhappy about the purchases.

Finally, our cases are crammed with food items. We have spices, strange noodles, bananas soaked in honey, some magical flour that will transform our meals into the exotic, and several packets of highly spiced snacks that should impress our neighbors when we get home. I should point out we were not traveling back to the US. If you are headed in that direction check with Customs and the FDA inspectors about what food items you can import.

Thai Massage

A very special part of Thai life is the massage. To soothe the body there are round-the-clock massages. Most major hotels have fancy spas; on most beaches there will be a tent set up where you can enjoy this most wonderful Thai ritual. There are even parlors at Bangkok Airport where weary travelers can enjoy a foot massage.

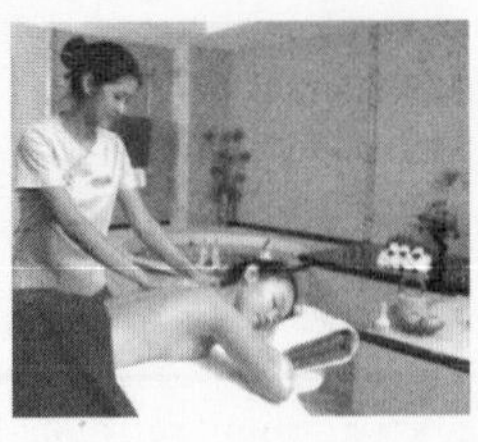

Thai massage comes in all kinds of packages, some even venturing to the erotic. Most, however, are simply therapeutic. The best exponents train for years to become qualified and have the ability to ease the effects of stress and tension. Prices vary according to where you are and what level of massage you seek. Special lotions and oils normally cost a little more. You can pay 200 Baht for a 45-minute treatment on the beach or up to 10 times that amount in an exclusive spa, where more exotic oils and aromas add to the pleasure.

We find that a daily massage – be it concentrated on feet and legs or the entire body – a very worthwhile experience. Thai massage is a very ancient form of healing; it came to Thailand from India as part of the Buddhist teachings in the second century BC.

Nightlife

Nightlife is as varied and vibrant as the colors of Thai silk. There are live sex shows in Bangkok to redden your cheeks, or Thai boxing, which brings out an unusual aggressive spirit in the locals. Classic Thai tunes are relaxing but the modern-day noises are much the same as the Western versions, and the words are totally incomprehensible. Discos abound and bar brawls are not unheard of in some of the less attractive neighborhoods. Bangkok has a full range of theatre and things cultural while other areas boast Disney-type theme parks and venues for rock concerts.

Most major hotels provide evening entertainment, which is certain to include traditional Thai dancing with its splendid silk costumes and delicate hand movements. The dancers appear to slide along the floor flexing their hands into the most impossible angles.

CAUTION: *Bootleg copies of the latest Hollywood movies manage to make it to Thailand street markets within days of their release. Quality copies sell for as little as 100 Baht. It may be illegal but there are always plenty of buyers. Surprisingly, though the vendors may not speak much English, they know a great deal about the films and the content. Normally the copies come in English without Thai subtitles. If you are tempted to buy, check that the audio is in English.*

Language

English is widely spoken but not everyone understands as much as you may think they do. Thais have a habit of smiling and saying yes to almost anything. That maybe one additional reason why foreign men find the Thai beauties so attractive.

The Thai language continues to be a problem for us. We have devoted some space to the subject later in the book (see page 387). It is important to learn a few basics – like the Thai greeting, *sa-wat-dee*, which means good morning, good afternoon, good evening, hello and goodbye.

Spoken Thai is a polite and non-offensive language. If you are a male speaker and just want to say hello, you say "sawatdee" and tack on the word *krup* to it. If you are female you add the word *kaa* (*sawatdee krup, sawatdee kaa*). These are polite after-words.

The word for thank you is *kop khun*. If you are a man you say *kop khun krup* and the woman says *kop khun kaa*. The Thai language is tonal, which means the same word can be pronounced with a rising, falling, high, low or level tone and could have five different meanings.

If you can master the Thai greeting – called a *wai*, pronounced "why" – by putting your hands in the prayer position and bowing your head, you will be well received. Normally a younger person *wais* an elder, who returns it. In the return greeting the hands come only to chest height, whereas in the full greeting the hands come to the nose. In the full Thai *wai* to a monk the hands come close to the forehead.

The written language, with its 44-letter alphabet of strange symbols, is even more complicated. The Thai alphabet looks like it has been ripped from a Paisley pattern and the letters appear to have lots of little irons above them.

AUTHOR'S NOTE: *You will notice that the English spelling of Thai words is inconsistent. Even street names can be "speld" differently from one end of the block to the other. The reason is that Thai, which has its own alphabet, is being transcribed phonetically into English. You can learn a little more about the language in the* Living in Thailand *chapter, page 387.*

Always carry the name of your hotel, or where you are staying, in the Thai alphabet. We had a problem once in Bangkok trying to get back to the Shangri-La Hotel. The driver did not understand us or the business card we showed him. Fortunately the hieroglyphics on the reverse were the name of the hotel in Thai – initially we thought some one had been doodling on the card – and we were whisked back to safety.

Spirit Houses

Most Thai homes have a small spirit house at their entrance. Thai people have been using spirit houses for thousands of years and they predate the spread of Theravada Buddhism to Thailand. It is believed that each dwelling or business will have spirits that inhabit it, and the best way to appease those spirits is to provide them with their own beautiful home in which to live. This will help keep the spirits from being mischievous.

They are often decorated with figures of married couples, furniture or even small figures of elephants – a symbol of good fortune and prosperity. Offerings of flower garlands, candles and incense are left nearby, on the veranda outside the spirit house.

Spirit houses are not only found in homes. They are often found at caves and bodies of water, such as local lakes, that play an important role in the life of villages. They are placed at the foot of trees considered sacred, and can also be seen at the site of accidents to appease the spirits of those who lost their lives. It is a grim reminder as you drive around Thailand of the spots prone to fatal accidents.

Where Do You Stay?

Thailand caters to everyone. There are the very finest accommodations in the major centers and less sophisticated places in the rural areas. The Thailand Tourism Authority (TAT) has grouped accommodation into four categories; these are the descriptions given by that agency.

Luxury Hotels

Luxury hotels in urban Thailand meet international standards and are renowned for their outstanding service and hospitality. Expect to be treated like royalty, living in elegantly furnished rooms with modern amenities, recreational facilities and an extensive choice of the best dining outlets in town right at your fingertips. Compared with similar establishments in the West, these hotels provide much more value for your money.

Resort Hotels

Similar to the luxury hotels, the resort hotels are unsurpassed in style, comfort and value, in comparison to their counterparts worldwide. Additionally, they offer astonishing scenic views of their surroundings, whether it's the azure blue waters of the south or the rolling hills and forests of the north. Most were specifically designed to be unique, heavenly oases, blending harmoniously with their environment, and offering a wide range of entertainment and gastronomic delights, with services provided by charming staff.

Guesthouses & Beach Bungalows

Dating primarily from the backpacker phenomenon of the 1970s, guesthouses offer superb value and charming memories for budget travelers. In Bangkok, these establishments are predominantly located on Khao San Road. In other major tourist cities and seaside towns, guesthouses and beach bungalows offer clean rooms and friendly service for a relatively cheap price, some as low as 100-400 Baht per night. Some may have air conditioned rooms and private bathrooms. Though the facilities may be basic, and beach bungalows may be prone to insect invasions, the quality of service has reputedly remained good.

Provincial Hotels

Found mainly in those rural areas not often frequented by foreign visitors, these are generally multi-story or a row of concrete block structures containing identical rooms with choice of either air conditioning or fan. Though cheap and clean they generally offer only basic facilities, most often equipped with squatting toilets, and lack eating facilities. They may be the only option available, especially in the remoter parts of Central and Northeastern Thailand.

Plus, Plus, Plus...

When you look at hotel rates and restaurant signs, beware of the little "plus" signs that follow the number. These indicate that service and government taxes (and possibly provincial taxes) will be added. For example 500 Baht +++ could take you closer to 600 Baht.

Most hotels charge the first "plus" for service (like tips, and normally 10% but we have seen it as high as 18.7%). This money goes to those smiling people who take care of you – or it is supposed to. We have heard of hotels and restaurants that do not pay the full amount to their employees; instead they pay a fixed fee to the employees and keep what's left for themselves.

The second "plus" is for government tax, which is 7.7% and should be charged on room rates only. The third "plus" is the additional provincial tax of 1%, and again should only be charged on the room rate. After the tsunami this tax was waived until September 30, 2005.

Where Do You Eat?

Thanks to the balmy tropical climate, the evening meal is best enjoyed outdoors. Major hotels will offer the choice of European or Thai menus and most have air conditioned restaurants for those who prefer to cool off at night. Prices in hotels will compare favorably to their US counterparts but the bargains are to be found at the local eateries. Where there's a beach there is certain to be a café or bar offering freshly caught seafood at very reasonable prices. Dining aboard a pleasure boat is an attractive alternative.

For those on a budget – or fearful of trying something from the street vendors – the major fast-food chains are well represented. The golden arches of McDonalds are everywhere, along with Burger King and KFC. For a quick snack, 7-Eleven stores, which abound in Thailand, offer a hot dog on a stick!

Fruit lovers are in for a special treat in Thailand. What Westerners consider exotic is commonplace here. And the art of fruit carving gives the luscious produce added appeal. Local bananas, small as a finger and creamy sweet, grow like weeds. Pineapples sell for pennies and papaya, mango, melons, guava and different citrus varieties are on show everywhere. Palms provide an abundance of coconuts and you'll find them with tops removed and straw inserted at roadside stalls, making a perfect mid-morning drink, or – with alcohol added – an out-of-the-ordinary cocktail.

Bangkok

Introduction

Bangkok is a wonderful city to visit but not a place in which we would choose to live. However, close to nine million people call this home and endure the traffic chaos, noise and air pollution with no apparent complaint. This is a city that is full of architectural wonders, ancient and modern, on both sides of a flourishing river. It is full of rare contrasts. The saffron-robed monks wander along congested sidewalks where ladies of the night ply their trade. The smartly dressed European businessperson towers over the short Thai street trader. It is religious and risqué. There is noise in the markets and silence in the temples.

IN THIS CHAPTER

This mega-metropolis is the starting point for most Thailand adventures. If you plan properly you can see the best of Bangkok in three or four hectic days and then get going to see to the wonders Thailand has to offer away from its capital.

The city's spacious new **Suvarnabhumi Airport** (pronounced soo-wan-na-poom), which comes into operation in 2006, replacing the **Don Muang** airport (dorn meu-ang), is to be the first point of arrival for 85% of all visitors to the kingdom. The airport is 30 kilometers east of Bangkok.

The ride from the airport will give you an idea of the traffic problems in the city, though it is far better now than it has been in the past. Bangkok has made great strides improving its transit systems since the 1997 financial disasters that hit Southeast Asia. Expressways have been completed; the elevated rail system, BTS SkyTrain, operates efficiently; and in July 2004 the King opened

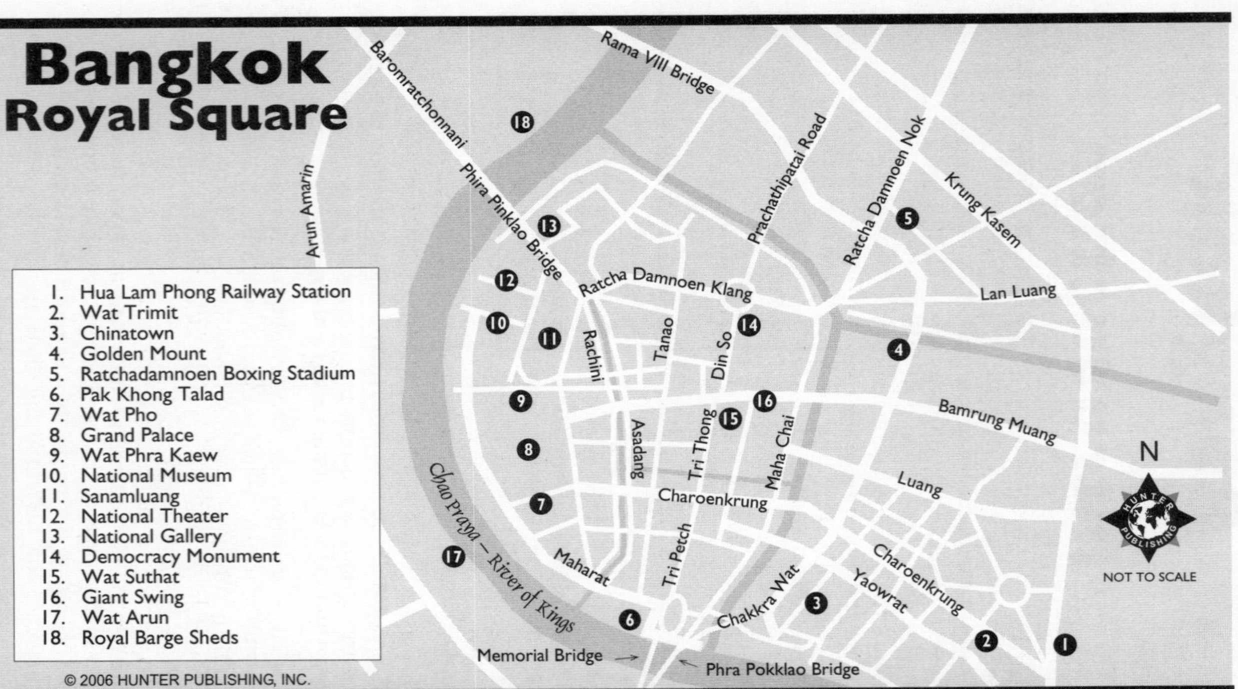

Bangkok
Royal Square
1. Hua Lam Phong Railway Station
2. Wat Trimit
3. Chinatown
4. Golden Mount
5. Ratchadamnoen Boxing Stadium
6. Pak Khong Talad
7. Wat Pho
8. Grand Palace
9. Wat Phra Kaew
10. National Museum
11. Sanamluang
12. National Theater
13. National Gallery
14. Democracy Monument
15. Wat Suthat
16. Giant Swing
17. Wat Arun
18. Royal Barge Sheds
© 2006 HUNTER PUBLISHING, INC.
Arun Amarin
Baromratchonnani
Phira Pinklao Bridge
Rama VIII Bridge
Prachathipatai Road
Ratcha Damnoen Nok
Krung Kasem
Lan Luang
Ratcha Damnoen Klang
Rachini
Tanao
Din So
Bamrung Muang
Asadang
Tri Thong
Maha Chai
Luang
Charoenkrung
Tri Petch
Maharat
Chakkra Wat
Yaowrat
Charoenkrung
Chao Praya – River of Kings
Memorial Bridge
Phra Pokklao Bridge
N
HUNTER PUBLISHING
NOT TO SCALE

an 18-station subway system – a month ahead of schedule. By the year 2010, the Thai government plans to expand these two mass transit systems to cover a total of 291 kilometers, linking all parts of the city. A budget of 446.6 billion Baht has already been approved for the projects.

Once secure in the air conditioned comfort of your hotel room, scour the list of tours available, or better still get a massage to relieve the agonies of long-distance air travel. Our biggest problem was leaving the opulence of our hotel room. There are now so many luxury hotels in Bangkok filled with spas, swimming pools and great restaurants that it takes a genuine effort to venture forth into the heat and crowds. Our advice is to get out early even if means rushing through a bountiful breakfast buffet.

USEFUL TELEPHONE NUMBERS

Tourist Police .... ☎ 1699
Tourist Service Center .... ☎ 1155
Bangkok General Hospital:
2 Soi Soonvijai 7
New Petchburi Road........ ☎ 02318 0066
Bumrungrad Hospital:
33 Sukhumvit Soi 3, Wattana .... ☎ 02667 1000
Emergencies........ ☎ 02667 2999
Samitivej Hospital:
133 Sukhumvit Soi 49
Klong Tan Nua, Vadhana........ ☎ 02392 0011
Tourist Authority of Thailand (TAT)
4 Ratchadamnoen Nok Avenue .... ☎ 02228 2977

Climate

Bangkok is hot throughout the year. Coolest and driest months to visit are November to March. April is hotter, but still relatively dry; the rains begin in May, continuing through October. Visiting during the rainy season need not be too unpleasant since showers are normally short with some dry and cloudless days. If there is flooding it will normally occur during September and October when the ground is saturated. Throughout the year temperatures in Bangkok often reach 35° Celsius (95° Fahrenheit).

History

From 1350 until 1767 the capital of **Siam**, the former name of Thailand, was **Ayutthaya**, 85 kilometers north of Bangkok. During this time Thai culture flourished, 33 different kings reigned, and the city became a major center for international commerce. The population grew to one million inhabitants. The present day Ayuthaya, at the confluence of the *Chao Phraya*, *Pa Sak* and *Lopburi* rivers, is well worth visiting since there are many historic ruins, two museums and numerous old temples and monasteries.

The Chakri Dynasty

KINGS OF SIAM

Rama I (*Budda Yat Fa Chulalok*) 1782-1809
Rama II (*Loet La Nabhalai*) 1809-1824
Rama III (*Nang Klao*) 1824-1851
Rama IV (*Mongkut*) 1851-1868
Rama V (*Chulalongkorn*) 1868-1910
Rama VI (*Vajiravudh*) 1910-1925
Rama VII (*Prajadhipok*) 1925-1935
Rama VIII (*Ananda Mahidol*) 1935-1946
Rama IX (*Bhumibol Adulyadej*) 1946-present

In 1782 the Burmese attacked Ayuthaya and King Rama I moved the capital down the river to *Bang Makok*, which translates to "Place of Olives." That town was founded as a trading post in the middle of the 16th century and soon became known as *Bangkok*. The King's thought was that Bangkok would be easier to defend against future invasion. In addition, his palace in Ayuthaya was sandwiched between two monasteries, making expandsion impossible there. With the help of thousands of prisoners of war, construction of the new city began. The canal system was expanded – much of that work remains today – and stout city walls constructed. The POWs were not to be trusted with temple building, however, so artisans from Ayuthaya were brought in for that job. When work on the new capital was completed in 1785 it was renamed *Krung Thep*, "City of Angels," but the name didn't catch on and people continued, and still continue, to call it Bangkok.

Chinese merchants were as much in evidence then as they are today. King Rama I wanted the land they occupied to build yet another temple, the Temple of the Emerald Buddha, ***Wat Phra Kaew*** (*wat* is the Thai word for temple). The Chinese accepted his offer to relocate to the area that is known as Chinatown today.

King Rama III was a great temple builder, and many of the temples you see today were completed during his reign in the first half of the 19th century. Fortunately the temple-building slowed when the next king arrived on the throne; Rama IV's initial undertaking was to build a road – the first in the city – alongside the river. That was completed in 1861; by the turn of the century more roads had been completed and the Bangkok elite were traveling in horse-drawn carriages and rickshaws.

Road construction and the introduction of the automobile were major trends at the start of the 20th century, and quickly got out of control as the century proceeded. Many of the canals built hundreds of years before were filled in to create more usable land. Still, travel on the river remained a favored mode of transport.

Thailand established a constitutional government in 1932 and its civil-service headquarters was in Thonburi, a town and province adjacent to Bangkok, to encourage development there. This growth slowed during the Second World War when the Japanese occupied parts of the city of Thonburi. At the same time the Thai resistance, the *Seri Thai*, came into being helping the allies to undermine the occupation.

During the '60s there was another invasion. American servicemen on R&R during the Vietnam War brought a dubiously welcome boom to the economy. The sex trade that was created, with its go-go bars, seedy nightclubs and massage parlors, continues today. Much of the money that found its way into the Thai treasury went to improve the city's infrastructure. However, not enough was spent on roads or public transit systems, which could not keep pace with the economic boom that was to come in the 1980s.

Bangkok, and Thailand in general, did not foresee the economic crash that was to strike Asia in 1997. But in typical Thai tradition the country bounced back and today the city is expanding at an incredible rate and establishing itself as the financial center of mainland Southeast Asia attracting both Western and Asian investment.

Getting Here

By Air

Bangkok's new $3 billion **Suvarnabhumi Airport**, 40 years in the planning, covers an area of 7,900 acres and was designed to challenge Singapore's Changi Airport and Malaysia's Kuala Lumpur International Airport as the major air-travel hub in Southeast Asia. It replaces the Don Muang Airport, which is overcrowded and outdated.

The main seven-story terminal building, a mammoth structure of glass and steel, will initially be able to process 45 million passengers a year but it has the capability of handling 100 million, more than 10 times the population of Bangkok. Initial aircraft movements are set at 76 per hour with the potential of 112. In its infancy the airport is expected to handle three million tons of cargo annually but is equipped to handle twice that amount. When the airport opened, access to the facility was only by road. Multi-lane elevated highways were constructed from five directions, north, northwest, west, south and northeast. An electric rail-link is under construction and should be completed by 2008. It will be an express line from Bangkok's Makkasan Station.

The airport has 15,000 parking spaces; its kitchens can produce 65,000 airline meals a day and the government claims it to be the most eco-friendly commercial airport in the world. "We have our own water-treatment and catering-waste-treatment facilities and the buildings have been designed to reflect heat outward to conserve energy," a spokesman explained. Thai Airways budgeted $15 million for setting up its operations here. Its 10,000-square-meter check-in facility includes a spa and a unique premium area, where passengers can relax on sofas while staff check them in via portable wireless terminals.

Opening of the 600-room Novotel Suvarnabhumi Airport Hotel coincided with the start of the airport operations. The $70 million hotel was created through the partnership of Airports of Thailand, Thai Airways International and Krung Thai Bank. The hotel is connected by a walkway to the airport's terminals and will also have access to the city rail-link when that is completed. Accor, the company that owns Novotel, won the contract to operate the hotel, beating competing companies including Marriott, Carlson and Amari.

AUTHOR'S NOTE: *The name of the airport, which means "golden land," was chosen by King Bhumibol when he laid the foundation stone in January, 2002. Other names that had been suggested, but fortunately rejected, were Nong Ngu Hao, which means cobra swamp, and the highly imaginative Second Bangkok International Airport.*

Getting Around

Despite its size and traffic problems Bangkok is easy to get around if you make use of the always-expanding public transport systems.

By Boat

Using boats and river taxis on the Chao Phraya River is probably the most pleasant way to traverse Bangkok. It's a busy river so there is always plenty to see, and you can get great views of many major attractions from the water. The best way to get around is to use the tourist boats that only stop at piers that are of interest to visitors. These boats are the most modern and comfortable, and the 75-Baht daily charge entitles you to as many trips as you can squeeze in. These boats leave every half-hour from Sathorn Pier. The non-tourist boats are a lot cheaper, you can go anywhere for 10 Baht, but they can get overloaded, particularly in the morning and evening rush hours.

If you simply want to cross the river there are numerous ferries that run from all the boat landings and charge a mere 2 Baht for the crossing. The river taxis are inexpensive and will take you anywhere on the river or along the neighboring canals. To get an understanding of living on the water you can hire a boat and take a tour along some of the canals. It's a far cry from the homes along the US Intracoastal Waterway or the charming abodes on England's River Thames.

By SkyTrain

Opened in 1999, the elevated rail system brought welcome relief to everyone who lives in or visits Bangkok. There are presently two lines – the **Sukhumvit Line** and the **Silom Line** – which cover most of the city center and many of the main tourist attractions (see the map on page 375). Extensions are planned for the outlying areas. The trains are safe and clean, and each one can carry over 1,000 people. They run on time and are a great way to sightsee above the congestion below. You can buy a three-day tourist pass for 280 Baht, which gives you unlimited use of the trains and the shuttle buses that link various routes to the system. Trains operate every few minutes from 6am until midnight. There are bilingual digital signs at the front and the sides of each telling you where you're going. SkyTrain has three tourist information offices, at Siam, Nana and Saphan Taksin stations. They are open from 8am to 8pm. Helpful English-speaking staff will explain the best tourist routes, provide maps, sell river tours and even hand out passes to temples.

By Subway

Bangkok's newest addition to its mass-transit system opened officially in July 2004 – a month ahead of schedule. At the official opening of the subway King Bhumibol Adulyadej named the initial section (the Blue Line) the *Chaloem Ratchamongkhon* Line, which means Celebration of the Auspicious Kingship. This is the first underground rail system in Thailand and took almost ten years to build. The initial section stretches over 20 kilometers beneath the city and passes under two major thoroughfares, Rama IV Road and Ratchadaphisek Road. The line begins at the city's main railway station, Hualampong and goes north. There are 18 stations, which provide a good link between many major hotels, the business district, shopping centers and the Queen Sirikit National Convention Center. Several of the stations connect with SkyTrain stations. Additions are already planned.

AUTHOR'S NOTE: *During the subway system's testing period, the train operators invited several groups of elderly and disabled people to try out the system to insure that all the special facilities worked for them.*

There are two park-and-ride facilities, one at Lat Phrao Station, the other at the Thailand Cultural Center station. Parking and travel costs are minor. Each station has ticket-vending machines, which accept coins and notes, and instructions are in Thai and English.

By Bus

Local buses are absurdly cheap and run everywhere, but they don't come high on our list of recommendations. They are color-coded to help you match them with the bus map but most of the signs are in Thai and once on board purses get snatched and valuables disappear. On the plus side there are lots of them, over 5,000, and some are air conditioned.

By Taxi

There are plenty of them and they are cheap compared to taxis in other large cities. Two other big pluses: The number of *tuk-tuks*, the three-wheeled terrors of Bangkok streets, is on the decline, as is the number of non-metered cabs where you have to haggle about prices. (There are still tuk-tuks around and if you feel like a ride of terror it comes cheap; you can get a fair distance for 30 Baht. Just don't carry the fragile ornament you bought for Aunt Mabel with you.) Minimum fare for metered taxis – the words Taxi Meter will be displayed on the roof – is 35 Baht for the first two kilometers and goes up by 5 Baht for subsequent kilometers. Rates are based on a speed of 6 kph. If you get stuck in a jam, not an uncommon happening, there is a surcharge of one Baht per minute. If you travel on the expressway you have to pay the toll charges, but they are minimal. Have change ready. Tipping is not essential but it is much appreciated; making a living driving a taxi in Bangkok is hardly ideal employment. If you do get a non-metered cab sort out the price before you start the journey. And don't forget, a lot of drivers do not speak or read English. Have something written in Thai that says where you want to go.

If you take a meter taxi make sure the meter gets turned on. Many drivers have the habit of not switching them on and making up their own prices. We found that, in Bangkok, as in many cities, the drivers come in two varieties: the first gives you a pleasant ride, and is courteous to other road users while the other, and quite prevalent here, feels he has to accelerate and brake with unpleasant regularity giving you a ride that is more suited to a Formula 1 race track than the heavily-traversed streets of a city.

By Limousine

Years ago, before the SkyTrain or subway existed, we discussed our shopping plans with the hotel concierge. He suggested we hire one of the hotel limousines. Our fears about the cost were quelled when he explained we would have change back from $20. Several hotels still provide this service and it is well worthwhile, even if the cost is higher today. If you have to travel through the traffic this is by far the best way to do it. Our liveried chauffeur, clad in spotless white, knew all the right places to go, some of which we would never have found without him. We offset the expensive day shopping with an evening visit to a street market, and returned to the hotel in a tuk-tuk clutching two very large suitcases. The tuk-tuk cost 50 Baht, which we felt excessive for the 20 minutes of terror we had to endure.

Touring the City

One of the best ways to get oriented is to take the early-morning three-hour boat trip along the **Chao Phraya**, the river of Kings, and the **Bangkok Noi Canal**. If you were fortunate enough to book a hotel overlooking the river you will already know what an active stretch of water it is. Thais have a tradition of setting up homes along rivers, and life on the river in Bangkok continues today in much the same way it did hundreds of years ago.

On most Bangkok tours there will be a stop at a temple. There are over 400 to see in the city, and if you decide to do some private sightseeing trips (an inexpensive way to select what you want to see) the guide will not be surprised or offended if you ask not to see any more temples. We have to wonder if temples were designed by Kodak since we have not met anyone who has visited Thailand without returning home with numerous photos of them, with or without people in them. However, if you like temples this is the place to be.

Bangkok stretches out over 600 square miles, making it one of the world's largest cities. Claims are made that the city is sinking an inch or so each year into the fertile delta on which it stands. Nobody seems too concerned, particularly developers, whose mega-structures continue to sprout up alongside ancient spires.

The main north-south railway line divides Bangkok in two. To the east of the railway are the main commercial and tourist areas. To the west is Old Bangkok with its palaces and temples, and the Chinese and Indian neighborhoods.

Getting Away

By Air

Thai Airways operates most of the domestic flights from Bangkok. In recent years several smaller carriers have started up to provide additional services, and some competition for the national carrier. Thai uses Boeing 737s or Airbus 300s on its domestic routes to Buriram, Chiang Mai, Chiang Rai, Chumphon, Hat Yai, Khon Kaen, Krabi, Lampang, Mae Hong Son, Mae Sot, Nakhon Phanom, Nakhon Ratchasima, Nan, Narathiwat, Phetchabun, Phitsanulok, Phrae, Phuket, Roi Et, Trang, Ubon Ratchathani and Udon Thani.

The no-frills carrier, **One-Two-GO**, operates daily services from Bangkok to Krabi and Surat Thani, using either a 444-seat Boeing B747 or a 216-seat B757, depending on demand. Krabi flights depart from Bangkok at 5pm daily except Thursday, when departure time will be 8:20am. Return flights leave Krabi at 6:45pm. Flights to Surat Thani leave Bangkok at 8am returning at 9:50am. One-way airfare for both flights is 1,650 Baht (US$41) per person, www.fly12go.com/en/main.

Bangkok Airways operates regular services to Chiang Mai, Hua Hin, Phuket, Samui, Sukhothai and Trat (for Ko Chang). Mainstay of the fleet is the Franco-Italian ATR-72, and the airline is introducing Boeing 717s on many of its services, www.bangkokair.com.

Tiger Airlines, another of Asia's no-frills operators, has several daily flights between Singapore's Changi Airport and Bangkok, using Airbus 320s with 180 seats in an all-economy configuration. Tickets are best bought on the Internet, www.tigerairways.com, or call ☎ 001800 656752.

Another budget carrier, **Thai AirAsia,** also offers service between Bangkok and Singapore. Tickets can be purchased online at www.airasia.com.

Rival no-frills carrier **Nok Air**, a subsidiary of Thai Airways, began twice-daily Bangkok-Phuket service in early 2005 with one-way ticket prices starting at 1,150 Baht including VAT, insurance and airport fees. Bookings may be made online at www.nokair.com.

The domestic terminal at the old (Don Muang) Bangkok airport tends to get a little chaotic, particularly in the early morning. Chances are you will be taken to your aircraft by bus. Don't be embarrassed to keep showing your boarding pass to insure you don't get flown to somewhere other than your chosen destination. It hasn't happened to us, but we have seen people heading for Phuket when they wanted to go to Chang Mai. With the new airport this should not be a problem.

There is a departure tax on domestic flights, which may be included in your ticket or may be collected when you check in. The charge is 60 Baht. The international departure tax of 500 Baht per person is not included in the price of airline tickets. Don't forget to keep sufficient cash for this charge at the end of your trip. This tax is not part of what you paid for in your ticket and must be paid – in cash – if you want to fly home.

FINE NO-FRILLS FLIGHT

Shortly after AirAsia introduced its low-cost flights to Bangkok from Phuket we bought two tickets on the Internet. They cost us $147, almost half what the scheduled flight would have cost. The flights ran on time, the flight attendants were helpful, the baggage was at the carousel before we were. There were soft drinks and sandwiches for sale onboard at very low prices. And we purchased good-quality polo shirts for 240 Baht each; the small Air Asia logo will be a talking point when we get home. One complaint: There is no seat selection; but surprisingly our fellow travelers, mostly Thai, made no mad dash for the aircraft when the flight was called. Just our luck: A week after we bought our tickets Thai Airways announced low fares for the same routing at almost the same price.

By Bus

Long-distance buses leave from one of three bus stations. **MoChit** is the North-and-Northeastern terminal, Kampaengphet 2 Road, ☎ 02936 3660. **Ekamai** is the Eastern Bus terminal, on Sukhumvit Road, ☎ 023912504. **Sai Tai Mai** is the Southern Bus terminal, Boromratchchonnani Road, ☎ 02435 1200.

AUTHOR'S NOTE: *The stretch of Sukhumvit Road from Asok Road to the Ekamai bus station is where many Westerners and Japanese live. There are some expensive restaurants here as well as an abundance of Western grocery stores. Traffic is an around-the-clock nightmare. Fortunately you can avoid it by taking the SkyTrain direct to the bus station.*

Here are some examples of the long-distance buses. In each case we have selected the most convenient time and vehicle.

For **Chiang Mai** there is a service that leaves MoChit at 9am and arrives at 7 pm. The cost is 625 Baht. **Lampang** buses also leave from MoChit. There is a bus departing at 9pm and arrives the following day at 5am. The cost: 405 Baht.

For travelers to **Pattaya** there is a service that leaves Ekamai every half-hour starting at 5am. The journey takes two hours and 20 minutes and costs 90 Baht.

For those heading south there is a daily VIP bus that leaves the Sai Tai Mai terminal at 7pm and arrives in **Phuket City** at 8:00 the following morning. The cost: 755 Baht. (Note: that trip takess 13 hours. The jet flight does it in 80 minutes but costs a lot more). The **Trang** VIP bus leaves at 7:30pm each night and takes 12 hours. The cost: 750 Baht.

AUTHOR'S NOTE: *According to the regulations a VIP bus is air conditioned, has no more than 24 reclining seats, provides food and drink service, has a hostess onboard and has a toilet.*

Bangkok

By Car

Driving yourself around Bangkok is as much fun as trying to learn the Thai alphabet. However, if you do want a car to travel out of town there are endless companies, many of them with desks in the major hotels. In case you hadn't noticed you drive on the left in Thailand (or at least you are supposed to).

CAR RENTAL COMPANIES

Avis Rent A Car	☎ 02255 5300
Budget	☎ 02203 0250
Central Car Rent Co.	☎ 02251 2778
Golden Car Rent	☎ 02267 8379
Grand Car Rent	☎ 02248 2991
Hertz	☎ 02722 6161
Highway Car Rent	☎ 02311 7867
Krungthai Car Rent Co.	☎ 02943 5800
Landmark Limousine	☎ 02255 8401
Lumpinee Car Rent	☎ 02255 1966
National Car Rental	☎ 02722 8487
Premier Inter Leasing	☎ 02391 0461
Q C Leasing Co.	☎ 02662 2431
Quality Rent A Car	☎ 02655 0080
SMT Rent A Car	☎ 02722 8484
Thai International Car	☎ 02954 3201
Winner Rent A Car	☎ 02251 0804

By Train

Bangkok's main rail station is **Hualamphong Station** on Rama IV Road. From here the tracks branch out in all directions. If you are traveling through Thailand you'll change trains here, since all lines end in Bangkok. Some of the trains, including the one that goes to the **Bridge on the River Kwai** (see page 116), operate from the **Thonburi** station, which is close to the Royal Barge museum and has great views over the river. Cost of train travel is about the same as going by bus. It tends to be slower by train but it can be more comfortable if you have a sleeping compartment. There are more details about train travel in the *Trains of Thailand* chapter (see page 351).

Things to See

Temples

The two most popular tourist attractions in Bangkok are the **Temple of the Emerald Buddha** (Wat Phra Kaew) and the **Grand Palace**. They are next to each other, and one ticket gets you into both places. The temple and the palace have something in common: they don't have full-time residents. No monks live in this temple, which makes it unique in Thailand, and the King doesn't live in the palace. His home is just a block or so away.

The usual way to visit these two incredible sights is with a city tour. However, you can make your own way here. If you do that, come first thing in the morning; the complex opens at 8:30am, and it will be less crowded and a little cooler. The entrance fee is 200 Baht and, should you make the error of arriving inappropriately clad – sleeveless tops and shorts are not acceptable – more appropriate clothing can be borrowed at the entrance gates.

> *The word* "wat" *means temple, and you will see it on road signs throughout Thailand. It is not a question; it's just to let you know that there's another temple coming up.*

Temple of the Emerald Buddha: If you see just one temple in Thailand, make it this one. The dozens of buildings that make up the complex are an architectural delight adorned with brilliant mosaics and golden spires.

> *You won't need to be reminded to remove your shoes before you enter a temple; the outside looks like Wal-Mart had a shoe sale.*

The main attraction is the temple that houses the Emerald Buddha, a tiny statue stuck up high and difficult to see. Three times a year the King comes to this temple to change the Buddha's robe. During the summer the robe is gold with diamonds; plain gold during the winter; and a monk's robe during the rainy season.

The **Grand Palace** that adjoins Wat Phra Kaew is made up of several very impressive halls, which have all played a role in Thai history. The **Amarinda Hall** is still used today for special occasions and houses the antique throne. The **Grand Palace Hall** is where the present king's elder brother was found shot dead in 1946; it has not been used as a royal residence since.

Wat Arun, Temple of Dawn, is probably the best known of all the Thai temples since it is featured in many of the ads promoting Thailand. Best views of the famous five-tower landmark are from the river. It stands majestically across from the Grand Palace. All river tours stop here for a short while; if you want more time, come on your own (take the 2-Baht ferry crossing from the **Tha Tien Pier** on Thai Wang Road). The temple's main feature is the 100-meter high central pagoda, which is covered in multi-colored Chinese porcelain chips – some of which were part of the ballast of the old Chinese ships that used to make crossings to Bangkok – that were donated by local people. Open daily from 7:30am to 5:30pm. Admission: 20 Baht. The ferry operates from 6am to 10pm. You can get great views by climbing up to the second tier of the base that supports the central tower.

DID YOU KNOW? *Up until 1785,* Wat Arun *was home to the Emerald Buddha.*

Wat Pho: South of the Grand Palace, and better known to the Thais as **Wat Phra Chetuphon**. A temple might seem to be an unlikely place to learn massage, but this is one of the skills taught at this temple, the oldest and largest in Bangkok. The temple is best known for its enormous reclining Buddha image that is covered in gold leaf, 46 meters long and 15 meters high. Within the 20 acres that the temple complex occupies there are more than 1,000 other Buddha images – a record number for any one Thai temple. The original *wat* was built in the 16th century – 200 years before Bangkok became Thailand's capital. It has been rebuilt several times since and bears little resemblance to the original structure. The *wat* has played an important role in teaching traditional Thai medicine, and Thai massage in particular. The temple offers one-hour (250 Baht) and half-hour (150 Baht) treatments. Foot reflexology and herbal treatments are also offered. For those who want to learn the art, 30-hour courses are available at a cost of 6,000 Baht. The lessons can be taken over a period of up to 15 days. The massage center is at the rear of the *wat*; there's normally a wait for massages unless you get here at opening time.

Open daily from 8am to 5pm; ☎ 02221 2974. Admission is 20 Baht and you can hire an English-speaking guide at the entrance for 150 Baht.

Museums

The National Museum, Bangkok: If you want to immerse yourself in Thai culture and history there is no better place than this. There is probably too much to see and it is easy to spend an entire day browsing and learning. With an admission fee of 40 Baht that includes a guide book and map, it is a Bangkok bargain. The place rarely gets crowded since it is not on many of the city tours. The museum (☎ 02224 1404) is on Naphra That Road between Thammasart University and the National Theater. It is opposite the *Sanam Luang*, that large oval field in front of the Grand Palace. Open every day from 9am to 4pm except Mondays, Tuesdays and national holidays (see page 33).

The collections of art and antiquities are phenomenal. The highlight for us was the royal family's funeral chariots that are housed in building 17. Yes, there are a lot of buildings many of which are not air conditioned. The chariot that caught our eye is named *Vejayant Rajarot* and was built in 1785 on the orders of Rama I. It was used to carry the urn containinghis remains at his funeral. It was last used in 1985 for the funeral of Queen Rambhai Bharni, wife of Rama VII. The chariot weighs 40 tons, stands 13 meters high and it takes 300 men to pull it.

As you wander around there are things ancient, and very ancient and modern. There are weapons and musical instruments, jewels and royal regalia, furniture and architectural wonders. Fortunately there is an inexpensive café in the center of things where you can regain your strength. Volunteers give free tours in English every Wednesday and Thursday starting at 9:30am. The museum is open from 9am to 4pm from Wednesday thru Sunday.

Vimanmek Mansion Museum: If you want to see some royal treasures without the crowds, then this largest-in-the-world teak building is the place to head for. The main three-story teak mansion and its associated buildings are in the **Dusit Palace** on Ratchawithi Road. The royal collection includes photography by the King and special handicrafts from around the country that have been collected by the Queen. There is a demonstration of Thai dancing twice a day, at 10:30am and 2pm. Open daily, except holidays, from 9:30am to 4pm; the 100-Baht admission charge includes a guided tour in English. Appropriate attire required. ☎ 02628 6300.

Jim Thompson's House: The life story of James Harrison Wilson Thompson is like a James Bond novel. His life was as colorful and exciting as the colors of the vast silk empire that he created. Born in Greenville, Delaware in 1906, he became an architect in New York. He volunteered to join the army when the Second World War began and was enrolled into the OSS, the Office of Strategic Services that later became the Central Intelligence Agency, and his clandestine work took him to North Africa and Asia. At the end of the war he was station head in Bangkok.

He became enamored of Thailand and at the end of the war decided to stay on. His first project was to help in the remodeling of the Oriental Hotel. And then he turned his attention to developing the silk industry, which at the time was a dying industry. His artistic and marketing skills created the Jim Thompson silk empire and have made Thailand a major source of quality silk today.

DID YOU KNOW? *Thompson's life ended mysteriously in 1967 while he was on holiday in Malaysia. He went for a walk in the jungle and was never seen again. The same year his sister was murdered in the US. Were their deaths linked?*

The home he created in Bangkok is a complex of six traditional Thai houses that were brought from different parts of Thailand and set in lavish grounds. If you wish to tour the property you must take a guide; the tour will give you an insight into the man who became known as the host with the most. He loved entertaining and his guests included people like Noel Coward and W. Somerset Maugham.

The house is in the center of Bangkok, opposite the National Stadium on Rama I Road. Open from 9am to 5pm. Admission: 100 Baht for adults and 50 Baht for students.

The Royal Barge Museum: Thailand's royal barges have played a major role in Bangkok's life for centuries. Today there is only a handful left and they are on display here. Originally used as ships of war, they date back as far as 1357. Back in the 1600s there were hundreds in use to ferry the nobility around but since then they have taken a battering. When the Burmese attacked the Thai capital in 1782 they burned the entire fleet, and King Rama I was only able to replace some of them. In more recent times most of the remaining fleet was damaged by bombing in World War II. The present King restored a number of those to the condition that you see them in today. Star of the fleet has to be the *Suphanahong* (Golden Swan), weighing fifteen tons and needing a crew of 80 to power her. She was carved out of one huge tree trunk. The royal family used to make an annual trip down the river to give robes to monks at the end of the Buddhist Lent, a time when the holy men are not allowed to travel. Easiest way to get to the museum is by boat; most of the river and canal tours stop here. Arun Amarin Road, ☎ 2424 0004. Admission is 30 Baht and the museum, more of a warehouse, is open from 8:30am until 4:30pm.

Kasetsart University: Exhibition of Thai textiles and traditional costumes. For those interested in learning about the history of textiles and costumes, the university has set up a permanent exhibition at its Office of Agricultural Museum & Culture, 50 Phahon Yothin Road, Chatuchak. Object of the exhibition is show how culture and traditions have been handed down through weaving and textiles. More info at ☎ 2942 8711, ext 108.

Around the City

Damnoen Saduak Floating Market: This is one of those little adventures you've got to make time for when you visit Bangkok. Yes, it is very touristy, but you'll see a slice of Thai life that has dominated this kingdom for centuries – living on the canals. Children born here are normally dunked into the murky water soon after birth to immunize them from the tropical diseases. And when you look around you'll see how well they survive. The big plus is the color of the whole thing. The fruits and vegetables that are grown in orchards and gardens around the water are piled high on rowing boats and traded between the river dwellers. There is a wide variety of produce – including cabbages, grapes, papayas, oranges and onions.

There are several ways to see this spectacle, which happens every day of the year, starting around 6am. It normally lasts around five hours and it is advisable to be here early to see the best of the produce, with fewer tourists, and cooler temperatures. You can come with a group tour, or drive down on your own; the market is just over 100 kilometers southwest of Bangkok and the drive will take about two hours. A private tour will cost about 3,500 Baht. For the economically minded there are buses leaving Bangkok's Southern

Bus Terminal every 40 minutes. The air conditioned bus costs 50 Baht, and one without A/C a mere 30 Baht.

If you take a tour it will begin at a staging area ahead of the market and be ferried in on a diesel-powered longtail boat. This gives you the advantage of being on the same level as the traders. When we took the ride we really thought we were in the middle of the wilderness until we saw an old tin sign hanging from a tree demanding that we *Drink Coca Cola*.

Most of the tours stop for lunch at the **Rose Garden** on the return journey. This retreat, though touristy, gives a great insight into Thai culture. There are demonstrations of Thai dancing and Thai boxing, a chance to see elephants at work and a ceremony involving monks. If you are going on your own it's worth a visit, and the food is good too.

If you buy the full-day tour it will include a visit to *Nakorn Pathom*, site of the world's largest Buddhist monument, and the most important in Thailand. You'll leave Bangkok at 7:30am and return at 6pm; the full-day tour will cost around 1,500 Baht, and it's a fun and educational day.

EATING AT THE MARKET: *Hygiene is not high on the priority list of those who cook from one of these canoes. Hands are dunked into the water and then used to mold chunks of dough, which are immersed in hot oil. The resulting steaming ball, resembling a gray dumpling, is offered for sale. We declined, but many didn't and they survived. Or least they made it back to the hotel that night without ill effect. These floating kitchens produce all manner of dishes from soups and curries to sweet dishes. As always there is a cool coconut, filled with its own water, to wash it down.*

Chinatown: You can't call the Chinese interlopers in Bangkok society. They were moved to this area almost 300 years ago when King Rama I moved the Thai capital from Ayutthaya and wanted the land the Chinese merchants occupied to build the Grand Palace.

And in all that time the place hasn't really entered the 20th century, let alone the current one. It is tough and grimy. Its traffic-choked streets are full of cheap markets and delightful smelly food stalls. If you came to see modern-day Bangkok you are in the wrong place. There is one tourist attraction here – yes, you guessed it, a temple. **Wat Traimit** attracts a lot of attention, not because it is a wonderful temple, but because it has a big solid-gold Buddha weighing in at five tons. Legend has it that the Buddha, covered in a thick coat of stucco, was being moved when it fell from a crane. The stucco fell apart to reveal the gold. It is believed that the coating was put on hundreds of years ago to stop the Buddha being stolen by the invading Burmese.

The entrance fee to Wat Traimit is 20 Baht, and it is open from 9am to 5pm. To avoid the constant traffic snarl, the easiest way to get here is by boat. Tha Ratchawong pier is only a couple of hundred yards from Yaowarat Road, Chinatown's main road, where the temple is located.

As you poke around the noisy streets of Chinatown you'll find the best prices in Bangkok for almost everything, from jewelry to auto parts, fabrics and paints. There are dozens of places selling gold and antiques, both old and newly antiquated. Then there are the fascinating Chinese medicine shops with something for anything that ails you. Few people here speak English and most of the Chinese don't speak Chinese. There's no such thing as a quiet time to visit. There are lots of good places to eat authentic Thai-Chinese food, which seems to have fewer of those dreaded tiny red bits.

Records show that 100 years ago the area had a green-light district (brothel keepers hung green lanterns to advertise their trade) with – in addition to the brothels – over 200 opium dens, plenty of pawn shops and countless gaming houses. Most of that stuff is illegal now. And we certainly didn't see any opium dens.

Pahurat: If you detected the aroma of curry in the area while you were in Chinatown, it was coming from here. *Pahurat* is just west of Chinatown; it is Bangkok's Little India, the site of the city's largest textile market.

Bargaining is expected at the enormous fabric market, which is known for its variety, everything from your basic white to the multi-colored cottons and silks for which it's famous. If you want fabrics for clothes or for covering furniture this is the place to find it. As you might expect, there are numerous excellent Indian restaurants in addition to the small stalls selling tidbits to munch while you shop. Great place to find those ornate sandals with large globs of colored glass and Indian jewelry. Other items worth buying are Indian spices and incense. Temple seekers do not despair. There is one in Pahurat – the largest Sikh temple outside of India. Here you not only have to remove your shoes before entering but you must also cover your head.

Rice-Barge Cruise: There are numerous ways to get between Bangkok and the kingdom's ancient capital of Ayutthaya, just 76 kilometers north. The most recent trip we made was aboard the luxury train *Eastern & Oriental Express* (see page 361). There are several enjoyable cruises, and it's an easy ride by bus.

Tharnatep Pintusan, owner of Educational Travel Center, has developed another way to make the journey using a converted rice barge, the *Thanatharee*. You can't call it luxury but you do get to live like the locals and learn Thai cooking – not in a luxury hotel kitchen under the supervision of a master chef, but on the stern of the barge as it chugs slowly up the Chao Phraya River.

Mr. Tharnatep feels that Thai life has changed dramatically in Bangkok. "I noticed that once you sail upstream, away from the city, the inseparable link between the river and Thai people reasserts itself. We can capture that on our barge trip," he says. For his efforts Mr. Tharnatep gained the 2004 Award of Excellence for inbound tours awarded by Tourism Authority of Thailand.

The *Thanatharee* carries 12 passengers who sleep in bunks, multi-share style, on the lower deck of the stout teakwood barge. There is just one shower and two toilets but, "Our guests have all day to shower so it is not an issue on a slow-moving barge," Mr. Tharnatep says.

While this is not the most luxurious of river barges, the price for the three-day, two-night adventure, including all meals, is a reasonable $196 per person. No fancy designer toiletries or lotions provided but you will get soap and towels.

Mr. Tharnatep says says his tours are meant to be a learning experience, an encounter with rural Thai values and heritage. He offers a hands-on approach to travel; guests can learn how to cook a meal in the small galley tucked into the stern of the barge. At an early-morning stop at the thriving market of *Prathum Thani*, 35 kilometers north of Bangkok, passengers can shop for fresh spices, vegetables and fruits, learning firsthand about the ingredients that make Thai cuisine so special.

"Passengers live for two and a half days almost as the villagers do, close to the river, dining on its fresh fish and the finest rice harvested in the vast emerald-green paddy fields of the Chao Phraya delta," he says. He has several itineraries; the one that follows was particularly appealing.

Day One: The *Thanatharee* departs Bangkok at 8:30am and heads to **Ko Kred**, an island in the middle of the Chao Phraya River. Here you explore the **Mon** pottery-making village before moving on to **Pathum Thani** market, where fresh meats, vegetables and various local goods are sold. Lunch is served on the way. There is a short stop at **Wat Pailom**, well known as a winter nesting ground of the Asian openbill stork, which migrates from Northern India and Siberia. The barge then heads upriver on *Maenam Noi*, a small branch of the main Chao Phraya River. You arrive at **Wat Singh** at approximately 6pm, tie up for the night and enjoy dinner on board.

Day Two: Before the cruise moves on there is an opportunity to give food to the monks on their morning alms round. After breakfast the cruise continues along the *Maenam Noi*. There are bicycles available, and you'll have time to explore the villages along the river, then rejoin the barge at **Wat Kophai**. The cruise continues to **Bang Sadej**, where it's back on the bikes to visit the town's famous temple and a local orphanage where hill-tribe children receive an education and vocational training. At the main village you'll meet the local people and see the cottage industries they engage in. The second night is spent at **Pamok**.

AUTHOR'S NOTE: *If cycling isn't appealing, you can always stay aboard and watch life on the river after having some village walks.*

Day Three: You can take a short morning bicycle ride to Pamok market and get some local food to add to your breakfast, if you wish. After breakfast there is time to visit the local **Pamok School**, and visits to a local family that makes drums and the local market are included before the cruise moves on to Ayutthaya, where it docks at the train-station pier around noon.

The Educational Travel Center can arrange transfers to and from Bangkok and sightseeing in the country's ancient capital. *Thanatharee* Rice Barge, Educational Travel Center, ☎ 02224 0043, www.thanatharee.com.

Red Cross Snake Farm: If you've looked ahead in the book and sneaked a peek at the *Phuket* chapter you'll know what we think about snake shows. However, this one does have some redeeming features. This is Bangkok's largest collection of those slithery creatures, and it is right in the city center at 1871 Rama IV Road, ☎ 02252 0161, across from the **Montien Hotel**. The redeeming feature is that the Red Cross sells a helpful medical guide and has a clinic where you can be immunized against some of those unpleasant tropical diseases like cholera and typhoid. Twice a day, at 10am and 2pm, there is a 20-minute slide presentation about Thailand's dangerous snakes and the antidotes produced by the Red Cross. If you stay on, you'll get to see a live show with professionals handling cobras, vipers and kraits. There is also a two-meter-long python you can play with. Fortunately this is not compulsory. Entrance fee is 70 Baht.

Erawan Shrine: The daily highjinks here are as bizarre as the history of this highly ornate shrine. It is at the corner of Ploenchit and Rajdamri Roads, one of Bangkok's noisiest and busiest intersections. Fifty years ago the Thai Hotel and Tourist Company was trying to build a hotel on the site. Everything went wrong. After numerous delays and labor disputes it was decided, as is the Thai way, to bring in a holy man to see if he could sort things out. He decided that they had picked the wrong date to lay the foundation stone and the only way to solve the problem was to erect a shrine dedicated to *Brahma*, the Hindu creation god, and *Erawan*, his three-headed elephant. It worked: the hotel, now the **Grand Hyatt Erawan Hotel**, was completed without a hitch.

This is the place to come seeking good fortune and to pay homage for receiving it. And come they do. Many bring gifts of flowers, miniature wooden elephants, and candles. Plenty of incense is burned, so much that it overpowers the traffic fumes. Should you forget to bring a gift there are nearby stalls selling suitable presents. And you can also hire dancers attired in traditional Thai costumes or an orchestra. The whole thing is a great photo opportunity and a wonderful way to watch Thai dancing. This is very true Thai and a big plus is that is free – provided you don't pay for the piper or presents. Closest SkyTrain station is Chit Lom.

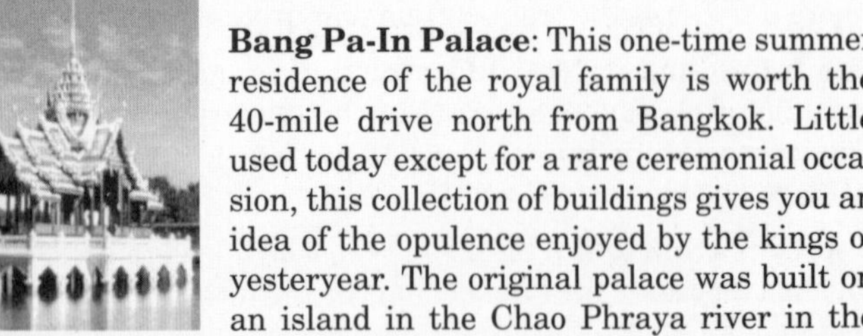

Bang Pa-In Palace: This one-time summer residence of the royal family is worth the 40-mile drive north from Bangkok. Little used today except for a rare ceremonial occasion, this collection of buildings gives you an idea of the opulence enjoyed by the kings of yesteryear. The original palace was built on an island in the Chao Phraya river in the

17th century by King Prasat Thong, who was shipwrecked here as a young man. The site was abandoned, and it was **King Mongkut** (King Rama IV) who began rebuilding the site in the 19th century. This is the king of *Anna and the King of Siam* fame. There has always been controversy in Thailand over the novel by Anna Leonowens and the films that were based on her writing, but certain things are fact. Mongkut did have over 80 children by dozens of wives. And he did have a huge harem. In 1862 he employed "Mrs. Anna" to educate his wives and children. What happened after that is a matter of opinion and myth. (In case you missed it, see pages 290 and 295 for more about Anna's life). Today there is a modern boat to take you round the island, which is home to yet another temple, Wat Niwettham Prawat. The boat departs every hour from Bang Pa-In Pier from 9am until 3pm and the cost is just 35 Baht.

Thai Boxing: We decided to list this under *Things to See* rather than *Things to Do*. There are indeed several gyms where you can learn or practice this ancient art of self-defense but we opted to be spectators rather than hospital patients. There are two main arenas where you can enjoy the spectacle. **Ratchadamnoen Stadium**, Ratchadamnoen Nok Avenue, ☎ 2281 4205, has fights on Mondays, Wednesdays, Thursdays and Sundays; the action switches to the **Lumphini Stadium** on Rama IV Road, ☎ 2251 4303 on Tuesdays, Fridays, and Saturdays. We use the word "spectacle" deliberately. It's not just the athletic kick-boxing that you get to see but the pre-fight ceremonies and the frantic betting. And it all comes with music from a small orchestra, which varies its program depending on the pace of the boxing.

CAUTION: *If you opt to check out Thai boxing on your own, be wary of ticket touts who will tell you they have the only good seats available.*

Thai boxing has been around for 500 years. The ancient rulers were masters of the art and insisted that all their fighting forces were trained in hand-to-hand combat; it is still used in military training today. What you see today is tame compared to the old days, when the fists became weapons of mega-destruction. The hands were bandaged with string and sprinkled with fragments of glass, then submerged in a gooey substance that eventually set rock hard. Then the battle commenced. It could be one of the reasons the country was never colonized.

Thai boxing, or *Muay Thai*, to use the local words, is big business in Thailand. There are over 60,000 professional fighters in the country and to perform at either of these two stadiums is considered a great honor. Each match consists of five three-minute rounds with a welcome two-minute breather between each round. The boxers battle with feet, fists, arms and anything else but their heads. It's exhausting even to watch. Ringside seats cost 1,000 Baht, but we were quite happy to sit farther away from the fighters and paid about half of that fee. You can arrive by taxi and purchase tickets at the windows, which are clearly marked with the price of tickets, or do as we did and have the hotel organize the tickets and transportation.

Dusit Zoo: Not only is it a zoo but a fine park, where you can rent paddleboats and dine under the shade of large trees. The zoo, also known as *Khao Din*, is between the Chitralada Royal Palace and the National Assembly. There's a good variety of African and Asian animals, including the royal white elephants, and tropical birds in an ornamental garden. Elephant rides for the younger ones. Open daily from 8am to 6 pm. Adults pay 30 Baht, children 5 Baht.

Siam Water Park: A visit to this attraction, northeast of Bangkok, is a good example of how much more you get for your money in Thailand. Admission for a child here is 100 Baht. We visited several water parks in southern Spain earlier in the year and spent almost four times that amount for admission. And then we had to pay for the extras: a sun bed, use of the changing rooms and a locker. That's all included here, and there's a lot more for everyone to do. There's an aviary, zoo, playground and botanical gardens, plus a full selection of water activities. It's open longer, from 10am to 10pm, the food and service are better and cheaper and, of course, it doesn't close in the winter. The park is in Munburi, a 30-minute drive east from the Lat Phrao flyover, ☎ 02919 7200.

Horse Racing: Bangkok has two race tracks. The **Royal Turf Club of Thailand** is on Phitsanulok Road, ☎ 2800 0020. The **Royal Bangkok Sports Club** track is on Henri Dunant Road, ☎ 2510 0181. Meetings alternate every Sunday between the two tracks. Admission charges range from 50 Baht to 100 Baht.

Benjasiri Park: This park was opened to commemorate the 60th birthday of Queen Sirikit in 1992. It adjoins the Queens Park Hotel on Sukhumvit Road and is close to the Emporium shopping complex. There are several contemporary sculptures and a Thai pavilion showing some of the work undertaken by the Queen. There is a children's playground, roller-skating rink, swimming pool and basketball and *takraw* courts. No charge for admission and open daily from 5am until 8pm.

> "Takraw" *is a popular game among young Thais. You'll see it played on street corners as well as on actual courts. It's a bit like volleyball, except you can't use your hands. The rattan ball is kept in the air by players using their feet, heads, elbows and knees – it will look familiar if you've ever seen a hacky sack, or footbag, game. Fascinating to watch, tricky to play.*

Suan Luang Rama IX Park: This royal park at Sukhumvit 103 Road opened in 1987 to commemorate the King's 60th birthday. The grounds are divided into six areas. There is a botanical garden on the north side and in another area there is a nine-sided tower honoring King Rama IX. There's a great use of water with ponds, streams and a waterfall. There is a reservoir that is used for water sports, and a large arena used for shows, both agricultural and cultural.

Seri Thai Park: This 145-acre park is the only lake park in Bangkok and was formerly known as *Bueng-ta-thong Pond*; it is named in honor of the *Seri Thai* movement, the World War II resistance group that worked with the allies during the Japanese occupation. For many years the area was an abandoned reservoir. When it was transformed into a park it became part of a flood-prevention project to help control water during the rainy season. There is a wide selection of Thai plants and trees. Among the tree varieties spread through the park are Borneo mahogany, cassia, banyan and royal poinciana in addition to numerous varieties of palm and fruit trees. Plants and flowers originating in Thailand dominate in the flower and fruit gardens. Admission is free and the park, open from 5am to 8pm, is near the Siam Water Park at Sukhaphiban 2 Road, Khlongkum.

The Princess Mother Memorial Park: This royal park, *Somdet Phra Sri Nagarindra*, also has a museum and a model of the house where the Princess Mother lived as a child. The main park area is filled with very old fig trees and numerous flowering shrubs. The exhibition halls display gifts given for the royal funeral as well as many of her personal effects. There is a paved jogging track. The park, on Somdet Chao Phraya Road, is open every from 6am to 6pm and the museum from 9am to 4pm but closed on public holidays. Admission is free. Nearby is the *Chao Phor Seua Shrine*, highly regarded by the Chinese community. The shrine, with a red and gold main arch, is covered with ornate carvings of fish, dragons and swords. Followers pay homage with flowers and garlands, which can be bought at the nearby street stalls.

Things to Do

Recreational Activities

■ Kite Flying

This is a favorite pastime for many Thais. Best time to see the action is at the end of February. Look to the skies at the parks and beaches around the country. Preferred spot in Bangkok is at the *Sanam Luang* in front of the Grand Palace. Contests are held throughout the country and if you want to have a try you'll find kites for sale at most street markets. The contests involve two teams. One has the larger male kite, called a *chula,* the other a female called *pakpaos*. The object is for the *chula* to trap the *pakpaos*.

Thailand's kite-flying tradition was not always a friendly activity. In the 13th century, kites were used in warfare. The kites were loaded with gunpowder, a long fuse was lit and they were flown over enemy lines. It was a sort of an air-to-ground missile. Kites that make lots of noise are still used today in religious ceremonies, and they have a more practical purpose in many parts of the country where farmers use them to keep birds away from their crops.

King Chulalongkorn (Rama V) is given credit for introducing kite-flying for pleasure. He described it as a "wholesome pastime." Rama V, the ninth surviving son of King Mongkut, came to the throne in 1868 when he was only 15; he was the king who abolished slavery in Thailand. Chulalongkorn Day is celebrated on October 23 each year in memory of his death.

■ Jogging

If you want to join the early morning fitness fans then make your way to **Lumphini Park**, a popular, peaceful sanctuary, in the middle of the city off Silom Road. Shortly after dawn you'll find dozens of Thais starting their day with aerobics, tai chi, and yoga, or simply strolling in the vast expanse of greenery. There is no charge for admission to the park, named after the Buddha's birthplace. Paddle-boats are available for rent and there are several inexpensive outdoor restaurants.

■ Walking

Bangkok is not ideally suited for pleasure walking. Distances may not look great on maps, but those don't take into account the heat, traffic or pollution. We have listed several parks where you are away from most of the noise, but do remember to drink plenty of liquids to avoid dehydration (sodas and anything containing alcohol do not count). Someone suggested it was an easy stroll from the Lumphini Park to the Erawan Shrine. It wasn't. Next time we'll take a cab and wait to do our walking in the countryside away from the city, or better still, along the beaches.

■ Bird Watching

Every year over the Christmas holidays thousands of rare Siberian grebes migrate from the bitter cold in Siberia to take refuge at *Bueng-ta-thong Pond* at the intersection of Phuttha Monthon Sai 3 and Bangwaek Road near Suan Saengtham Monastery. Apparently they are attracted by the vegetation of the area, which ranges from tall trees to field of different grasses. Lots of other birds and wild animals also thrive here.

■ Horseback Riding

There are two locations for those who want to hit the saddle in Bangkok. The **Bangkok Equestrian Center** at 20/1 Moo 2 Soi Chadsanthahanrue, Sukhumvit, ☎ 02328 0273, has horses for hire starting at 600 Baht an hour and offers lessons and monthly memberships. A little farther out of town is the **Garden City Polo Club** at 37 Moo 5, Bangna-Trad Road, Bangpu, ☎ 02317 1431. Fees are similar and they offer polo lessons as well.

■ Golf

There are dozens of golf courses around Bangkok. We have limited our list to those that are open to non-members, are less than an hour by car from the city center, and have a minimum of 18 holes. Green fees shown at the end of each listing are for non-members playing on a weekend.

Alpine Golf & Sports Club, 9 Bang Khan Sathani Vitthayu T. Klong 5, A. Klongluang, Pathumthani, ☎ 02577 3333. 7,000-yard par 72 course that was the venue for the 13th Asian Games. 4,000 Baht.

Bangkok Golf Club, 2 Tiwanon Road, Bangkradi, Pathumthani, ☎ 02501 2771. 6,918-yard par 72 course popular with the ex-pat community. Night golf available. 2,100 Baht.

Bangpoo Country Club, 191 Moo 3, Pragsa, Muang, ☎ 02324 0320. 7,048-yard par 72 course designed by Arnold Palmer with large and fast-sloping greens. 2,000 Baht.

Chuan Chuen Golf Club, Chuan Chuen Flora Ville, Bangkok-Pathumthani Road, Pathumthani, ☎ 02598 2839. 6,178-yard par 18 course designed by Nick Faldo with many water hazards, 80 bunkers and lots and lots of trees. 700 Baht.

Dynasty Golf & Country Club, Poldamri Road, Amphur Bang Lane, Nakhonpathom, ☎ 03439 1076. Built on a reclaimed rice paddy, this 6,792-yard par 72 course has water hazards on most holes. 850 Baht.

Kiarti Thanee Country Club, 199-200 Moo, 5 Bangna-Trad Highway, Samutprakarn, ☎ 02707 1700. Fairly flat 6,730-yard par 72 course with lots of bunkers and water hazards. 1,800 Baht.

Krungthep Kreetha Sports Club, 516 Krungthep Kreetha Road, Huamark, Bangkapi, ☎ 02379 3716. Accurate tee shots needed, as trees run along most fairways on this 6,874-yard par 72 course. 1,900 Baht.

Lakewood Country Club, 99/1 Moo 11, Bangna-Trad Highway, Samutprakarn, ☎ 02312 6276. Located at kilometer-marker 18 of the Bangna-to-Trad highway this course has 27 holes, each nine a 36 par. Noted for its dog-legs, flowers and shrubs. 2,700 Baht.

Lam Lukka Country Club, 29 Moo 7, Klong 11, Tambol Lamlukka, Pathumthani, ☎ 02995 2300. Accuracy rather than power is called for at this 36-hole course (each 18 is a par 72), 27 kilometers east of the Don Muang airport. 1,800 Baht.

Muang Kaew Golf Course, 52 Moo 8, Km. 7.7, Bangna-Trad Highway, Samutprakarn, ☎ 02316 3918. Only 20 minutes from the city center, this 7,015-yard par 72 course gets busy at weekends. 2,700 Baht.

Muang-Ake Golf Club, 52 Moo 7, Phaholyothin Road, Pathumthani, ☎ 02533 9335. Just 10 minutes north of the airport, this 6,398-yard par 72 course, with wide fairways and large greens, is well suited to beginners. 1,030 Baht.

Muang-Ake Vista Golf Course, 52/999 Phaholyothin Road, Luk 6, Pathumthani, ☎ 02997 8501. Another good course for the beginner, and sister course to the club above. The canals make great water hazards on this 5,572-yard par 72 course. 1,030 Baht.

Navatanee Golf Course, 22 Navathanee Serithai Road, Kannayao, ☎ 02376 1034. This 6,902-yard par 72 course was designed by Robert Trent Jones, Jr., for the 1975 World Cup. Within metropolitan Bangkok. 2,200 Baht.

Panya Indra Golf Club, 99 Moo 6, Ramindra Road, Km. 9, Kannayao, ☎ 02519 5840. Lakes and lagoons make this floodlit 27-hole course opened in 1991 (each nine is a par 36) a challenge. 3,000 Baht.

Panya Park Golf Course, 46 Moo 8, Suwintawong Road, Km. 9, Nong Chok, ☎ 02989 4200. Another 27 holes – each nine a par 36 – set in magnificent landscaping with water to contend with on most holes. 1,000 Baht.

Pinehurst Golf & Country Club, 73 Moo 17, Phaholyothin Road, Phathumthani, ☎ 02516 8679. One of Thailand's better courses this 27-hole club has hosted many international tournaments. 2,300 Baht.

Rajpruek Club, 100 Moo 3, Vibhvadi-Rangsit Road, Don Muang, ☎ 02955 0555. This 6,568-yard par 72 course has several dog-leg holes and makes good use of bunkers and water hazards. 2,000 Baht.

Rose Garden Golf Club, 53/1 Moo 4, Tha Talad Sub-district, Nakhon Pathom, ☎ 03432 2769. Clever mix of natural and man-made features on this 7,085 par 72 course. 1,300 Baht.

Royal Bangkok Sport Club, Henri Dunant Road, Pathumwan, ☎ 02251 0181. One of the area's oldest and shortest courses with a par of 66 for the 4,992-yards. 180 Baht.

Royal Gems Golf & Sport Club, 98 Moo 3, Salaya-Banglane Road, Nakhon Pathom, ☎ 02441 9314. This is a tough 7,155-yard par 72 course with deep rough and big bunkers. The large greens help out. 2,600 Baht.

Royal Thai Air Force Golf Course, 14 Moo 8 Tambol Koo-Kod Amphur Lamlukka, Pathumthani, ☎ 02531 1484. The following three courses were designed by the Thailand Army Office for the use of the military. They are all par 72 and open to the public. This one adjoins Don Muang airport, and on several occasions we have watched golfers in action as our jet has landed. They always appear to be unaware of us. Might a set of earplugs be included with your golf clubs? 600 Baht.

Royal Thai Army Sports Center (East Course), 459 Ramintra Road, Bangkhen, ☎ 02521 5338. This 6,372-yard course is the newer of the two Royal Thai Army courses. Well designed for beginners and very busy at weekends. A Dutch friend had an unusual experience while playing here: He was under a tree when a large green snake fell to the ground. It slithered away rapidly, and the Thai golfers he was playing with found it amusing. Our friend didn't. 1,200 Baht.

Royal Thai Army Sports Center (West Course), 459 Ramintra Road, Bangkhen, ☎ 02521 5338. Built in 1965 for army officers, this 6,924-yard course is now open to the public. 800 Baht.

Subhapruek Country Club, 102 Moo 7, Bangna-Trad Road, Km. 26, Bang Bor, Bang Plee, Samutprakarn, ☎ 02317 0801. This 7,010-yard par 72 course was formerly the Bangna Country Club. Water hazards on most holes and lots of palm-tree-lined fairways. 1,500 Baht.

Summit Windmill Golf Club, 72 Moo 14, Km. 10.5, Bangna-Trad Road, Bang Plee, Samutprakarn, ☎ 02750 2112. Designed by Nick Faldo, this 6,956-yard par 72 course is upmarket and attracts a lot of foreigners working in Bangkok. Unusual touch: The clubhouse sits on an island. 3,000 Baht.

Thana City Golf & Country Club, 100 Moo 4, Km. 0.14, Bangna-Trad Road, Bangchalong, Bangplee, Samutprakarn, ☎ 02336 1968. This 6,905-yard par 72 course was designed by Greg Norman, who has created the fantasy of a seaside links course in the middle of one of Thailand's biggest housing developments. 2,300 Baht.

The Legacy Golf Club, 10 Moo 7, Klong Samwa, ☎ 02914 1930. Formerly the Natural Park Ramindra Golf Club, this 7,073-yard course is within 30 minutes of downtown. It's a tough course, and at the 16th players have to hit their approach to an island green. I wonder where Florida-based designer Jack Nicklaus got that idea from? 2,200 Baht.

The Royal Golf and Country Club, 69 Moo 7, Sukhumvit 77, Samutprakarn, ☎ 02738 1010. Water comes into play on 17 of the holes at this 6,807-yard par 72 course, which is well suited for all players, novice and experienced. 2,400 Baht.

The Vintage Club, Panviti Road, Klongdan, Bangbor, ☎ 02707 3820. This 6,580-yard, par 72 course is fairly flat and in delightful countryside with well-placed water hazards. 1,800 Baht.

HAPPINESS IS A HAIRCUT - THAI STYLE

Getting your hair cut is no big deal, particularly if you are like me and have very little on top. But here in Thailand it can be something you look forward to with enthusiasm.

Such was the case the day I arranged for a taxi to take me to a hotel spa. Despite jokes from the the pool attendants at our hotel, who promised me a good short-back-and-sides from their barber for a mere 50 Baht, I headed out into the crawling traffic.

A typical cheery Thai greeting awaited me at the spa from three young ladies, who burst into giggles when I said I had come for a haircut. They reminded me of the three little maids from *The Mikado*. The leader of the trio approached quietly and said the normal price would be 700 Baht but the translation of what she said next was that they would come up with a better price since there was so little hair to cut. Discussions followed, a glass of iced water was placed at my side, and then the leader returned with a calculator that revealed 400. "This price okay?" she asked. I nodded agreement. I would have happily paid full price but never turn down a bargain.

The program began. I was ushered into a very chilly air conditioned salon where I was assisted into the barber's chair, dusted off and presented with another glass of cold water.

The hairdresser appeared, probably towering to five feet if she stretched on tip-toes and weighing in at no more than a case of Coca Cola.

She spoke no English. When she asked, "where you from?" I knew that was the extent of her vocabulary except for "thank you" and "hello." I told her that I had just dropped in for the day from Outer Mongolia. She smiled sweetly.

The scissors appeared and she chopped merrily away for some minutes until the few strands on my head were reduced to stubble. She chipped around my ears, nose and throat. A razor appeared and she gently removed growth from lower neck and sideburns.

"Shampoo!" she said, or asked. This was the bit I had been waiting for. All very nice having a sweet young thing hovering around your head with razor and scissors but now came the icing on the cake.

I was ushered into the adjoining room where I was invited to stretch out onto a bed, which had a wash basin at one end, where my head was positioned. Then came wash and rinse. And massage, scalp and neck. Wash and rinse again with heavy massage on the scalp. My temples were massaged and then again down my neck. All very pleasant. Another wash and rinse. Then ears got a treatment. I gave up counting the washes and rinses. The delightful aromas of lotus and lemon grass filled the room.

The shampoo is over and it is back to the chair, where my untouched ice-water has been replaced with a fresh glass. The dryer comes out and the remnants of hair are dried. The final touch is a shoulder and arm massage. All too soon the 50-minute haircut is over. The rest of the day was a little anti-climatic. I did look several times to see if my hair was growing. How long will it be before it needs cutting again?

Shopping

Bangkok has become one of the top shopping areas in Southeast Asia. In recent years, numerous modern shopping malls have been built and these attract top name stores with quality merchandise. Fortunately the wonderful street markets continue to flourish where price outperforms quality and bargaining is common practice. Hypermarkets (superstores), notably the British **Tesco** and the French **Carrefour**, are everywhere, and have unfortunately forced many small retailers out of business. If you can't be bothered to venture outside, most of the major hotels have shopping arcades with quality stores and merchandise with prices to match.

■ Chatuchak Weekend Market

This is the granddaddy of all street markets. If you can't find it here you don't need it. There are 35 acres of stalls selling everything from hardware to handicrafts. Animal lovers please turn a blind eye; the live animals are not always cared for in the best manner. The bargaining begins each Saturday and Sunday morning soon after 9am, and some stalls stay open until the sun goes down. It gets hot and crowded. Over 200,000 people are expected each day. Watch out for pickpockets and not-so-old antiques, and do not expect to cover everything in one visit. Clothes and handicrafts are a great buy but you must bargain. There's also food and flowers, CDs and luggage. We doubt you'll find a better selection of goodies anywhere else in Thailand. Best way to get here is by SkyTrain or subway; get off at Mo Chit and follow the crowd.

■ Siam Center & Siam Discovery Center

Double your shopping pleasure with two giant malls, joined by a fourth-floor walkway. Avoid the weekends when the area gets very busy, as this is the place where the younger, trendy Thais like to hang out. The Siam SkyTrain station is right at the door and there is a 2,500 space parking garage for those brave enough to drive. There are close to 400 stores, a mammoth movie complex and too many restaurants to mention. There are always special events and sales taking place. Like most of Bangkok's malls this complex is open from 10am to 9pm seven days a week. The Siam side of things is more young and trendy, and the Discovery tends to be a little more exclusive. The movie theater is on the sixth floor of the Discovery Center; call ☎ 02658 0454 to discover what comes in English or with English subtitles. Movie times are shown every day in both *The Bangkok Post* and *The Nation*.

A THAI CHRISTMAS

We were concerned that on our first Christmas visit to Thailand, a Buddhist/Muslim country, we might miss the Western-style celebrations. We took with us decorations and pre-wrapped gifts to make it more like home. We need not have bothered. The large stores in Bangkok were full of gift ideas for Christmas and published glossy inserts suggesting gifts for him, her and the younger ones. We saw many Thai spirit houses decorated with tinsel, and in a Muslim village in Phuket we saw men wandering around with Santa hats on. The Tesco stores throughout the kingdom sold everything from fake trees to wrapping paper and make-believe snow balls. One truly cosmopolitan touch: Heard over the holidays at the Italian restaurant at the Shangri-La Hotel, Bangkok – Bing Crosby singing *White Christmas*.

■ The Emporium Shopping Center

If you're looking for quality (not bargain prices) then this upmarket, trendy complex with six floors of stores, cinemas, art galleries and restaurants may be the place to spend a few hours. To give you an idea of size there are two Starbucks here, along with numerous boutiques, bookstores, a supermarket and some fine dining. What surprised us most was the number of top-quality jewelry stores, which are grouped together on the first floor. We saw very few customers, though, and that could not be blamed on lack of selection; choice was abundant in all of the top-name shops. Closest train station is Phrom Phong and there is a large parking lot if you come by car. Sukhumvit 24, ☎ 2664 8000.

■ The Patpong Night-Bazaar

It's hard to know whether this area comes under shopping or nightlife, but since we only came here to shop we'll leave it here. These two roads – **Patpong 1** and **Patpong 2** – are jammed with stalls selling clothing, ceramics, wood carvings, genuine fake watches, leather goods and lots of luggage. We bargained hard, but not enough, for two suitcases (we bought an identical one for less in Phuket). Alongside the stalls are a mass of bars, discos and the "a-go" dancing joints, so named for those who go in for a dance and then depart with their dance partner for a few additional steps. It's a sort of lending library of ladies. We didn't venture into any though we received plenty of invitations. We asked why the place was so popular and were told, "The girls are so friendly." Enough said. There is a McDonalds on the corner and they do sell hamburgers. Just off Rama IV, and every taxi driver understands "Patpong."

■ Seacon Square

This place is "far out" in more ways than one. First, it is the largest shopping mall in Southeast Asia, with more than 400 outlets to shop, dine and even ice-skate. And it is far from the city center in a new eastern suburb on Srinakarin Road. To get here from downtown you take the SkyTrain, then a bus; if you're driving from Silom you take Rama IV expressway to Bang Na Road, turn left into Srinakarin Road and make a U-turn into the complex. Once you're here there's enough to occupy most folk for a week. There's a book store with a million books (hopefully this volume will find shelf space one day), a theme park with boat rides and a roller coaster, a bowling alley, multi-screen move theater and mini-golf course. Then there are shops, hundreds of them. Feeling a little hungry? You'll find the all-American Sizzler among the eateries on the fourth-floor restaurant area.

■ World Trade Center

At the intersection of Ratchadamri Road and Rama I Road, ☎ 02222 9855, this eight-story shoppers' delight is home to numerous trendy shops in addition to the **Zen** and **Isetan** department stores. Lots to keep you busy: a movie house, ice-skating rink and restaurants. The government-owned **Thailand Duty Free Shop** is on the seventh floor. Outside you are in the midst of Bangkok's fashionable Ratchaprasong shopping area. For-top-of-the-line items step inside **Gaysorn Plaza**, home to such names as Louis Vuitton, Gucci, Prada, Christian Dior, Fendi, Salvatore Ferragamo, Burberry, Christian Lacroix, Lanvin, Celine, Loewe, La Perla, Tag Heuer, Hugo Boss, Omega, Aigner, Alfred Dunhill, Daks and Bally. Nearby are the **Peninsula Plaza** and the **Amarin Plaza**, both listed below.

■ Narayana Phand Pavilion

Across the street from the World Trade Center, this operation is partly owned by the government to promote and sell official handicrafts from throughout the kingdom. Everything here – items in bronze, silk, wood and ceramic – is made in Thailand. 127 Ratchadamri Road, ☎ 02252 4670.

■ The Peninsula Plaza

Highly-priced and -prized fashions from local designers, top imported brands and gourmet shops make this plaza upscale in every way. 153 Ratchadamri Road, ☎ 02253 9672.

■ Amarin Plaza & Sogo

Homesick Americans can find solace here, site of the first McDonalds to open in Thailand. There is also a Starbucks and a Radio Shack. Sogo brings you the best in Japanese merchandise. 494 Ploenchit Road, ☎ 02255 0831.

■ River City

This four-story complex claims to be the largest art-and-antique center in Southeast Asia, with close to 200 shops selling top-of-the-line art, antiques, jewelry, handicrafts and a better class of souvenirs. It's a great location, overlooking the Chao Phraya River, and the well-priced restaurants are worth a visit. Auctions take place every month. There is a free river-shuttle service for those staying at any of the riverfront hotels. On Si Phraya Road, ☎ 02237 0077, close to the Royal Orchid Sheraton hotel.

■ Pantip Plaza

This is the shopping spot if you are looking for anything related to computers. Pirated software is a big seller at this five-story mall; however, it is often closed, after a police crackdown to stop the illegal sales. Unfortunately without the illicit products this place would cease to exist. Computer peripherals – the mouse I am using right now cost $3 – and computer repairs are cheap. Many of the store operatives do not speak English but they have an uncanny knowledge of computers and all the latest software. Many times new programs are available here before they hit the US or European markets. You'll also find computer books, DVDs of the latest US movies, cameras and small appliances at bargain prices. The plaza is near the Amari Watergate Hotel on Petchburi Road in the Pratunam district, a central area well served with good street markets and good hotels. 604 Phetchburi Road, ☎ 02254 9797.

> *Buying electronics in Thailand does have advantages. Telephones and some computer equipment are so cheap that it is worth taking the risk that it will not work well when you get home. We discovered that things assembled in Thailand, like desktop computers, can be very cheap, but items imported into Thailand fully assembled, like laptops, are expensive. If you have a problem when you get back home, do not expect a smile from the repairman when you say you bought it in Thailand.*

■ MBK Center

Hard to believe, but this seven-story mall used to be the biggest shopping center in Bangkok. It's still huge, with enough space to house a 40-lane bowling alley and a seven-screen movie theater. The stores are noted for women's fashions, food, jewelry, luggage

The Eastern & Oriental Express *crosses the River Kwai*

Above: Seafront gardens, Hua Hin
©2006 Marriott Hotels

Below: The delicate art of fruit carving

Above: Learning the basics of Thai cuisine

Below: A whistling chef, Bangkok

Above: Children in traditional festival costumes

Below: Siamese dancers at the White Elephant Restauran JW Marriott Resort

Courtesy of Marriott Hotels

Above and Below: The challenge of a boat race, a favorite at any Thai festivals

Above: Hilltribe children, Golden Triangle

Below: The ever-present, pleasant elephant

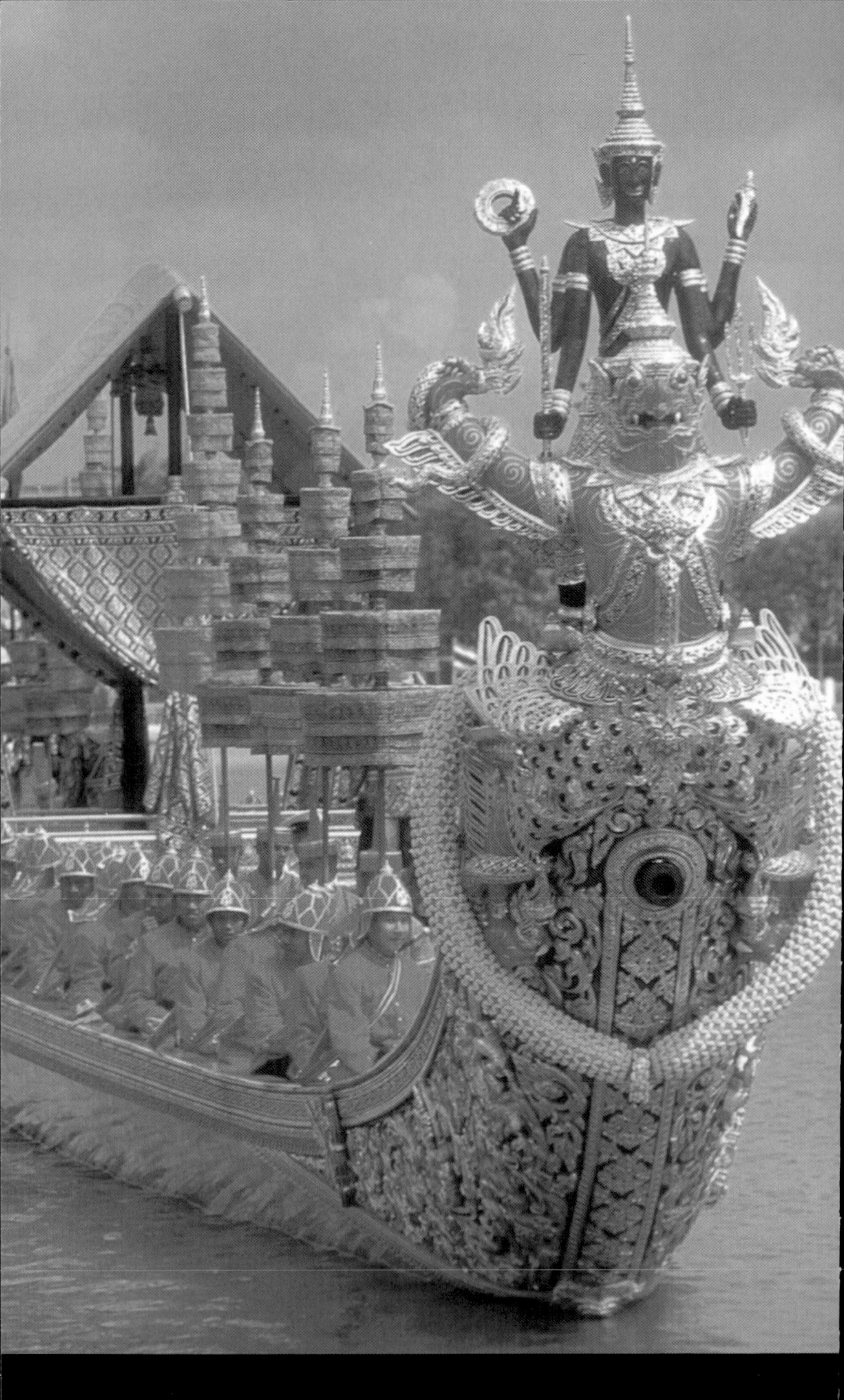

Royal Barge, River of Kings

and electronic gadgets. MBK is easy to get to; it adjoins the quality department store **Tokyu**, which has a bridge linking it to the National Stadium SkyTrain station. 444 Phayathai Road, on the corner of Rama I and Phaya Thai, ☎ 02217 9111.

■ Pak Khlong Flower Market

The major hotels all have astounding displays of fresh flowers, and this is the market where most of them come from. The market takes place every day in the early morning hours, next to the **Memorial Bridge**, where the Chao Phraya River meets the Khlong Lawt, one of the city's major canals. This is Thailand's largest fruit, vegetable and flower market and you need to be here at 2am to watch the boats and trucks arrive laden with produce. The sights and smells are worth the early-morning visit.

■ Memorial Bridge Night-Market

If you decide to visit the Pak Khlong flower market, described above, you might consider a visit to this nearby bazaar beforehand. Trading starts around 7pm and closes at 2am, and you'll find it a lot cooler than the Chatuchak weekend market thanks to the gentle wind from the river. Not a popular tourist spot, and you'll find clothing prices equal to or better than Chatuchak. Despite the late hour, do not forget that bargaining is still expected.

Check clothing sizes carefully. Thai people are generally small, and what they consider a large size might not be large enough. We bought a pair of underpants in a Bangkok department store. The label said "extra, extra large" but when unwrapped the item proved to be a perfect fit for a small boy.

■ Collectors' Corner

Stamp Market

Stamp collectors are in for a treat every Saturday and Sunday morning, when there is a stamp market in front of the **General Post Office** at 1160 Charoen Krung Road. Over a dozen stamp dealers set up shop under a tent in the parking lot. The trading starts around noon and continues until 5pm. Chairs are provided so that you can scan the collections in relative comfort. There's a full assortment of philatelic items, first-day covers and souvenir sheets, as well as individual stamps.

While you're here, the post office itself is worth a visit. It's a large building with 36 serving positions and even opens on Sundays. Normal hours are from 8am to 10pm on weekdays and from 8am to 1pm on weekends. There is a pack-and-wrap department in case you want to mail something home, and a special counter for philatelists (that's stamp collectors). You'll find a heavy concentration of stamp-dealers' shops near the post office, but most of the dealers who frequent the market do not have shops. We wonder how the stamps keep their quality in these hot and humid conditions.

AUTHOR'S NOTE: *The post office is presently phasing out its telegram-and-telegraph section. We wonder w-w-w- why?*

There is a stamp museum on the first floor of the **Metropolitan Postal Bureau** behind **Sam Sen Nai Post Office**, ☎ 2712439 or 2331050, right outside the Saphan Kwai SkyTrain station. In addition to viewing stamps of the world, you can buy stamps and plenty of philatelic paraphernalia. The post office is . If you find yourself in front of the Paola Memorial Hospital you are on the wrong side of the tracks. Admission is free and the museum is open from 9am to 4pm, Tuesday thru Saturday. If your traveling companions aren't into stamps they can visit the nearby **Sapha Kwai market**, open every day from the wee hours, with every kind of fresh food. There are several dressmaking and tailor stores next to stalls selling a range of textiles.

Flag Market

If flag- or emblem-collecting is more your scene, you need to visit an area they call the flag market behind Wat Bowon Niwet on Phra Suman Road, in the Bang Lamphu area. There are a half-dozen shops here that specialize in flags and related paraphernalia. And the houses in the area are an architectural quirk. They appear to be single-story from the outside but they are actually two stories once you get inside. The temple is important too; King Rama IV was chief abbot before he became king, and King Rama VII and the present king were monks here.

■ Central Chidlom

It would be wrong to leave the shopping section without mention of **Central Department Stores**, Thailand's biggest department store chain (1027 Ploenchit Road, ☎ 02655 7777). This is their flagship store near the Chit Lom SkyTrain station; there are numerous branches in Bangkok and throughout the nation. Everything you would expect to see in a popular department store including excellent children's clothes, everything for the home and well-priced designer fashions. You'll also find a Jim Thompson silk shop here, a name synonymous with the best in Thai shopping. These stores are normally open from 10am to 10pm.

Festivals

■ February

River of Kings Light & Sound Show: A happy blend of old Thai cultural performance together with modern-day pyrotechnics light up the Chao Phraya River for two weeks every February. The festival is sponsored by the Bangkok Tourist Bureau, the Royal Household and the Tourism Authority of Thailand. Generally there are two shows nightly, at 7pm and 9pm, and tickets at 400 Baht for a seat on a floating stadium can be reserved by calling the Grand Palace office, ☎ 02222 8181.

■ April

The Thai New Year: *Songkran* is probably the best-known and most-enjoyed festival in Thailand. The date varies according to the solar calendar but is normally in the middle of April, when the days and nights are the same length. Thais spend the morning visiting temples to honor their relatives and then spring-cleaning their homes. Then everyone hits the streets and starts water fights. It is lots of fun if you don't mind getting soaked. In Bangkok look for heavy action on the main tourist thoroughfares.

■ May

Royal Ploughing Ceremony: This Bangkok festival is held in mid-May and marks the start of the rice-growing season. This ancient Brahmin festival was reintroduced in 1960 by King Bhumibol Adulyadej and takes place at Sanam Luang, the large oval field in front of the Grand Palace. Both the King and Queen attend so there are lots of colorful traditional costumes. Object of the ceremony is to make predictions about the year ahead.

Visakha Puja: This nationwide festival on May 17 marks the birth and death of Buddha and is considered to be the holiest of days. Sermons are given at all temples, and in the evening candlelit processions move around the places of worship.

■ July

Khao Phansa: This day marks the start of the Buddhist Lent, which lasts for approximately three months, from the first day of the waning moon of the 8th lunar month (July) to the fifteenth day of the waxing moon of the 11th lunar month (October). During this time, monks stay inside their temples to meditate and study. It is no coincidence that this is also the height of the rice-growing season, which extends from May to November – the tradition was begun to prevent monks from trampling upon rice paddies when they ventured out to receive alms.

■ August

The Queen's Birthday: A nationwide celebration on August 12 to mark Queen Sirikit's birthday. Thais everywhere decorate their homes, but the decorations are particularly spectacular in Bangkok around the Grand Palace. The day is also Mother's Day in Thailand.

■ October

Thai Beer Festival: The Thai breweries organize this event annually between October and December to show how well their products go with Thai food. Tourists are expected to join in the eating and drinking, and to watch the musical performances that are staged all over the city. Most of the activity takes place at the World Trade Center.

■ November

***Loy Krathong*, Festival of Lights**: This nationwide festival is celebrated when the moon is full, sometime in mid-November. Around the kingdom, floats – called *krathongs* – are decorated with flowers and candles and set adrift in the sea, on rivers and in canals. As the floats drift away prayers are offered that everything bad will float away too. It's also a time for thanking the water for all the good things it has brought. Parties abound once the floats are gone. This is one of the most moving and attractive of all Thai festivals.

■ December

Trooping of the Color: Brits won't need telling what this all about. It takes place in December every year in The Royal Plaza, Bangkok. Plenty of pomp and pageantry as the royal guards swear allegiance to the King and march in full ceremonial dress.

The King's Birthday: There is celebration throughout the land on December 5 when the King celebrates his birthday. In Bangkok there is a spectacular firework display near the Grand Palace.

River of Kings Festival: A new event promoting the wonders of the Chao Phraya river is sponsored by an alliance of the six luxury hotels with riverside locations – the Royal Orchid Sheraton Hotel, the Shangri-La, the Millennium Hilton, the Peninsula Bangkok, the Oriental and the Bangkok Marriott Resort & Spa. The alliance points out this event will be different and a separate event from the annual River of Kings Light & Sound Show, which is put on by the Royal Household in February (see page 91).

Where to Stay

ACCOMMODATIONS PRICE SCALE	
Indicates rates charged per night during high-season for a double room, including breakfast and all service charges. Prices vary according to the exchange rate between the US dollar and Thai Baht. Most hotels offer discounts from their published rack rates during low season. All those listed accept major credit cards; rooms have direct-dial telephones and private bathrooms.	
$	Under $50
$$	$51 to $100
$$$	$101 to $175
$$$$	Over $175

Shangri-La Hotel, 89 Soi Wat Suan Plu, New Road, ☎ 02236 7777, www.shangri-la.com/bangkok, $$$$. At the end of the last century there were only two super-luxury hotels in Bangkok – this one and the legendary Oriental. Now that has changed dramatically with the addition of all the hotels listed in this category. The business traveler and the tourist not on a budget are spoiled by the vast choice. We continue to be amazed by the high standard of the Shangri-La, which consistently rates as one of the top ten hotels in the world. Highlights for us were the impressive lobby, great restaurants, speedy and special room service and the views of the always-busy Chao Phraya River. The hotel has a total of 799 rooms and suites. Expect to pay more in the new wing, with added benefits. There's enough going on to spend an entire vacation in the hotel without venturing outside.

THE NAME OF THE CHAIN

Hotels in Thailand, particularly in Bangkok, change brand names with alarming regularity. So we apologize now if the hotel we've listed is operated by another of the world's innkeepers when you go searching for it.

Some well-intentioned friends told us that we must take tea at the Regent when in Bangkok. "Everybody does it," they told us. "It's the real thing there with scones, strawberry jam and cream." But there isn't a Regent – there was, but now it's a Four Seasons. We had a problem finding our way to the InterContinental until someone told us it used to be Le Meriden and before that... We learned later that the InterContinental PR folk produced thousands of keychains explaining the name change and gave them as gifts to taxi drivers in the hope of helping with the brand change. Our cab driver must have been out of town at the time.

The good news is the Regent is coming back to Bangkok. A new 327-room Regent hotel is to be built on Sukhumvit Road and is scheduled to be open for business, and hopefully afternoon tea, in early 2007. In the meantime if it's afternoon tea you seek try the **Author's Lounge** at the **Oriental** or the slap-up high tea every Sunday at the **Shangri-La**.

The Oriental, 48 Oriental Avenue, ☎ 02659 9000, www.mandarin-oriental.com, $$$$. All of Bangkok's luxury hotels have large rooms, excellent employees, elaborate business centers and outstanding restaurants. Only one, the Oriental, has so rich a history. It started as a seaman's lodge along the Chao Phraya River over a century ago. It set high standards then and maintains them today. There are 358 rooms, 35 suites and five restaurants. There is a sense of old-world charm and style that is unique in Bangkok. You don't just stay at the Oriental, you experience it. A special Thai luncheon buffet and set-dinner feasts are a tradition.

InterContinental Bangkok, 973 Ploenchit Road, Lumpini, ☎ 02656 0444, fax 02656 0555, www.intercontinental.com, $$$$. If you have enjoyed an InterContinental hotel elsewhere in the world, you're going to be thrilled with this one. It's got space, style, super service and a great location in the best shopping district. Rack rates start at $300 a night for a very large room and go up to $2,000 for the royal suite, though you may get lucky with an Internet booking for just under $200. The buffet breakfast, no bargain at 780 Baht, beats anything we've ever seen with exotic dishes from around the world. An economic and good alternative is the deli on the ground floor where two can have a delicious Danish with coffee and have change from 300 Baht. Swift and stylish room service with reasonable prices. The swimming pool on the 37th floor is a haven away from the busy city below for those who can handle the height. Word of warning to those who like to stay close to sea level – the guest rooms are all above the 18th floor.

There is a full-sized ironing board and iron in every room at the InterContinental, which avoids the call to housekeeping each time there's a collar or sleeve that needs a quick press. If you're a priority-club member there's no better place to accumulate points, or spend them.

The Peninsula Hotel, 333 Charoennakorn Road, Klongsan, ☎ 02861 2888, www.peninsula.com, $$$$. With a spectacular view of Bangkok's skyline from the west bank of the Chao Phraya River, The Peninsula is close to the Taksin Bridge, with easy access to major business districts, shopping areas and the airport. The hotel has an exclusive lounge facility at the **Peninsula Pier** on the opposite bank of the river, only minutes away by the hotel's private river-shuttle boat. Completed in November 1998, The Peninsula Bangkok features 370 guest rooms and a selection of suites, including 60 one-bedroom and five grand suites.

JW Marriott Hotel Bangkok, 4 Sukhumvit Road, Soi 2, ☎ 02656 7700, fax 02656 7711, www.marriott.com, $$$$. All the bells and whistles that you would expect from a Marriott, and the only hotel in Bangkok with direct access to the expressway system. If you time it right, Internet specials can get the room rate below the $$$$ level, making this a very reasonable place to stay.

There are 441 rooms, including 39 suites, all elegantly furnished and fully equipped. As at other top hotels, you touch the phone and someone knows your name and wants to help. Excellent swimming pool, spa and health club, with the largest fitness gymnasium of any Bangkok hotel. It's worth the extra Baht to organize a meet-and-greet at the airport. Within seconds of leaving baggage claim our cases were taken, and we were whisked away in a shiny white limousine. The next time we touched a suitcase was in our room. We used the limo service again when we left the hotel to join the *Eastern & Oriental Express* train. We felt quite regal and relaxed arriving at Hualampong station with a liveried chauffeur. Much better than getting there white-knuckled, curled up in a tuk-tuk. It is 30 minutes by car to the airport, a big plus if you are a traveler who leaves catching a flight to the last minute. The hotel is close to the Queen Sirikit National Convention Center, the World Trade Center and most of the major embassies.

> *The **Bangkok Baking Company**, on the ground floor of the JW Marriott, produces wonderful sandwiches and is a great place to have an inexpensive coffee and Danish if you can't handle the bountiful breakfast buffet nearby.*

The Westin Banyan Tree, 21/100 South Sathorn Road, ☎ 02679 1200, fax 02679 1199, www.banyantree.com, $$$$. Tallest hotel in town, this 216-all-suites complex is in the center of the business district, and its height allows views of the entire city. Spa, sauna, swimming pool and 24-hour coffee shop. Check the Internet for special packages, which include treatments at the hotel's **Spa Bliss** and limo transfers. Not for the traveler on a budget.

> *Don't miss **Vertigo**, the restaurant on the 61st floor of the Banyan Tree (see page 102).*

Hotel Plaza Athénée, Wireless Road, ☎ 02650 8800, fax 02650 8500, www.hotel-plaza-athenee.com, $$$. One of the latest and largest additions to the five-star Bangkok hotel list, the Plaza Athénée has 354 guest rooms and 28 suites, and is designed for business conferences that can cater to up to 1,200 guests. Among the myriad facilities is a squash court. Walking distance to the major embassies and only 300 meters from a SkyTrain station.

The Grand Hyatt Erawan, 494 Rajdamri Road, ☎ 02254 1234, fax 02254 6308, www.bangkok.grand.hyatt.com, $$$. Stunning lobby with a stream and jungle welcomes you to this 400-room businessman's resort. Families too can enjoy the extensive facilities. The hotel is surrounded by shopping centers and across from the World Trade Center. Again, lots of restaurants.

Montien Hotel Bangkok, 54 Surawongse Road, ☎ 02233 7060, fax 02236 5218, www.montien.com, $$$. Centrally located top-quality hotel with 475 rooms that frequently has special deals for businessmen. The price, around 6,500 Baht includes airport transfers, breakfast, cocktails between 6pm and 7pm and they press your clothes. There's a 24-hour coffee shop, and the Patpong market is right outside. There is a sister hotel, the **Montien Riverside**, 272 Rama III Road, ☎ 02292 2999. You pay more here but you get great views over the river.

The Sukothai Hotel, 13/3 South Sathorn Road, ☎ 02344 8888, fax 02344 8899, www.sukhothai.com, $$$. Six acres of tropical gardens provide a tranquil setting for this businessman's favorite. The 226-room hotel boasts an extensive library for the traveling executive, and the décor is heavy on teak, granite and Thai silk. Close by is Silom Road for shopping and nightlife.

Nai Lert Park, 2 Wireless Road, ☎ 02253 0123, fax 02253 6509, www.nailertpark.swissotel.com, $$$. This Raffles International Hotel, formerly the Hilton, is nestled in the **Nai Lert Botanical Park**. The 338-room resort is convenient for the business and entertainment districts and just moments away from great department stores. The botanical gardens are home to hundreds of tropical plants, flowers and animals.

Royal Orchid Sheraton, 2 Captain Bush Lane, New Road, ☎ 02266 0123, fax 02236 8320, www.sheraton.com/royalorchid, $$$. The riverfront location of this 740-room resort enables guests to visit many of Bangkok's historic attractions by boat. In addition to all the usual facilities the hotel has a children's swimming pool, a golf driving range and a tennis court. There are also daily aerobatic classes.

Holiday Inn Silom, 981 Silom Road, ☎ 02238 4300, fax 02238 5289, www.holidayinnsilom.com, $$$. Set in a busy area in the center of the city's commercial hub but a superb hotel with all facilities including a tennis court and swimming pool. Coffee shop, restaurant and hairdressing salon inside and lots of activity outside.

Sofitel Silom Bangkok, 188 Silom Road, ☎ 02238 1991, fax 02238 1988, www.sofitel.com, $$$. Internet rates range from $76 to $310 for this well-located hotel, which has 422 rooms and 32 suites. Design is a blend of Thai and French, there are four good restaurants, a swimming pool, fitness center and spa. The club lounge is a popular after hours meeting spot for businessmen and women.

Metropolitan Hotel, 27 South Sathorn Road, ☎ 02625 3333 fax 02625 3300, www.metropolitan.como.bz, $$. Huge rooms – all 171 of them are over 50 square meters – the Metropolitan, in the middle of the financial district, caters to the yuppie market by employing a younger service team full of information on the latest happenings in the Thai capital. As in most quality hotels, the décor makes good use of teak and Thai silk.

Conrad Hotel, All Seasons Place, 87 Wireless Road, ☎ 02690 9999, fax 02690 9000, www.ConradHotels.com, $$. Great for the athletic executive, this 393-room hotel with two entrances is in the middle of the business district and boasts a rooftop jogging track and two floodlit tennis courts. Lots of bars and restaurants, some dedicated to healthy dining. Near the embassies and SkyTrain station.

Emporium Suites, 622 Sukhumvit Road, ☎ 02664 9999 fax 02664 9990, www.emporiumsuites.com, $$. The 374 suites sit above the extravagant Emporium shopping and entertainment center. Nearby are Benjasiri Park and the Phrom Pong SkyTrain station. Price includes full American breakfast, daily newspaper, welcome drink and fruit basket.

Merchant Court at Le Concorde, 202 Ratchadaphisek Road, ☎ 02694 2222, fax 02694 2223, www.bangkok-leconcorde.swissotel.com, $$. Set in the central business district but only a 10-minute drive from the main tourist sights, this 224-room hotel is well equipped for conferences and banquets, boasting an 822-square-meter ballroom.

The Evergreen Laurel Hotel, 88 North Sathorn Road, ☎ 02266 9988, fax 02237 8400, www.evergreen-hotels.com, $$. Like so many of Bangkok's business hotels, the Evergreen with 160 rooms, including 45 suites, has an elaborate business center with translation and secretarial services in addition to computers, fax and copying machines. It claims to be the city's first boutique property. There is a full-service health club if the work gets too much.

President Solitaire, Sukhumvit Soi 11, ☎ 02255 7200, fax 02253 2330, www.solitaire-bkk.bangkok.com, $$. If you like things state-of-the-art, this is the place you need to stay. All 128 suites, including the penthouses, are connected to the Internet with LAN (that's local area network for those who aren't in a high-tech frame of mind). All connections are on DSL lines, that's broadband to me, and the connection speed is 128kbs. Interesting to note that is the same number of rooms in the hotel (or a typographical error somewhere). And that's not the end of it. There is wireless Internet service too, available on all guest floors, in the lobby, library, lounge and dining room. And outside in the swimming pool area. If you didn't know, wireless connection means just that – here are no wires, just laser beams. And all this Internet wizardry is free to guests. Get surfing.

Amari Watergate Hotel, 847 Petchburi Road, ☎ 02653 9000, fax 02653 9045, www.amari.com, $$. Don't let the name "Watergate" put you off. This 575-room hotel gets its name from the nearby *Pratunam* market: "*Pratu*" means gate and "*Nam*" means water. Shoppers and businessmen have the best of both worlds. The hotel is close to both the World Trade Center and the Siam Square shopping mall. Sukhumvit Road and Silom are a short distance away. There's plenty of space if you want to give a party. The grand ballroom can handle up to 1,000 guests for a cocktail party or seat 800 for a banquet.

The Imperial Queen's Park Hotel, 199 Sukhumvit Soi 22, ☎ 02261 9000, fax 02261 9530, www.imperialqueenspark.com, $$. A mammoth 37-story, twin tower hotel with 1,400 rooms, the Imperial Queen's Park has six different restaurants and, as its name suggests, adjoins Queens Park. Well suited for the businessman or tourist family. Close by is the Emporium shopping center.

The Grand President, 16 Sukhumvit Soi 11, ☎ 02651 1200, $$. More of an apartment complex than a hotel, the Grand President has 437 studios and suites that come with fully equipped kitchens. The building is billed as a perfect retreat from the noise and bustle of the streets below.

The Radisson Hotel, 92 Soi Saengcham, Rama IX Road, ☎ 02641 4777, www.radisson.com, $$. This 431-room hotel on 24 floors adjoins Bangkok's Royal City Avenue entertainment district. All rooms feature quality teak furniture. There are four restaurants and the complex is convenient for shopping. Nearest SkyTrain station is Makkasan.

Novotel Lotus, 1 Soi Daeng Udom, Soi 33 Sukhumvit Road, ☎ 02261 0111, fax 02262 1700, www.accorhotels-asia.com, $$. Quality Novotel property, this 224-room hotel is in the center of the business and entertainment area of Sukhumvit Road. Within walking distance is the Phrom Phong SkyTrain station, the Emporium shopping mall, the Queen Sirikit National Convention Center and Benjasiri Park.

Rama Gardens Hotel, 9/9 Vibhavadi Rangsit Road, Laksi, ☎ 02561 0022, fax 02561 1025, www.ramagardenshotel.com, $$. This 500-room resort gives you the best of both worlds. It is only five minutes from the old airport and 20 minutes from downtown.

And the big plus is that it is set in 26 acres of parkland and gardens. There are two swimming pools and a sports center.

Pathumwan Princess, MBK Center, 444 Phayathai Road, ☎ 02216 3700, fax 02216 3730, www.pprincess.com, $$. If you want to shop until you drop, this is place to stay. Bangkok's best shopping surrounds this 29-story complex with 458 rooms and suites. Amid the cafés and restaurants there is an Olympic-sized swimming pool.

Zenith Sukhumvit Hotel, 29/117 Sukhumvit Soi 3, ☎ 02655 4999, fax 02255 3109, www.zenithsukhumvithotel.com, $$. Functional businessman's hotel in the city center with a pleasant restaurant offering Thai and European cuisine. Expect to pay $70 a night.

Thanpuying Suites, 88 Soi Thanpuyingpahol, Ngamwongwan Road, ☎ 02941 2020, fax 02941 2021, www.thanpuyingsuite.com, $. Good price, between $30 and $50 a night, for a good location near Bangkok's business district. Just 32 rooms and special rates for long-term rentals.

Ambassador Royal Suite Hotel, 171 Sukhumvit Road, Soi 11-15, ☎ 02254 0444, fax 02254 7509, www.amtel.co.th, $. This 750-room hotel has been serving the needs of Bangkok visitors for over 25 years. It is in the center of the commercial and entertainment district and is within easy walking distance of the bargain-filled street markets.

Viengtai Hotel, 42 Rambuttri Road, ☎ 02280 5434, fax 02280 5392, www.viengtai.co.th, $. The Viengtai is within the inner city of old Bangkok. Its 200 rooms are well equipped, considering the price of under $30 a night, including breakfast. It is within easy walking distance of many popular historic sites and the Chao Phraya River.

Royal City Hotel, 800 Borom Ratchonni Road, Bangplad, ☎ 02435 8888, fax 02434 3636, www.royalrivergroup.com $. You'll pay a little over $30 a night for one of the 400 rooms at this hotel, which is on the Thonburi side of the Chao Phraya River. The hotel is within walking distance of the Temple of the Emerald Buddha (Wat Phra Kaew) and the Grand Palace. The hotel has a fitness center and swimming pool.

Where to Eat

There are so many places to eat in Bangkok that if we ate at a different place every night for 10 years we would barely cover the territory. We must confess that we have always been so pleased with the restaurants in the hotels where we have stayed that we seldom wander far. We have listed some of the city's favorite spots as well as some of those in hotels where we have dined. If you want to try something different watch for the regular restaurant reviews in the *Bangkok Post* or *The Nation*, both daily newspapers give good opinions, far better than those that appear in many of the tourist guides where the amount of advertising determines the amount of space and praise given in the review. Also we found the eating spots in the shopping plazas offered good value and service. For some reason even the fried chicken and hamburgers taste better than they do at home.

DINING PRICE SCALE	
Per person, based on a two-course dinner (a main course with either a starter or dessert), with a glass of wine and coffee. Wine is expensive and will affect the bill accordingly.	
$	Under $10
$$	$11 to $20
$$$	$21 to $30
$$$$	Over $30

Summer Palace, the Chinese restaurant at the InterContinental Hotel, 973 Ploenchit Road, ☎ 02656 0444, $$$. This is Cantonese cuisine at its best, with a level of service you'd expect at an Inter-Continental property. Portions are large, so we suggest splitting even the small dishes. Helpful advice from the order-takers makes sifting through the large menu a lot easier. We were well pleased with our fried pork ribs, chicken in a red bean sauce served with the restaurant's special fried rice, so light it almost floated from the bowl. Tangy pear sorbet and mango pancakes completed an excellent meal. Another fine location to dine in the hotel is the **Espresso**, which offers all-day dining at reasonable prices. We had an early dinner there one night and came away with change from 1,000 Baht. Lindsey had an Indonesian rice dish with pork satays, chicken, and an unexpected fried egg while I braved a Thai soup that was politely spicy for Western consumption.

The Marriott Café, inside the JW Marriott, 4 Sukhumvit Road, Soi 2, ☎ 02656 7700, $$$. We had planned to dine away from the hotel, but when we saw the astonishing buffet laid out in this restaurant just off the lobby we quickly changed our minds. It was a truly international spread, with lots of items we didn't recognize but many more that we did. I can't think of a meat or fish that was not available. The shellfish was extraordinary and the dessert display would have given a calorie counter nightmares. This feast didn't come cheap at 800 Baht (++), but it was well worth it. This restaurant has deservedly won numerous awards for its buffets. The hotel's other dining spots have also earned recognition. These include the **Man Ho Chinese Restaurant**, noted for its Cantonese and Szechwan specialties; the elegant **New York Steakhouse** – the name speaks for itself although you could add the words juicy and tender; and the **White Elephant Thai Restaurant**, open for lunch or dinner, where the waiters are specially trained to explain in good English about all of the dishes. If you want to enjoy a little Thai music and dance come in the evening. As we said at the start of this section, with hotels offering this wide selection it was hard to be tempted away from the hotel portals.

Shortly after we left the Marriott hotel, a new Japanese restaurant was opened and is receiving rave reviews for its modern-day approach to Japanese cuisine.

Sirocco, 64th floor, State Tower Building, 1055/111 Silom Road, ☎ 02624 9576, fax 02630 8464; and **Vertigo**, in the Westin Banyan Tree (see page 96), 61st Floor, Thai Wah II Tower, 21/100 South Sathorn Road, ☎ 02679 1200, fax 02679 1199, www.banyantree.com, $$$$. I have put these two together since they are the highest dining spots in the city. And they are two places that I will never dine at since I have a fear of heights and can have a dizzy spell looking down from a kitchen stool. I am told the view from either one is mind-boggling. Both have earned awards and reputations for excellent food and service. The Sirocco is noted for its far-reaching Mediterranean cuisine and includes dishes from Lebanon and Morocco. Most main dishes, like the grilled lamb chops with garlic, rosemary and sun-dried tomato, are over 1,200 Baht. Vertigo is also pricy and concentrates on sophisticated barbecued seafood dishes. On its menu are red mullet *en papillote* with thyme, grilled scallops in a shell with toasted hazelnut and coriander butter, and grilled oysters with parmesan cheese. Tempting, but I'll try my luck in the lobby lounge.

Lemongrass, 5/1 Sukhumvit Soi 24, ☎ 02258 8637, fax 02258 3888, $$. This a perennial favorite with locals and visitors is in an old Thai house smothered in Asian antiques. Here is the place to enjoy delicate Thai food at its best, although we are told that the cuisine has been cooled down over the years to make the meals more palatable for the numerous Western clients. Open for lunch from 11am to 2pm and for dinner from 6pm to 11pm. The place is small and reservations are recommended.

Wang Tien, 98/102 Panawongse Building, Surawong Road, ☎ 02236 8470, $$. Very short on ambience and sophistication but the food here makes up for that. Top Cantonese seafood at a very reasonable price. Special dishes feature scallops, prawns, snow fish and crab. Good value set lunches (between 11am and 2pm), which solves the ordering problem. At nighttime (opening hours 5:30pm to 11:30pm) two can dine very well and come away with change from 2,000 Baht.

Baan Khanitha, Klong Toey, near the Asok train station, ☎ 02258 4181, $$. This is an award-winning Thai restaurant where once only a few farangs came. Now it seems that there are more foreigners than Thais. Helping the foreigners is a good team of English-speaking waiters happy to explain the dishes. There are inexpensive lunch specials (every day from 11am to 2pm) starting at 190 Baht. Popular dishes on the dinner menu (6 to 11pm) are squid stuffed with crab, pork in a red curry, green curry with chicken and aubergine, and soft-shell crabs, fried and served in a hot and sour sauce. All those dishes were under 200 Baht. Nice night ambience and a place you can relax. The restaurant has another location at 49 Soi Ruamrudee 2, ☎ 02253 4638, fax 02253 4634.

Cabbages & Condoms, next to the PDA head office in Soi 12, Sukhumvit Road, ☎ 02229 4611, www.pda.or.th, $. Yep, that's the name of the restaurant; it's part of a chain that is growing rapidly and now has two resorts with the same name. The operations are run by the Thai Population and Community Development Association (PDA) whose founder selected the name, saying that birth control should be as cheap in Thailand as its vegetables. The vast array of high-quality Thai dishes has been adapted for Western palates. The food, service and prices are all excellent if you can handle the décor, which is, not surprisingly, displays of the world's different condoms. It claims to be the world's largest collection, which nobody would dispute. They're displayed on the walls, and the carpet up the stairs has cartoons about condoms woven into it.

In keeping with the birth-control theme, drinks are available at the Vasectomy Bar, and those things that are offered after you've dined aren't after-dinner mints.

To raise funds for its projects, the PDA operates a handicraft shop jointly with Oxfam, which sells carved wooden figurines and woven silk items all made in Northeastern Thai villages. The other C&C restaurants are in Chiang Rai, Korat and Nang Rong. The resorts are in Pattaya and Saptai.

Cyrano, 26 Sukhumvit Road, Klongtoey, ☎ 02258 1590, $$$. Elegant new French restaurant and club that received rave reviews when it opened its doors. Both décor and menu are extravagant, although the owners insist it should be like dining in your own home.

Bacchus, 20/6-7 Ruam Rudee, Ploenchit, ☎ 02650 8096, www.baccus.tv, $$. The main attraction of this wine bar, restaurant and lounge is the vast selection of French and Italian wines. Owner Koji Hara says he created the place to be fun and relaxing as well, providing an intimate atmosphere for diners and wine connoisseurs.

TEA TIME

Many of the nicer hotels in the city make a big thing about afternoon tea. Although the country was never a British colony, many traditions, like afternoon tea, snuck in from Malaya and Singapore, and famous visitors like Noel Coward and W. Somerset Maugham would have insisted upon it. Perhaps the best place to take tea is in the **Authors' Lounge** at the **Oriental Hotel** where tea, virtually every kind available, is served from 2 to 6pm along with dainty sandwiches and an assortment of cakes and cookies (biscuits to the British visitor). Other hotels who follow the tradition are the **Shangri-La**, where on Sundays they have an elaborate high tea buffet, and the **Sukhothai Hotel**. Prices vary but expect to pay 500 Baht for the experience.

Zen Japanese Restaurant, $.You will find these restaurants all over Thailand. They are in most of the major shopping malls and we find them to be tremendous value, with good food and attentive service. The pictorial menu makes it easy to select a complete meal without making embarrassing mistakes. On our first visit I opted for the snow fish in soy sauce (255 Baht) and Lindsey had the deep-fried prawns (150 Baht). The meals came with soup and an assortment of tasty side dishes. We mentioned the word "fork," and quickly the chopsticks were replaced with western cutlery. Excellent value and somewhere we would visit again. There is a frequent-diners program. Some confusion on how it works, but we have two points towards a free meal.

Hard Rock Café, on Soi 11 near the Siam Square shopping area, ☎ 02254 0830, $. You'll find all your favorite dishes here plus some Thai ones. Big plus is that they stay open until 2am when most places are closed. Keeping more reasonable hours is the nearby **S & P Restaurant & Bakery**, which serves well-priced snacks and quality ice creams as well as offering a good breakfast for 75 Baht.

Black Canyon Coffee Shop, $. This is another chain that appears at all the major shopping malls in Thailand. If you're out shopping and fancy a change from the normal mall cuisine offered by KFC, McDonalds, Pizza Hut and similar eating spots, then this little bistro might fit the bill. They offer a large menu but have a half-dozen daily specials. We opted for two of these: fettuccine with chicken curry cooked in coconut milk (65 Baht), and spaghetti and minced pork with chilies and basil (60 Baht). Remarkably cheap and remarkably tasty, although the spaghetti was almost in the too-hot-to-handle department. The countless specialty coffees cost from 45 Baht and we highly recommend the fruit smoothie at 60 Baht.

And finally a little place that is incredibly popular with locals and as far as we know has not made it into a guide book before: **Ba Mee Nam Ped**, which translates to "duck soup," an astonishing eatery that has been in the same family for generations. It's at the corner of Sukhumvit Road and Soi 15. The location is noisy and busy but the food comes highly rated. One snag: They close at 6pm, so either have dinner early or take a late lunch.

Nightlife

Bangkok is known as the city that never sleeps. It buzzes with everything from the classical to the comic. It is notorious for its prostitution and pornography. Both are illegal in Thailand but both attract visitors in huge numbers. Should you indulge in either activity, expect no sympathy or help if things go wrong. This is a perfect example of when the buyer better beware.

Calypso Cabaret: Typical Thai cabaret, featuring transvestites. Close to 50 performers, most of them deceivingly delightful in gorgeous gowns. Lots of comedy acts, singing, dancing and a fun night out. The theater is in the Asia Hotel, 296 Phayathai Road. Two shows nightly at 8:15pm and 9:45pm. ☎ 2216 8937 for reservations, important since the place fills up. The 800 Baht admission price includes one drink.

Joe Louis Puppet Theatre: A fascinating evening of Thai entertainment where the puppeteers are as much part of the show as the puppets. Every evening the troupe performs a condensed version of Ramakian, the story of Rama, the Thai adaptation of the Indian epic, Ramayana. Rama was a prince forced into exile with his brother, Prince Lak, and his wife, Nang Seeda. She is abducted by the demon ruler Totsakan. Comic hero of the piece is Hanuman, a white monkey, who helps Rama recover his wife. Fun evening for all ages. There is a puppet-and-mask-making demonstration at 7pm and the show begins at 7:30pm. It's all over at 8:45, in time for a visit to the nearby night-market. 1875 Rama IV Road, near the Bangkok Suan-lum night-bazaar, ☎ 02252 9683, fax 02252 9685, www.joelouis-theater.com/eng. Admission: 600 Baht.

Siam Niramit Show: This lavish spectacular opened its doors to the public in May 2005. The nightly show starts at 7:30pm. Ratchada Grand Theater, one kilometer from the Thailand Cultural subway station, www.siamniramit.com. Admission: 1,500 Baht. The Website is a show in itself. The theater cost $38 million and seats 2,000.

Beyond Bangkok

North

Ayutthaya

A 90-minute drive north of Bangkok brings you to the ancient city of Ayutthaya – pronounced eye-YOU-teeuh – which was the Thai capital for 417 years before it was destroyed by the Burmese in 1767. Up until that time it was a bustling metropolis attracting both European and Asian traders. Its population grew to more than a million, double that of London at the time, and many of its inhabitants used the waterways that surrounded the city for homes and transport.

IN THIS CHAPTER

The city was established by Prince Ramathibodi of U-Thong, on an island formed by the confluence of the Lopburi, Pa Sak, and Chao Phraya rivers. Today the rivers provide an ideal spot from which to view the city. After the vicious attack the city became a ghost town. The inhabitants were either killed or taken away as slaves.

Today it stands as an historic landmark with little to show for its glorious past except for shreds of ancient temples and museums, which tell the lengthy history of a city ruled by 33 different kings since its inception in 1350. It is just 75 kilometers north of Bangkok, which makes it an easy day-trip by road, rail or boat.

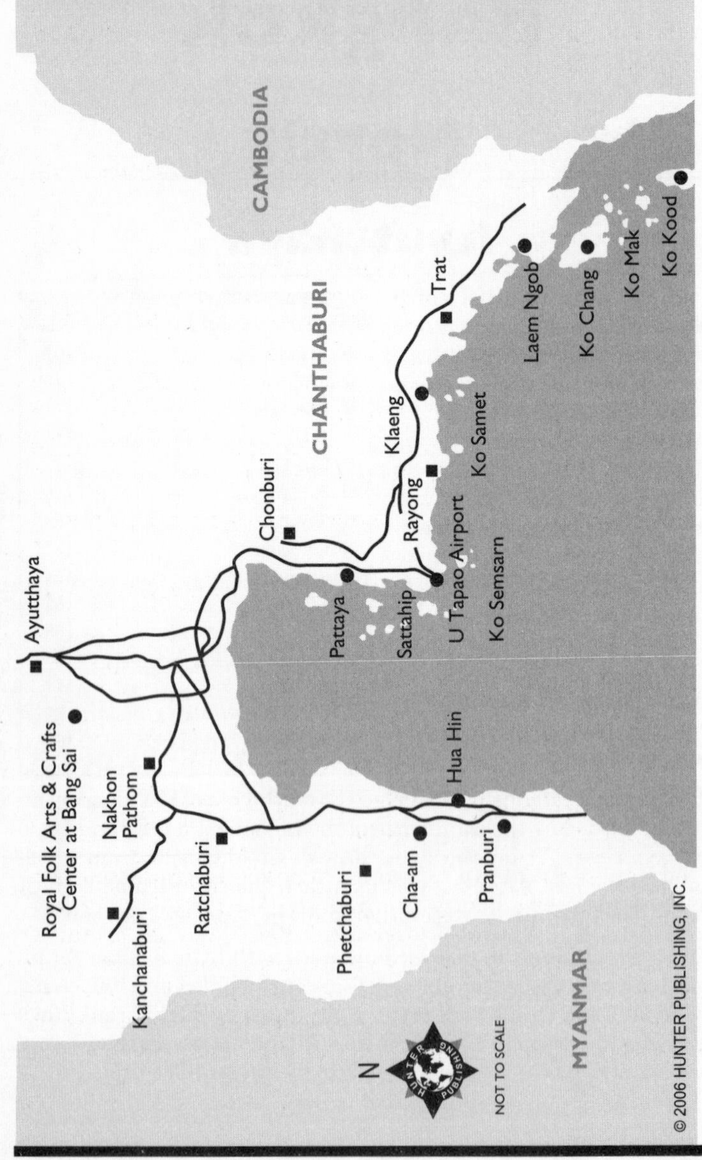
Beyond Bangkok
CAMBODIA
CHANTHABURI
Chonburi
Ayutthaya
Royal Folk Arts & Crafts
Center at Bang Sai
Nakhon
Pathom
Kanchanaburi
Ratchaburi
Phetchaburi
Cha-am
Pranburi
Hua Hin
Pattaya
Sattahip
U Tapao Airport
Ko Semsarn
Rayong
Ko Samet
Klaeng
Trat
Laem Ngob
Ko Chang
Ko Mak
Ko Kood
MYANMAR
N
NOT TO SCALE
HUNTER PUBLISHING
© 2006 HUNTER PUBLISHING, INC.

■ Getting Here

By Bus

Direct air conditioned buses leave Bangkok every half-hour from the **Northern bus terminal** on Phaholyothin Road (☎ 02537 8055) from 5:30am until 7:30pm.

By Train

Trains leave Bangkok's **Hualampong station** (☎ 0223 0710) every hour from 6:40am until 10pm.

AUTHOR'S NOTE: *The journey from Bangkok to Ayutthaya by bus or train is about 90 minutes.*

By Boat

There are no public boats making trips here, but you can book an excursion with one of the following companies:

Oriental Queen (☎ 02236 0400) leaves at 8am from the Oriental Hotel; 1,800 Baht.

River Sun Cruise (☎ 02266 9125) departs at the same time from the River City Shopping complex; 1,500 Baht.

Horizon Cruise (☎ 02266 8164) departs the Shangri-La hotel and costs 1,490 Baht.

The *Chao Phraya Express* Boat (☎ 02222 5330) has a Sunday tour that starts at 8am from Maharat Pier and costs 300 Baht.

***Mit Chao Phraya Express* Boat** (☎ 02225 6179) has a similar Sunday trip starting at the Tha Chang Pier at 8:30am; 300 Baht.

If you want to spend two days and a night on the trip, **Manohra Cruises** operates a luxury trip from the Marriott Resort Hotel (☎ 02476 0021), that costs over 6,000 Baht. Another operator, **Mekhala** (☎ 02256 7168), has a similar trip, which departs from pier in Soi Charoen Nakhon 59 and costs between 5,000 and 6,000 Baht depending upon the accommodation. An interesting and inexpensive option is the **Rice-Barge Cruise** (see page 72).

■ Getting Around

Ayutthaya is one of those places that is famous for what it was, not what it is now or will be in the future. Once you've wandered around the remains and taken a boat trip, there's not a lot to do here. It makes a pleasant break from the buzz of Bangkok, but we found that after a few hours we wanted to go back to the Thailand of today.

■ Where to Stay & Eat

Best accommodation, should you want to spend more time studying the history, is at the **Krungsri River Hotel**, Pa-Sak River Bank, ☎ 03524 4333, fax 03524 3777, $. Plenty of things to do after sightseeing, including a bowling center, swimming pool, snooker club, and fitness center. The 200-room complex also has a pub, restaurant, cafeteria and karaoke lounge. The hotel is on the eastern side of the Pridi Damrong Bridge and not too far from the railway station.

■ Things to See & Do

Museums

The city became a **UNESCO World Heritage Site** in 1991 and attracts historians and temple lovers as a result. The **Ayutthaya Historical Study Center** on Rochana Road is a national research institute devoted to the study of Ayutthaya. The center is also responsible for Ayutthaya's history museum, **Chai Sam Phraya National Museum**. Both the center and museum are open Wednesday through Sunday from 9am until 4pm; admission 40 Baht for both.

Temples & Palaces

Ayutthaya is a temple-lover's dream come true. Although most were destroyed during the 1767 attack, many have been rebuilt over the years. Most of the city's treasures and gold were taken by the Burmese, but surprisingly, during the rebuilding of some of the temples, treasures were found buried underground and are now on display, either on-site, at the Chai Sam Phraya museum (see above) or at the National Museum in Bangkok (see page 67).

Today there are a dozen temples to visit, all spectacular in their way. One that did survive the Burmese attack was **Wat Phra**

Meru, which has an impressive carved wooden ceiling, and an 18-foot-high Ayutthaya-style Buddha image that is covered in gold leaf.

The ***Viharn Phra Mongkol Bophit*** temple was originally built in 1610 and rebuilt in 1956. Its giant Buddha, one of the biggest in Thailand, spent 200 years in the open air before a new home was built. This is a favorite area for festivals (see below), and the adjoining park provides the perfect rest areas for locals and tourists. Look for elephants that provide rides around the park.

AUTHOR'S NOTE: *Based on our observations, elephant-riding here seems a popular pastime with camera-clutching Japanese visitors.*

If you want to take a break from the tour of temples take a look at the **Chankasem Palace**, originally built during the reign of King Maha Thammaraja, the 17th Ayutthayan monarch. Destroyed in the 1767 attack, it remained a ruin until King Mongkut rebuilt it about 100 years later for his use during occasional visits to Ayutthaya.

One of the attractions that used to bring the royal family here was the rounding up of the wild elephants. The large enclosure, the elephant *kraal*, is made up of massive teak logs and provides an unusual photo opportunity although the last use of the *kraal* for capturing elephants was in May 1903 during King Chulalongkorn's reign.

AUTHOR'S NOTE: *One item that caught us by surprise was the large* **Roman Catholic Church of St. Joseph**, *which looked out of place among the numerous temples.*

Festivals

January

Bang Sai Arts and Crafts Fair: This annual week-long fair held at the end of January showcases products from all districts of Ayutthaya province and is part of the Queen's **Promotion of Supplementary Occupations and Related Techniques** (SUPPORT) project to promote local products and handwork. In addition to the exhibitions and displays of crafts, there are numerous performances of folk music and dancing.

April

Songkran: The Thai New Year festival is celebrated in grand style here in Ayutthaya, with the main celebrations on April 13 taking place in front of the giant Buddha, *Viharn Phra Mongkol Bophut*.

November

***Bang Sai Loi Krathong* (Festival of Lights) & International Boat Racing**: This festival takes place all over Thailand. Here, the highlight occurs in front of the **Chantakasem National Museum**. In addition to the setting adrift of little candlelit boats under the full moon, there are exhibits of local handiwork, street parties and boat racing.

December

World Heritage Site Festival: To commemorate its designation as a World Heritage Site in 1991 by UNESCO, Ayutthaya holds a week-long celebration before Christmas with numerous events, including a sound-and-light show highlighting the city ruins, fireworks, exhibitions and parades.

Bang Sai

■ Getting Here

By Bus

Buses leave from the Northern Bus Terminal on Bangkok's Phaholyothin Road every 30 minutes between 5:30am and 6pm. Tickets are 25 Baht by air conditioned bus, and 17 Baht by ordinary buses.

By Car

If you are driving north from Bangkok, take the Bang Sai-Sam Khok road, which branches off before the Bang Pa-In Intersection.

By Boat

Many of the boat services mentioned earlier in the section on Ayutthaya stop at the pier in Bang Sai.

■ Things to See & Do

The Royal Folk Arts & Crafts Center at Bang Sai: In an effort to keep traditional Thai crafts as a major cottage industry, the Queen established this arts and crafts center in 1976. Today it thrives. And it is not just tourists who support the center; crowds of Thais make their way here on weekends to take advantage of the shopping opportunities and to enjoy the attractions.

The workshops and parks are spread out over 14 acres alongside the Chao Phraya River, some 30 kilometers north of Bangkok. Best time to visit is mid-week when it is less crowded.

Starting point to tour the center is the **museum shop**, where a full range of handicrafts are displayed. There are also galleries of art and ceramics. The workshops where the items are produced are inland, away from the river, and many of them have demonstrations on how the various products are made. Items you can buy and see produced include furniture, sculpture, Thai dolls, basketry, wooden carvings, masks, artificial flowers and hand-woven silk and cotton products. Apart from the handicrafts there are gardens to enjoy as well as aviaries and an aquarium. The center is part of the SUPPORT project, designed not only to foster the Thai handicraft industry but also to train those in need of employment. For more information, ☎ 03536 6092.

The center is open daily from 8:30am until 4:30pm, but there are no demonstrations on Monday. Admission is 20 Baht.

West

Kanchanaburi

The city of Kanchanaburi, 150 kilometers west of Bangkok, is a lively picturesque spot best known as the home of the *Bridge on the River Kwai*; it's a pleasant drive from Bangkok on a good scenic highway. Kanchanaburi Province is full of wonderful vistas, probably the best waterfalls in Thailand, and endless lakes, jungles and its fair share of temples and golf courses.

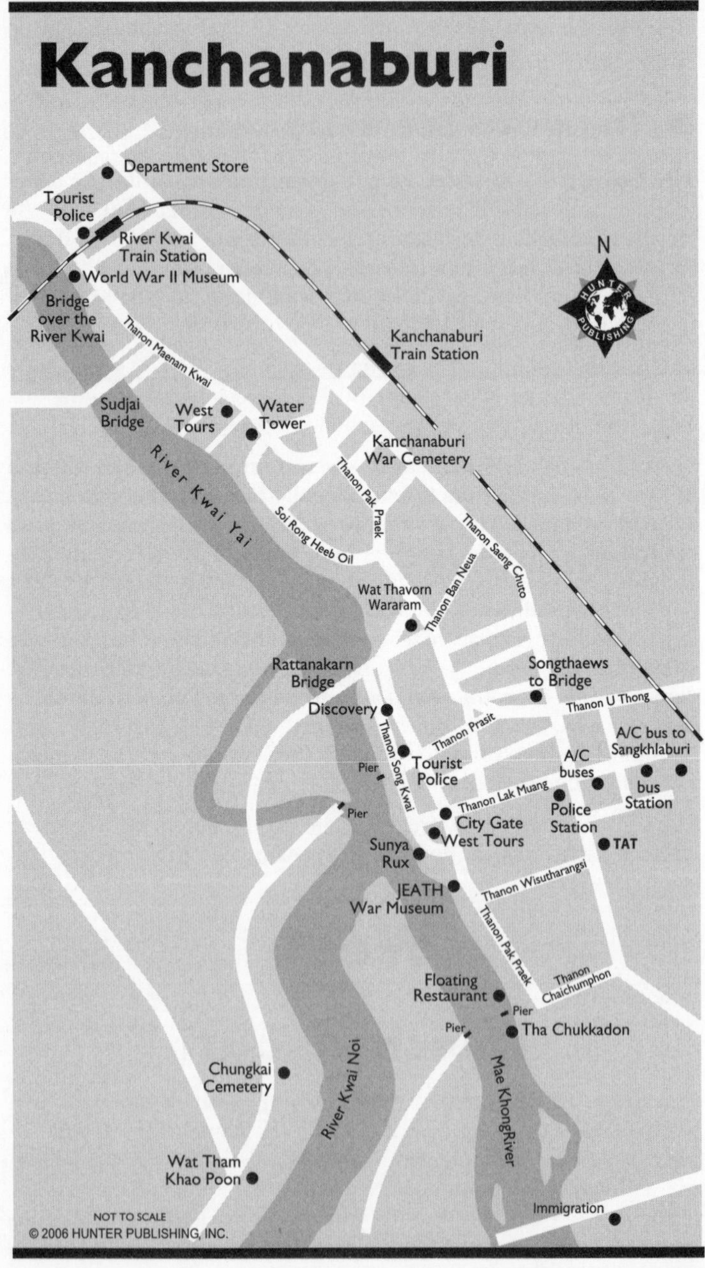
Kanchanaburi
Department Store
Tourist Police
River Kwai Train Station
World War II Museum
Bridge over the River Kwai
Thanon Maenam Kwai
Kanchanaburi Train Station
Sudjai Bridge
West Tours
Water Tower
Kanchanaburi War Cemetery
River Kwai Yai
Thanon Pak Praek
Soi Rong Heeb Oil
Thanon Saeng Chuto
Thanon Ban Neua
Wat Thavorn Wararam
Rattanakarn Bridge
Songthaews to Bridge
Thanon U Thong
Discovery
Thanon Prasit
A/C bus to Sangkhlaburi
Thanon Song Kwai
Pier
Tourist Police
A/C buses
bus Station
Thanon Lak Muang
Pier
City Gate
West Tours
Police Station
Sunya Rux
TAT
JEATH War Museum
Thanon Wisutharangsi
Thanon Pak Praek
Thanon Chaichumphon
Floating Restaurant
Pier
Pier
Tha Chukkadon
Chungkai Cemetery
River Kwai Noi
Mae KhongRiver
Wat Tham Khao Poon
NOT TO SCALE
© 2006 HUNTER PUBLISHING, INC.
Immigration
N
HUNTER PUBLISHING

■ Getting Here

By Bus

There are services throughout the day from Bangkok's Sai Tai Mai Southern Bus Terminal on Boromratchchonnani Road, ☎ 02435 1200. First-class fare is 86 Baht, and the journey takes two hours.

By Car

Driving time from Bangkok is around two hours on a good, surfaced road. The easiest route is on Highway 4 (the Phetkasem Highway) via Nakhon Chaisi, Nakhon Pathom, Ban Pong, Tha Maka and Tha Muang.

By Train

There is limited service from Bangkok with just two trains a day. However there are numerous day-excursions from Bangkok and it may be worth checking with a tour operator or with the Thonburi Station, ☎ 02411-3102, where the services originate. First-class, one-way tickets cost 123 Baht, second-class 64 Baht and third-class 28 Baht.

Similar excursions are offered by **Thai Focus**, and tickets can be purchased on the Internet at www.thaifocus.com.

■ Getting Around

There are numerous combinations of ways to get around. For detailed information visit one of the tour operators in town who organize long and short trips around the area.

Kanchanaburi province has a good road system, which enables you to traverse the jungle in relative ease and has also enabled several jungle-style resorts to open. The province – noted for its numerous sugar plantations – also has great areas for fishing and hiking. If you're driving there is a spectacular journey towards the border with Myanmar, following the same course as the "railway from hell," a route that put this province on the tourism map.

■ Things to See & Do

The Bridge on the River Kwai

The main reason we headed out here, along with millions of others each year, was to see the infamous bridge. The bridge itself is disappointing, but the history of the place makes a visit here a moving and memorable experience. As you stroll among the graves of those who died here, still and serene, it is hard to imagine the barbaric and cruel scenes of the 1940s.

The first thing you have to realize is that Pierre Boulle's book about the construction of the Thailand-to-Burma railway was a novel, not an historical document (you can read more in the *Death Railway* section, page 371). When David Lean's blockbuster movie was released in 1957, further changes were made to make the film more entertaining than factual. And the film was not made here in Thailand, but in Sri Lanka.

The most surprising thing is that there never was a bridge over the River Kwai. Boulle (who also wrote *Planet of the Apes*) made the assumption that the railway crossed the Kwai since it followed its path for so long. The railway actually crossed the *Mae Klong* River.

This fact really did not matter until the tourists started arriving in droves after the movie's release. The sleepy town was transformed almost overnight. And the Thais quickly solved the problem. The Mae Klong, where it passes under the bridge, was renamed the *Kwai Yai* (the big Kwai), which then flows into the *Kwai Noi* (the original little Kwai).

The prisoners actually built two bridges. Neither of them are anything like the massive bamboo-and-wood structure shown in the movie. The one you see today, a rather squat unimpressive bridge with concrete piers and steel spans, is much like it was in the 1940s. The steel spans were brought from Java by the Japanese; some of those were destroyed by allied bombing and replaced after the war. Records show that the prisoners completed a wooden bridge in February1943 but the Japanese, concerned about its strength, replaced it with the steel bridge a few months later.

You can't get this close to the bridge without making a crossing. Despite warnings of its dangers, tourists do it every day, most of them whistling *Colonel Bogey*, the wartime song made famous by the film. If you do make the crossing, watch out for the trains. They do cross slowly and there are several escape spots on the bridge where you can step aside as the train passes.

And *Colonel Bogey*? That part is authentic and the march was probably sung, rather than whistled, a great deal during those horrific days. It was composed by Lieutenant F.J. Ricketts (1881-1945) who was director of music for the Royal Marines at Plymouth in southwest England. The music was first published in 1914 when the military frowned upon its officers having any outside professional pursuits, so he used the pseudonym Kenneth Alford.

A Railway Excursion

For some extreme scenery, the train ride beyond the **River Kwai Bridge station** to the end of the line at **Nam Tok** is a must-see journey. It takes about two hours, and will take you down the **Kwai Noi valley** over the impressive **Wampo Viaduct**, the scary trestle bridge that clings to the rock face. Few of the POWs who helped construct this bridge lived to tell the tale. Your thoughts here have to be that it has stood like this for 60 years and surely can handle a couple more crossings.

The rest of the journey is very scenic, without the scary bits, and the tiny stations on the route are bedecked with flowers. The journey can be done there and back in a day; you can organize a taxi out and ride the train back, or vice versa. Train schedules are not always adhered to, and a telephone call to the Tourism Authority of Thailand (TAT) office, ☎ 03451 1200, is advisable. Their office is south of the bus station, which is on the south side of Kanchanaburi.

Beyond Nam Tok on the disused section of the railway is **Konyu Cutting**, named Hellfire Pass by the POWs because of the torchlight that illuminated it during the nighttime construction. Here the Australians have cleared a five-kilometer stretch of track as a memorial to those who died. There are ample places where you can walk along the disused track bed and imagine the hardship that the workers endured.

Museums

There are three museums in the town dedicated to the death railway. The one we found most interesting is the newest, opened in 2003, the **Thailand Burma Railway Center** (☎ 03451 0067, www.tbrconline.com), which is alongside the main cemetery. Here you learn why the railway was so important to the Japanese and get a grim insight into how the prisoners lived and died. The story of the railroad is enhanced by accounts of what happened after the war and what is happening today to remember those who died. The center is open daily from 9am to 5pm. Admission 60 Baht.

AUTHOR'S NOTE: *Curators of the center, Hugh Cope and Rod Beattie, admit to having an ironic problem. They have an incredible amount of information on those who died building the Thailand-Burma railway but very little on those who survived.*

There may be lots of things about the book and the film that are not historically accurate. But that is not so important. What is important is that without them the world's attention would not have been focused on the death railway. The tale of a small bridge opened our eyes to a very sad saga. The bridge here at Kanchanaburi was one of 688 constructed along the railway. Do you know the names of any of the others?

Kanchanaburi's other museums are the **JEATH Museum**, which is three kilometers south of the main railway station and open daily from 8:30am to 4:30pm, admission 30 Baht; and the **World War II Museum**, which is close to the bridge and opens daily from 8am to 6pm, admission 30 Baht. The JEATH museum (the letters JEATH represent the first letter of Japan, England, America, Australia, Thailand and Holland, the countries who lost soldiers during the railway construction) is filled with World War II memorabilia, including frightening sketches some of the prisoners made of the various forms of torture they endured. The World War II museum is a bit like a Robinson's department store, with such a wide range of items on view. Although there are numerous exhibits about the death railway you can also view pictures of Miss Thailand from the 1930s as well as portraits of the museum founders. Probably one of the most important items is a glass tomb containing the remains of some of the Asian laborers, who are often not as well remembered as the allied POWs. You'll find more about the Railway from Hell in the *Trains of Thailand* chapter, page 351.

Festivals

April

The Thai New Year: The Songkran festival in April has an added dimension here. The ***Ban Nong Khao*** **Fair**, held at the same time, promoting the traditions and cultures of village life with demonstrations of handicrafts as well as a beauty-queen contest and some local theatrical performances. It is also a time when the locals perform the ***Yoei*** **Dance**, a 500-year-old folk play with lots of dancing, hand-clapping, drum-banging and colorful costumes.

November

Boat & Raft Festival: You can't be this close to a famous river without having a festival of races and water sports. This event takes place early in November near the Khun Phan Dam.

River Kwai Bridge Week: This annual event at the end of November, sponsored by the Kanchanaburi Provincial Authority, commemorates the death railway with a fair that includes a light-and-sound show, stalls selling local handicrafts, and historical and archaeological exhibitions.

Shopping

You'll find all the typical Thai souvenirs and handicrafts available at the spots where tourists gather, both on the main street and near the bridge. As might be expected, postcards and books about the bridge are big sellers. One local specialty worth considering are the Thai **blue sapphires**, which are mined in Kanchanaburi's **Bo Phloi** district, as are topaz and onyx.

National Parks

There are two major national parks in Kanchanaburi: The **Thungyai National Park**, claimed to be the most unspoiled jungle park in Thailand and covering more than 600,000 hectares along the Myanmar border; and the **Erawan National Park**, 65 kilometers northwest of Kanchanaburi city, which is home to the Erawan falls the seven tiered waterfall that appears in Thailand promotions almost as often as temples.

Most of Thailand's national parks charge a modest entrance fee – the highest we've paid is 200 Baht for car and passengers – and the most helpful Website we've found for researching the parks is www.amazing-thailand.com/parks.

Golf

Mission Hills Golf Club, 27/7 Moo 7 Thambol Pang-Thru Amphur Thamuang, Kanchanaburi, ☎ 03464 4147, www.golfmissionhills.com. Claimed to be one of the best courses designed by Jack Nicklaus, this 18-hole, par 72, 6,364-yard course attracts players from Bangkok, just an hour-and-45-minute drive, as well as those from Kanchanaburi province. Luxury lakeside lodges are available if you want to stay overnight. Visitor green fees: 1,200 Baht for weekdays and 1,900 on weekends.

Evergreen Hills Golf Club & Resort, 152 Moo 2 Rangsali, Thamuang, Kanchanaburi, ☎ 03465 7094, www.evergreenhills-golfclub.com. This club has a 72-room resort nestled in one the province's jungle-covered valleys, which attracts visitors who want to stay overnight and play more than one round. This 6,879-yard 18-hole par 72 course caters to golfers of all levels. Visitor green fees: 800 Baht for weekdays and 1,200 for weekends.

Nichigo Resort & Country Club, 106 Moo 4, Thambol Wang-dong, Kanchanaburi, ☎ 03451 8518, fax 03451 3334, www.nichigoresortcc.com. The 27 holes of golf are just part of this country-club complex, set between the mountainous border with Myanmar and the River Kwai. Many of the 100 rooms and suites have views of the three 36-par nine-hole courses. Visitor green fees: 1,000 Baht for weekdays and 1,500 for weekends.

■ Where to Stay

ACCOMMODATIONS PRICE SCALE	
Indicates rates charged per night during high-season for a double room, including breakfast and all service charges. Prices vary according to the exchange rate between the US dollar and Thai Baht. Most hotels offer discounts from their published rack rates during low season. All those listed accept major credit cards; rooms have direct-dial telephones and private bathrooms.	
$	Under $50
$$	$51 to $100
$$$	$101 to $175
$$$$	Over $175

The Felix River Kwai, on the river across from the Bridge over the River Kwai train station, ☎ 03451 5061, fax 03451 5095, www.felixriverkwai.co.th, $$$. The Felix occupies a prime location just north of the bridge and has the best accommodation in the area. Most expensive rooms have a view of the river, and you can walk down to the bridge, albeit the wrong side from the station, in a couple of minutes. The rooms are large and well equipped and there are two swimming pools and a choice of restaurants.

Duen Shine Resort, close to the Felix, ☎ 03465 3345, fax 03645 3346, $$. Similar standard but slightly cheaper than the Felix and you do get a choice of cottage, hotel room or raft house, an upmarket version of what you'll find elsewhere on the river. Nice gardens, with a swimming pool and very acceptable restaurant.

River Kwai Hotel, 284/3 Thanon Sang Chuto, ☎ 03451 3348, fax 03451 1269, $. The best hotel in the town center, a fair distance from the river but it is close to the restaurants and shops. The hotel has a nightclub and swimming pool.

Pavilion Rim Kwai Resort, 79/2 Moo 4, Ladya-Erawan Road, ☎ 03451 3800, fax 03451 5774, www.pavilionhotels.com, $$. This 194-room resort is set in the heart of River Kwai valley, midway between Kanchanaburi and the Erawan National Park. Rates for the fully equipped and nicely decorated rooms run from 3,100 Baht for a superior room up to 5,900 Baht for the prestigious two-bedroom pavilion-suite bungalows. If you don't get to visit the nearby famed Erawan Waterfall you can enjoy a miniature version in one of the hotel's two swimming pools. It's a 30-minute drive back to the infamous bridge. There are Pavilion hotels and resorts at Phuket, Krabi and Songkhla.

Comsaed River Kwai Resort, 18/9 Moo 5, Ladya, ☎ 03463 1443, fax 03458 9094, www.comsaedriverkwai.com, $$. If you don't mind being 19 kilometers out of town, then this award-winning resort is the place to stay. The 91-room complex offers a range of accommodation with luxury rooms, suites or one- or two-bedroom villas, all with views of the River Kwai. The villas have fully equipped kitchens if you want to cook for yourself, and there is an excellent restaurant. Opened in 1994, the Comsaed has a good spa and is set in very pleasant gardens. This is luxury in the country-side within a 20-minute drive to downtown.

■ Where to Eat

There are many fine spots offering the best of Thai and Chinese cuisine. Needless to say, most local menus feature freshly caught fish from the river. Most popular dining areas are the **Song Kwae Road waterfront** area and the **riverside** restaurants.

South

Hua Hin

■ Introduction

Hua Hin, a two-and-a-half-hour drive south from Bangkok, is Thailand's oldest seaside resort and in some ways remains a regal and charming place to stay. It does not have the sex trade that has smothered Pattaya or the overdevelopment that threatens Phuket. Twenty minutes' drive along the coast to the north is **Cha-am**, an enjoyable resort not yet as extensive as Hua Hin.

We were disappointed when we first arrived in Hua Hin. It was far more developed than we had realized. Because of all the buildings, many of them high-rise hotels, it is difficult to see the beach unless you happen to be in one of the hotels.

In some ways we were reminded of Miami Beach and the vast expanse of Collins Avenue, where you can only assume there is a beach and an ocean beyond the maze of concrete structures. And when we did get to see the beach we were let down again. These beaches may be nice by European standards but they are certainly nothing special in Thailand. Better than Pattaya perhaps, but nothing compared to the wonderful white, powdery sand farther south.

■ History & Character

Hua Hin's development is not dissimilar to that of south Florida. The town was transformed from a sleepy fishing village in the 1920s when a railway station was built (as, in Florida, Henry Flagler built the railroad to Palm Beach), thus enabling the northern elite to reach their winter palaces in style. The railway line was followed by a summer palace for King Rama VII. He found it the ideal escape from Bangkok, and when he set up here the capital's high society followed. It didn't take long for the aristocratic visitors to discover nearby Cha-am and subtly develop that area as well.

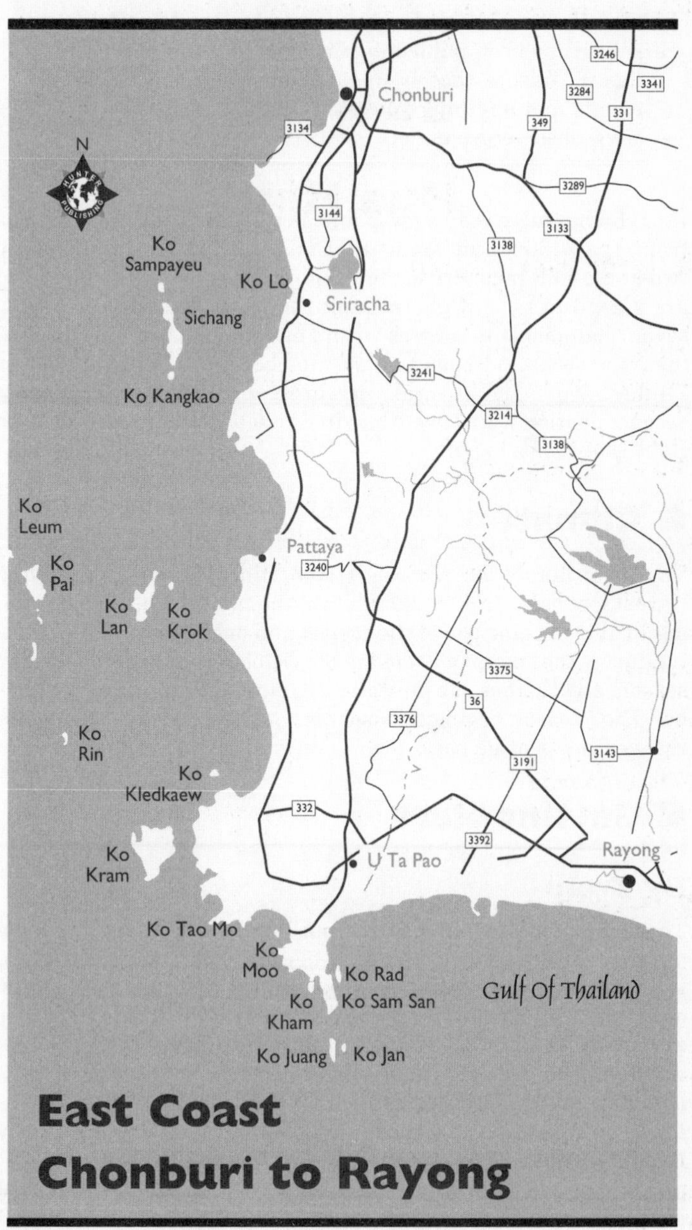

East Coast Chonburi to Rayong

THE LOCAL PERIODICAL

Hua Hin has its own English magazine, the *Hua Hin Observer*. It's been publishing for over 10 years and now it has a Website that is updated monthly showing local events and anything you need to know about the area, www.observergroup.net.

Hua Hin has more than a few points in its favor. It's a great retreat from the snarl and smog of Bangkok, within a pleasant two-and-a-half-hour drive. And the facilities, once you get here, are second to none. Golfers think they're in links heaven, with seven championship courses within easy reach. And the choice of luxury resorts and spas is only matched by those available in Phuket. We found several instances where prices for luxury accommodation were lower than in Phuket. Getting more for your Baht is always a big plus.

■ Climate

The royal family did not select Hua Hin as a summer holiday retreat just because of its closeness to the capital. The area has the distinction of being one of the coolest and driest parts of the country during the summer. From May to October is considered the low season, and there is substantial rain, most of it falling in September. High season begins in November and extends to April when the weather is at its best.

■ Getting Here

By Train

There are a dozen trains daily from Bangkok to Hua Hin. Some are slow third-class-only trains, so beware. The 7:45am departure is an express with second-class air conditioned carriages, which arrives in Hua Hin at 11am. The cost is 302 Baht. There's another express at 2:45pm that makes a stop at Hua Hin at 6:30pm on its way to the border with Malaysia. Departures at the time of writing are from Hualampong Station on Rama IV Road near Chinatown. Tickets can be purchased up to 90 days in advance at any Bangkok station. The advance ticket office at Hualampong Station is open every day from 7am to 4pm, ☎ 02223 0341, 02223 7010 or 02223 7020. If you want to avoid the wait, Bangkok travel agents will arrange tickets and charge 100 Baht for providing the service. The station office in Hua Hin is on Damnoenkasem Road, ☎ 03251 1073.

By Air

Bangkok Airways, www.bangkokair.com, has daily flights from the capital utilizing the turbo-prop Franco-Italian ATR-72. Flight time is 40 minutes. The Bangkok Airways office in Hua Hin is on Phetchkasem Road, ☎ 03251 2083.

Guests at the two **Evason Hua Hin** resorts have their own express shuttle from Bangkok. The service was created by Evason in partnership with airline operator **SGA Airlines**. They operate a 12-passenger Cessna 208B Caravan aircraft fitted with plush leather seating. The operation is designed to grow with demand, but initial flights were timed to connect with international arrivals to and from Europe, with daily departures from Bangkok at 8am, ll:30am, 3:30pm and 6:30pm. Flights depart Hua Hin at 9:30am, 1pm, 4:30pm and 8pm. Round-trip airfare is 5,200 Baht. Reservations, ☎ 03261 8200. The airport is five kilometers north of the town, and taxis are always available when flights arrive.

By Bus

Air conditioned buses leave Bangkok's Southern Bus Terminal, Sai Tai Mai, on Boromratchchonnani Road, ☎ 2435 1200, every 30 minutes between 5am and 10pm for Hua Hin. Advance reservations are not required. Travel time is three hours and costs about the same as the train. The bus terminal in Hua Hin is at the Siripetchkasem Hotel on Srasong Road, ☎ 03251 1654. There are also overnight buses to other cities in southern Thailand. Most leave Hua Hin before midnight. Among the places served are Phuket, Ko Samui and Hat Yai.

Some of the major hotel chains do offer a mini-bus service between their properties in Bangkok and Hua Hin.

By Taxi

If you prefer going it on your own, some taxis will bring you to Hua Hin from Bangkok. It's quick – about two-and-a-half hours if you don't stop. Arrange the price before you leave, or ask the hotel concierge to do it for you. Expect to pay about 2,500 Baht.

USEFUL TELEPHONE NUMBERS

Tourist police 24-hour hotline .... ☎ 1699
Tourist police office:
Thanon Damern Kasem .... ☎ 03251 5995
Hua Han Police:
Thanon Damern Kasem. .... ☎ 03251 1027
Tourist information
Hua Hin .... ☎ 03253 2433
Cha-am .... ☎ 03247 1005
Thonburi Hua Hin Hospital:
17/155 Thanon Phetchkasem. .... ☎ 03252 0900
San Paulo Private Hospital:
222 Thanon Phetchkasem .... ☎ 03253 2576
Thonburi Cha-am Hospital:
Narathip Road .... ☎ 03243 3903
Main post office, Damnoenkasem Road
near the Phetchkasem intersection .... ☎ 03251 1350

■ Getting Around

Rental-car agencies do a good business in Hua Hin for those wanting to get out and explore the surrounding countryside. Most hotel reception desks can arrange car rentals, or you can call **Avis**, ☎ 03251 2021, or **Budget**, ☎ 03251 4220. There are also cars for hire from stands on Damnoenkasem Road. Prices there may be lower. Check to see you have insurance. A small vehicle will cost about 1,000 Baht per day.

You'll find lots of motorcycles for rent around town. Be warned about lack of insurance and be sure and wear a crash helmet if you can't resist the temptation. Expect to pay 200 Baht for the dubious pleasure.

Tuk-tuks, motorcycle taxis, and trishaws are readily available in both Hua Hin and Cha-am. Cost of a trip between the two areas will be up to 200 Baht.

■ Things to See & Do

Festivals & Events

June

Jazz Festival: Annual event taking place at the beginning of June, which attracts more people – players and spectators – each year. The festival is normally held over a three-day Friday to Sunday period. Main performances are held each night on the Red Cross Stage and the Beach Stage. Petchkaseam Road up to the railway station becomes Jazz Alley and a venue for more performances. The main stage performances finish at midnight on Friday and Saturday and 10pm on Sundays but the music continues elsewhere until the wee hours. Performers, and spectators, come from around the globe.

September

Hua Hin's biggest annual event has to be **elephant polo**, a five-day extravaganza held in mid-September that is gaining worldwide notoriety since its inception in 2000. There are numerous lighthearted matches followed by a serious tournament that brings players from around the world. It's held at the **Pradiphat Pine Forest** at Suan Son, south of Hua Hin, with headquarters at the **Anantara Resort & Spa**, where a gala dinner is held on one of the evenings (see page 128).

In addition to the fun matches, there is a parade of elephants and competitors and an exhibition match before the actual tournament begins. The mallets used are two meters long – it varies somewhat according to the height of the elephant – but the ball is the same size as the one used in regular polo. Played according to **World Elephant Polo Association** rules, the Thai tournament is played with three elephants per team on a pitch one-third the size of a standard polo field. A game is comprised of two seven-minute chukkas.

Money is raised from the gala dinner's charity auction where unusual prizes, like being a hot-air-balloon pilot or driving the world's best sports cars, bring in large amounts of money. The event raises millions of Baht for the **National Elephant Institute**, which cares for old animals and retired *mahouts* (elephant trainers). There is no charge for watching the tournament.

The finals are normally held on a Sunday, an all-day affair that is highlighted by a jazz brunch. Attendees at the event usually include members of the National Elephant Institute's elephant orchestra making a jumbo noise, and the paintbrush-wielding elephants, whose artwork regularly sells at the charity auction for up to $800. Tickets for the gala dinner and the jazz brunch are available from the **Anantara Resort & Spa**, ☎ 03252 0250. In previous years the tickets cost 4,500 and 800 Baht respectively, plus service and taxes. The resort has special packages for the tournament week, as do other hotels in the area.

The Royal Palaces

There are two palaces in the area well worth a visit. The elder of the two is **Maruekkhathayawan Palace**, 14 kilometers north of Hua Hin. This was built in 1924 as a holiday home for King Rama VI who is credited with much of the design incorporated in the residence. The palace is made entirely of teak with lots of long walkways and open rooms. Sadly the king did not spend a great deal of time here; he died in 1925. The palace is open to the public every day from 8am to 4pm.

The second palace, **Klai Kangwong**, is the present royal family's summer palace and can only be visited when they are not in residence. This was built by King Rama VII in 1926, and has a Spanish flair. The Maruekkhathayawan palace, by comparison, is in a Victorian style. *Klai Kangwon* translates to "far from worries," which is what King Rama VII wanted when he stayed here. The most historic event to occur at the palace was when the change was made from absolute monarchy to the present constitutional monarchy. The king was in residence when news came from Bangkok of the takeover by the People's Party. To avoid any possible bloodshed the king accepted the news and returned to the capital as the first king under the new system. Unfortunately there is nothing to see in the palace that marks the event. The present king has made great use of the palace and it has been his headquarters when initiating development projects. When the royal family is not in residence, the palace is open from 9am to 4pm. Phetchkasem Beach Road, ☎ 03251 1155, fax 03251 0979. There is a 20-Baht admission charge.

Massage

All the walking around the stores and stalls downtown plays havoc with the feet. There is nothing like an hour-long Thai foot-massage to ease the pains and strains of shopping. We found an excellent parlor at 182/9 Naresdamri Road. The **Elephant Thai Massage**, ☎ 03253 3455, offers the complete range of massage and beauty salon services at prices a fraction of what you'd pay in a hotel spa. Our foot massage cost 300 Baht and a full two-hour Thai massage costs 400 Baht. Quality operators perform in a very pleasant environment.

Golf

There are now seven world-class golf courses within easy reach of Hua Hin. It's become a major attraction for the area. So important is it that most courses include free pick-up from area hotels in their green fees. And if they don't there's a good chance that your hotel will provide a similar service.

Royal Hua Hin Golf Course, Damnoenkasem Road near the Hua Hin Railway Station, ☎ 03251 2475. We start with this one since it was the first championship golf course in Thailand. (The Gymkhana Club in Chiang Mai was founded earlier but what they have hardly qualifies as championship.) The course – 18 holes, 6,678 yards, par 72 – was designed by a Mr. O.A. Robins, a Scottish railway engineer, and opened in 1924. Be warned there are lots of trees, which attract many a ball, and the heavy grass fairways keep the ball from running on. Because of its location and historic interest this is very popular course so be sure and call for a tee time. Play starts at 6am when it is relatively cool. Green fees for visitors: 1,200 Baht.

Springfield Royal Country Club, 193 Huay-Sai Nua, Phetchkasem Road, Cha-am, ☎ 03247 1303. Quality course that was designed by Jack Nicklaus in 1993, and he left his trademark with good use of bunkers and water hazards. The setting, clubhouse and practice facilities are all superb. The course, an 18-hole par 72, playing over 7,000 yards, is a 25-minute drive north from Hua Hin. Green fees for visitors: 2,500 Baht.

Palm Hills Resort & Country Club, 1444 Phetchkasem Road, Cha-am, ☎ 03252 0800, fax 03252 0820. Palm Hills is a little closer to Hua Hin than Springfield and was opened two years earlier, in 1991. Designed by another American, Max Wexler, the course is part of a 650-acre resort that boasts tennis, badminton and squash courts. There is a gymnasium and a swimming pool for those who would rather dive than hit divots into the air. The course has introduced a package price of 2,000 Baht per person, good on any day of the week, which includes green fees, caddy and round-trip transfers to any hotel in the area. Didn't bring your clubs? You can rent a set for 350 Baht.

Palm Hills is a scenic resort among rolling hills and jagged escarpments. Coastal views from parts of the course are truly spectacular. The 18 holes are arranged in two halves, which are separated by the clubhouse with its Thai-style architecture coupled with American-style facilities. Most of the course enjoys gentle terrain but be prepared for the tenth hole, where the tee shot is at the side of a very large limestone mountain.

Hua Hin Seoul Country Club, formerly the Milford, 174 Moo 1, Prnomparn. Pranburi, www.golfhuahin.com/seoul. Hua Hin Seoul Country Club offers a pleasant change from the longer championship courses, with fantastic sea views. This 18-hole, 6,614-yard par 72 was designed by Robert McFarland and opened in 1992, and is a 20-minute drive south of Hua Hin. It is not an easy course. The front nine holes, with their strikingly raised tees, are the major challenge. The weekday 1,600 Baht package includes green fees, caddy and transfers from local hotels. The price increases by 200 Baht on weekends and public holidays.

Majestic Creek Country Club, 164 Moo 4 Tambol Tabtai. The 30-minute drive inland to this course is almost as enjoyable as playing golf. The road heads towards the border with Myanmar and passes through small Thai farms that produce bananas, mangos, sugar cane and pineapples. It's an interesting insight into rural living before you arrive at the 18-hole, 6,961 yard, par 72 that was designed by local architect Sukitti Klangvisai and opened in 1993. Majestic offers superb holes in an exciting layout beneath the mountains. There are a lot of natural hazards to watch out for as well as numerous man-made ones. It's a challenging course, starting with the first hole par-four with its dog-leg corners. Most good Thai course import grasses for fairways and greens. Here they have used the indigenous zoysia grass to good effect. There is 2,000-Baht-per-person package, which includes transport to and from area hotels, green fees and caddy. The rate applies seven days a week.

Imperial Lake View Hotel & Golf Club, 79 Moo 4, Tambol Sampraya, Cha-am, ☎ 032 45 6233, fax 03245 6235. A total of 27 holes here to test your skill. The older 18 holes, par 72, cover 6,915 yards while the nine-holes, known as the desert course, is a par 9 measuring 3,417 yards. Designer Roger Packard had adventure in mind when he created these courses, where many of the greens are hidden from the tees.

The clubhouse is part of a 75-room hotel complex, which offers quality amenities such as a swimming pool that overlooks the 18th green. There are also tennis courts, for those who brought rackets instead of clubs. Lake View has an any-day-of-the-week 2,000 Baht package.

Sawang Resort Golf Club, 99 Moo 2, Sapang. Kaoyoi. Petchaburi. This is another course incorporating a hotel; it is the farthest from Hua Hin of the clubs we have listed. It takes about an hour driving north on the road to Bangkok to reach this course, which is set in a private valley surrounded by freshwater lakes. The 18-hole, 6,959-yard par 72 course was designed by Isao Ikatsumata and opened 1993. In addition to the driving range there are chipping greens, a putting green and a pro shop all designed to help improve your game. The club has a 1,400-Baht package deal for weekday players. The price includes green fees, caddy and round-trip transportation to area hotels. Clubs are available for rent starting from 450 Baht.

Water Sports

Hua Hin Water-Sports Center on Takiab Beach, ☎ 01857 4328, fax 03252 1014, offers what it terms the ultimate water sports package with 15 minutes on a personal watercraft, 15 minutes waterskiing, 10 minutes whirling around in a doughnut, 30 minutes on a banana boat followed by an hour-long boat ride. They also include body boarding, beach volleyball, a barbecue lunch and use of beach chairs and umbrellas. When we called for a price we were told they were still working that out. However we did get some prices: A one-hour boat trip was 600 Baht and a two-hour island excursion cost 1,000 Baht and included fresh coconut water and a tropical fruit platter. A four-hour fishing trip, including a packed lunch, fishing equipment and bait was available for 5,000 Baht with additional hours charged at 800 Baht. The company offers free pick-up and drop-off from Hua Hin hotels.

Windsurfing is a popular pastime both in Hua Hin and Cha-am. Best times are in the early summer during the Southwest monsoon when the wind is side-shore and in the winter, during the Northeast monsoon when the wind is side-on shore. Wind strength is usually a few knots stronger here than in Pattaya, a major spot for windsurfers, except from July to October when Pattaya is better. Big plus for Hua Hin is the cleaner water. Main center for surfers is next to the Cha-am Regent resort where there is a small club with board storage facilities and a restaurant. The Windsurfing Association of Thailand occasionally organizes fun board races on this beach. Boards can be rented at several resorts, including the **Royal Village** in Hua Hin, the **Regent** in Cha-am and **Club Aldiana** in Pranburi.

AUTHOR'S TIP: *If you want a break from the beach or pool, there is a reasonably priced and well-kept go-cart track near the airport.*

■ Where to Stay

ACCOMMODATIONS PRICE SCALE	
Indicates rates charged per night during high-season for a double room, including breakfast and all service charges. Prices vary according to the exchange rate between the US dollar and Thai Baht. Most hotels offer discounts from their published rack rates during low season. All those listed accept major credit cards; rooms have direct-dial telephones and private bathrooms.	
$	Under $50
$$	$51 to $100
$$$	$101 to $175
$$$$	Over $175

The only place to stay here in 1923 was the **Railway Hotel** (see page 133), built by Prince Purachatra, a son of King Rama V, when he was in charge of the State Railway, and completed after the Southern Railroad was built linking Bangkok with Malaysia. Bangkok's elite filled the hotel, an elegant Victorian building with formal gardens, and enormous rooms with appropriate décor of the period. It is still a wonderful place to stay.

With the hotel in great demand, bungalows sprang up along the beaches and other members of the royal family built retreats. A golf course was started that claims to be the first in Thailand, something the Gymkhana Club in Chiang Mai would dispute.

Although modern hotels have filled the waterfront, the area still retains a regal air. It still is a fishing village in part, with excellent seafood restaurants where you can sit and gaze out to sea (trying to avoid the lights of the concrete jungle farther along the bay).

Driving around the countryside can be a rewarding experience. Heading inland towards the border with Myanmar will give you a true insight into Thai-style agriculture. Within minutes you can be in a tropical wonderland of rubber trees and banana, pineapple or mango plantations. Then there are the scenic coastal routes to explore.

Back in Hua Hin there are quiet quaint streets – and a couple of bar alleys that aren't quite so quiet – where you can meander safely, and a night-market that isn't as frantic as those in the capital.

Many farangs have decided to retire here; others have invested in bars or guesthouses. The Thais accept that with gratitude rather than seeing it as an intrusion. It gives the area a more stable and international feeling. It's the sort of place that you can come back to, that improves the more you try it. Maybe our initial disappointment was ill-founded. We'll know better after another visit or two.

We have not limited our listings to Hua Hin but have included the resorts of **Cha-am** to the north and **Pranburi** to the south. There are now more than 100 places to stay in the area. If you don't want the luxury – and expense – of a full-service hotel, there are numerous guesthouses that offer basic rooms at low prices. The price guide is for a double room, with breakfast and taxes included, in the high season. Over the Christmas and New Year Holiday most resorts require you purchase their gala dinners.

Hotel Sofitel Central Hua Hin, 1 Damnoenkasem Road, ☎ 03251 2021, fax 03251 1014, www.sofitel.com, $$$$. This is the first in our list since this is where it all began. The oldest and most famous hotel in Hua Hin the Sofitel was formerly the Railway Hotel, built in 1924 by the Southern Railway. It retains its Victorian charm despite all its modern facilities. Sip afternoon tea in the Museum or wander in the 40 acres of gardens amid well-manicured topiary. It is amazingly quiet considering the crowds and street vendors beyond the hotel walls. Depending on the season, expect to pay from 5,000 to 7,100 Baht for one of the gorgeous high-ceilinged rooms. The resort is right on the beach and has three swimming pools, two putting greens, tennis courts and a snooker room.

The **Evason Hua Hin**, 9 Parknampran Beach, ☎ 03263 2111, www.evasonhuahin.com, $$$$. Wonderful choice of accommodation is offered at this five-star resort in Pranburi, a 20-minute drive south of Hua Hin. In addition to 61 rooms, the Evason has suites, studios, and even villas with private pools and gardens. Prices range from 4,800 Baht per night up to 12,000 Baht for a villa with a pool. Breakfast, 450 Baht per person, is extra. Most rooms have open-style bathrooms, which create more space and light.

Families with children are well accommodated. There are suites with interconnecting rooms, and the resort has a professionally managed **Kids Club**, where younger visitors can spend the entire day enjoying special meals and adventure games in addition to the normal seaside activities. Great spa, fitness center and shops.

Chiva Som, 73/4 Phetchkasem Road, ☎ 03253 6536, fax 03251 1154, www.chivasom.net, $$$$. This is one of the world's top spas, with 15 treatment rooms offering everything from massages to body reshaping, aromatherapy and reflexology. Set amid seven acres of seafront gardens just south of Hua Hin, the resort only has 37 bungalows and rooms, with the staff outnumbering guests by four-to-one. Two pools – one inside, the other by the beach – saunas and steam rooms insure that the spa lives up to its name, *Chiva Som*, which translates to Haven of Life. All-inclusive packages, including meals (these are special, since the spa has its own organic gardens north of town) and a variety of treatments, start at around $300 a day, per person. Perhaps this is not the place to bring the entire family.

Evason Hideaway & Six Senses Spa at Hua Hin, 9/22 Moo 5 Parknampran Beach, Pranburi, ☎ 03261 8200, fax 03261 8201, www.evasonhideaways.com, $$$$. This is one of the newest and most expensive resorts in Hua Hin, with just 55 villas, each with its own infinity pool. Lowest prices we've seen start at 11,000 Baht +++. The villas are lavishly furnished, have outdoor bathrooms and private gardens that are surrounded by a brick wall for greater privacy. There is a highly rated Just Kids club and a choice of fine dining. The resort is managed by Six Senses Resorts & Spas, which also owns and operates the Soneva Fushi Resort and Soneva Gili Resort in the Maldives.

DID YOU KNOW? *Most traditional Thai homes have an outdoor* sala *– a covered open-air structure set in a quiet corner of a garden – where one can lie on a raffia mat, relax, meditate or even receive a massage. Emphasis is on peace and quiet rather than comfort, unless you feel at ease on a hard wooden floor. Hotels with spas and wellness centers often copy this tradition.*

Marriott Resort & Spa, 107/1 Phetchkasem Beach Road, ☎ 03251 1881, fax 03251 2422, www.marriott.com/HHQMC, $$$$. A favorite spot for families and golfers, this luxury resort with stunning Thai architecture has 220 rooms that face either the sea, the pool or landscaped tropical gardens. Sports facilities include volleyball and tennis courts, windsurfing, parasailing and waterskiing. The outdoor fitness center is a classic Thai *sala*, which overlooks the pools and beach. Good restaurants and excellent spa. It's a 10-minute walk to the center of Hua Hin, either along the road or the beach. We have seen $99-per-night specials, but they excluded taxes and service charges, which when added brought the total to over $120. Great place to spend your Marriott rewards points, or earn more. We stayed here when the hotel was full and finding a spot near the swimming pool was a problem.

Aleenta Resort Hua Hin, 183 Moo 4, Parknampran, Pranburi, $$$$. At the southern end of Pranburi beach, a 30-minute drive south of Hua Hin, this lavish resort has incredible views out over the beach to the sea in one direction and to the mountains in the other. The name *Aleenta* comes from the ancient Sanskrit and means "a rewarding life." There is an assortment of accommodation and everything faces the sea. Some of the 10 luxury suites, all with private decks and beautiful views, have their own plunge pools. There is a private villa, which can accommodate six people; the rate includes a housekeeper and chef. The beach in front of the resort faces east and stretches for five kilometers, making it ideal for jogging or long walks. There is a freshwater infinity pool on the second floor of the Clubhouse. The resort has plenty of bicycles for guests who want to explore the surrounding countryside. The spa offers a combination of Thai and Swedish therapies. You can dine in your suite or at the open-air restaurant, or enjoy a beach barbecue. The restaurant is open to non-residents for lunch and dinner but you have to make a reservation. Prices range from 7,000 Baht for the garden suite up to 16,000 Baht for the Palm Villa.

Dusit Resort Hua Hin (formerly the Dusit Resort & Polo Club), 1349 Phetchkasem Road, Cha-am, ☎ 03252 0009, fax 03252 0296, www.huahin.dusit.com, $$$$. All 300 well-equipped rooms and suites at this five-star resort have private balconies overlooking either the sea or splendid gardens. It boasts one of the largest swimming pools in Thailand and a full range of land- and water sports. There are tennis and squash courts, fitness center, horse-back riding track and the Palm Hills Golf Club is right across the street. There are five restaurants and four bars – two of them with live music. The resort opened the biggest convention hall in the area in mid-2005 at a cost of $4 million. The ballroom can accommodate up to 1,500 guests. Banquet facilities can accommodate 850 diners and there is theater-style seating for 1,200. There is a low-season special of $125 per night, plus taxes and service charge, which includes an elaborate buffet breakfast, fruit, flowers and a half-hour spa treatment as well as discounts on food and drinks. For an additional $100 a night you can upgrade to a suite.

Hilton Hua Hin Resort & Spa, 33 Naresdamri Road, ☎ 03251 1612, fax 03251 1135, www.hilton.com, $$$$ There had to be one high rise to hit central Hua Hin and this is it. It towers somewhat unpleasantly over the town and seafront but provides the most spectacular views for hotel guests. There are 296 rooms including 41 suites along with every possible facility including a spectacular pool. Look for packages that include a spa treatment and breakfast. To get the best deals, around $150 per night per couple, you have to stay a minimum of seven nights and book a week in advance, in which case this hotel turns from a $$$$ to a $$$.

Anantara Resort & Spa, 43/1 Phetchkasem Beach Road, ☎ 03252 0250, fax 03252 0259, www.anantara.com, $$$. Set in 14 acres of landscaped gardens, the Anantara has 162 rooms and suites, each with a balcony overlooking either the gardens or the beach. Rates vary widely depending on accommodation and time of year. A garden-view room costs 5,000 Baht and goes to 7,500 over the Christmas holidays. The one-bedroom suites cost as much as 16,500 Baht for that same holiday period. Great beach-front location, free-form swimming pool and sumptuous spa. The Anantara hosts the annual elephant-polo tournament. For more information about this wonderful contest look under *Festivals & Events*, page 127.

Praseban Resort, 173 Moo 4 Parknampran, Pranburi, ☎ 03263 0590, fax 03263 0589, www.prasebanresort.com, $$$. A very new, very small and very special resort with just 14 delightfully deco-

Housekeeping, Thai style

Above: Thailand is renowned for its floating markets

Below: Night markets are everywhere in Thailand

Above: Chinese herbalist at work

Below: Patong, on Phuket island, comes alive at night

Both photos courtesy of Phuket International Hospital

Above: Tour boat, River of Kings, Bangkok

Below: Bangkok's impressive SkyTrain

Above: Manohra Song dinner cruise, Bangkok

Below: Street dining in Bangkok

Above: Vegetable market, Phuket
Courtesy of Phuket International Hospital

Below: Transportation in Bangkok at a bargain price

Above: Kayaking is a favorite sport for visitors

Below: Thailand is a paradise for divers

Siamese dancing, always a delight

rated suites and villas, all with sea view and private balcony, and just steps away from the sea. The mini-resort is at the southern end of Pranburi, 30 kilometers south of Hua Hin. Internet rates start at an all-inclusive 4,000 Baht for a weekday night climbing to 7,500 Baht for a weekend night in a suite. They also have several well-priced packages. For 14,900 Baht two people can enjoy three nights in a Sawanya Villa, daily American breakfast, a candlelight dinner and an 80-minute session of aromatherapy. Despite its size the resort offers a choice of dining. There is the Kanang Sari Restaurant on the deck open for breakfast, lunch and dinner with Thai and international dishes and the Praseban Seafood Terrace for candlelit dinners specializing in locally caught seafood.

Hua Hin Grand Hotel & Plaza, 222/2 Phetchkasem Road, ☎ 03251 1391, $$. This is a reasonably priced hotel that has numerous eating spots all with different themes, including Japanese and European. If you can't find what you want among them there is a 24-hour coffee shop. This high-rise hotel with 168 rooms and suites has a fitness center, swimming pool, snooker club, beer garden, karaoke lounge and a discotheque.

Regent Cha-am Beach Resort, 849/21 Phetchkasem Road, Cha-am , ☎ 03245 1240, fax 03247 1491, www.regent-chaam.com, $$. This is the biggest property we've found in the area with a total of 650 rooms, suites and cottages. The resort is 20 kilometers out of Hua Hin and is made up of a low-rise hotel, a three-story Mediterranean-style complex and – the latest addition – the Regent cottages, thatch-roofed villas with beach views, which will take you out of our $$ category. With all this accommodation there are numerous facilities including a shopping arcade, three swimming pools, fitness center, putting green and mini-golf and well as water sports on the beach. The restaurants offer Chinese, French, Italian and Thai cuisine.

Peony Hotel, 172/4 Naresdamri Road, ☎ 03253 3491, fax 03253 2599, www.peonyhotel.com, $$. This is a new small economy hotel seeking business from families and golfers and within easy walking distance of the beach, shops and restaurants. All rooms are fully equipped and have balconies overlooking the pool. The restaurant is in front of the hotel and is open from 7am to 11pm with an international menu. Breakfast baskets are available for golfers who want to get to the courses for an early tee time. Some courses are open from 6am. A variety of room sizes are designed for families. Rates range from 1,500 Baht for a double up to 3,000 for a two-bedroom suite. The hotel has a total of 34 rooms and its own pro shop, and offers discounts to some of the area golf courses.

Ban Duangkaew Resort, 83/158 Soi Talay 12, Takiab Road, ☎ 03251 5307, fax 03251 5532, $. Pleasant mini-village of Thai cottages set amid trees and gardens, with pool and access to the beach. Over the Christmas holidays the resort slips out of the $ category when rates go to 3,400 Baht a night. Out-of-season promotions give free nights for stay over six nights.

The Long Beach Inn, Phu Noi, ☎ 03255 9068, Canada ☎ 604-937-3121, $. An intimate guesthouse, designed in Canada, and set in the tiny fishing village of Phu Noi, a 30-minute drive south from Hua Hin. The inn is close to the Khao Sam Roi Yot National Park and the eight-kilometer-long beach at Dolphin Bay is a three-minute walk away. The package rate of €30 a day includes breakfast. There's a café, bar and swimming pool. The inn can arrange a local fishing charter to Monkey Island or book a dinner cruise in nearby Parknampran. The Thai and Canadian hosts even offer a pickup service from your hotel in Bangkok.

Fu-Lay Guest House, 110/1 Naresdamri Road, ☎ 03251 3670, $. The location on a jetty make this guesthouse with well-kept air conditioned rooms and nice bathrooms, a pleasant and inexpensive place to stay.

The Dougherty Home, 263/72 Soi Jamjuree, off Phetchkasem Road, ☎ 03253 2715, fax 03253 2297, $. You'll get an American and Thai welcome at this guesthouse, which is a five-minute walk from the beach. Spacious rooms, all with air conditioning and cable TV. There's a restaurant and swimming pool.

Royal Beach Guest House, 113/12-13 Phetchkasem Road, ☎ 03253 2210, $. Close to the beach and one kilometer from the town center, all rooms come with air conditioning, cable TV and video. The guesthouse has a bar, swimming pool and coffee shop.

PP Villa, 11 Damnoenkasem Road, ☎ 03253 3785, fax 03251 1216, $. A small, friendly hotel that is close to the beach, and a bargain at under $30 a night. All 33 rooms have balconies, and there is a pool and cozy restaurant.

All Nations, 10/1 Deachanuchit Road, ☎ 0 3251 2747, fax 03253 0474, $. If you want something neat, clean and cheap, and are prepared to share a bathroom, this may be the place for you. Best of the 12 rooms goes for 600 Baht a night and comes with air conditioning and TV. All rooms have balconies and the upper back rooms have panoramic views of the sea and mountains. During Songkran, the Thai New Year, there is a 50% surcharge on all rooms, a common practice. The bar is popular with the local ex-pat farangs and the restaurant offers both Thai and Western dishes.

All Nations set up the first cyber café in Hua Hin, and a movie is shown every night around 7:30pm.

■ Where to Eat

One thing is for sure – you don't need to go hungry in Hua Hin. You can spend a lot of money in the hotel restaurants, or dine on the beach and enjoy the area's specialty, fresh seafood, for a fraction of what you'll pay in those establishments. We have kept our listings brief just to give you an idea of what is available. All the restaurants are very inexpensive by Western standards.

Between the time we write this and when you read it a dozen more eateries will have opened up or changed hands or closed down. It's a similar story with the bars. Businesses changing hands seems to be more prevalent in Hua Hin. It could be that some ex-pats come here and get disenchanted. Thailand is a great place to vacation but not as much fun when you have to work hard for little return.

From our wanderings we doubt any Michelin stars will be placed here but it is a fun place to eat, especially at the seafood eateries along the water. The **Ketsarin Restaurant** is a good example; they serve European food too. **Satukarn Square** is the place to go if you want variety. The best authentic Thai restaurants are on Naebkehard Road – **Baan Hua Hin** and **Sara Janes** are two that are recommended – and if you want Thai at silly prices go to the night-market and see what the street hawkers are cooking up.

Buffalo Bill's @ Fisherman's Wharf, 8 Chomsin Road, ☎ 03253 0087. If you can handle a full English breakfast, you will not find a better place than this. The first time we ate here it was because of a convenient parking spot. We were so impressed with the eggs Benedict that we returned to try other early-morning meals, and we were not disappointed. Succulent ham and the best bacon we've eaten in Thailand. The restaurant is down by the fishing pier and is open all day. We never found time to sample a lunch or dinner but will on our next visit. Fair prices and friendly service insure this place will still be in business.

The Bali-Thai Restaurant, Soi Tanawit, between Satukarn Square and Hua Hin Shopping Center and the night-market. Yes, it is a bit touristy with its nightly show, but everyone we saw here was smiling. And it wasn't just the staff. Open every day from 5pm until midnight. The Delights of Asia three-course dinner is a bargain at 180 Baht, not including drinks, taxes and service. The cuisine is a mixture of Thai and Asian, much the same as the show. Great place to bring the family and spend less than you would back home at McDonalds. There is a sister operation in Cha-am on Soi Tanawit, ☎ 03253 6442.

Sunshine Restaurant, 130/5 Naresdamri Road, ☎ 03253 2475, fax 03253 2602. This is a European restaurant, German bakery, a delicatessen, Internet café and you can reserve a Budget rental car. And it's hard to find, even though it's across from the Hilton Hotel. Stand in front of the Beautiful Optic Shop and look to the right; that small entrance is where you are headed. Great place if you want a break from noodles and tiny little red bits in your food. The garden restaurant features European cuisine with great steaks. There are Thai dishes as well. Check out the menu before you go at www.sunshine-restaurant.com. Their delicatessen shop has Thai-made German sausages, imported cheeses and hams. They advertise European bean coffee but where that is grown we do not know. And don't forget while you're dining or checking your e-mail you can rent a car. Open every day of the year from 9am until 10:30pm.

And here are some others – all inexpensive – that come with recommendations: **Amadeus Restaurant**, 23 Naresdamri Road, ☎ 03253 0489, Austrian, as you would expect; **Koo on the Beach**, at the junction of the Fishing Pier Road and Naresdamri Road, ☎ 03251 4625, trendy Thai with great views and service; **Meekaruna Seafood**, 26/1 Naresdamri Road, ☎ 03251 1932, a smaller, family-run Thai restaurant overlooking the fishing pier and with very personal service; **Taj Mahal**, 31/1 Naresdamri Road, ☎ 03251 6615, Indian at its best; **Ban Nong Kae**, Phetchkasem Road, opposite Nirvana Retreat, where the Thais go to eat; **Itsara**, 7 Napkehard Street, ☎ 03253 0514, in a 1920s seaside home, good choice of fish and meat dishes, where the most expensive main courses are less than 300 Baht.

■ Nightlife

Hua Hin is not renowned for its nightlife but there is plenty going on, although it may seem a little tame after Bangkok, Pattaya or Patong Beach.

> *You won't find any go-go bars, yet the girls associated with those establishments do exist in Hua Hin if you know where to look.*

Most visitors are so well catered to in their hotels that few venture out after dinner. However, if you want to sample Hua Hin's nightlife we suggest you head for **Soi BintaBaht**. This street is the home of **Jungle Juice** and **All Nations** – both popular with local farangs – and a dozen other bars. Other places worth a visit are **Johnny Walkers** – good when the barbecue is going; **The Ship** – great juke box; and the **London Lounge**, popular with longtime residents. For pool players, try the **U-Turn**, **El Toro** or **Bamboo Grove**. **Billy's Bar**, in the bazaar area, is more of a sports bar, with a pool table.

If you want the disco scene you need go into the **City Beach Hotel** where **Star Planet** operates, or to the Grand Hotel where you'll find **Stepz**. Opposite the City Beach Hotel is the **Admirals Pub**, more British than Thai, and the place to go if you'd rather drink than dance. The towering Hilton Hotel has a striking bar with live music and a good selection of beers, homegrown and imported. If you're with the family and just want somewhere to have a quiet drink, try the **Mai Tai**, a pleasant outside spot next to the Hilton.

Most bars close between 1am and 2am depending on trade and local law officers. One that seems to be open the latest is the Nice n' Easy, which is small but still manages to squeeze in a pool table. Prices on Soi BintaBaht: Expect to pay less than 100 Baht for a beer and up to 300 Baht for something stronger.

■ A Street Party - Thai Style

We were surprised and delighted when two Thai friends invited us to spend a weekend in their home at Hua Hin. We had seen how the rich and famous luxuriate in wondrous spas and how the poor eke out a living from the hillside or dwell on the banks of unpleasantly polluted canals. But now we had the chance to see how normal middle-class Thai families lived, and it was a fascinating experience that made us even more eager to spend more time living in the kingdom of silk and smiles.

Our Hosts

The family lives in a two-bedroom brick home just a couple of blocks inland from Hua Hin's plush waterfront hotels. The home is a typical modern structure that you see in new housing developments throughout the country.

Husband Tong works as a tour-bus driver, and his wife is an executive at the local hospital. They have a 10-year-old son who spoke English almost as well as his parents. We had been invited for **Children's Day**, when the neighborhood was staging a street party. The following day was to be another celebration when monks were coming to bless the neighborhood.

Preparations

Children's Day in Thailand is akin to Three Kings Day in Spain, when parties are held and the young ones all get gifts. When we arrived the street had already been blocked to traffic. A large stage was being erected at one end of the road and chairs and tables were spread across the carriageway. Fish were slowly cooking on a large barbecue and at the street-sides, under the shade of what looked like sea-grape trees, the ladies of the neighborhood were all busy preparing cauldrons of food. Judging by the aromas, a mighty amount of those tiny little red bits was being used.

As the preparations continued we took a stroll and watched an unusual game on a nearby playing field. It looked like volleyball but the players, all teenage boys, did not use their hands, just heads and feet. It took great agility. We learned later that this was the favorite Asian game of *takraw*.

On our return the party was underway and we were introduced to the neighbors. Nobody except our hosts spoke English, but the welcome smiles we got were genuine. These people were truly pleased to be entertaining farangs. The president of the homeowners association made a brief speech and then ushered us to sit with him at the center table. He said he spoke English and was a retired headmaster. And that's about all the English we understood. He continued to chatter on but it was a complete blur. We would have a better chance of understanding a Glaswegian on a Saturday night after the pubs have closed than making sense of what we were hearing. Still, we smiled, and he smiled and the food began to arrive.

There were all kinds of seafood, chunks of the barbecued fish, rice and noodles and things we did not recognize but ate and enjoyed. Somebody was looking after us because nothing we had was to hot to handle.

Out of nowhere another farang, a German, who spoke no English, was introduced to us, and the Thais wrongly assumed we would be able to communicate with him. We just smiled at each other and agreed the whole party is very good. Ya, good, very good. We learned later that he was about to take a Thai wife, a daughter of one of the neighbors, and we are invited to return for that celebration.

The Celebrations

Meanwhile the show began on the newly erected stage, complete with a high-tech sound-and-light system. The children were the first to appear with displays of dancing, both modern and the traditional Thai where hands move to fantastic angles. This was followed by a comic fashion show presented by the really young ones. All the neighborhood children got to perform in the show and all were rewarded with prizes at the end.

Numerous speakers followed, who we discovered are local politicians who visit street parties such as this to get the attention of the voters. But this neighborhood has introduced a rule that keeps their numbers to a minimum: anyone who speaks has to finish with a karaoke solo. That proved an amusing break. Meanwhile the food kept coming, and the bottles of whiskey were replenished. The men were the only ones drinking the whisky. The women appeared content with tea, soft drinks and the occasional beer.

Once all the speeches were over and the children's performances completed the neighbors took it in turns to perform karaoke. The whole event was a cross between a Spanish fiesta and an English street party of bygone years. The most remarkable part was how welcome everyone made us. We felt like family visiting for the weekend, not intruding foreigners. It was long past midnight when we made our way to bed (remembering to remove our shoes as we entered the house).

AUTHOR'S NOTE: *We were given the boy's bedroom; this was air conditioned, but as in most Thai homes there was no hot water. The reasoning is that because it is always hot you shower or bathe to cool down and clean yourself. So you do it with cold water. Try telling that to the farangs in the hotels down the street.*

The Second Day

I woke early just as the sun was rising and walked out onto the street. Tong and his neighbors were busy cleaning the area in preparation for the day's celebrations, when the monks would come to the neighborhood. A large tent was erected to house the holy men and once again the women were busily preparing another feast. Nobody appeared to be affected by last night's festivities although the children were a little late on parade. When they did appear they were playing and boasting about the gifts they'd received, and too busy to notice the preparations going on around them.

The Blessing

When the men in the saffron robes arrived, the neighbors took their seats in front of the shaded tent and the holy men began chanting. Their performance was almost hypnotic and it continued for a long, long time. It was a very soothing sound, and from what I was told the words of the chant are equivalent to the Christian Ten Commandments. It takes years to learn the words, which are in the ancient *Pali* language, and never once does a monk make a mistake. A single thread of cotton was run from one side of the monks' tent around the homes and back to the tent. It was the area within the cotton that received the blessings.

The ceremony complete, it was time to eat. Custom has it that the monks eat first, much to the dismay of the children. We sat outside Tong's home and dish after dish was brought to us to try. I remember one dish that sounded terrible but was very tasty – it was boiled fish roe. There were all kinds of dumplings and pork dishes and some unexpected sweet courses. This breakfast went on for several hours while the children played on the street. When we first arrived they had looked at us as oddities, but now they accepted us and smiled as we struggled to consume more food.

The Community

The camaraderie of the neighborhood is common in Thai villages. The people look out for each other and accept with gratitude whatever they have, without resenting others having more.

Tong and his wife have, we estimate, a combined income of around $10,000 a year, and they consider themselves well blessed. They rarely eat at home. Eating at neighborhood restaurants is so cheap – the family of three normally eats for less than 100 Baht – and with both working odd hours there isn't time for cooking at home. Tong takes care of all the housework, which is not the norm, to give his wife free time with their son when she gets through with her job. When there is work, Tong works seven days a week, sometimes more than 12 hours a day. Their living expenses are ridiculously low by western standards. Their monthly utility bills total little more than 200 or 300 Baht. They don't have a land-line telephone, which is expensive to them, but both have cell phones, which are incredibly cheap to buy and operate.

They observe all the Buddhist traditions and are frequent visitors to their local temple. They spend a lot of time taking care of older people, not only family members, but elderly people who are on their own.

A Temple Visit

During our stay we visited the local temple with the family. They make a point of a special temple visit when a family member celebrates a birthday. Before going we made a market stop and purchased a variety of fruit and flowers, which were presented to a monk. We sat around him while a prayer was chanted then we all received a sprinkling of water from a brush the monk waved above us.

A Reminder

Our next visit was the most incredible of all. The family makes it part of any birthday celebration to buy a casket at the local temple for some unfortunate who has died penniless. For 300 Baht a coffin and shrouds are bought, blessed and placed in readiness for the next pauper. The surrounding walls of the temple were covered in horrific pictures of accident victims, mostly from motorcycle accidents, who had been recipients of the donated coffins. It was a very grim reminder of the dangers of motorcycle-riding throughout the kingdom.

> *Perhaps if more people viewed this sort of pictures their driving practices would be less risky. The family seemed unshaken by the awful photographs. Perhaps they have come to accept it as tragic part of Thai life, but it is something we will not forget.*

Past & Future

Like most middle-class Thais, our friends never take a Western-style vacation. If they have a day or two without work, they'll visit their families, who are scattered throughout Thailand. Both of them come from rural areas and very humble beginnings. Their childhood homes were in bamboo huts amid rubber plantations and close to rice paddies, and the modest concrete home with running water is considered a great luxury. Their main concern is the future of their son. Schooling in most of Thailand is excellent, and it's free. Their dreams are that he will eventually go on to university and be a major player in the Thailand of tomorrow. And that is dream that most people in the world share.

Pattaya

■ History

Pattaya, 147 kilometers southeast of Bangkok on the eastern side of the Gulf of Thailand, had a totally different origin from that of Hua Hin, across the Gulf. The staid and regal resort of Hua Hin (see page 122) began its life as a popular beach venue favored by the Thai royal family. Pattaya, on the other hand began its transition from a sleepy village to what it is today back in the late '50s, with the arrival of several truckloads of American GIs who were seeking some serious R&R away from their military duties.

The elite of Thailand followed the royals to Hua Hin. It was folk of a different ilk who followed the US servicemen to Pattaya. Not surprisingly, the prostitutes, pimps, pill pushers and pornography purveyors moved in as more and more US soldiers discovered that Pattaya was the place to party. Today the original strip where it all began still exists but the once-sleepy village around it has expanded into a metropolis, complete with hotels, resorts and theme parks, catering not only to footloose males looking for companionship but to families looking for fun on their annual beach vacation.

Pattaya has become one of Asia's major playgrounds. It has the buzz and brashness of Bangkok with the added advantage of being on the beach. Laid back and quiet it isn't. There is the occasional oasis of solitude but Pattaya is brimming with activity around the clock. It is open in all seasons with every kind of attraction.

■ Community

Pattaya surrounds three separate bays. In the center is **Pattaya Beach**, where it all began, and everything still happens there. To the north is **Naklua Bay**, quietest of the trio; and to the south, with its string of oceanfront high rises, is **Jomtien Beach**, famous for its windsurfing.

There is a large expatriate community here. Those we have spoken to love living here, not because of the seedy side of life that surrounds them, but because of the infrastructure that tourism has created. They've turned a blind eye to the sex trade and enjoy wonderful medical services, great shopping and quality restaurants.

THE PATTAYA MAIL

Pattaya has its own English-language newspaper, the ***Pattaya Mail***, which is available every Friday; if you want to keep abreast of local events you can browse the Internet edition at www.pattayamail.com. The newspaper began in 1993 and is widely read by the large ex-pat population that has set up home in the area. The last issue I saw had some exciting pictures of the Chonburi buffalo races, an event that has been taking place each October for over 130 years. The *Mail's* main office: 370/7-8 Pattaya Second Road, Pattaya City, ☎ 03841 1240, fax 03842 7596.

Pattaya city has been administered under a special independent system since 1978. It has a status comparable to a municipality and is separately administered by a mayor who is responsible for making policies, organizing public services, and supervising all employees of Pattaya city administration. Other developing areas, particularly Ko Chang (see page 171), are hoping to be afforded a similar status.

The population of Pattaya in 2003 was said to be 92,878. Surprisingly there is a lower percentage of Buddhists (80%) than the national average. Muslims account for 16% of the population and Christians make up the other 4%. Not surprising are the statistics that 90% of the labor force is involved in tourism and the city has no native products.

■ Climate

Pattaya and its environs enjoy three seasons: It's hot and humid from March to May, hot with the addition of lots of rain from June to October and cooler and clearer from November to February.

■ Getting Here

By Air

Pattaya is served by **U-Tapao Airport**, which is south of the city. **Bangkok Airways**, www.bangkokair.com, has regular service here from points throughout Thailand. The Qantas-backed no-frills airline **Jetstar Asia** has daily flights between Singapore and Pattaya, www.jetstarasia.com.

By Bus

Air conditioned coaches regularly depart from Ekkami, the Eastern Bus Terminal, ☎ 02391 2504, and also from Mo Chit, the Northern Bus Terminal throughout the day. There are also minibuses that go directly from Bangkok Airport, ☎ 02535 1111. Fares from Ekkami for the 136-kilometer, 2½-hour journey start at 66 Baht. Fares are similar from other departure points.

By Train

The State Railway of Thailand offers one daily service departing Bangkok's Hualampong Station at 6:55am, ☎ 02621 8701. The trip takes over three hours. First-class fare for the 155-kilometer journey is 140 Baht, second-class is 72 Baht and third-class is 31 Baht.

By Car

From Bangkok it is a two-and-a-half-hour journey on the **Bangna-Trat Highway**, via Bang Pakong, Chonburi and Sri Racha. A new motorway signposted for Pattaya and Rayong bypasses Chonburi and saves a few minutes on the journey.

■ Getting Around

By Bus

Pattaya City has introduced a new bus service to help visitors get around the resort city. The service consists of three color-coded lines – green, red and yellow – which cover the main streets of Pattaya, Naklua and Jomtien. Bus stops are also color-coded to make it easier to identify the routes. Each line has a fixed clockwise and counter-clockwise route, for a total of six, served by three air conditioned buses per route, from 6:00am til 2:00am. All routes begin at the Big C supermarket on Sukhumvit Road, Pattaya.

A 30-Baht one-way ticket can be used on any of the routes. Day passes are also available; a one-day pass is 90 Baht, three-day is 180 Baht and a one-month pass is 900 Baht. The service is operated by **Pattaya Beach Bus Co., Ltd.**, in a joint venture with the state-run Office of SME Promotion, ☎ 03875 7340.

By Car

Rental cars are readily available but, as everywhere else in Thailand, beware of the lower-priced Jeeps you'll find along Beach Road; some may not have insurance. These are the rental agencies we can recommend.

ARC, 389/114 Moo 5, Sukhumvit Road, ☎ 03842 0252.

Avis, Dusit Resort on Beach Road, ☎ 03836 1627, fax 02254 6718.

Budget, 331/1 Moo 6, Sukhumvit Road, ☎ 03872 6185, fax 03872 6362.

Pattaya Car Rent Center, 437/157 Soi Yodsak, ☎ 03842 0863, fax 03842 0863.

PP Car Rent, 193/156 Rungland Village, South Pattaya, ☎ 03842 6552.

VIA, 215/15-18 2nd Road, opposite the Royal Garden Plaza, ☎ 03842 6242, fax 03842 6243.

USEFUL TELEPHONE NUMBERS

Tourism Authority of Thailand (TAT)	☎ 03842 8750
Tourist Police	☎ 03842 9371 or 1699
Police station	☎ 191
Pattaya police	☎ 03842 0802
Banglamung	☎ 03822 1800
Highway police	☎ 03839 2021
Fire brigade	☎ 199
Pattaya International Hospital	☎ 03842 8374
Bangkok Pattaya Hospital	☎ 03825 9911

■ Things to See

Temples

There are two temples in the area worth seeing. **Wat Yan Sangwararam**, 12 kilometers south of Pattaya (three kilometers from Nong Nooch gardens, see page 150) is a collection of temples built around a lake in the styles of various dynasties and nations including Thai, Burmese, Indian and Chinese. Meditation courses are available here at 6am and 6pm. Nearby is the **Wihan Sian** building, which houses Chinese art objects and antiques. The second temple is **Wat Chaimongkol** on South Pattaya Road, whose standing Buddha image, named *Buddha Chaimongkol*, is thought to have been made 350 years ago.

Museums & Attractions

Bottle Art Museum: 100 meters south of the bus station on Sukhumvit Road at Km. 145, ☎ 03842 2957. An unusual one-man show with some 300 bottles containing models of world sights and transportation. The one man is Dutchman Peter Bedelais who has spent most of his life putting art into bottles – everything from Thai temples to Dutch windmills. He's on hand to show you how it's done. Open daily from 10am to 10pm. Admission 100 Baht.

Nong Nooch Orchid Village: A couple of hours spent here is well worth the 15-kilometer drive out from the city. The tropical gardens are a delight, with emphasis on the orchid house. But what brings the crowds is the Thai cultural show. A visit here helps you get to know a little more about life in the kingdom. There are displays of Thai boxing, Thai dancing and an elephant show all mixed with an assortment of ceremonies and rituals. There are 500 acres to explore, and the easiest way to visit is buy a morning or afternoon tour from any hotel in town. Pick-up times are around 8:30am and 1:30pm, depending where you're located. Total cost for the trip is 550 Baht. If you come on your own there are three 90-minute shows daily at 10:15am, 2pm and 3:45pm.

Ripley's Believe It Or Not: Located in the Royal Garden Shopping Plaza on Pattaya Beach Road, ☎ 03871 0294. Open daily from 10am to midnight. Admission: 280 Baht. This weird collection of over 300 intriguing examples of the world's oddities includes everything from sharks to masks, and from tools of torture to models of the world's smallest and largest men. Adjoining amusement arcade has high-tech cars and the latest video games.

World Gems Collection, 98 Moo 6, North Pattaya Road, Naklua, ☎ 03837 1222. Every tourist town in Thailand has its gem factory but this one, just five minutes north of town, is the best for showmanship; it's a visit the whole family can enjoy. And it's free, provided you're not tempted to purchase. But that's not easy when you see the selection. The approach is more like a theme park (without turnstiles) than an overgrown jewelry store. After the customary free drinks and "where you from" greeting it's a train ride in a tunnel, with stops along the way showing the mining and processing of gemstones, all very Disney-like with animated characters and informative soundtrack, in English. Then you get to see the craftsmen at work before emerging into the vast sales area, where temptation to purchase is hard to resist. Whether prices are better than downtown we can't tell but the trip out here is worthwhile even if you might pay more. Taxi or bus rides to the collection are free from any area hotel.

Mini Siam, Sukhumvit Highway at Km. 143, ☎ 03842 1628. This is an amazing model village featuring many great Thai landmarks, which makes it a popular spot for Thai tourists. Among the Thai models is the Bridge over the River Kwai, the Democracy Monument and the Temple of the Emerald Buddha. Europeans aren't forgotten, with models of the Eiffel Tower, the leaning tower of Pisa and London's Tower Bridge. All the models are at a scale of 1-to-25. Open daily from 7am to 10pm.

Animal Shows

Alangkarn, Sukhumvit Road Km. 155, Jomtien, ☎ 03825 6000, www.alangkarnthailand.com. If you've wondered why the Thai people think so highly of elephants you'll get a better understanding if you attend this mega show, a recent addition to the attractions of Pattaya. In days of yore elephants were crucial in Thailand's military victories, and today these battles are recreated on the giant stage here. The attraction is similar to the FantaSea show in Phuket. The theater has everything from laser to water spectacles and can seat 2,000. (The adjoining restaurant can seat half that number.) This is full evening of entertainment with some culture, gorgeous girls, and handicrafts thrown in for good measure.

Sri Racha Tiger Zoo, 341 Moo 3, Highway 7 Km. 20, Sri Racha, ☎ 03829 6556, fax 03829 6559, www.tigerzoo.com. This popular tourist stop 30 kilometers north of Pattaya was forced to close its doors for several weeks at the end of 2004 when 83 tigers at the zoo either died or were culled after becoming infected with bird flu. The tigers were found to have been fed raw chicken carcasses infected with avian influenza. The incident attracted worldwide publicity, but at the time of writing the zoo was reopened and reported that things were back to normal. Despite their loss, the zoo claims to have the largest number of Bengal tigers in captivity. In addition to the tigers there are numerous attractions, including a circus, which can accommodate more than 1,500 visitors daily, women wrestling alligators, pig-racing contests, and a variety of animals, from camels to crocodiles, thousands of them, which create ideal photo opportunities. There is also a "happy family" exhibit where a tiger, a pig and a dog coexist. The zoo is open every day from 8am to 6pm. Admission 250 Baht, children 150 Baht.

Pattaya Elephant Village, ☎ 03842 8648. Phonprapha Nimit Road, six kilometers northeast of Pattaya off Highway 3 at Km. 145. There's a one-hour elephant show every afternoon at 2:30pm when the mighty beasts show how they work in the jungle and play football for fun. Admission to the show is 400 Baht or you can take a 90-minute trek for 700 Baht. There is also a rafting option.

■ Things to Do

Festivals

Pattaya celebrates all the traditional Thai festivals but, as expected, does have some of its own and variations on the national celebrations.

April

Thai New Year: After all the Songkran festivals are finished elsewhere Pattaya City holds its annual ***Wan Lai*** festival on April 19 with lots of processions and dousing one another with water. Friends tell us that each year an ever-increasing number of farangs take part.

Pattaya Festival: Normally held in April following the New Year celebrations, and designed to promote tourism. This is when the Miss Pattaya Beauty pageant is held, and floats covered in floral displays traverse the streets. Lots of activities along the beaches with water-sports and sandcastle-building competitions. Arts and crafts are exhibited and sold, and there are numerous cultural performances. The whole thing culminates with a massive firework show on the beach.

October

Chonburi Buffalo Races: A little out of town perhaps, but the beach brigade make the journey to join in the fun in October as Thai farmers show off their buffalos in races and also contests where man takes on the beasts of burden in battles of fun. There are beauty contests and local vendors provide a wonderful array of food stalls.

Shopping

You'll find shops and stalls throughout the Pattaya area. There are three major malls including a large **Central Festival**, a **Tesco Lotus** and a **Big C**. To give you an idea of the shopping size of the area, there are a total of 77 **7-Eleven** stores. Along the beachfront and in the side alleys there is the normal array of tourist trinkets, and don't think you can hide from shopping by sitting on the beach. Pattaya and the other beach areas are noted for the vast number of vendors who ply their wares along the sand. You are more likely to find the better stores, fashionable boutiques and clothes shops with ready-to-wear garments in the main street of Central and South Pattaya. The major hotels have shopping arcades where prices might be a little higher and it's not so comfortable to bargain.

Bargain Hunting

We did some shopping one day at **Big C**, the Thai subsidiary of the French supermarket chain Carrefour. We were moving into a partially furnished apartment so our purchases were a little strange but it will give an idea of the bargain prices. We spent a total of 640 Baht at today's exchange rates that was $15.71, or €12.11. And this is what we bought: A two-slice electric toaster, nine quarts of drinking water, two liters of Coca Cola (the real thing), two coconuts, two ceramic coffee mugs, a large packet of Oriental spiced potato chips, a liter of purple carrot-and-grape juice, a packet of sliced green mango that came with a bag of sugar, peppers and salt for dipping, three small cartons of chocolate milk and a bag of hot-and-sour pickled mustard. Also included in our purchases were a variety of good-quality plastic storage jars, three ice trays and several plastic glasses. Many of the items bought are not normally found in your local Winn Dixie.

Recreational Activities

Windsurfing & Sailing

Pattaya is Thailand's capital for windsurfers. Top event of the year is in December when the town hosts the **Siam Cup**. Best months for action are March-April and July-August. **Jomtien Beach**, a 10-minute drive from the center of Pattaya, is the main hub for action. Equipment can be rented at **Amara Sailing Center**, **Club Loong Chat**, and the **Starboard Club**. All three are on Jomtien. Another popular spot for windsurfers is **Tabsai**, 30 kilometers north of Pattaya on the road from Bangkok, where the water is generally calmer.

Diving

There are dozens of dive sites along the coast and the nearby islands. Two of the most popular sites are wreck dives. One is off the coast of Pattaya Beach, the ***Khram* Wreck**; the second, a good deal farther south near Ko Lam, is the ***Hardeep* Wreck**. The Khram is a man-made reef created by a 200-foot World-War-II US Navy vessel that was deliberately sunk by the Thai Navy in 2003. The keel sits at 30 meters below the surface and the top of the wreck just 15 meters below. The site is already yielding some coral and attracting a full range of fish, and is recommended for more experienced divers.

The *Hardeep* Wreck, also more suited to experienced divers, is the remains of a Thai coastal freighter sunk during World War II. Maximum depth is 26 meters. The vessel's power plant was deliberately removed to allow access to the engine room, and it is possible to swim the entire length of the coral-encrusted hull. Full range of fish to view including turtles, stingrays and puffer fish.

Aquanauts Dive Center has two offices. The main office – 437/17 Moo 6, Soi Yodsak, Beach Road, Pattaya, ☎ 03836 1724, fax 03841 2097, www.aquanautsdive.com – is 100 meters from the beach on Soi Yodsak, between Pattaya Central Road and Pattaya North Road and open from 8am to 6pm. The second office, open from 11am to 9:30pm, is at Montana Court, ☎ 03871 0727, fax 038710-727, close to the beach on Pattayaland Soi 1 near the heart of Pattaya's nightlife area, just north of the Pattaya pier.

Ihtiander, 280/1 Beach Road, South Pattaya, ☎ 03871 0208, fax 03871 0208, www.ihtiander.com. This organization claims to be the only combined scuba-diving and meditation center in the world, devoted to introducing and helping its clients explore the mysteries of the underwater world and their inner being at the same time. For a decade the company has been teaching diving and meditation in the waters around Thailand, and operates dive centers in both Pattaya and Ko Chang. The company has two dive boats, the larger of which is equipped to handle live-aboard cruises. If you are not up to the meditation diving, the company organizes a full range of courses, starting with snorkeling for beginners.

Golf

There are 15 international-standard courses within 40 minutes of Pattaya. We have listed five here and you'll find more in the *Rayong* section, page 159.

Laem Chabang International Country Club, 106/8 Moo 4, Bueng, Sri Racha, ☎ 03837 2273, fax 03837 2275, www.laemchabanggolf.com. This 27-hole course – each of the nines is a par 36 – was designed by Jack Nicklaus, and many think it is one of Thailand's best courses. The three courses – lake, mountain and valley – are linked to an upmarket lodge. Check the Internet for package deals. Visitor green fees: Weekend, 2,500 Baht.

Pattaya Country Club and Resort, Km. 30 Highway 331, Tambon Kaomaikiew, Banglamung, ☎ 03842 3718, www.thailandgolfparadise.com/pattaya. About 25 kilometers inland from Pattaya, this 18-hole, par 72 course plays over 6,341 yards. The course, opened in 1994, attracts a lot of players from Bangkok since it's only a 90-minute drive from the capital. Wide fairways and slightly hilly terrain make it a popular course with beginners as well as more seasoned players. There is a small hotel with a swimming pool and the club house offers a full-service restaurant. Visitor green fees: Weekend 1,410 Baht and weekdays 840 Baht.

Phoenix Golf & Country Club, Km. 158 Sukhumvit Road, Huai Yai, Banglamung, ☎ 03823 9391, fax 03823 9402, www.thailandgolfparadise.com/phoenix. Three nine-hole courses – ocean, lakes and mountains – designed by Denis Griffiths and opened in 1993. Great scenery and landscaping, with the lakes course being the most challenging. Swimming pool, tennis courts and restaurant are all within the club grounds. Visitor green fees: Weekend 1,800 Baht and weekdays 1,000 Baht.

Plutaluang Navy Golf Course, Moo 6, Sattahip District, ☎ 02466 1180, fax 03870 1843, www.thailandgolfparadise.com/plutaluang. This older course with 36 holes was designed by the Royal Thai Navy, who took full advantage of the Chonburi Province hills to make this a challenging course. The clubhouse is in the center of the four nine-holes and serves both Thai and Western food in its restaurant. Well priced considering the quality of the course. Visitor green fees: Weekend 750 Baht and weekdays 450 Baht.

The Rayong Green Valley Country Club, 23 Moo 7, Ban Chang, ☎ 03889 3838, fax 03889 3845, www.thailandgolfparadise.com/rayonggreen. Hilly terrain is the attraction of this 18-hole, par 72, 7,131-yard course designed by Peter W. Thomson and opened in 1992. Other attractions here are the large clubhouse, polo club and equestrian track. Visitor green fees: Weekends 1,200 Baht and weekdays 1,000 Baht.

The Offshore Islands

There are numerous islands offshore from Pattaya well worth visiting for their fine beaches and coral. The area is renowned for sailing and you'll find dozens of yachts cruising or racing around the islands. Pattaya and the surrounding area have numerous world-class marinas as well as anchorages for smaller vessels. The **promenade pier** at **South Pattaya** is where you'll find a boat to take you to the various islands. Large boats can carry up to 200 passengers, and the much faster speedboats carry about a dozen. Expect to pay up to 1,500 Baht if you select one of the more distant islands. Travel time can be up to two hours, depending on the boat and the island.

Ko Lan, eight kilometers from the shore, is ideal for divers and has an abundance of coral; but if you prefer not to go over the side you can take a glass-bottom boat to view the underwater scenery. Most of the boats dock at Ta Waen Beach, situated on the northern end of the island and dotted with stalls and bars. There are several other smaller less crowded beaches on the island. Waterskis, parasails and personal watercraft are available for hire. The island tends to get busy at weekends with lots of visitors from Bangkok.

Quieter and smaller is **Ko Krok** with just one small sandy beach on the east of the island. The island has an abundance of coral heads ideal for snorkeling.

Farther west is the Ko Pai group of islands, which includes **Ko Pai** and **Ko Leum**. These islands also offer good swimming and several good opportunities for snorkeling or scuba diving. Since they are a little farther out – some 13 kilometers from shore – these islands tend to attract fewer visitors.

■ Where to Stay & Eat

Pattaya Marriott Resort & Spa, 218/2 Moo 10, Beach Road, ☎ 03841 2120, fax 03842 9926, www.marriott.com, $$$$. All the luxury you expect in a Thai Marriott, this 10-story resort has 286 rooms and seven suites set in wonderful gardens. You can retreat from the nearby bustle of entertainment and shopping to the elegance and calm of the resort, which has a 2,000-square-meter spa and fitness center, numerous bars and restaurants, swimming pool, and rooms to suit the businessman determined to work or families on vacation. Special Internet rates for advance purchases can save you money. The hotel, with high-speed Internet access in every room, is equipped to handle large groups and seminars.

Sugar Hut Resort, 391/18 Moo 10 Tappraya Road, Pattaya, ☎ 03825 1686, fax 03836 4186, $$$$. Not directly on the beach, but this resort – a five-minute drive to Pattaya Town on the way to Jomtien Beach – is probably one of the best places to stay in the area. The Sugar Hut has 28 authentic Thai-style villas and eight Thai houses sitting around three swimming pools in luxuriant tropical gardens. Everything is top quality including the special indoor/outdoor bathrooms. Expect to pay over $150 a night for the pleasure of staying here. The **Sugar Hut Restaurant** is highly recommended too.

Hard Rock Hotel Pattaya, 429 Moo 9, Pattaya Beach, ☎ 03842 8755, fax 03842 1673, $$$$. Big and brash, and fits in perfectly with the Pattaya scene. The 320 rooms have loud décor with lots of rock-star pictures and blue or orange carpets. Full in-room entertainment centers with wall-mounted televisions, and in case you forget where you are all the bed linens come with the Hard Rock logo. Pattaya's largest swimming pool is here, of course, along with a **Hard Rock Café** on the beachfront. Also on the nine-acre site is a 280-seat restaurant with show kitchens serving Japanese, Mediterranean, Thai and Chinese cuisines, a deli counter, E-Bar (Internet café), banquet facilities that accommodate 380, Lil' Rock club for kids, gym, spa and massage salon, and a sand island for pool activities. A word to the wise: The word "peaceful" does not appear in their promotional materials.

Amari Orchid Resort, 240 Moo 5 Beach Road, ☎ 03842 8161, fax 03842 8165, www.amari.com, $$$. Set in 10 acres of tropical gardens at the quieter northern end of Pattaya's crescent-shaped bay, the 236-room Amari is equipped for conferences and banquets but is a popular spot for a quieter vacation. The resort has its own shopping arcade, a pleasing swimming pool and two restaurants, plus the new free-standing **Mantra** restaurant. Internet rates, particularly its all-inclusive packages, keep it out of the $$$$ category.

Dusit Resort Pattaya Beach, 240/2 Pattaya Beach Road, North Pattaya, ☎ 03842 5611, fax 03825 0496, www.dusit.com, $$$. This resort, with all of its 464 quality rooms and suites having private balconies with sea views, has its own beach at the more exclusive northern end of Pattaya Beach amid the numerous concrete high-rises. There's a choice of dining with three separate restaurants, two swimming pools, three tennis courts and a fitness center and spa. And it's only a 10-minute walk to the center of activity in Pattaya.

Royal Cliff Beach Resort, 353 Pratamnak Road, Pattaya, ☎ 03825 0421, fax 03825 0511, www.royalcliff.com, $$. This is a group of four stylish hotels in one mega-resort set on 64 acres of parkland on a quiet headland overlooking the sea. There is something to suit everyone, with 12 different types of rooms, and we have seen Internet rates as low as $85. Best value for money is the 527-room **Royal Cliff Beach Hotel**, at the heart of the resort, with accommodation geared towards the package holiday-maker.

Royal Cliff Terrace, which opened in 1973, was the original hotel within the resort. The 88 rooms here are in a low-rise building tucked into the cliff face and facing the sea; they are designed for families and honeymooners.

The **Royal Cliff Grand**, which opened in 1992, is for the conference and incentive market and boasts an atrium lobby with uninterrupted views of the outlying islands.

Top of the quartet is the 85-room all-suites **Royal Wing & Spa** where the prices soar along with the service and room facilities.

If you stay anywhere within the resort you have a large array of attractions. If you don't enjoy the private beach there are five swimming pools, six tennis courts, 10 restaurants, four bars, three ballrooms and 15 meeting rooms. The complex also has its own catamaran for cruising the islands around the Gulf, shops, a clinic and all the executive services. And if you want to experience the nightlife in Pattaya, that is a five-minute drive away.

Asia Pattaya Beach Hotel, 325 Moo 12 Pratamnak Road, South Pattaya, ☎ 03825 0491, fax 03825 0496, www.asiahotel.co.th, $. Another large hotel with 314 rooms, well priced, three kilometers south of Pattaya on a cliff overlooking the Gulf of Thailand. The well-equipped rooms are all the same size, the only difference is the views either to the ocean or hillside. You pay more to see the sea. In addition there are some suites and executive rooms with more space. There are three bars and three restaurants, and a nine-hole golf course. In addition to the swimming pool there is a tennis court and snooker room. At night there is a disco, or you can walk to town along the beachfront in ten minutes or take a five-minute taxi ride. Want a change from hotel dining? There are several small restaurants near the hotel entrance.

A large well-stocked aquarium greets you in the lobby of the Asia Pattaya Beach Hotel.

Cholchan Pattaya Resort, 19 Moo 1, Pattaya, Banglamung, ☎ 03870 2777, 03870 2778, $. Another large resort – this one has 550 rooms – with a great beachfront location, just a short courtesy-bus ride to the center of town. And well priced, with rooms as low as $38. The Cholchan caters to both business and leisure travelers with the full range of bars and a restaurant with traditional Western meals as well as Asian delicacies. The resort sits in 10 acres of great gardens, with swimming pool, tennis and squash courts, driving range, massage and business center, and operates a children's club on weekends. They can hold meetings for 1,000 people, too.

Rayong

■ Introduction

Once you leave Pattaya and head south along Highway 3 the road takes you close to the **Sattahip Thai** naval base and the **U-Tapao Airport**, which is also a military installation but is used for commercial flights. The airport was an important one for the US military during the Vietnam War and not surprisingly still gets visited by vets.

Rayong is the capital of Rayong Province, a 3,500-square-kilometer area with 100 kilometers of coastline, somewhat neglected as a tourist destination. The town is more of a staging area for its offshore islands, predominately **Ko Samet** (see page 163), or a spot to stop if you're traveling farther east to **Ko Chang** in the National Marine Park. It is a popular area for Thais since it is less than 200 kilometers from Bangkok. The province has the full range of terrain including mountains, rolling hills, pleasant beaches and fertile plains, on which grow some of the country's finest fruit.

One of the province's claims to fame is that it produces most of the country's fish sauce, the condiment that replaces salt in most Thai cooking. It is also well known for its shrimp paste, dried prawns and dried squid. You'll find good displays of these items at any of the Rayong markets. Reed mats are another local specialty. They can be found at the markets too along with other items made from reeds, including hats and bags.

■ Climate

Best time to visit is from November until February when it is least likely to rain.

■ Getting Here

By Bus

Air conditioned buses leave every 40 minutes from Bangkok's Eastern Bus Terminal on Sukhumvit Road, ☎ 02391 2504. Cost for the 182-kilometer journey is 85 Baht; it takes about 3½ hours.

By Car

Driving from Bangkok should take about three hours on Hughway 3 (Sukhumvit Road).

By Taxi

The fare for the three-hour ride should be in the 2,000-Baht range; be sure to negotiate the price before you leave Bangkok.

USEFUL TELEPHONE NUMBER

Tourism Authority of Thailand (TAT) ☎ 03865 5420

■ Things to See & Do

Attractions

Sri Muang Park: Located in the center of town behind the city hall. The most prominent feature is the Buddhist shrine with the lengthy name of *Ho Phra Phut Tha*, which is built over an artificial lake. The park has lots of trees and flowers, a small zoo, a basketball court and a takraw court.

The Sobha Botanical Gardens: There is a combination of homes and gardens here, just three kilometers from the ferry pier at Ban Phe. The gardens claim to have amassed one of the biggest collections of plants and trees in Thailand. They also have acquired three homes, each one over 100 years old, which are decorated and furnished with items of yesteryear.

Lotus Crystal: Seeking a different sort of Thai souvenir? The Lotus Crystal Company on Highway 3375, 30 kilometers northeast of Rayong, opens its doors to visitors daily except Sunday from 8am to 5pm, to show the wide variety of the crystal products it produces. 161 Moo 6, Nikorn Soi 4, Highway 3375, Nikornpattana Bankhai, ☎ 03863 6372.

Suphattra Land: Opposite Ban Mab Tong School in the Bankhai district about 18 kilometers from Rayong Town. This is a colorful, modern working fruit orchard and botanical garden, with electric trams to show visitors around. Main products grown here are mangosteens, durians and rambutans.

Golf

Eastern Star Golf Resort, 24/5 Moo 3, Ban Chang, ☎ 03863 0410, fax 03863 0418, www.thailandgolfparadise.com/eastern-star. Challenging links-style 18-hole course just west of Rayong playing over 7,134 yards on an area that was once a coconut grove. Designed by Robert Trent Jones, Jr., the course is part of a larger complex that includes a tennis court and swimming pool, and a restaurant that offers a choice of Thai, European and Japanese cuisine. Weekend visitor green fees: 1,250 Baht.

Great Lake Golf & Country Club, 77 Moo 5, Off Highway 36, Bangkok-Rayong Road, Mab Yang, ☎ and fax 03862 2630, www.thailandgolfparadise.com/greatlake. Nick Faldo designed this excellent course on the banks of the Dok Krai Reservoir, a half-hour north of Rayong. In addition to the reservoir hazard Faldo managed to incorporate 120 bunkers into the 6,807-yard course. Weekend visitor green fees: 1,320 Baht.

Festivals

May

Rayong Fruit Fair: Held at the end of May each year to promote the area's produce, which includes some of the kingdom's best fruits, notably rambutans, mangosteens and the dreaded delicious durians.

> *Why dreaded? We've been in a couple of hotels where there are signs forbidding you to bring the fruit into the room because of the stench it can cause.*

The fair has its share of contests and exhibitions and brightly colored floats, decorated with fruit, compete for prizes.

June

Sunthon Phu Day: Sunthon Phu is considered to have been one of Thailand's foremost poets and, since he hailed from Rayong, the people mark his birthday, June 26, with numerous events, including poetry writing, art involving scenes from the poet's works, and a car cavalcade. Sunthon Phu's work dates from the early

Rattanakosin Period, which began in 1782 when Rama I became king (he was the first monarch of the current *Chakri* royal dynasty). Best known of his poems is the epic romance *Phra Aphai Mani*. In 1986, UNESCO named him as a Person of International Literary Distinction.

November

The Robing of the *Phra Chedi Klang Nam*: This traditional fair coincides with the national ***Loi Krathong* Fesitval**, when Thais launch small decorated floats into the water. The ceremony takes place at **Wat Pak Nam** in Rayong's Mueang district. In addition to the religious activities there is a variety of entertainment, lots of food stalls and boat racing.

December

The Red Cross Fair: Annual event held during the New Year holiday from December 28 until January 3, featuring exhibitions promoting the province, as well as a variety of shows and entertainment for young and old.

■ Where to Stay & Eat

Rayong Resort, 186 Laem Tarn, Ban Phe, ☎ 03865 1000, fax 03865 1007, www.rayongresort.com, $$$. Older, larger resort with 169 rooms split in three sections, the main, smaller cape wing and 10 beach rooms. Its location on Cape Laem Tarn with great views to Ko Samet and loads of activities, especially for younger ones, makes this a pleasant break from the bustle of Pattaya, an hour's drive north. Good package deals are available from its Website and it's worth paying the extra for one of the rooms on the beach.

The Rayong Resort offers a sunset cruise around Ko Samet.

Purimas Beach Hotel, 34 Payoon–Namrin Road, Bangchang, ☎ 03863 0382, fax 03863 0380, www.purimas.com, $$$. Upmarket resort with a spa, on the beach about seven kilometers before the town of Rayong if you're driving along Highway 3 from Pattaya. All the 79 suites have great sea views and are completely equipped. Top-quality spa operated by Sothys of Paris. Large pool, fitness center and beauty salon and a choice of restaurants. Rack rates are close to 6,000 Baht for a regular suite and 11,000 for the deluxe version but we have seen rates half this price on the Internet.

■ Ko Samet

After you leave Rayong, head east towards Chanthaburi; the turn-off to **Ban Phe** and the ferry pier for Ko Samet will be on your right. If you haven't had a chance to buy any local products or produce you'll find plenty of opportunity around the pier.

Ko Samet used to be called the "island of crushed crystal," since so many of its beaches sparkled. It's a place that has suffered somewhat from overuse but it still remains popular with tourists, particularly younger Thais eager to escape from Bangkok. The ferry crossing from Ban Phe takes 40 minutes, operates from 6am to 5pm and costs 30 Baht. Most of the accommodation is along the beaches on the island's east coast. Since the island, which is six kilometers long and very skinny in parts, is designated a national park, you get to pay a 200-Baht admission fee. The national park visitor center, police headquarters (such as they are), and health clinic are near the ferry dock.

Where to Stay & Eat

Amid the 30 or so places of accommodation on Ko Samet we have selected three properties that can be considered luxury at an affordable price. They are related and share the same Website, which makes comparing them easier. The first two are on the island's much quieter western shore, on **Prao Beach**, which is a wonderful place to view the sunsets, and the third is on **Sai Kaew Beach**, on the northeast shore of the island. The Website they share is www.aopraoresort.com.

Le Vimarn Cottages & Spa, Ao Prao, ☎ 03864 4105, fax 03864 4099. Presently the best place to stay on the island. The 17 deluxe thatched-roofed cottages are set on stilts amid tall trees on a slope that leads down to the beach. They are simply but elegantly furnished with all the mod cons you'd find on the mainland. Several packages available: A two-night stay here in the honeymoon cottage – including spa treatments, dinner, and transfers to and from the mainland by ferry – costs 26,800 Baht.

Ao Prao Resort, sharing the same beach as Le Vimarn, ☎ 03864 4100, fax 03864 4099. Larger than its neighboring resort with 52 rooms, this is happy a mix of rooms, bungalows, and suites. The resort is less expensive than La Vimarn. The two-night package here could be yours for less than 10,000 Baht. Ao Prao does have large luxury family suites with two bedrooms as well as executive suites that offer great views of the bay – even if you're sitting in the bathtub. The **Seaview Restaurant** at the water's edge offers both Thai and Western cuisine.

Sai Kaew Beach Resort, On Sai Kaew beach across the island from the two previous resorts, ☎ 03864 4193, fax 03864 4194. There's more activity on this side of the island and you'll pay less. The package here runs at under 9,000 Baht. We've mentioned spa packages but the Website has other options, including a diving package. There are 40 rooms here, all having large windows so you get great views of the tropical gardens or the beach even when you're in bed. The **Rim Talay Restaurant** caters to both Western and Thai tastes.

Klaeng

This town, capital of the province of the same name, makes an ideal rural stopping place if you are driving from Bangkok to Trat. It has a pleasant beach resort, is quieter and less expensive than the big-time palaces of Pattaya, and the town is close to the **Khao Chamao National Park** (see below), noted for its eight-level waterfall.

■ Getting Here

By Bus

Air conditioned buses leave from Bangkok's Eastern Bus Terminal on Sukhumvit Road. There are 10 departures daily, between 5am and 10pm. The trip takes just over three hours, and the fare is 85 Baht.

By Car

The trip from Bangkok on Highway 3 (Sukhumvit Road) takes under three hours. Once clear of the turnoff for Ban Phe ferry (see page 163), Klaeng is the next major spot on the road to Chanthaburi.

■ Things to See & Do

This is the closest town to **Khao Chamao National Park**. It is well organized for visitors with several nature trails, a campsite, bungalows for rent, and a food mart and visitor center.

To get here you drive seven kilometers east from Klaeng along Highway 3 to the junction with route 3377, where you turn left (you're now heading north) and continue to Nam Sai village. Here you turn right and drive one kilometer to the park headquarters. The park, which spreads into both Rayong and Chanthaburi provinces, has several waterfalls to visit in addition to the famous eight-level one, and the forest is crammed with an enormous collection of plant life. Another park, **Khao Wong National Park**, less than 20 kilometers from Khao Chamao, is noted for its numerous caves, streams and strange rock formations.

■ Where to Stay & Eat

Novotel Coralia Rim Pae, 4/5 Moo 3, Pae Klaeng, Kram Road, Klaeng, ☎ 03864 8008, fax 03864 8431, www.novotel.com, $$. This beachfront resort with 189 rooms is 35 kilometers from Rayong and 80 kilometers from Chanthaburi. Rooms booked on the hotel Website cost 2,200 Baht ++ and breakfast is an additional 290 Baht. The rooms are fully equipped, and there are two restaurants, a swimming pool and a karaoke bar.

Chanthaburi

■ Introduction

Our drive along Highway 3 brings us to the fascinating, bustling ancient town of Chanthaburi, the provincial capital of an area that is steeped in history and famous for its gems. If you want to see gemstone trading, try to arrange your visit to be here on a Friday, Saturday or Sunday morning. The main area for gems is **Si Chan Road**, where tables are rented out by the hour for sellers and buyers to swap cash for gems.

In earlier times most of the stones that were traded here were locally mined, but today most of the gems are imported. On these weekend mornings, traders come from Bangkok and meet with the local merchants. The area is full of gem shops and factories where stones are cut, polished and mounted into jewelry. The lapidaries of Chanthaburi are rated as among the world's best. If you know gem stones, then this is probably a good place to buy them. But you need to know what you're doing. We've heard lots of stories of how glass and plain rocks can be treated, heated and presented as passable gems.

Thailand's main cities are full of grand jewelry emporiums, where you first see craftsmen hunched over benches blending sparkling gems with precious metals. Moments later you glide into lavish, brightly illuminated showrooms stocked with shiny creations that can cost anything from a few dollars to millions. The sales force, resplendent in dark suits and fluent in most modern languages, descend armed with calculators that convert the Baht price tags into every imaginable currency. They know every birthstone, the right gems for every anniversary, and they have a natural talent to know a genuine buyer from a curious visitor who is content to leave with a business card. Several executives at these super stores told us that their basic training was here in Chanthaburi, and the best artisans came from here too.

Aside from the gems, a major attraction of Chanthaburi is the amazing mix of cultures and people that the area has attracted. Back in the 1850s, with stories rife that the hills were alive with rubies and sapphires, Cambodians, Chinese and Burmese moved here. They were joined later by refugees from Vietnam escaping from religious persecution. The French occupied the city for over a decade at the end of the 19th century when they rebuilt the Catholic cathedral. The population of the province is estimated at about a half-million. Annual average temperature for the province is a balmy 28.13 degrees Celsius.

■ Getting Here

By Bus

Air conditioned buses leave every 30 minutes from Bangkok's Eastern Bus Terminal, ☎ 02391 2504. The fare is 106 Baht, the 106-kilometer journey takes about four hours.

By Car

It's under four hours total driving time from Bangkok on Highway 3 (Sukhumvit Road).

■ Things to See & Do

Attractions

King Taksin Monument: King Taksin was the monarch who expelled the Burmese from Thailand after they had destroyed the ancient capital of Ayutthaya in 1767. Chanthaburi was the last

Burmese stronghold. A bronze statue of the king on horseback was erected here in 1893. It is in the city park on Thaluang Road, opposite the old governor's office.

Catholic Cathedral: The Church of the Immaculate Conception is said to be the most beautiful Catholic church in Asia and the largest Christian church in Thailand. The cathedral was rebuilt by the French during the time they occupied Chanthaburi; that work was completed in 1909. The church contains some intricate stained glass and several exceptional murals. There has been a church on this site since a small missionary chapel was built here in 1711.

Festivals

Chanthaburi Fruit Fair: This annual event in mid-May allows the city and the province to show off their produce – notably durian, mangosteens, and rambutans – when it is in its peak condition. In addition to selling produce from the orchards the province uses the fair for lots of cultural displays, as well as promoting local handicrafts.

■ Where to Stay & Eat

Maneechan Resort & Sport Club, 110 Moo 11, Plubpla, ☎ 03934 3777, $$. Good family hotel with 72 pleasant rooms and it is part of the city's largest sports club, which includes a large swimming pool, fully equipped gym, fitness center and tennis courts. Popular with Thais; not everyone here speaks English. There is a massage service, and for shoppers it is a short walk to Robinson Department Store. Internet rates run between 2,500 Baht and 3,500 Baht.

K.P. Grand Hotel, 35/200-201 Theerat Road, ☎ 03932 3201, www.chanthaburi-hotel.com, $$. There are 202 well-appointed rooms at this 18-story hotel, reasonably priced at 1,600 Baht, although the very large (105-square-meter) executive suite has a rack rate of 8,000 Baht. Choice of dining: the upmarket **Sky Room Restaurant**, noted for its creative European, cooking is on the 18th floor. Closer to ground level is the Mei-san Restaurant, which offers good Chinese cuisine. Nice swimming pool and fitness center and, as you would expect, a Thai massage service is available.

Caribou Highland Hotel, Chawana-Uthids Road, ☎ 03932 3431, fax 03932 1584, www.caribou-hotel.com, $. Probably the best value in town. The 112 standard rooms, well equipped, sell for

990 Baht a night; the larger junior suites cost 1,600 Baht; and the two-bedroom grand suite on the seventh floor, with great views of the city, sells for 4,000 Baht a night. The prices include breakfast. Bargain prices too at the hotel's **Sunflower Chinese Restaurant** on the second floor, which is open from 6am until midnight. There is an international lunch buffet three times a week for 90 Baht and on Friday nights the buffet dinner costs 120 Baht per person.

The Caribou Highland Hotel Website has two movies, one about the hotel and the other about the city. One snag – the commentary is in Thai.

New Travel Lodge Hotel, 14/5 M 3 Raksachamoon Road, ☎ 03930 1888, fax 03930 1555 $. Well-priced rooms, all selling at less than 2,000 Baht a night, considering the facilities and bright décor. If you're driving, you'll appreciate the spacious guarded car park, and the pleasant swimming pool is a plus.

Chanthaburi Riverside, 69 Moo 9, Chanthanimit Road, ☎ 03931 1726, $. Very basic small hotel where you can get a room for under $6. Breakfast not included. The only reason we list it is that it has a great location overlooking the River Chanthaburi and within shouting distance of the gem shops. What you save here can be spent on a few more rubies or sapphires.

Trat

■ Introduction

Trat, the fourth-smallest province in Thailand with a population of less than a quarter of a million people, is more a place you pass through rather than stop in. It is best known as the gateway to the islands of the National Marine Park, including **Ko Chang**, **Ko Laoya**, **Ko Mak** and **Ko Kood**. Departure point for those is at Laem Ngob, which is 17 kilometers south of the town of Trat, the provincial capital.

The eastern part of the province is separated from Cambodia by the **Buntud Mountains**, and the **River Weru** separates it in the west from Chanthaburi.

The town of Trat, 70 kilometers east of Chanthaburi, is also the last major place to get supplies if you're heading south to the border with Cambodia.

■ Getting Here

The new **Trat Airport**, belonging to Bangkok Airways (☎ 03957 9767), is 35 kilometers northwest of the city, and looks like a carbon copy of the airline's facility at Ko Samui. Most passengers are destined for the islands but, with demand growing, the airline says it will add services and probably other destinations.

■ Where to Stay & Eat

There are a dozen guesthouses in Trat offering basic accommodation, several restaurants and a handful of souvenir shops, and a well frequented KFC. Topping the list of places to stay is the **Trat Hotel** on Soi Thanacharoen, ☎ 03951 2233, with a variety of riime; air conditioned doubles from 400 to 600 Baht. The Tourism Authority of Thailand (TAT) has an office here, at 100 Moo 1, ☎ 03959 7255, tattrat@tat.or.th.

■ Things to See & Do

Festivals

Trat Memorial Day: Annual event celebrated on March 23, the day the province returned to Thai sovereignty after the French occupation. The celebrations are held at the provincial town hall.

Trat Fruit Fair: Held at the end of May or beginning of June and featuring exhibitions and displays of agricultural produce from the region. Lots of contests about who grew the biggest and best.

National Marine Park Islands

The islands in the marine park include Ko Chang, Ko Laoya, Ko Mak and Ko Kood.

■ Introduction & History

Ko Chang and its surrounding 50 smaller islands are poised to become the next Phuket of Thailand. That's the way some politicians view it, including the Prime Minister. Others fear that this group of islands, which were designated as a National Marine Park back in 1982 in the hope of preserving their natural beauty, will be ruined by new development in much the same way that befell the Phi Phi islands.

DID YOU KNOW? *The word* chang *means elephant in Thai, though the big beasts never roamed here – until now, when elephant trekking is one of the options afforded visitors. It's possible the name came as a result of the island's shape but to us it looks more like a tortoise with a hat on.*

Probably the most important part of the island's history took place offshore in an area near **Salak Petch** beach known as the **Naval Battle Ground**, or ***Boriwaen Yutthanavee***. It was here, during the time the French held colonies in Southeast Asia, that the French and Thai navies clashed and on January 17, 1941, the Royal Thai Navy's ship *Thonburi* was sunk. The wreck has become a popular dive site. And every year the people of Trat Province remember the attack by holding memorial services and floating garlands out to sea to honor those who died. A museum with an exhibition of naval history has been built on the mainland at **Laem Ngob Beach**.

Geography

The national marine park area spreads over 650 square kilometers off the **Ngob Headland** of Trat Province, which borders on Cambodia. The islands have been a favorite spot for Thai holidaymakers and a few nature-loving foreigners. The last published figures showed that only 118,000 people visited the islands in the year 2003. By comparison, two million people visited Phuket in the first six months of 2004.

Tourism

The area got a boost in tourism when the tsunami hit Phuket and its surroundings. Some of those who switched resorts told us later that they were impressed with Ko Chang but felt it had yet to reach the international standards of other major Thai resort areas.

Until the big resorts opened for business, the only accommodation that was available on the islands was basic bamboo huts. Most of them offered a mattress on the floor – beds put you in a higher price bracket – and power was only available at certain times of the day when the generator ran. Today it is still possible to get a room for under 100 Baht but it is very basic living, and one needs a tough skin to withstand the mosquito and sand-fly bites.

■ Ko Chang

Ko Chang is the major island in the marine park, and the second-largest in Thailand – Phuket is the largest, and Samui the third – at 30 kilometers in length from north to south and 8 kilometers across at its widest point. The island is covered in dense virgin rain forest and skirted by white sand beaches, the best of which are on the island's west coast.

The two biggest communities on Ko Chang are **Ban Salak Petch** and **Ban Long Than**, both on the south end of the island. Most of the islanders are fishermen, and Salak Petch is the perfect harbor for boats; this is where you'll find all the piers with ferry services to other islands in the archipelago, as well as to Laem Ngob on the mainland.

It still lacks many modern conveniences, but they are coming. The new airport on the mainland at Trat (see above), built by Bangkok Airways, and the good superhighway from Bangkok, 360 kilometers away, make getting here easier. The airport, which is a 15-minute drive from the ferry terminal, has service to Bangkok, Phuket and Samui. A new telecom system has been installed and this has prompted the opening of several Internet cafés on the island. There are small medical clinics on the island but the closest hospital is at Trat. Plans are also underway to link up the island's road so it will be possible to make a circular tour.

The government has also announced several development programs for the island, which include a yacht marina, an area set aside for boat racing and an expansive undersea aquarium. Critics claim that the aquarium project is not worthwhile since the water is not clear enough to support such a scheme.

Before the current growth of tourism, the main industry here was fishing; to supplement their meager incomes the islanders are adapt at fruit farming as well as tapping the rubber trees for their sap.

Cars, jeeps and motorcycles are available for rent on Ko Chang to explore the coastal regions of the islands. And there are plenty of inexpensive restaurants and bars scattered around.

Attractions

Away from the resorts, the main attractions on Chang are fishing, diving and snorkeling. Or you can go hiking in the rain forests and find the two multi-level waterfalls where you can swim in the fresh, cool pools below. The flora and fauna awaiting the intrepid trekker are spectacular. It's possible to see more than 70 species of birds, as well as wild boar, monkeys and barking deer.

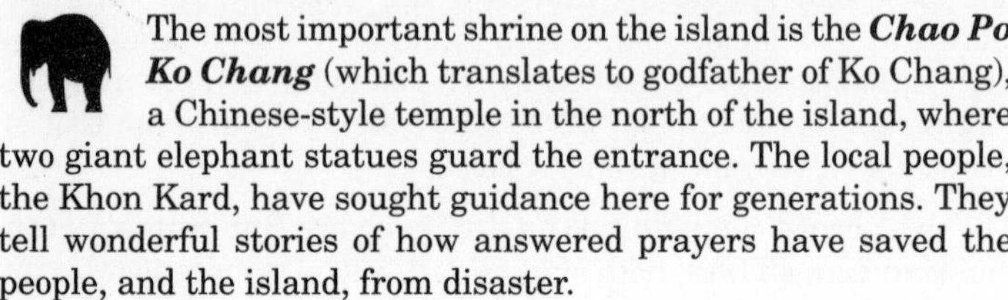

The most important shrine on the island is the ***Chao Po Ko Chang*** (which translates to godfather of Ko Chang), a Chinese-style temple in the north of the island, where two giant elephant statues guard the entrance. The local people, the Khon Kard, have sought guidance here for generations. They tell wonderful stories of how answered prayers have saved the people, and the island, from disaster.

Where to Stay & Eat

Amari Emerald Cove Resort, 88/8 Moo 4, Klong Prao Beach, ☎ 03955 2000, fax 03955 2001, www.amari.com, $$$. This was the first luxury chain resort to open on Ko Chang. It was in full swing for the 2004-2005 Christmas and New Year holidays. It is one of the largest resorts on the Chang Islands, with 165 rooms and suites. Amari went for quality with all its accommodation having fine-looking solid wood furniture and modern Thai décor. The rooms have great views of either the cove or nearby mountains. Guests have a choice of three restaurants, one with an outdoor terrace, as well as two bars. The resort has a 50-meter pool, a rarity in the archipelago, a Jacuzzi, a children's pool and a scuba diving center. There is also the **Sivara Spa** and a fitness room. High-season Internet rates started at $136 +++ for the deluxe rooms with suites costing as much as $400 a night.

Ramayana Koh Chang Resort, 19/9 Moo 4, Klong Prao beach. Bangkok sales office, ☎ 02261 6364, fax 02261 6367, www.ramayana-kohchang.com, $$$. Elegant new luxury resort set inland amid the island's finest gardens. The 64 fully equipped rooms and suites all have private patios and are beautifully furnished. The resort has its own beach where it maintains a club with a sundeck terrace, and provides an hourly minibus service to get you there and back; a scuba and snorkeling center, a snack bar and traditional Thai massages are available at the resort. There is a swimming pool and several restaurants. Complimentary shuttle services are provided to the **Bang Bao** fishing village as well as to the island's pier. There's an upmarket spa at the resort as well as a library and Internet center. An elaborate buffet breakfast is provided at the **Sritandorn Restaurant** from sunrise until 11:30am. Room rates start at 5,000 Baht for the room and go as high as 12,000 Baht for the two-bedroom family suites. The resort does offer several attractive package deals on its Website.

Aiyapura Resort & Spa, 29 Moo 3, Klong Son Beach, ☎ and fax 03955 5118, www.aiyapura.com, $$$. A large leaf-shaped infinity swimming pool with a swim-up bar is a focal point for this upmarket resort, which has 77 rooms, including villas and suites – all equipped with in-room tea and coffee making facilities. There are three restaurants and there has been an emphasis on things Thai in décor and design. The decks have been constructed with the kingdom's teak and the umbrellas that adorn the area came from Chiang Mai. Rates, which include breakfast and taxes, vary from a low-season standard room at 4,200 Baht to 14,000 Baht for the honeymoon suite in high season. The resort has one of the best spas on the island, where you can expect to pay 3,000 Baht for a two-hour session. There's a nightly barbecue (750 Baht) or a set dinner (650 Baht).

KC Grande Resort, 1/1 Moo 4, Ban Had Sai Khao, ☎ 01833 1010, fax 01939 5857, www.kcresortkohchang.com, $$. This popular inexpensive resort on White Sand Beach (*Had Sai Khao*) has undergone some major improvements to its 50 beachside bungalows, and its new lobby, which has facilities including a room for Internet access, safe deposit boxes and a coffee corner where you can drink as much as you want as long as you want. The resort is within walking distance of the busy settlement that White Sand Beach has become with its numerous stalls, bars, restaurants, the police booth and clinic. The main street also houses Ko Chang's only two ATMs. Rates range from 1,700 Baht for the older standard bungalows in low season, to 4,100 Baht for the more modern beachfront bungalows in high season. The prices include breakfast and taxes. The resort's **Beach Café** is open all day and has become a favorite spot for its fresh grilled seafood.

Banpu Ko Chang Hotel, 9/11 Moo 4, White Sand Beach, ☎ 01863 7314, www.banpuresort.com, $$. A pleasant, well-priced private resort where you have a choice of bungalow location. For those in groups and looking for fun and frolic, the bungalows around the lake are the place to be. If it's peace and quiet you seek then the bungalows near the sea are the ones to book. Each of the chalets have been hand-crafted with local woods and ceramic tiles and are surround by tropical gardens. The resort has a spa and swimming pool, and the views from the property are inspiring. All the accommodation comes fully equipped; expect to pay 3,400 Baht a night for the best chalets.

Sea View Resort & Spa, 10/2 Moo 4, Kai Bae Beach, ☎ 03938 2279, fax 03955 1153, www.seaviewkohchang.com, $$. It's the location on a cliff near the viewpoint at the southern end of **Kai Bae Beach** that attracts visitors to this well-established resort. Inexpensive for most of the accommodation (as low as 1,200 Baht for a standard cottage in low season, June to September) although the best suite does sell for 14,000 Baht in high season, from October to May. Those rates include taxes and breakfast. Nice beach and comfortable, not luxurious, accommodation makes it a great value.

Barali Beach Resort, 77 Moo 4, Klong Prao Beach, ☎ 03955 1238, fax 03955 1239, $$. Reasonably priced new, larger beachfront resort with all the Asian-style villas well equipped with TVs, stereo and minibar. Great location for sunset-watching on the west coast of the island. Two pools, the smaller one for children, coffee shop, lobby lounge and room service. There is a mangrove canal nearby and the resort rents out canoes so you can paddle your way through it. Rates for a deluxe villa start at 2,400 Baht and top price is 7,800 Baht for a junior suite villa over the Christmas period.

Ko Chang Grand Lagoona, ☎ 03950 1605, fax 03950 1067, www.grandlagoona.com, $$. This resort gets the prize for the oddest assortment of accommodation, ranging from a room on a seven-deck floating hotel to quaint floating chalets or pleasant Lanna-style hillside villas.

> *The* Lanna Kingdom *was the original name of an area of northern Thailand; Lanna-style is the architectural tradition of that area.*

The resort is spread over 400 rais which, it claims, makes it the biggest resort on Ko Chang (the *rai*, a unit of land measurement, is difficult to convert, so we will take their word for it). This place has as it name implies, a large lagoon as well as a white sand beach, streams and an area of tropical rain forest. The resort's unusual floating hotel, the **Galaxy**, is built on an old wooden barge; you can stay here for 4,500 Baht on weekdays or 5,500 Baht on weekend nights. The Galaxy has 125 rooms and a banqueting room to handle 200 diners; weekday prices here are 1,500 Baht. If you want to stay on dry land, the homes on the hill sell for 4,500 Baht week nights and 6,500 Baht at weekends. Focal point here is the bathrooms have a transparent roof so you can stargaze while you shower.

■ Ko Laoya

There are in fact three small islands, **Ko Laoya Nai**, **Ko Laoya Klang** and **Ko Laoya Nok**. The islands are close to the southern tip of Ko Chang and noted for wonderful coral heads and fine white beaches. There is a bridge that links Laoya Klang to Laoya Nai. There is only one resort here, **Laoya Resort**, ☎ 02673 0966, fax 02211 9656. They offer an all-inclusive three-day, two-night package for 5,000 Baht per person, which includes the return boat trip between Laem Ngob ferry and the resort, the accommodation, and six set meals. The resort boasts 24-hour uninterrupted electricity, and all rooms have air conditioning and TV. There's not a lot to do here but fish, swim, sail and snorkel.

■ Ko Mak

This island, off the south coast of Ko Chang, has long been inhabited by farmers and fishermen, and was once occupied by the French. It only covers 15 square kilometers but is full of rubber tree and coconut plantations and noted for its fine beaches. The first tourists began coming here in 1974 when some bungalows for tourists were built at **Ban Ao Nid** on the east of the island. Poor communications and transport halted further development until 1987, when small basic resorts were built on some of the island's beach areas. Today there are close to a dozen different places to stay, most of them very basic, but it has become the most popular of the small islands in the marine park.

Getting Here

The ferry from Laem Ngob to Ko Mak leaves the mainland every day at 3pm and returns every morning at 8am. The crossing takes three hours.

Where to Stay

Koh Mak Resort, ☎ 03950 1013, fax 03950 1013, www.geocities.com/kohmaak. The 28 bungalows, some air conditioned, that comprise this resort are on **Suan Yai** beach on the western side of this island, facing the tiny island of Ko Kham, with a distant view of Ko Chang and Ko Wai. There is a diving school, and dives are arranged for nearby sites. Most are suitable for students, though more experienced divers can go down as far as 30 meters. The restaurant offers good Thai food but says its cook will attempt western dishes. The resort offers all kinds of boat rentals, archery and windsurfing lessons and operates a small post office with Internet and regular phone connections. There is a convenience store, pool table and a library. The type-B bungalow with air conditioning costs 4,200 Baht for a three-day, two-night stay. The price includes the boat transfer, six meals and a snorkeling trip.

Cococape, Koh Mak, www.koh-chang.com/kohmakcococape. The best bet here of the 28 bungalows is the Laguna Cottage that comes with a private bathroom and air conditioning for 2,800 Baht a night. The thatched-roof wooden cottages sit on stilts and are scattered neatly along a nice beach that is bounded by coconut palms. The resort has bikes, boats, kayaks and fishing tackle to rent and offers help in learning windsurfing, kite-surfing and archery. There is a speed-boat available for hire that can take you to the neighboring islands including Ko Rayang, Ko Wai, Ko Kood and the three Laoya islands.

■ Ko Kood

Ko Kood is the second-largest island in the National Marine Park, the fourth-largest in Thailand, and the farthest from the Trat coast. Its resorts are a little more upmarket than on most of the other marine park islands, but they are still well priced even if you have to travel a little farther to reach them. The terrain consists mostly of hills covered in wild vegetation sloping down to wonderful beaches. There are also some breathtaking coral reefs offshore. Perhaps the most important visitor here was King Rama V who came to see the **Klong Chao waterfall**.

Until the resorts came the few villagers depended on fishing and farming. At last count only 1,500 were considered residents on the island, which covers 130 square kilometers.

Getting Here

Ferries depart either from **Ao Thammachat** or **Ko Chang Center Point** landings, from 7:30m to 4:30pm. Private boat charters can be arranged at the Laem Ngob landing or in advance at Ko Chang Center Point, ☎ 03953 8055.

Where to Stay & Eat

Some of the resorts close during the off-season and many are fully booked way in advance during the most popular season, which is from early November until the end of February.

Ko Kood Island Resort, Moo 6, Yai Kerd Beach, ☎ Bangkok reservations ☎ 02211 9656. E-mail koodlaguna@thai-tour.com. The resort on Yai Kerd Bay, the northernmost part of the island, offers the choice of two areas to stay. The more expensive **Ban Klang Nam** has 20 sturdy wood-finished cottages built over the shallow sea. A two-night, three-day package costs 4,350 Baht per person and includes the accommodation, nine meals, and boat transfers to the mainland. The second choice is **Ban Cherng Kao**, where each of the eight cottages can accommodate up to seven persons. Per-person package cost for these is 3,600 Baht.

Ko Kood Laguna, www.kokoodlaguna.com. There are five different accommodation types at different locations, depending on the size of your party and how much comfort you want. There's no swimming pool; the resort says the sea is a better alternative and it has powerboats to rent for skiing or a sport-fishing boat for day- or night-trolling. The good-looking Seaside cottage costs 4,300 Baht per night/per person if you stay for two nights, and thereafter 1,000 Baht per night/per person. That price includes air conditioning, TV and refrigerator, round-trip transfers to the mainland by speedboat and four meals a day. There is 24-hour power but the air conditioners are only turned on between 6pm and 7am – just when you most need them.

Koh Kood Cabana, Tapow Beach, ☎ Bangkok reservations 02211 9656, e-mail kohkoodcabana@thai-tour.com. Situated on the west coast of the island at Tapow Beach, claiming to be the most beautiful beach on Ko Kood, and close to the Klong Chao waterfall this resort has the facilities to handle groups up to 200. Ko Kood Cabana offers a good variety of accommodation. These are the single- or double-occupancy bungalows; the larger ones can house from six to 12 people. All bungalows have their own bathrooms and all face the beach. A VIP room here with air conditioning costs 3,200 (plus 7% VAT) Baht per day and includes four meals a day, a trip to the Klong Chao waterfall, round-trip transfer to the mainland by speed boat.

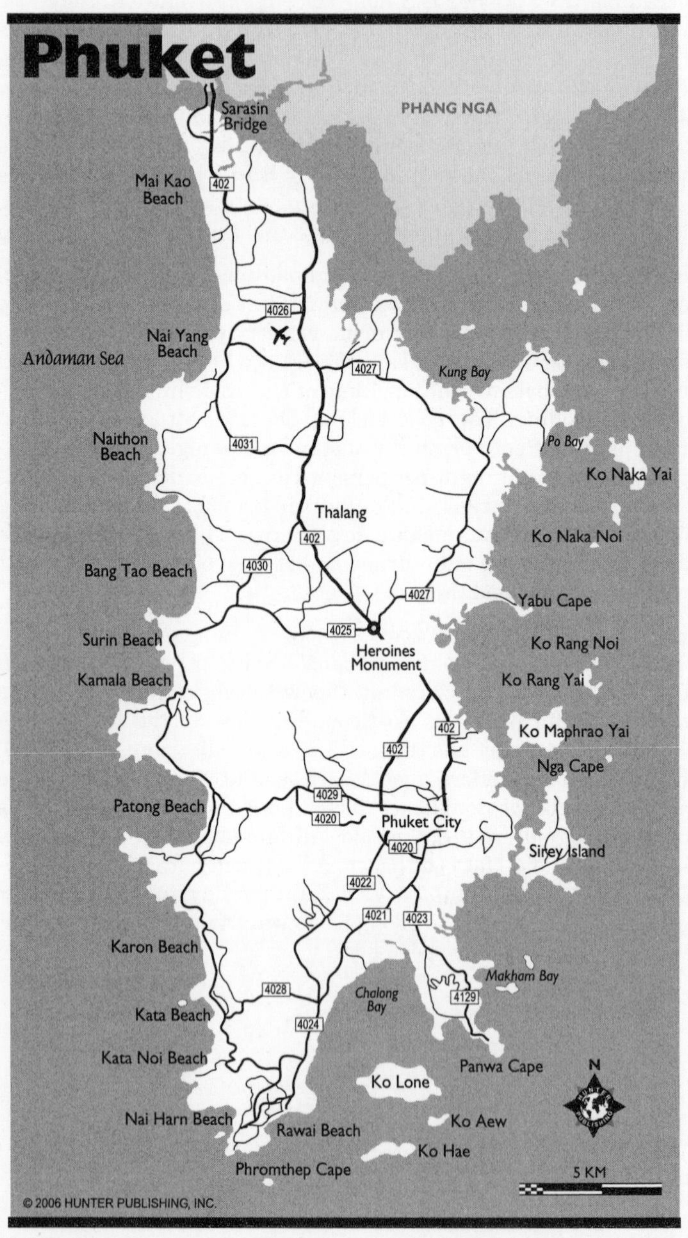
Phuket
Sarasin Bridge
PHANG NGA
Mai Kao Beach
402
4026
Nai Yang Beach
Andaman Sea
4027
Kung Bay
Po Bay
Naithon Beach
4031
Ko Naka Yai
Thalang
402
Ko Naka Noi
Bang Tao Beach
4030
4027
Yabu Cape
4025
Surin Beach
Heroines Monument
Ko Rang Noi
Kamala Beach
Ko Rang Yai
402
Ko Maphrao Yai
402
Nga Cape
4029
Patong Beach
4020
Phuket City
4020
Sirey Island
4022
4021
4023
Karon Beach
Makham Bay
Chalong Bay
4028
4129
Kata Beach
4024
Kata Noi Beach
Panwa Cape
N
Ko Lone
Nai Harn Beach
Rawai Beach
Ko Aew
Ko Hae
Phromthep Cape
5 KM
© 2006 HUNTER PUBLISHING, INC.

Phuket

Introduction

Phuket – a tropical paradise jammed with endless pleasures and treasures – has long been Thailand's top tourist destination. The island, which is approximately the size of Singapore, has everything from ancient relics to zoos. There is something to please any adventure seeker. There are crowded beaches, or secluded coves. Festivals and regattas cram the calendar.

IN THIS CHAPTER

The island was cruelly hit by the tsunami that hit Southeast Asia on December 26, 2004. We were here when that happened and if you have already read our account in *The Tsunami*, page 9, you will know how lucky we were.

Despite the deaths and destruction it did not take the island long to fight back the tears and grief and rebuild the broken bits of this holiday paradise. We stayed for several months after that sad Sunday and learned firsthand what resilient and fine people the Thais are. Although so many suffered it was hard to find someone complaining. The attitude was: Things will get better. And they did.

The island got a minor jolt early in 2004 when a major travel publication dubbed it one of the world's ugliest tourist destinations. In true Thai style, local officials – including the governor – did not dispute the claim, but vowed to make changes. The good news was that Chiang Mai got good marks in the same poll.

But it wasn't long before numerous very not-ugly resorts began opening. Some of them far exceeded our affordable-luxury theme. By 2005 the new resorts that were opened included the very expensive and exclusive Trisara on the northwest side of the island, and the world-class The Racha resort, technically within the province of Phuket but located on an island to the south. More in our price range was the TwinPalms, which opened at Surin Beach, and the Crowne Plaza, which replaced an older hotel on Karon Beach. Another top quality boutique resort, Arahmas now graces the beach at Nai Yang. You can read about all these new resorts in the *Where to Stay* section, page 223.

Climate

First, it never gets cold. Temperatures never drop below 22 degrees Celsius and never get much higher than 34. There are two distinct seasons – the rainy one from May through October (September is the wettest month) and the hot one from November through April. There are lots of sunny days during the rainy season and the showers are normally short. However, monsoons are not unknown. The best months to visit – and the high season for hotel rates – are November through February.

History

Burmese Invasions

Every British child knows what happened in the year 1066 when William the Conqueror defeated King Harold at the Battle of Hastings. Likewise, American youngsters remember the year 1492 when Columbus sailed the ocean blue and discovered America, or to be more precise a small island in the Bahamas called San Salvador. For the people of Phuket the year to remember is 1785, when two women thwarted an invasion of Burmese with artificial guns made of wood.

A British sea captain, Francis Light, knew that the Burmese fleet with 3,000 men was preparing to invade and wrote to the governor of Phuket who, in fact, had just died. Captain Light thought, like many historians, that the Burmese wanted to capture Thais and take them back to Burma as slaves. The governor's wife, Kunying Jan, a granddaughter of the Sultan of Kedah, intercepted the message and with the help of her sister Mook rallied the islanders into action. There was a shortage of men so she ordered several hundred women to dress as soldiers. There was also a shortage of weapons so they were armed with coconut palms and sticks. For a month the Burmese tried to establish a foothold near Bang Tao

Bay but continual Thai sorties prevented that. After a month, on March 13, 1785, the Burmese were facing starvation and retreated.

Francis Light was an employee of the British East India Trading Company and had been sent out to find a strategic port to control shipping in the Straits of Malacca. The company eventually decided to set up shop in Penang but Captain Light fell in love with a Phuket girl, married her and stayed on the island.

King Rama I, amazed by their exploits, bestowed noble titles on the sisters. Kunying Jan became *Thao Thepkrasatri* and her sister was named *Thao Srisunthorn*. Today the two heroines are remembered by statues, erected in 1966, that adorn a roundabout on the highway to the airport. You will notice that many local people make the Thai wai greeting as they pass the roundabout, which is at the Tha Ruea intersection, 12 kilometers north of Phuket City.

But the Burmese were not done with their visits to Phuket. When King Rama II was new to the throne they pillaged the area three more times between 1809 and 1812. Takua Pha and Takua Tung were destroyed and Thalang and Tha Rua port left in ruins. Armed forces from Bangkok arrived in time to repel further onslaughts. Then the British took over Burma and the Burmese raids stopped.

In 1825 many of the islanders who had fled to Phang Nga and Krabi returned to re-establish Thalang and concentrated on rice growing. Meanwhile an area south of Thalang was becoming more important as the center of the tin trade and in 1850 was elevated to town status and became Phuket Town. In 2004 that status was elevated again and it became Phuket City.

The Sea Gypsies

The sea gypsies – the semi-nomadic Moken people known as the *chao ley* (people of the sea) – have lived as hunter-gatherers, dwelling on boats or in stilted dwellings along the coasts of Thailand and Myanmar for hundreds of years. Today their main centers in Thailand are in the Surin Islands, on Sirey Island (a small islet off Phuket City), and at Rawai Beach, on the southern end of Phuket. They are probably the oldest inhabitants of Phuket. It is unfortunate that their culture is being eroded because of the tourist invasion. Now they get visitors to their settlements and some of their traditional habits are vanishing. They used to exist without money, managing to barter their way through life with their skills as fishermen. Now those photo opportunities bring cash and they have homes with electricity and running water.

They are gentle, friendly people whose future looks like being further transformed as local government tries to integrate them into regular Thai society. They are still of great interest to scientists and anthropologists because of their uncertain background. There are no written records of where they came from and yet they have a unique language and their own form of spirit worship.

The sea gypsies are very involved in the collection of birds' nests, which is a very lucrative and dangerous enterprise. You can learn more about the harvesting of these nests needed for the authentic Chinese birds' nest soup in the *Phi Phi Islands* section, page 263.

Scientists have discovered that the sea gypsies' children have incredible underwater vision, twice as good as a European child, which enables them to find the tiny shells and shellfish when they dive to the sea bed. The men normally fish with roughly made harpoons and use nets only to store their catch while they are underwater. Many of them can dive to depths of 75 feet and it is only recently that they have used snorkels in their search for food. The sea gypsies welcome visitors to their settlements and going on your own seems a more peaceful way to see what remains of a culture that will one day disappear.

Chinese Immigrants

Tin mining attracted large numbers of Chinese workers but, because they came from different cultures within China, bloody battles ensued. In 1876 two sects fought each other and then went on a rampage of murder and theft throughout the island. The temple at Chalong became a meeting point for islanders trying to stop the uprising. When the Chinese gangs arrived at the temple the islanders, normally peaceful, battled with the Chinese. More Thais joined the fight and eventually the uprising was quelled.

The Chinese played an important role in Phuket's development. Praya Rasda, a Chinese grandee, governed Phuket from 1890 to 1909. During his term of office European-style houses were built in the town, new roads constructed and poor people were encouraged to become livestock farmers. At Praya Rasda's request the Standard Chartered Bank set up its first Thailand branch in Phuket. In 1901 he was credited with introducing the first rubber tree into Thailand. The kingdom became the largest exporter of rubber in the world.

King Rama V later made Phuket a *monthon*, a Thai governing authority, giving it control over Phang Nga, Krabi, Ranong, Trang, Satun and Takua Pha. Since 1933 Phuket, like all other provinces, has been ruled by an appointed governor of the Interior Ministry. It was not until 1967 that the Sarasin Bridge was built to connect the main land with Phuket. With the opening of an international airport in 1976, Phuket turned its attention to the fast-growing tourist industry.

Getting Here

By Air

Most air arrivals to Phuket are from Bangkok. **Thai Airways** (www.thaiairways.com), **Bangkok Airlines** (www.bangkok-air.com), **AirAsia** (www.airasia.com) and **Nok Air** (www.nok-air.com), a subsidiary of Thai Airways, all offer services from the capital. Flying time is 80 minutes. There are several charter airlines that fly direct from Europe to Phuket and there also services from Kuala Lumpur, Hong Kong, Penang, Singapore, and Sydney. **Tiger Airlines**, one of Asia's no-frills operators, has a daily morning flight between Singapore's Changi Airport and Phuket using Airbus 320s with 180 seats in an all-economy configuration. Tickets can be bought on the Internet (www.tigerairways.com) or by phone (☎ 001800 656752). Budget carrier **AirAsia** (www.airasia.com) also offers service from Singapore.

The airport works well and there are nice bars and shops to peruse. Normally, airports are expensive places to eat. Not so Phuket, where the prices are the same as elsewhere on the island. We're not suggesting you add the airport to your sightseeing agenda but if you do get delayed there are worse places to spend an hour or so. However, once you pass through the immigration control and pay your 500 Baht departure tax, the shops and bars on the airside are not as pleasant as those inside the terminal.

If you fly into Bangkok from a foreign destination and are in transit to Phuket, customs and immigration facilities are avoided in Bangkok and you take care of the formalities in Phuket. Because of the large number of people arriving in this manner, and the shortage of immigration officers on the island, there were delays in the past of up to two hours. It is a problem the airport is struggling to solve. The government does respond to complaints but not always as quickly as it should. After flying halfway around the world, nobody enjoys standing in line waiting for your official welcome to the land of silk and smiles.

By Bus

Buses, both with and without air conditioning, leave Bangkok's Southern Bus Terminal for Phuket several times daily. The trip, normally leaving in the evening, takes about 13 hours, ☎ 02434 7192, 02435 1199.

By Car

From Bangkok take **Highway No. 4** (Phetchakasem Road) through Phetchaburi, Prachuap Khiri Khan, Chumphon, Surat Thani and Phang-nga, then cross Sarasin Bridge to Phuket Island. The total distance is 862 kilometers and will take about 12 hours. There are several small inexpensive hotels en route if you want to break the journey. Even the most adventurous traveler might need a couple of days to recover from this trip!

By Rail

There is no direct train service to Phuket. Travelers by train must get off at Phun Phin railway station in Surat Thani and continue by regular bus to Phuket. State Railway of Thailand, ☎ 02223 7010 or 02223 7020.

Getting Around

By Car

You will have no problem finding somewhere to rent a car, either at the airport or at any of the major resorts. Most rental companies will accept a valid US or European license but some may ask for an International Driving Permit. If you want one of these you have to obtain it in your home country before traveling. Minimum age is 21, although some companies may require an older driver. Beware of companies, and sometimes individuals, renting vehicles without insurance. The lower price may seem attractive but it could prove costly if you have an accident. If you haven't driven in

Monks in Northern Thailand

Above: It's not always sunny in Thailand
Courtesy of Phuket International Hospital

Below: View of the Mekong River
Courtesy of Tohsang Resort

Above: Always bargain when you shop in the markets

Below: The buzz of Bangkok at night

Above: Take time to relax in a hammock

Below: The beauty of a waterfall

Above and Below: Only Thailand could produce something as ornate as this royal barge...

...or these carved fruits & vegetables

Above: Children at play
Courtesy of Tohsang Resort

Below: Kayaks ready to go

Above and Below:
Royal barges at night

The Marriott Resort at Pattaya
Courtesy of Marriott Hotels

Phuket before we suggest you get driven around a little before you venture off on your own. Remember to drive on the left and remember that motorcycles have the right of way. Rates are reasonable and you can expect to pay an inclusive price of about $30 per day, depending on the vehicle you select.

Here are some of the companies that rent cars: **Avis**, Kata Beach Resort, ☎ 07638 1530-1533; **Boomerang Travel & Tour**, 71/13 Patak Road, Chalong Bay, ☎ 07638 1690; **Hertz**, with offices at Thavorn Palm Beach Hotel, Karon Beach, ☎ 07638 1034-7; Holiday Inn, Patong Beach, ☎ 07634 0608; Le Meridian, Karon Noi Beach, ☎ 07634 0480-0485; Pearl Village, Nai Yang Beach, ☎ 07632 7006; Phuket Arcadia, Karon Beach, ☎ 07638 1038 40; Phuket Airport, ☎ 07632 7258; and Phuket Cabana, Patong Beach, ☎ 07634 0138; **Phuket Horizon Car Rent**, 235/4 Yaowarat Road, Tambon Talat Nua, ☎ 07621 5200; **Pure Car Rent**, opposite Thavorn Hotel, Ratsada Road, ☎ 07621 1002; **Via Rent A Car**, 70/85 Rat U-Thit, Patong Beach, ☎ 07634 0160.

We have rented from Pure Car Rent several times and found their rates to be a little lower even if the cars are a little older. Also Pure has said it will offer a discount off its published rates to anyone who has a copy of our guidebook.

By Motorcycle

These are available all over the island at ridiculously low prices, but we strongly recommend that you do not rent one. We have seen too many accidents and too many injuries to justify the low cost. Hundreds of people die on the roads of Phuket each year and most of them were riding motorcycles. Most come without insurance, and when there is an accident involving a tourist and a local vehicle the traffic police understandably tend to favor their fellow countrymen.

By Taxi

Both legal and not so legal. A vehicle with the word "taxi" fixed permanently to it is probably legal, particularly if it has a meter. Those that have a cardboard sign sitting on the hood or trunk that is removed when you drive off are not. Either way, negotiate a price before your journey begins. Illegal drivers, making full use of the family vehicle, are frequently given tickets as you travel. They accept these with a shrug and consider them part of the cost of doing business. Most drivers are very friendly; many speak a strange version of English and will gladly accept a tip.

USEFUL TELEPHONE NUMBERS

Tourism Authority of Thailand (TAT) . . ☎ 07621 1036
Emergency . . . . ☎ 199
Tourist Police . . . . ☎ 07621 9878 or 1155
Marine Police . . . . ☎ 07621 1883
Phuket Provincial Office . . . . ☎ 07621 1366
Immigration Office . . . . ☎ 07621 2108
Phuket Adventist Hospital . . . . ☎ 07621 2386
Phuket Ruamphaet Hospital . . . . ☎ 07621 2950
Sirirot Hospital (Phuket International) . . ☎ 07624 9400, 07621 0935
Bangkok Phuket Hospital . . . . ☎ 07625 4421
Kathu Patong Hospital . . . . ☎ 07634 0444
Paet Sompoj Hospital . . . . ☎ 07621 4428
Thalang Hospital . . . . ☎ 07631 1033
Vachira Phuket Hospital . . . . ☎ 07621 7294
Overseas Phone Service . . . . ☎ 100
Phone directory assistance . . . . ☎ 13
Police . . . . ☎ 07621 2046
Post office . . . . ☎ 07621 1020

AIRLINES

Phuket Airport . . . . ☎ 07632 7230
Air Lanka . . . . ☎ 07621 2892
Bangkok Airways . . . . ☎ 07622 5033
China Airlines . . . . ☎ 07632 7099
Emirates Air . . . . ☎ 07621 2892
Malaysia Airlines . . . . ☎ 07621 6675
Silk Air . . . . ☎ 07621 6675
Thai Airways . . . . ☎ 07621 1195, 07621 2946, 07621 2499
Tiger Airlines . . . . ☎ 001800 656752

By Tuk-tuk

These are small, brightly painted pickup trucks with bench seats in the rear. This is the cheapest form of four-wheeled transport. Again, negotiate the price before you travel and expect to stop and pick up or drop off other passengers on your journey. Not recommended if you are traveling with fragile items.

Courtesy Buses

There are many ways to travel around Phuket for nothing. Free **minibuses** and **water taxis** link the major hotels and the Canal Point Shopping Center in the Laguna Beach complex. Many of the better stores and restaurants will send a car or bus to pick you up from your hotel if you are a potential client. Free transportation is normally provided when you buy a boat excursion. **FantaSea** – the island's biggest attraction, a Disney-style show and play area with an eating emporium the size of a Cape Canaveral hangar – includes transportation from most island hotels with its admission price (see page 208).

Patong

This heavily populated area on the western shore of Phuket was devastated by the tsunami. Patong, which attracts tourists in vast numbers, is jammed with hotels and cheap inns. Its streets are choked with bars and tiny stores. The area caters to everyone. Quiet English families mingle with Australian youths bent on beer binging. Transvestites sit in seedy bars, and tiny Thai girls seek customers for massage parlors that do not always follow the ancient rules of healing. Gay couples stroll arm-in-arm alongside petite camera-clutching Orientals. Street markets offer the full range of inexpensive "copies" of watches, designer clothes, CDs and luggage. Tourist trinkets feature elephants and colorful but cheap silk products. If it wasn't for the heat or the chatter of the Thai traders this could be Blackpool or Southend, two of Britain's major holiday centers. We are also reminded of San Antonio, on the Spanish island of Ibiza, which tends to attract the British lager louts. Locals expect the summer brawls and bravado. One told us, "Football hooligans have to holiday somewhere. At least we know where they are!"

We have stayed in Patong, in the new wing of the Holiday Inn, and were very impressed with the quality of the accommodation and friendly service. We often shop in the area because prices in the street markets are lower, thanks to the huge volume the vendors enjoy. And there are several art studios where talented Thai artists produce excellent work. They have a wonderful ability to copy any picture you request: Want your own Mona Lisa? This is the place to get it. They also produce good portraits of family or pets at fair prices. Again, do expect to bargain.

If you like things loud, with crowds and late nights, and being jam-packed on a beach infested with personal watercraft, this is the place to be. We prefer the tranquility found just a mile or so north or south.

> *This was an area that rated high in the "ugliest tourist destinations" poll mentioned at the beginning of this chapter. It compares with Torremolinos, on Spain's Costa del Sol (another spot that got the "ugly" award), or parts of Florida's panhandle better known as the "redneck Riviera." The rebuilding that is going on here, described in more detail in* The Tsunami *(see page 16) will eliminate some of the more unsightly aspects of the area.*

Phuket City

The most populous part of the island is on the western coast and around Phuket City, known as **Phuket Town** until 2004 when its size warranted the name change. Many signs have not been changed and most people still refer to it as Phuket Town. This is the center of trade and commerce on the island and most government offices are here. Remarkable examples of Sino-Portuguese buildings recall earlier days when tin-mining was an important part of island life. Many Chinese came to the area to work in the mines, followed by Portuguese traders who set up shop.

The main Phuket market is held daily in the city center and if you can arrive early – it's open from 1am to 5am – you will be enthralled by the varieties of food that is traded. Trucks rumble into town loaded with pineapples and bananas. Others come with chicken or pork carcasses. The aroma of spices and fresh produce makes it a morning to remember. You will find many hotel chefs, or their assistants, selecting provisions for their kitchens. Finding someone who speaks English will be a problem. Finding somewhere to have breakfast will not. Numerous cafés, mostly run by Chinese, offer interesting cuisine at very low prices and are open throughout the night.

The population of the island is around 400,000 of which 80% is Buddhist and 15% Muslim. Mountains cover 70% of the island. The major tourist hotels are on the western shores, starting just north of the airport on Nai Yang Beach. If your flight arrives from the west you feel like you're about to land among the beach chairs on the final approach.

Most northerly major hotel is the new **JW Marriott Resort & Spa**, a giant complex with a lobby the size of Grand Central Station. A huge infinity pool at the side of the lobby would serve as an Olympic site but this feature is for decoration, not for swimming. Adjoining the hotel is the **Marriott Vacation Village**, probably the finest time-share project that Marriott operates. It feels like nobody was watching the pennies when this Marriott project was constructed. The complex is on Malkhao Beach. The only beach north of this is Sai Kaew Beach, which is close to the Sarasin Bridge.

One snag with staying at the Marriott is its location away from town. The major boating centers on the eastern shore, the **Yacht Haven** and the **Boat Lagoon**, are not too far away but it will take at least an hour to get to the southern end of the island.

Closest quality hotel to the airport is the **Pearl Village Resort**, which adjoins the **Nai Yang National Park** on Nai Yang Beach.

The park is well worth the 20 Baht admission charge and makes an ideal spot for a picnic and just watching local fisherman at work. It's a simple drive from the airport if you follow the coast rather than heading inland for the faster route to town.

To the south is **Nai Thon Beach**, one of the few less developed areas on the island. This exceptional beach is shared by three small hotels: The **Andaman White Beach Resort**, the **Phuket Naithon Resort** and the **Phuket Nature Home Resort**. This is a quiet, relaxing area with pleasing beach restaurants. Farther along is the fantastic **Trisara**. Driving around the side roads in the area will give you a good insight into typical Thai village life.

Bang Tao Beach is farther to the south and home to the luxury resorts set in the Laguna area. Laguna is a whole world on its own. It is not unlike the Lucayan concept on Freeport, Grand Bahama Island. The area has everything. There are luxury hotels, apartments, a shopping center, lagoons, a by product from the bygone days of tin mining, restaurants, a golf course and several new housing projects. Expect to pay more for everything here. It is mostly new and growing rapidly.

Farther to the south are the beaches of **Surin** and **Kamala**. Surin was the site of the first golf course constructed in Thailand but is now a park and grazing area for buffalo. The beach is ideal for water sports of all kinds but can be very dangerous during the monsoon season because of a strong undercurrent. There are several very expensive housing projects in the area and also some quality hotels.

Kamala was until recently a quiet village. The opening of the multi-million dollar theme park **FantaSea**, which is one of the most popular tourist attractions for evening entertainment, has changed that, and the road has changed that. The road follows the coast to Patong. On the way you will see more new housing projects. At the start of 2005 there were 125 different developments under construction on the island. Most are aimed at foreigners, like us, who are seeking a holiday home or a planning a new life on this tropical isle. There are prices to suit everyone, from luxury homes like the glamorous Surin Hills costing over one million dollars to the more affordable three-bedroom home for $85,000 at **Land & House** in Chalong. The name of the development is not exactly mind boggling but the prices are. The price includes a nicely landscaped garden with each having a special feature like a pond and fountain or a Thai sala. There is no pool with the home but there is an enormous clubhouse which, among other things, contains an indoor basketball court.

The drive towards Patong takes you past **Nakalay Beach** and **Kalim Beach**. The beachside road in Patong is never quiet, though there is usually a lull at dawn as the revelers stagger home and the joggers begin their morning exercise. On the south side of that metropolis of fun and frolic you pass the **Simon Cabaret**, home of the very popular transvestite show. Every night the vast parking area is crammed with mega-coaches and you wonder where all the people have come from. There are two more sandy bays concealed from the road, **Tritrang Beach** and **Freedom Beach**, before you arrive at Karon, a town that has grown rapidly from a peaceful village to its present day status as a popular tourist area. If you booked your room because of a picture that showed your hotel on the beach you are in for a disappointment. Somehow the camera omitted the road that separates hotels from sand and that road is a busy one with a continual stream of tuk-tuks and motorcycles. And remember traffic here drives on the left, or is supposed to.

> *The "drive-on-the-left" rule does not apply to the motorcycles that come from all directions with an assortment of attachments; these are capable of carrying entire families or mobile kitchens purveying spicy meals on wheels.*

Crime In Phuket

Monthly crime figures issued by Phuket police usually put gambling as the top transgression, followed by being an illegal immigrant and involvement with drugs coming in third place.

We have a friend here, Kuhn Noi, a tailor who operates from the Crystal Hotel in Karon. He moved here from Bangkok 16 years ago to leave the crowds. Then there were fields and no hotels. Today he thinks he is back in Bangkok. Not true. This is like a deserted suburb compared to the capital city. Incidentally, *Kuhn* is a wonderful word and the polite way to address any Thai. It means Mr. or Mrs. or Ms. or Miss. If you're Fred, you become Kuhn Fred and the wife is Kuhn Mabel, if her name is Mabel.

As you reach the village of Kata Noi you have the choice of following the coast along Kata Beach or cutting off the corner. In the triangle that is created by the shortcut lie the massive **Club Med** complex and the smaller **Kata Beach Hotel**.

Once you pass **The Boathouse**, our favorite place to stay, and the very inexpensive **Kata Sun Hotel**, with large rooms at small prices, the road takes you up over the mountain ridge. Atop is the **View Point**. This is the place for views, obviously. You can look back at the beaches of Kata Noi, Kata and Karon and ahead towards Nai Harn beach. The picturesque island in front of you is Ko Pu Island.

You can then drive down to Nai Harn beach and make your way out to **Phromthep Cape**, the island's southernmost point. This is the perfect, and most popular, place to view the sunset. Advice: Linger a little longer after the sun has gone down to avoid the traffic that heads back towards town.

A Medical Moment

Like many men I do not suffer sickness lightly. On a visit to Phuket I was coughing and sneezing and was convinced that I was seriously ill. I was not, but nobody could convince me otherwise and a suggestion that I visit the doctor was acted upon promptly.

I was driven to the offices of a Dr. Chusak in Kata, ☎ 07633 0115. The front of the clinic is a counter, open to the world, where medicines are dispensed. At the side of that, just two steps from the street, a half-dozen flimsy white plastic chairs served as the doctor's waiting room. The wait to see the physician was brief. A mother with two sons departed his office and I was in. There were no forms to fill in about health and welfare and nobody even asked my name or age. In perfect English the doctor asked a half-dozen questions about previous health problems while he checked my vital signs. He then announced I had a cold and cough, no fever, and if I took the medicine he was prescribing I would recover quickly. In our short encounter he convinced me he knew his business and I was feeling better already. I asked about payment and he said that would be included with the medication. Back on the street the attractive young pharmacist counted out three different pills, labeled them in English and added a bottle of an American cough suppressant. She then presented a bill, which amounted to a little less than $11 – about half of what I would have paid in the US for the cough medicine. There are two international hospitals in Phuket that take care of visitors and they have excellent English-speaking staffs. You pay a bit more than at the clinics but it is wise to go to the hospital if you are very ill.

She offered a receipt, which she explained I could use to reclaim against any insurance I might have. I did not have the nerve to submit the bill. Nobody would have believed it and anyway it did not come anywhere close to the deductible. Why so cheap? I doubt the doctor needs malpractice insurance, he doesn't operate in a high-rent district and there were no old magazines cluttering up the waiting area. I did recover quickly but later bought another bottle of the cough medicine. For that I paid the equivalent of 30 cents.

The unusual Thai sense of humor came into play the following morning at breakfast.

"You must be seven today," a waiter told me. "Seven," I said. "I don't understand."

"Well, you were sick yesterday so you must be seven today."

Lots of giggling from the waitresses followed. I returned to my eggs and bacon.

A Driving Tour

The drive along the eastern side of the island will take you past Chalong and into Phuket City. Other major points farther along the eastern shore are the Boat Lagoon complex, home to some floating mega-palaces, and farther on the more tranquil Yacht Haven. Phang Nga Bay is off to our right. This is the vast stretch of water on the eastern side of Phuket that is home to those strange little limestone islands. Huge fingers extend from the aqua green waters and point to the brilliant blue sky. **James Bond** and **Phi Phi** are among the islands. Others contain eerie caves, which you can visit by inflatable kayak. In the center of some of the islands (hongs in Thai) are secluded lagoons ringed by the high craggy cliffs.

This journey around the island can take three or four hours, depending on when and where you stop. There's a lot more to see away from the major highways. It's easy to get lost – as we well know. Fortunately a smiling face has always appeared to point us in the right direction.

Things to See

■ Temples

These edifices with their ornate gold and red trimmings crop up everywhere with the same regularity as those hamburger havens with the golden arches. It would not surprise me if McDonalds got their entrance idea from here. The most frequently visited temple in Phuket is **Wat Chalong**. We climbed four or five flights of stairs in the main building and were faced with a large glass dome. This, we were told, contained some of the bones of Buddha and it was a great honor that such a treasure was here in Phuket.

A week-long fair is held in the temple grounds every year, normally at the end of January. Our visit there showed once again how well priced things are. The attractions for younger members of the family were incredibly inexpensive. Most of the rides and side shows cost about a dime. Another plus was that the stalls selling clothes and assorted goodies all displayed prices and there was no haggling. And no tailor touts. There were numerous stalls selling food that was cooked while you waited.

Wat Phra Thong (Golden Buddha Temple) in Thalang contains a Buddha that is partially buried in the temple floor. According to legend, those who try to dig it up will die. There is small museum alongside the main building featuring an unusual collection of curios and crafts. Most temples have a shop selling film, postcards and souvenirs.

Wat Phranangsang, also in Thalang, was the rallying point for the islanders when the two heroines took on the Burmese in 1785. **Wat Cherngtalay**, just east of Cherng Talay town, features many large and colorful murals depicting Buddhist themes. There are numerous Chinese temples and shrines throughout Phuket City, and are at their busiest during Chinese New Year and the Phuket Vegetarian Festival. A gigantic Chinese temple is under construction on the main road that links the airport and Phuket City. Due to the tremendous amount of work to be done nobody is giving a completion day.

We came upon a very small and friendly Chinese temple hidden away in Phuket City, the **Shrine of the Serene Light**, down an alleyway across from the Thai Farmers Bank on Phang Nga Road. After visiting the shrine we were offered tea by the ladies looking after the temple, who asked if we would like to join them for lunch. We declined but were invited to return on another day to share a meal with them. During our brief visit several of the neighborhood Chinese families came by to bow their heads at the shrine while burning incense sticks. The temple had a very ornately carved and painted wooden façade, and the interior walls were decorated with intricate murals. It was a hushed little enclave just yards from the hectic city traffic.

Most people visit temples as part of a sightseeing tour but you are welcome to go on your own. Remember to wear sensible, modest clothes that show respect. And take off your shoes before entering the temples. You will note the monks wear slip-on sandals and are able to enter the places of worship without stopping.

■ Nai Thon Beach

We discovered this quiet beach on our way to Trisara and the Andaman White Beach Resort. It is a little off the beaten track but the journey is well worth the effort. Taking the road to the airport from town, drive past Thalang and look for a flashing-light intersection before the airport turnoff. The road is signposted for Nai Thon Beach and it takes you through some lush countryside past rubber plantations before coming to the coast. The beach itself remains quiet throughout the year and there are sun-beds available for rent. The sea is calm during the November-to-April high season and there is ample parking alongside the beach. There are low-cost houses and bungalows to rent along the road, which also has several shops and cafés. Neat place if you want to enjoy swimming away from the crowds. If you continue along the road it will take you past the Andaman White Beach Resort and Trisara. Continuing along will bring you to either the road back to Thalang or into the Laguna area.

■ Snake shows

This rates on the same level as bungee jumping. However, Thailand is home to more than 50 species of snakes, including several poisonous varieties, something that nobody trying to sell us a home has mentioned. There is a safe way to view these squiggling critters and that is a snake show. These are held throughout the day at various points on the island: **The Phuket Shooting Range**, admission 300 Baht, ☎ 07628 0130, in Chalong, just west of the Chalong circle on Route 4028; the **Andaman Cobra Show** on Soi Ta-iad, off Chao Fa East Road, a few kilometers north of Chalong Circle; and at the small **Snake Farm** near Simon Cabaret, just south of Patong. Those who have attended tell us that the snake handlers charm, caress, harass and even kiss various species of snakes, including spitting vipers and king cobras.

■ The Yellow Line

Painting a yellow stripe down the center of a road may not be your idea of fun, but here in Kata Beach is was an all-day attraction that in my opinion was more enjoyable than elephant trekking or watching orchids grow (both of those events are considered big time in Phuket).

The six-man Thai team arrived carrying bundles of fraying string, a good supply of traffic cones, a large tin of gooey yellow paint and a machine that may well have been salvaged from the Ark.

As the day progressed more joined the team, not I think as fully paid members but as a means of passing the time. For some it was a welcome break from standing outside tailors' shops asking unknown visitors where they were from and suggesting their wardrobes could handle an upgrade. Not an inappropriate comment since most of the victims wore T-shirts celebrating events decades passed with shorts stained and burned from cheap Thai curry.

The painting program started with a nail being dug into the existing yellow line, which had almost faded away. A string was attached to the nail and stretched out to another nail a good fifteen paces away. The cones were duly scattered and the machine, hauled by one man, pushed by another into the center of the thoroughfare. A generous dollop of the yellow substance was poured into the machine allowing a little to spill onto the road surface not due to be painted. This small amount was sufficient for several of the workers to step in and spread at random creating a not unattractive pattern to the road. It appeared that the road to Kata Beach was not exactly paved with gold, but more spattered by a dose of yellow measles.

The line-painting proceeded at a pace surpassed by sleepy snails. Passing traffic was curtailed to one-way only and a healthy tail-back developed at both ends of the town. It enabled many of the drivers to exit their vehicles and have lengthy discussions with their fellow countrymen about the previous evening's Thai boxing bouts, TV soaps or whatever it is that Thai people deem important.

It should be noted that the road is extremely narrow. There is just room for two small cars to pass at the best of times. Now we have the problem of an approaching bus which, by virtue of its girth, needs to straddle the center line. The nails and string are removed and cones, machine, and manpower move to the side. The bus passes and manages to flatten the yellow line to a much grander width than the machine had managed to do.

Like any spectacle interest wanes and we decided to move on. We left our taxi at one end of the proceedings, walked to the other and took another taxi, saving ourselves a good 45 minutes. When we returned that evening the job was completed and the crew made another appearance the following day at Karon Beach. We will not be available to attend. They move towards Phuket City in the New Year.

Many years ago we visited a cathedral in Toledo, Spain, where our tour guide showed us part of the choir stalls. The wood carving was extraordinary. It had been the life's work of one man who had eventually gone blind in the ill-lit environment. I thought at the time what a tremendous thing for future generations to think that their forebear had created such a wonderful piece of work. Hard to think of a Thai in years to come telling a boy that his granddad's life had been spent splattering yellow lines around the island.

■ Seashell Museum

We almost gave this place a miss but glad that we did not. Located on the southern end of the island, across from the Evason resort, the displays of shells and fossils were extremely well done and worth the 200 Baht admission. There are over 2,000 species of shells on display that include a left-handed noble volute – a one-of-a-kind goodie for shell collectors – golden pearl, giant clams large enough to engulf a child and fossils dating back 350 million years. It has taken the Patamahanthin brothers over 30 years to amass the collection. Typical souvenir shop attached, but with everything coated in shells.

■ Gibbon Rehabilitation Center

Thailand's wild gibbon population suffers from the poaching of baby gibbons for illegal sale as pets. This often involves killing the fiercely protective mother gibbons, and later, the abandonment or killing of matured aggressive pets. The Gibbon Rehabilitation project, a research division of the **Wild Animal Rescue Foundation of Thailand**, located in the Khao Pha Theaw National Park near Bang Pae Waterfall, tries to rehabilitate abandoned pet gibbons to the wild. Donations and T-shirt purchases will help keep the project, the only one of its kind in the world, going. We were delighted to see so many tourists taking an interest in the project during our visit. Their urgent need is for more volunteer helpers as the work is all done by these hard-working non-paid conservationists. They also stress the importance of not having your photo taken with a gibbon, a popular tourist attraction, as this simply adds to the reduction of wild gibbon numbers. More info: e-mail gibbon@samart.co.th or www.wartai.org, ☎ 07626 0492. There is a 200 Baht per-person charge to enter the national park, but none of that money is for the gibbon project, just for the maintenance of the park which, we are pleased to report, was being used by local people for picnicking and swimming in the river that tumbles through the rocks from the nearby Bang Pae Waterfall.

■ Phuket Orchid Garden and Thai Village

The large orchid nursery with a number of rare and exotic varieties is just one of the attractions here. There are four restaurant pavilions, a children's playground, handicraft shops and a twice-daily cultural show featuring demonstrations of Thai dancing and Thai martial arts. Show times: 11am and 5:30pm. You can arrange to have boxes of orchids delivered to your hotel on your departure date. The cut blooms last well and make ideal presents. Located off Thepkasattri Road on the north end of Phuket City. Open daily 9am-9pm. Admission: 400 Baht, ☎ 07621 4860, 07623 7400.

■ Butterfly & Insect Farm

Small but pleasant attraction with nice gardens, lots of bugs, butterflies, birds and a waterfall. If you're driving, leave Tesco Lotus in the direction of Phuket City; go one kilometer and turn left. The attraction is signposted and will be a half-kilometer down on the right. Open daily from 9am-5:30pm. Adult admission 150 Baht; children under 10, 60 Baht. 71/6 Soi Phaniang, Phuket City, ☎ 07621 5616, 07621 0861, www.phuketbutterfly.com.

■ What does a massage cost?

This is a question similar to, How much is a bottle of perfume? It depends on quality, location and time. Most popular are the beach massages, normally lasting an hour and giving you a head-to-toe treatment. As a rule of thumb, or rather rule of magical massaging fingers, the more expensive the hotel the more expensive the massage will be on the beach in front of it. Prices range from 200 Baht along the busy Patong waterfront to 400 Baht in front of the upmarket Laguna resorts. On the beach in front of the JW Marriott we paid 300 Baht for the best 60-minute beach massage we have ever enjoyed.

Again prices vary widely once you step inside an air conditioned parlor. There are dozens of them scattered around the island as well as the top of the line spas in the luxury resorts. So much about a massage depends upon the training and proficiency of the masseuse. And the best are not necessarily employed at the top spas. Many times it is a question of trial and error. And, somewhat like Scotch whisky, there's no such thing as a bad one, some are just better than others.

A good example of a massage center with low prices but with well-trained operators is the **Tum Rub Thai Massage Center** at the southern end of Kata Beach. Here's a brief run down on their prices: Regular Thai massage, one hour 200 Baht, two hours 300 Baht; foot-reflexology one hour, 250 Baht (our favorite, and the hour passes all too quickly); aroma oil massage (their most expensive treatment), 400 Baht for an hour. They have "side-orders" of manicure and pedicure for 100 Baht each. The center is open daily from 10am to 11pm, ☎ 09599 1487 or 09464 6695.

■ Phuket Zoo

The daily shows featuring elephants, crocodiles and monkeys are the main attraction. Wide variety of birds and animals make this a popular spots for locals as well as tourists. On Soi Phalai, near Chalong. Open daily 8:30am-6pm. Admission: foreign adults 400 Baht; foreign children 200 Baht; Thais 80 Baht, ☎ 07638 1227 or 07638 1337.

AUTHOR'S TIP: *All children are admitted free to the Phuket Zoo on Children's Day in January.*

■ Phuket Aquarium

The Phuket Aquarium reopened in April 2005 after undergoing a two-year, $2 million renovation. The aquarium's major attraction is a 10-meter-long underwater glass tunnel similar to the one at Singapore's Underworld aquarium. The attraction is open every day from 8:30am until 4pm. Admission is 100 Baht for adults and 50 Baht for children, ☎ 07639 1128.

■ Khao Phra Thaeo National Park

It is hard to believe that 70% of Phuket is mountains and, despite all the development, much of the island is still forest. But this park in the northern part of the island is Phuket's last significant virgin rain forest. If you only have a short time to spend then the walk up to the Tonsai waterfall is a must. For those who want a longer spell in the tropical forest there is an eight-kilometer trek right through the park from Bang Pae waterfall to Ton Sai. Guides are available at the park, and if you opt for the longer trek a guide is highly recommended, particularly if you hope to see some of the wildlife that abides in the forest. A small museum and information center is near the bottom of the waterfall. To get here take Route 4027 east from the Heroines' Roundabout for seven kilometers. The entrance is well signposted on the left. National parks in Thailand charge foreigners a 200 Baht entrance fee.

Things to Do

■ Golf

Phuket has six excellent golf courses and all are open to non-members. Forgot your clubs? They all rent out equipment, everything from shoes to umbrellas. Most insist you take a caddy and that will cost you about 200 Baht.

Laguna Phuket Golf Course, 34 Moo 4, Srisoonthorn Road, Cherng, Talay, ☎ 07632 4350, fax 07632 4351, www.lagunaphuket.com. This 18-hole par 72 course was designed by Max Wexler and opened in December 1991. The course, in the Laguna complex, features lagoons, coconut groves and generous, undulating fairways. Facilities include a driving range, putting greens, practice bunkers and chipping areas. The front nine holes, a par 36, meander through a once flourishing coconut plantation. Players must be exact on their tee shots, as water comes into play on five out of the nine holes. Eight of the back nine holes provide water hazards. Additional balls can be purchased at the pro shop. Golf instruction is available at the driving range and practice area. Golf carts are not available. Dress code: golf shirts with collars, short or long tailored trousers, socks and golf shoes. Green fees start at 2,900 Baht.

Blue Canyon Country Club, 165 Moo 1, Thepkassatri Road, Thalang, ☎ 07632 7440, fax 07632 7449, www.bluecanyonclub.com. The club has two courses set in 730 acres in a secluded valley. Canyon Course: The original 18 holes, par 72, was designed by Yoshikazo Kato in 1991. This championship course has featured in many major golf tournaments including the Johnnie Walker Classic. The Lakes Course runs through a landscape of lakes and natural canyons with a constant gentle 10 mph wind providing an added dimension to the game. Among those who have played here are Tiger Woods, Greg Norman and Ernie Els. Green fees start at 2,400 Baht.

Loch Palm Golf Club, 38 Moo 5, Vichit Songkram Road, Kathu, ☎ 07632 1929, fax 07632 1927, www.lochpalm.com. This 18-hole par 72 course was designed by Dr. Sukitti Klangwisai and opened in November 1998. The course is built around Phuket's largest lake, Crystal Lake, and has more than 1,400 palms lining its fairways. The course has smooth slopes and dramatic elevation changes to test all levels of skill. Optional golf carts are available. Green fees start at 2,600 Baht.

Phuket Country Club, 80/1 Vichit Songkram, Kathu, ☎ 07632 1038, fax 07632 1721, www.phuketcountryclub.com. The club is made up of two courses totaling 27 holes and was opened in May 1989. They were designed by Dr. Sukitti Klangvisai and built over a reclaimed tin mine. The Old Course, par 72, is set in a valley with fairways meandering through the hills. The Country Club Course is a challenging 3,575 yards par 37, 9-hole course, particularly suitable for the low handicap golfer. Green fees start at 2,350 Baht.

Mission Hills Phuket Golf Club Resort & Spa, 195 Moo 4 Para, Pha-Khlok, Thalang, ☎ 07631 0888, fax 07631 0899, www.missionhillsphuket.com. Newest of the Phuket courses, Mission Hills opened the first 18 of its 27 holes at the end of 2004. The course, which has spectacular views of Phang Nga Bay is part of a homes and hotel complex and was designed by Nicklaus Design associate John Cope. Odd touch: Project manager for the golf course was aptly named Kuhn Golf. Green fees for hotel guests: 3,000 Baht for the 18-hole ocean view course and 1,500 for the nine-hole bay view course. Visitors pay 3,800 and 1,900 Baht.

Thai Muang Golf Course & Marina, ☎ 07657 1533, fax 07657 1214, www.thaimuangbeach.com. Not on Phuket Island but just 30 minutes by car from Phuket International Airport in Phang Nga province. This 18-hole par 72 course was designed by Perry Dye and opened in December 1958. It has a superb location along 2.5 kilometers of immaculate beach. For those who want to stay longer the Thai Muang Beach Chalets adjoin the course. When we visited the course looked in great shape but unfortunately the chalets did not. Green fees from 2,200 Baht.

■ Submarine Dive

The Phuket Submarine Co. Ltd., at Chalong Pier, ☎ 07628 1560, www.phuketsubmarine.com offers five submarine trips a day starting at 8am. The submarine takes you down 30 meters of Phuket's southeast coast to get close to fish, reefs and coral. Cost of the trip, including transfers to the pier, is 2,500 Baht for adults and 1,800 Baht for children. Go on one of the early morning trips and the company includes a speed boat trip to Coral Island with lunch included.

■ Bungee Jumping

This is something we have not tried, nor do we care to. But if your idea of fun is jumping from a great height there are two places to have at it in Phuket. **Jungle Bungy Jump** in Kathu District promises "The best fun you can have with your pants on!" There you jump from a 50-meter tower over water. The second venue, **World Bungy Patong**, claims to be Southern Thailand's highest bungee. Located on Sai Namyen Road at the back of Patong, ☎ 07634 5185. Open daily 10am-7pm. Price: 1,400 Baht per jump. Hard to believe you have to pay for this. And that's enough money for four dinners in Phuket City.

Mini-golf

Fire-breathing dragons, an active volcano, T-Rex and brontosaurus replicas and eerie jungle sounds make for an exciting round of mini-golf. And a welcome relief from bungee jumping. **Dino Park Mini Golf** says it is great fun for the whole family, which is more than can said for the bungee jumping. The Jurassic-themed restaurant and bar suggested for a post-game drink or meal. Look for the hungry elephant. Open from 10am-midnight; best enjoyed in the cooler evening hours. 119 Patak Road, Karon Beach. Admission: Adults 240 Baht; Children (ages four-12) 180 Baht, ☎ 07633 0625, www.dinopark.com.

Whitewater Rafting

Closest spot for this adventure is north in Phang Nga Province on the Songproak River. **Phuket Sealand Co. Ltd.**, 125/1 Phang Nga Road, Phuket, ☎ 07622 2900, fax 07623 2905, www.phuketsealand.com, offers the rafting as part of an all-day adventure and will arrange pick-up from your hotel in Khao Lak, (75 kilometers from the starting camp) Krabi (80 kilometers) or Phuket (85 kilometers). In addition to the four kilometers of rafting through some choppy waters the day out includes elephant trekking, a four-wheel-drive visit to a waterfall and a Thai lunch. Cost is 2,500 Baht for adults and 1,800 Baht for children.

Scuba

Phuket rates in the top 10 scuba diving destinations in the world. There are lots of reasons why, but the three main ones are the warm water (it averages 28 degrees Celsius), great underwater visibility and spectacular reef and rock formations. There are dive centers all over the island offering all manner of diving opportunities. You can take day-trips or live-aboard cruises to the **Similan Islands** and **Burma Banks**. Here are some of the top sites:

Shark Point (Hin Musang)

About 25 kilometers east of Chalong, about one hour by speedboat. The reef gets its name from the leopard sharks that settle on the sandy bottom. One of the three limestone pinnacles of the reef breaks the surface. Spectacular soft corals and sea fans highlight the site. This is a government-protected marine sanctuary where commercial and spear fishing are prohibited, as is the collection of marine life.

The Racha Islands

There are two major areas south of Phuket to explore, **Racha Yai** and then farther south **Racha Noi**. Racha Yai, with 10 dive sites, is a perfect spot for beginners, where schools of false barracuda circle over a reef. Racha Noi suits more experienced divers because the currents are stronger, and to fully enjoy the site, which includes a wooden shipwreck, you need to dive deeper.

Ko Doc Mai

Stopping-off point heading to Shark Point, this site does not always have the greatest visibility but the dive is worthwhile since it offers one of the best wall dives around, plus a couple of caves and an abundance of marine life including turtles, leopard sharks, moray eels and yellow tube coral.

Anemone Reef

A massive limestone pinnacle that rises 30 meters from the sea bottom but never comes to the surface, and presents a major navigation problem, as you will see from our next listing. As the name suggests, the area abounds with sea anemones as well as myriad tropical fish, plus grouper, snappers and the larger game fish. The pinnacle is less than a mile north of Shark Point.

King Cruiser

Phuket divers have the anemone reef to thank for this exceptional artificial reef. In 1997 the car ferry *King Cruiser*, on its way to Phi Phi Island, strayed off course, hit the reef and sank in less than an hour. It's a relatively safe dive to explore the ship from stem to stern and top to bottom. Not only is the location popular with divers but an enormous number of fish are now making their home here.

Here are some of Phuket's diver centers: **Sea Bees Diving**, 1/3 Moo 9, Viset Road, Chalong, ☎ and fax 07638 1765; **Aqua Master (Thailand) Co. Ltd.**, 273-277 Patak Road, Karon Beach, ☎ 07628 6190, fax 07628 6191; **Dive Asia**, 24 Karon Road, Kata Beach, ☎ 07633 0598, fax 07628 4033; **West Coast Divers**, 120/1-3 Rat-U-Tit 200 Pee, Patong Beach, ☎ 07634 1673, fax 07634 1515; **Genesis Liveaboards**, 18/17-18 Moo 8, Chaofa Road, Chalong, ☎ 07638 1221, fax 07638 1221; **Kata Diving Service**, Kata Garden Resort, 121/1 Moo 4, Patak Road, Karon, ☎ 07633 0392, fax 07633 0393; **Scandinavian Diver Co., Ltd.**, 58/6 Soi Patong Resort, Bangla Road, Patong Beach, ☎ 07629 4225, fax 07629

2408; **Scuba Cat Diving**, 94 Taweewong Road, Patong, ☎ 07629 3120, fax 07629 3122; **White And Blue Dive Club**, 71/5 Moo 10, Chao-Fa Road, Chalong, ☎ 07628 1007, fax 07628 1280.

■ Horseback Riding

There are two riding clubs in Phuket, both offering tours and instruction for people of all ages and abilities. **Phuket Bang Tao Riding Club**, 394 Moo 1, Bangtao Beach, at the entrance to Laguna Resorts. Cost 660 Baht per hour, ☎ 07632 4199 or 07632 4099. **Phuket Riding Club**, 95 Viset Road, Rawai. Charges between 300 Baht and 500 Baht an hour, depending on degree of instruction required. Open 7am-6:30pm, ☎ 07628 8213.

■ The Elephant Trek

There were those in our family who were determined to elephant trek. I was not one of them. I had the task of making the bookings. We had selected a trekking site that was relatively flat, as we had been warned ahead of time that the more mountainous the trek the more uncomfortable it would be. I was shown a multitude of pictures of folk with fake smiles enjoying their ride on jumbo's back. The two-hour safari was suggested and I eventually bartered the ticket tout down to a bare 30 minutes. For this the majority of those who took the trek were later truly thankful.

Price was then discussed and I discovered there was only one class available, upgrades did not exist, frequent traveler programs were out but smoking was permitted. Water was available for an extra charge and should be purchased prior to boarding since there was no on-trek service. Granddaughter Lindsey Ana did not measure high enough on the ruler provided and therefore would travel free. Since she was the only one who enjoyed the trip this was a nice bonus.

We had not made reservations and that was no problem since we were the only people there. However, minutes after our two elephants began their 30-minute plod; a bus load of Japanese tourists arrived and caused a minor panic at the check-in area.

Lindsey, daughter-in-law Belén and Lindsey Ana boarded the first of the two animals assigned to the Evans family. Watching Lindsey step from boarding gate to seat in a most uncomfortable manner convinced me that I had done the right thing by staying on the ground. Son Chuck traveled on the second beast, which appeared to be a somewhat smaller model and a little younger. This appeared to be of little benefit since he seemed as uncomfortable as the others on the larger version. The seats I believed to be salvaged from pre-war (World War II, not Iraqi) London buses and were held into place by a series of cords, the last of which was very thin and extended under the elephant's tail.

When the transport moved from sight, our guide suggested we adjourn to the coffee shop. To achieve this we had to cross a very uncertain-looking rickety wooden bridge. My concerns were allayed when I was told that the elephants crossed the bridge on a regular basis. What they did not tell me was that only very tiny new-born elephants weighing little more than a bale of hay were allowed on the bridge – one at a time.

The coffee shop was unique and an ideal stop on any safari. Coffee was not served or any other kind of drink or refreshment. The only amenities were ample shade, an assortment of antique chairs and a ready supply of Thai newspapers written in that weird alphabet that looks like your children have gone haywire with the Crayolas.

I made a polite inquiry about the lack of coffee. I was told you could bring your own or purchase it from the entrance area, which was still clogged with Japanese tourists smothered in cameras. It would mean crossing back on the bridge. I felt more comfortable peering at the newspapers and I could understand the pictures.

Soon our trekkers returned. As some kind of punishment the elephant drivers, sitting scrunched up on the elephant's head with their legs and feet vanished somewhere beneath them, had lengthened the journey by a few minutes. The three adults agreed that it was an uncomfortable experience never to be repeated. The best part was when the animals stopped for a drink of water and the ancient seats stayed still for a few welcome minutes. The rocking motion of the elephant had all the pleasure of riding on a motorcycle with square wheels. Their admiration for the kings of Siam who regularly traveled by elephant was greatly enhanced. Since we were not interested in making a further booking we departed.

Several companies on the island organize elephant trekking together with additional attractions. **Siam Safari**, ☎ 07628 0116; **Phuket Sea Land**, ☎ 07622 2900; and **Island Safari**, ☎ 07828 1281, have English-speaking operators to take your calls.

■ Kite Surfing

Roger Van Den Akker, ☎ 07628 8258, runs a kite surfing school. Students learn the basics in shallow water before taking off to secluded beaches and bays to master this sport.

■ Target Shooting

The **Phuket Shooting Range** has a variety of weapons to rent from .22 handguns to shotguns. The place is understandably noisy. Expect to pay around 500 Baht for 10 shots depending on the weapon. Instruction is included. The range also has paintball sessions for those not wanting to use live ammo. Located in Chalong just west of the traffic circle. Open daily from 9am-6pm, ☎ 07628 0130.

■ Bowling

A popular pastime for locals. There are six bowling alleys on the island with several more under construction. Patong: **Ocean Plaza Bowling**, 31 Bangla Road, ☎ 076341 163/7. **Rock & Bowl**, Soi Kepsub 2, Sai Nam Yen Road, ☎ 07634 5165. Phuket City: **CS Bowl**, 2nd floor, Big C Supercenter, 72 Moo 5 Chalermprakiat Ror 9 Road, ☎ 07624 9260. **Ocean Bowling**, Ocean Shopping Mall, 38/1-15 Tilok-U-Thit Road, ☎ 07622 3057. **Pearl Bowling Lanes**, intersection of Montri and Phang Nga roads, ☎ 07621 1418.

■ Movies

The **Coliseum Paradise** multiplex cinema, near Robinsons department store in Phuket City, used to be the only movie house on the island. The new **Central Festival** shopping plaza changed all that in 2005 with its very lavish and comfortable six-screen operation. Seats normally cost 100 Baht a person but for 400 Baht on weekends, 300 Baht weekdays, you get a two-seater reclining couch in the back row. Or go first class for 500 Baht and get a large reclining armchair complete with blanket should you find the air conditioning just a little chilly. That price includes sodas and pop-corn during the film. You can use the facilities of a comfortable pre-movie lounge an hour prior to show time and enjoy free drinks (non-alcoholic) and a variety of munchies. Most of the films are the latest Hollywood productions in English with Thai sub titles. Times and listings appear daily in the *Bangkok Post* or *The*

Nation. Advance bookings can be made for Central Festival, ☎ 07620 9000, or for the Coliseum, ☎ 07622 0174, where the admission charge is 90 Baht. We have never watched movies in such comfort, or so inexpensively, as those we enjoyed at Festival.

■ Go-karting

There is one track on the island at Kathu at the end of Patong Hill and we have passed it several times and never seen it busy. The 600-meter track opens every day from 10am-7pm. **Patong Go-Kart** Speedway, 118/5 Vichitsongkram Road, Kathu. Charges start at 390 Baht for 10 minutes, ☎ 07632 1949.

■ Martial Arts

The combat martial art of Thai boxing or Muay Thai is both exciting to watch and a challenging sport to try. **Saphan Hin Stadium** in Phuket City has regular matches; instruction is available at several locations, including the **Phuket Thai Boxing Gym**, 82/5 Moo 4 Patak Road, Kata, ☎ 07628 1090, 07628 1200, and **Abang Marts**, Rawai, on the road leading to Kata from Chalong Circle. Instruction costs about 300 Baht per session.

■ ATV Off-roading

This is a great way to see the non-tourist side of Phuket. The two-hour program starts with a training session. Groups are small and everything is provided. First stop is at a rubber workshop in the forest to see local people collect resin from the trees and start the process of rubber production. After riding in the forests it's onto a deserted beach for a speed run. Special emphasis is given to viewing local flora and fauna. Cost 2,500 Baht, which includes pick-up from your hotel as well as refreshment en route. Bookings can be made with **Phuket Dot Com**, 4th Floor, Land Rover Building, 9/17 Moo 6, Thepkasattri Road, Phuket City, ☎ 07623 6550, fax 07623 6542.

■ Cabaret & Live Theater

Simon Cabaret: We were both raised in England where the annual Christmas pantomimes were one of the highlights of the festive season. In those productions the principal boy was always played by a woman. She was the most attractive female in the cast and always had wonderful legs and wore calf-length leather boots.

And the comic dame was always played by a man. As a result we should not have been surprised by the men dressed as women in the Simon Cabaret, Phuket's largest and most lavish transvestite show. But we were. The men look stunning in exquisite costumes as they lip-synch popular songs from around the world. The show has been a success for over a decade and most nights the 600-seat theatre is filled for the two shows. Admission is 600 Baht for the posh seats and 500 Baht for the regular ones. Show times: 7:30pm and 9:30pm. 8 Sirirach Road, Patong Beach, ☎ 07634 2011. Other transvestite performances can be enjoyed at **Andaman Queen Cabaret** and in many of the neighboring open air bars in Patong. More western-style and low-key is the **Sphinx Restaurant and Theatre**, ☎ 07634 1500 on Rat-U-Thit Road in Patong, with twice-nightly dance shows of Broadway hits and other catchy songs in its classy and intimate upstairs theatre, for only 300 Baht per show.

■ Phuket FantaSea Show

This show can truly be called a mega-extravaganza. This is a 140-acre theme park that will keep you busy from opening time at 5:30pm until they shut the gates at 11:30pm. They've tried to keep it Thai but it tends to be more like Las Vegas, with décor resembling Fort Lauderdale-Chinese. You enter through a festival village with dozens of stalls offering games, handicrafts and souvenir shopping. A buffet dinner starts at 6pm in a gigantic 4,000-seat restaurant where the food is as varied as the clientele. We stuck it out for an hour and still did not get to see all the different things on the vast buffet tables. I think they aim for quantity rather than quality. The show starts at 9pm but they ask that you be seated ahead of time in the 3,000-seat theater, which is aptly named **Palace of the Elephants**. The 75-minute show has everything from fireworks to elephants, fantastic sound and visual effects. It's not a place you need to visit twice but the kids will love it. Admission for just the show is 1,100 Baht, 800 Baht for children under 12, and if you want show and dinner the prices are 1,600 Baht for adults and 1,200 Baht for children. The show closed and reopened several times after the tsunami allowing the organization to undertake additional maintenance work and staff training. Normally in high season some 3,000 people would visit the attraction every night. That number dropped to single digits. By the time the Chinese New Year celebrations started in 2005 FantaSea reopened and the numbers began to improve.

■ Bare-boat charters

Thai Marine, with offices at the Boat Lagoon and at the Yacht Haven, has a variety of catamaran and single-hull sailboats for charter. They also have the Thai-built Prowler-powered catamaran. Rental rates include a boat boy with good local knowledge. The company also has a large range of crewed yachts available for charter, ☎ 07623 9111, fax 07623 8974, www.thaimarine.com.

■ Cruising

Phang Nga Bay is a wonderful place for sailing or power-boating since the waters are well protected. It was amazing how many boats were out in the bay when the tsunami hit on December 26, 2004, and were in no way affected. We met a couple from South Africa who had been out sailing all day. They had no idea of the devastation that had been caused until they came in to dock and saw so many vessels washed up on the shoreline. In general, even when the Andaman Sea is too rough to navigate – such as during the monsoon season – you'll find comfortable waters in the bay.

■ Deep-sea Fishing

The available fishing grounds in the Phuket area extend far beyond the nearby waters, to **Krabi**, a province about 75 kilometers to the east of Phuket, the two **Phi Phi Islands** and the **Similan Islands**. To meet the needs of the ever-increasing game fishers, dozens of charter companies have sprung up in Phuket, Krabi and Phi Phi offering boats and equipment for hire. Phuket has become the top game-fishing destination in Southeast Asia. Fighting fish species available in the Andaman Sea include marlin, sailfish, tuna, dolphin, wahoo, barracuda, king mackerel, cobia, queen fish and African pompano. The **Wahoo Big Game Fishing Co. Ltd.**, 48/20 Moo 9, Chalong, ☎ 07628 1510, fax 07628 0775, www.wahoo.ws, operates four big-game fishing boats offering day charters and night charters in addition to extended live-on-board safaris. They also have an office in Patong at 108/3 Thaweewong Road, ☎ 07634 1379, fax 07629 3040.

Phuket Island Hopper Co. Ltd., 29/12 Moo 1, Thepprathan Road, Rasada, Sirey Island, ☎ 07625 2606, www.phuket-island-hopper.com. This small company operates a fascinating combination of sea and land adventures from a tiny island off Phuket City. Even if you don't use their services the beach in front of their operation provides stunning views of numerous islands in Phang Nga

Bay. The beach is not suitable for swimming, but sitting under the shade trees with the views is a welcome break from the nearby hassle of Phuket City. The company operates different half-day and full-day trips for snorkeling and sightseeing to Yao Yai Island, the Phi Phi Islands, Raya Islands or Krabi. Costs start at 1,200 Baht for a six-hour outing. The company also has a small bungalow, restaurant and swimming pool close to the beach and can organize longer trips with an overnight stay. They can custom-build a trip depending upon your interest, be it bird watching or wildlife study.

The joy of boating, on your own, or with a crew, is that you can avoid the islands on the normal tourist itinerary. Some of the islands – there are at least 40 – are inhabited but not visited by day-trippers. On Ko Maak there is a small fishing community whose lifestyle remains unchanged despite the busy goings on in Phuket. If you do drop anchor here don't be surprised that you can't buy souvenirs or supplies.

Some of the islands do have accommodation if you want to get away from the Phuket scene. See the Island listings at the end of the *Where to Stay* section, page 234.

There are several places to stay on Ko Yao Noi, which is right in the middle of the bay, halfway between Phuket and Krabi. As you would expect there is not a lot to do on the island except enjoy its natural wonders, but the local residents will happily show you their prowess as fishing folk and how they work with rubber trees. They are anxious to preserve their way of life and expect visitors to show decorum by dressing modestly and not drinking alcohol in public. It's perfectly acceptable to imbibe at the resorts.

■ Coral Island Crowds

Jaruwan Foosaksomboon has developed an incredible marine business on the shores of Phang Nga Bay. From her office adjoining the Chalong Pier, Kuhn Jaruwan, general manager of **Nikorn Marine Company**, operates a fleet of boats to suit any tourist need. Perhaps her biggest claim to fame is the development of Coral Island, better known locally as Hey Island, where her organization takes as many as 500 visitors a day to swim, snorkel, and parasail. Guests get an elaborate lunch with a whole steamed fish shared between four, soup, tempura vegetables, rice and chicken followed by a plate of tropical fruit. The whole day out sells for 950 Baht, including transfers between any Phuket hotel and the 15-minute speed-boat trip to the island. Snorkel equipment is loaned free of charge and for a few Baht more you can sample parasailing, helmet diving or water skiing.

The trip is a bargain but you get to share the fine beach with lots of people. In addition to the guests that Nikorn handles, other operators use the island too and on a busy day over 1,000 people can flock to its shores. Despite the vast number there is an incredible variety of tropical fish swimming close to shore, the perfect place for beginners to gain confidence with a mask and snorkel.

We enjoyed our day relaxing in a deck chair – also included in the price – but next time we visit the island we'll do it after 3pm when most of the day-trippers are on their way back to Phuket.

The island is deserted at night except for a handful of illegal aliens and everything for the numerous visitors – food, staff and equipment – is ferried out each morning by longtail boat. It takes some organizing but to Kuhn Jaruwan it is just a part of her daily job, since she also organizes fishing charters and hires out speed boats. She offers anyone who turns up at her office with a copy of this guide a discount from her published tariff. Nikorn's Website: www.phuketmarinetour.com, ☎ 07638 3951, fax 07628 0371.

Longtail-boat ferries make daily trips to Ko Yao Noi from Bang Rong Pier on the east cost of Phuket. The fare is 50 Baht for the hour-long journey. Departures are at 9:30am, noon and 5pm. Return times are one hour later. That means if you can handle four hours of longtail-boat riding you could make a day-trip there for 100 Baht, which is one of the cheapest cruises we know of. It is also possible to charter longtail boats, or faster vessels, elsewhere in Phuket.

To get to Bang Rong pier take route 4027 east from the Heroines' Roundabout, then turn right at the sign for Bang Rong. A few kilometers down the lane and you'll see the pier. It was in need of repair when we saw it but we were promised it was about to be fixed. Hopefully it will be repaired by the time you get there.

■ Sea-canoe Adventure

Perched precipitously on a flimsy small flat inflatable canoe and being pushed through narrow caves may not seem much like fun. But this is what we did and it proved to be one of our more memorable days spent in Phuket. It's an early-morning pick-up from hotels for the sea canoe adventure, which departs from the eastern side of the island from a rustic, rickety pier, the crossing of which was the most perilous part of the day. A low tide meant going right to the end of the pier where we were lowered into a longtail boat, which took us into deeper water where the mother ship was moored.

Once aboard the lead guide, J.J., explained the rules and regulations about our day-long adventure as our vessel chugged towards some of those grotesque giant fingers that appear to be growing from the water. The group, limited to 30, was mostly northern European with some Orientals. All conversations were conducted in English, which we appreciated but made life a little harder for the others. The rules were all pretty basic about not jumping overboard or partaking of alcohol. Smoking was permitted and ashtrays provided (these were of no use since the wind blew ash everywhere as one approached the receptacle).

We reached the first series of caves and slid down onto the tiny bright yellow canoes that came with no mod cons. Each couple had been assigned a guide and we had the good fortune to have J.J. as our paddle master. He deftly maneuvered the canoe towards the island and lo and behold a small opening came into sight. The order to lie down was given and we passed through a little cave that leads to a small lagoon. The scene was awesome as we gazed skyward at massive limestone cliffs faces splattered with green foliage. Our earlier instructions had been that we should be quiet at all times. That order was not necessary as everyone was silent with the wonder of it all.

The inside of these islands are known as hongs. They were only discovered when aerial photography was made of the Phang Nga Islands. They are filled with unspoiled flora and fauna that has to be seen to be believed.

We moved farther down the island and entered the bat cave, an enormous cavern housing thousands of those night-flying creatures. We had been warned not to look up for fear of catching something coming down. It was extremely dark inside the cave and J.J. had given Lindsey a lantern so that she could help him navigate. He suggested she might like to shine the beam upwards to view the thousands of bats. Much to my delight she declined. The lagoon here not only had small trees growing in the cliffs but there were numerous monkeys scurrying around. We got to traverse another cave and lagoon before returning to the boat for lunch. The vessel had two decks. The guests occupied the upper one while the lower one was a large galley where chefs had been busy preparing our meal. And what a spread it was. We started with a slightly spicy fish soup, which the Thais would consider bland. There was barbecued fish, fried chicken and a few plates of unknown but tasty contents and a massive mountain of rice. Freshly baked cookies and a variety of local fruits finished off the repast. Cold drinks and coffee were available throughout the day.

After lunch we had the choice of relaxing onboard, taking a canoe for a paddle, or just swimming. We opted for the rest. Then it was time to return to the canoes for the final cave and lagoon. Granddaughter Lindsey Ana had fallen asleep and I volunteered to stay aboard with her while the rest of the family paddled off for the final adventure. It was a decision I will never regret. This is the cave where the entrance is very, very small. Not only does one have to lie down but air is taken out of the canoe so that it can be squeezed through the cave and into the lagoon. Several of our fellow adventurers turned back with mild cases of panic and claustrophobia. For some just the hissing of the escaping air had been enough to deter them from the passage.

By the time we returned to Phuket the tide had risen and we did not have to face the rickety pier. It was a wonderful excursion even if I did have to forgo the last cave. For that I have to thank Lindsey Ana.

The adventure we went on was organized by **Sea Canoe (Thailand) Co., Ltd.**, 367/4 Yaowarat Road, Phuket City, ☎ 07621 2252, fax 07621 217, www.seacanoe.net, who have been making the trip every day since 1989. Total cost for our day out, including transfers between our hotel and the pier was 2,970 Baht per adult.

For those who prefer not to make such an early-morning start the company offers a similar excursion that leaves the pier at noon and returns at 7pm. That trip includes a seafood buffet dinner and costs 3,450 Baht.

For those more adventurous the company has two- and three-day trips that combine kayaking with trekking on some of the remote islands in the bay with the nights spent in a raft house. The three-day/two-night expedition costs 13,950 Baht per person.

Shopping

Shopping in Phuket took on a new dimension in 2005 when the gigantic **Central Festival Plaza**, in the center of the island, was completed. Spread out over three levels with 246 stores, spas, and seven cinemas with stadium-type seating and wall-to-wall screens, this place cannot be covered in one day.

We went looking for a mobile phone. There were 20 stores that sold nothing but mobile or cell phones. After a lot of comparison shopping we bought a Nokia phone for under $60. The real bargain was that for an additional $15 we were able to make unlimited calls to any phone in Thailand for 100 days.

Some of the opening specials were incredible: A Black & Decker electric drill for $2 (regular price is $20) and a complete computer setup for $260. Some other prices worth noting: Contact lenses and solution were less than half the price you'd pay in Europe. Most local food items in the giant Market Place food store were everyday low. A pineapple, sliced, carved and packed, was 50¢, as were other local fruits. Wine was considerably higher than US or European prices but a bottle of Sang Som Thai rum seemed a spirited deal at $2.50.

Before Central Festival was opened many said the only places to shop in Thailand were Bangkok and Chiang Mai. But Central Festival changed that. Central is Thailand's biggest department store chain and its shares the plaza with all the great names in fashion and home care. Others with a big presence are Office Depot, Power Buy, a major retailer in electronics and appliances, and HomeWorks, a do-it-yourself center. There are more than two dozen food outlets including such American favorites as KFC, Sizzler, Pizza Hut and Starbucks.

Shortly after Festival opened its doors, another large plaza opened, the **Index Indoor Living Mall**, just a few hundred yards north. The main store here features all kinds of home furnishings in a range of prices, from expensive teak and leather to economical particle-board office furniture. Among the stores here is one of America's favorites – a TrueValue hardware store.

Shopping elsewhere there is the full array of merchandise available, from the cheap and cheerful copies of designer clothes in the street markets to fabulous gold and diamond jewelry. Here are some of the items worth buying in Phuket.

■ Jewelry & Gems

Thailand became a major player in the world of gems and jewelry in the 1980's. The **Gem Factory**, on the bypass road in the center of the island, claims to be the world's biggest gem shop. Here you can see jewelry being made and the vast showroom has something for every pocketbook. Smaller jewelry shops abound in Phuket City and in Patong Beach. Low labor costs added to the skill of Thai jewelers make custom jewelry an excellent buy.

■ Pearls

Phuket is known as the Pearl of the South and produces international-standard natural, cultured, teardrop and artificial pearls that are made from pearl dust. You can buy pearls individually, as a strand or as part of an ornament. The Japanese were the pioneers of pearl culture and set up a farm to culture pearls in Thailand on Naga Noi Island off Phuket in the 1980s. Since then, many pearl farms run by Thais have been established on islands around Phuket and some offer trips to their facilities.

■ Seashells

You'll find numerous souvenirs coated in local seashells. New legislation is limiting the shells that can be used but right now there is an ample supply of items. For a vast selection visit the stalls and shops near the **Gypsy Village** at the southern end of the island. There they make almost everything from shells – cutlery, combs and clock faces.

■ Silk

A product synonymous with Thailand. The silk is produced in the north and northeast of the country but is available here at comparable prices. Like most things, silk comes in a range of qualities. If you want the best there are several stores where you are assured of the best. At the top of the list is **Jim Thompson**, who has several shops in Phuket, throughout Thailand and elsewhere in the world. There is an outlet store in the center of the island where prices are slightly lower if you are looking for material by the yard, rather than clothes or completed products. Another excellent store is the **Shinawatra Home Mart**, not far from the Gem Factory. Our only problem with the Home Mart is the overzealous sales staff who follow inches behind you and keep putting products in your face. If you are looking for cheaper silk products, head for the street markets, where colorful scarves and squares can be purchased for just a few Baht, making ideal inexpensive gifts.

> *Beware of cheap cotton imports from India that look and sometimes feel like silk. There is a federation of Thai silk producers whose sole interest is protecting the industry and their logos will be on genuine silk products. They also include detailed instructions for the care of silk products.*

■ Batik

This cloth is produced in Phuket in brilliant colors and distinctive designs inspired by the natural surroundings, the sea and marine life. Besides cloth, there are numerous batik products – shirts, sarongs, skirts, bags and handkerchiefs – that can be purchased at shops and stalls throughout the island as well as from beach vendors.

■ Cashew Nuts

Thanks to the Phuket climate, the cashew nuts grown here are said to have a better quality than those grown elsewhere in the world. Numerous products are on sale – roasted cashew nuts with salt, cashew nuts fried with garlic, cashew nuts coated with chocolate, honeyed cashew-nut brittle and cashew apple juice. Locally produced cashews appear with good regularity in Thai dishes.

■ Nielloware

Phuket is one of several Thai cities where nielloware is produced on a commercial scale. Thai nielloware is very attractive in appearance and very durable to use because the niello alloy inlay, looking like blackish enamel, is fused and not just welded to the silver object.

■ Local Treasures

Pewter

Phuket has always been a large producer of tin. It follows that pewter ware, an amalgam of lead and tin, is a traditional craft here. Prices for plates, mugs and other items are cheaper here than other parts of Thailand.

Nang Thalung

Brightly colored shadow puppets cut from buffalo hide make excellent wall decorations.

Ceramics

Ceramics of Phuket on Wichitsongkram Road has a complete range of locally produced souvenirs.

Purses

Yan lipao is a fine grass that local women weave into beautiful purses. The art has been revived by Queen Sirikit as part of her SUPPORT project to bring prosperity to village women.

Furniture

There is an excellent selection of locally made furniture, but hardly the thing you can pass off as hand-luggage on your return flight.

Food & Household Goods

For food and daily essentials you have to visit the huge supermarkets – **Tesco, Lotus** and **Big C** – on the edge of town. Both have many other stores grouped around them. We particularly enjoy shopping at Tesco. Both the range of items and the low prices are hard to believe.

AUTHORS' TIP: *Avoid visiting Tesco on a weekend. It gets very busy. And on weekdays it's a lot quieter if you arrive early when the store opens. With the opening of the new stores at Central Festival we were told Tesco would be less crowded. Not true!*

Markets

The stalls and shops in Phuket City and at the beach resorts are full of inexpensive beachwear, bric-a-brac and souvenirs that look wonderful here but are destined to end up at a garage sale when you get home. The major shopping areas are on **Ratsada Road**, **Montri Road**, **Yaowarat Road**, **Phang Nga Road**, **Thalang Road**, **Thepkasattri Road** in Phuket City; and in Patong, **Kata** and **Karon** beaches.

Arts & Antiques

For an interesting array of arty items from Thailand, Mynamar and Cambodia take a look inside **The Palace of Art Company**, 103/3 Moo 4 Banbangjoe, Thalang, ☎ 07627 3533, fax 07627 3535. It's on the road that links the heroines' monument roundabout and the Laguna complex.

Robinsons department store in Phuket City is the place that Thais shop on a regular basis. It is has umpteen floors, all relatively small and without air conditioning but it's one of those places that if they ain't got it you don't need it.

Kata Beach

A new market full of shops and restaurants is being established at Kata Beach across the street from the Club Med and Kata Beach Resort. In addition to the existing stalls selling the normal souvenirs and beach items, several better quality shops and air conditioned restaurants are slated to operate from here. Traders are hoping that this new complex will keep tourists in the area and stop them from taking the 15-minute tuk-tuk trip to the larger shopping areas of Patong.

■ From Rockets to Rawai

We are sitting in **Don's Café** sipping coffee from an American-sized coffee cup and eating eggs sunny-side-up with home-made hash-brown potatoes and crispy bacon. At the next table three men analyze the Monday night football game with a distinctive Southern drawl. No, you didn't skip a page or pick up the wrong book. We are still in Phuket, not a Waffle House in the Deep South, just a jungle-covered mountain away from the Andaman Sea on the road to Rawai Beach.

AUTHOR'S TIP: *Incidentally, one of the advantages of being 12 hours ahead of the US East Coast is that you get to watch Monday-night football at 9am on Monday morning.*

The café is part of a mini-food empire developed by one-time rocket scientist Donald D. Battles, who deserted the US space program and landed not on the moon but in Bangkok, running a high-tech business. When the Thai economy collapsed in 1997, instead of retreating to his native Alabama, Don decided to come south to a holiday home he had established and try to find employment for his employees at a time when jobs vanished as fast as the value of the Baht.

He started with one concrete table, a barbecue grill and employees who knew as little about the catering business as he did. Today he has 35 full-time employees, a flourishing shopping mall, a first-class restaurant and a wholesale food business that is the envy of the industry.

Don says he is in his sunset years watching the area around him prosper and proudly telling of how many Thai students are getting university educations thanks to the generous welfare and benefit programs he has started through the business. He is even prouder that some of his key people now own part of this business, which is very high-tech despite its location in the middle of a tropical island. Waiters and waitresses take orders with hand-held computers and the café and restaurant area has wireless Internet access.

In addition to the café the mall has a very respectable wine cellar, a bakery providing an international assortment of breads and pastries, meat processing plant producing everything from top steaks to excellent British sausages, an international food store and an Internet café.

Festivals & Events

■ January

Phuket Gay Festival: It started as small community project and is now an annual event attracting large numbers of visitors. It takes place at the end of January at Patong Beach. Lots of beach events to take part in and strange and outrageous costumes and stage shows to watch.

Andaman Sea Rally: An annual boating event from Phuket to the Andaman Islands, open to both power and sail. Explore the spectacular sailing grounds of the Andaman Islands and enjoy it in a social atmosphere. A fun event with some serious offshore racing for those inclined.

■ March

Two Heroine Sisters' Festival: Held in March every year in memory of the two heroines who led the defense of the island against the Burmese in 1785. Each year a variety of events and parties are held over a four- or five-day period.

■ April

Songkran: Thailand's most famous April festival celebrates the Thai New Year. Phuket celebrates in grand style with lots of noise and lots of water-throwing in the streets. If you want to stay dry, stay indoors.

Turtle Releasing Festival: Part of the April New Year celebrations. In order to help preserve and protect the turtle they are bred at the Phuket Aquarium. When they are mature enough, they are released into the sea. The ceremony is usually held at Phanwa Cape and Nai Yang and Mai Khao Beaches to coincide with the Songkran Festival.

Phuket Bike Week: As if you haven't seen enough motorcycles! These annual April get-togethers started in 1994 and bring together all the super machines including the huge Harleys and little Hondas. Events include charity rides around the island, music concerts, contests and parties. More info: www.phuketbikeweek.com.

Annual Cricket Tournament: The Lighthouse Phuket International Cricket Sixes tournament, www.phuketsixes.com, started in 2004, attracts teams from Australia, Thailand, Macau, Borneo, India, Pakistan and Malaysia. The event, held in April at the Karon Sports Stadium was expanded to a four-day event in 2005 when 18 teams attended. In addition to the tournament, the organizers stage lessons and hold matches for all-comers on the beach.

■ May

Phuket International 10s Rugby Tournament: Held at the Karon Municipal Stadium, Karon Beach. Teams come from all over Southeast Asia and Europe to compete for the Clive Williamson Memorial Trophy. More info: e-mail phuketvagabondsrfc@yahoo.co.uk.

■ July

Phuket Race Week: First of these sailing regattas began in 2004. Organizers Image Asia promise five days of great breezes, yacht racing and parties.

■ August

Por Tor Festival: An important merit-making festival held in Phuket City for ethnic Chinese. Special food, flowers and candles are presented to the ancestor's altars. Cakes in the shape of turtles are made from flour. This is done because turtles live to great age and it is believed that by making such offering worshippers may extend the length of their lives.

Phuket Fireworks Festival: Thousands of fireworks light the sky in a dazzling display at Sapan Hin in Phuket City in mid-August. This is a large park area and a very popular place for picnics and sports activities.

Hotelex Exhibition Food & Beverage Show: This event takes place in mid-August. Designed for those in the catering business but the contests are worth watching. Competitions include speedy bed making, cocktail mixing and a beauty pageant. Entry to the show is free, ☎ 07622 2801.

■ October

Vegetarian Festival: Celebrated by Phuket's Chinese community, this highly popular festival continues for 10 days. The events includes unpleasant body piercing, strange processions of people under trances with endless amounts of fire crackers exploding. The festival was started in the 19th century by immigrant miners from China who were lured to Phuket in search of tin. Phuket residents of Chinese ancestry and many Thais too, go on a vegetarian diet and attend ceremonies at local Chinese temples. Parades take place throughout the island although the center of the event is in Phuket City. Look for people who have pierced holes in cheeks and tongues as part of a cleansing ritual. One contestant told me that the holes soon heal – in plenty of time for next year's event. A plus part for visitors is that a wonderful array of vegetarian food is on sale in the streets of Phuket City.

■ November

Patong Beach Tourist Festival: This annual event, first held in 1985, marks the beginning of the tourist season in Phuket. It is held in the first week of November and organized by the tourist trade community of Patong Beach to promote tourism in the province. Its aim is to create unity among those who work in tourism. If the hope was to stop tuk-tuk drivers fighting over clients, then it is not working! However it is good reason for a party. Activities include water sports and tourist beauty contests. Each year the organizers add something unusual. Since it is in Patong you can expect it to be loud and colorful in addition to a lengthy parade, shows and concerts.

Laguna Phuket Triathlon: This event attracts top athletes from around the world. The race starts with a 1,800-meter swim followed by a cycle along a 55-kilometer course up a coastal road, and ends with a 12-kilometer run. All this is in extreme heat, even if they do start early in the morning. The finish is normally at the entrance of the Banyan Tree resort. That's the place to be if you want to see a lot of tired and sweaty athletes cross the finish line. There is a prettier sight for spectators. There are usually a lot of lovely Thai maidens clad in their silk gowns to present the prizes. More info on the race e-mail: triathlon@lagunaphuket.com. In recent years Australians have dominated the list of winners.

Phuket International Sport fishing Classic: Fishermen from all over the globe compete in this November classic event. The competition with its headquarters in Chalong Bay emphasizes "catch and release" policy and promotes sport fishing around Phuket's waters.

***Loy Kratong*, or Full Moon Day**: This is a nationwide annual festival but has special significance here, since Phuket is an island. Floats made from banana trees with candles and incense are launched into the water at night to take away bad luck. Events held at all of Phuket's major beaches and in Phuket City. A couple of places where it gets crowded but is worth watching are at Chalong Bay and Wat Chalong.

■ December

Phuket King's Cup International Regatta: This event attracts yachtsmen from all over the world. It was first held in 1987 to celebrate the King's 60th birthday. Final night is normally on December 5 with presentation of prizes and a massive party on Kata Beach. At exactly 7:27pm everyone holds an illuminated candle and observes a one-minute silence. Local choirs sing celebration songs and the foreigners finish things off with a rousing rendition of *Happy Birthday To You*. Best place to view this yachting spectacle is from Phromthep Cape, the southernmost tip of the island. It is impossible to judge who is doing well because all classes race at the same time. The bay in Kata Beach is an exciting spectacle at sun up as the dozens of crews are ferried out to their racing yachts in the Thai longtail boats. Each year the party venues and race days change.

Phuket International Marine Expo: This exhibition of boats and other marine products made its debut in 2003 and promises to be successful after attracting so many top marine industry personnel and potential buyers from all over Asia. The event, organized by Image Asia, takes place early in December and normally coincides with the King's Cup Regatta.

Phuket International Seafood Festival: Where better than Phuket to have a seafood festival. This annual seafood lover's event held at Patong Beach is mostly a competition by hotels and restaurants to show off their skills. In addition to mouth watering displays there are cooking demonstrations. Competitions include ice sculpting and events for bartending skills.

Cultural Festival: Every year, shortly after Christmas, the city takes on a festive air. The streets are closed to traffic, and food vendors and other sellers erect stalls on the sidewalks. Thais come from far and wide to enjoy the week-long historical and cultural festival. Many of the older buildings are open to the public and demonstrations of local handicrafts are given. Other buildings have exhibitions portraying the history of the island before the days of tourism. Bands and choirs from local schools give concerts in floodlit gardens. Few tourists attend and it is an ideal place to sample the varied fare from the food stalls. There are several clean, neat hotels in the city and they attract a lot of businessmen as well as visitors on a budget.

Where to Stay

There are now over 500 hotels in Phuket and the number continues to grow. The letters NTD after a listing indicate that the property was not damaged by the tsunami.

ACCOMMODATIONS PRICE SCALE	
Indicates rates charged per night during high-season for a double room, including breakfast and all service charges. Prices vary according to the exchange rate between the US dollar and Thai Baht. Most hotels offer discounts from their published rack rates during low season. All those listed accept major credit cards; rooms have direct-dial telephones and private bathrooms.	
$	Under $50
$$	$51 to $100
$$$	$101 to $175
$$$$	Over $175

Trisara, 60/1 Moo 6, Srisoonthorn Road, Cherngtalay, ☎ 07631 0100, fax 07631 0300, www.trisara.com, $$$$. This is first in our list since these are the finest hotel rooms we have seen anywhere. Forget about luxury at an affordable price. Staying here is mega-expensive, and you can expect to pay $1,000 a night especially if you include breakfast at $25 a person, plus a hefty 17.8% service charge, plus taxes. Each of the 33 rooms covers 240 square meters of well-planned luxury; rooms are loaded with teak and silk and feature a large infinity swimming pool (yes, one for each room), huge flat-screen TV, spacious bathroom and an outdoor terrace with shower. There are numerous steps to climb as you traverse the resort but with 250 friendly employees there is always someone to help you along. If you want even more space there are 12 luxury residential villas adjoining the resort. The bedrooms are just as huge, and you get a full kitchen in addition to full use of the Trisara's hotel services. There's a choice of restaurants, and two lobbies – one for arrivals, the second for departures. The resort went into full operation at the end of 2004.

The air conditioning system is hidden under the rooms to insure they stay quiet and cold. Many of the site's original trees were spared during construction and have been built around. You'll find them poking through pools and walkways. There's no charge for the 15-minute transfer from the airport.

For directions to Trisara, look under Nai Thon Beach listing in the *Things to See* section of this chapter, page 194. The tsunami had little effect here since so much of the resort is high above the beach. There was damage to the beach pool but that was repaired within a few days. The only casualties were the beach chairs and a few ornamental pots.

JW Marriott Resort & Spa, 231 Moo 3, Mai Khao, ☎ 07633 8000, fax 07634 8348, www.marriott.com, $$$$. Spectacular. Design and décor are delightful. Expect to pay $300 a night for sampling life in this new resort. And if you want one of the spacious suites double that number. On our first visit here shortly after its opening we were offered a discounted rate of $150 since the room count was low. Later we spent three weeks in the adjoining Marriott Vacation Village time-share project. The two-bedroom apartments there are similarly lush and lavish and we had access to the hotel's extensive facilities. One snag is that you are cut off from the rest of Phuket. But if all you want is to be pampered and relax in a tropical haven that really doesn't matter. The beachfront restaurant, pool bars, swimming pools were damaged by the tsunami but everything was operating normally within a few weeks.

Amanpuri Resort, 118 Moo 3 Cherngtalay Road, Pansea Beach, ☎ 07632 4333, fax 07632 2100, $$$$. The most expensive place to stay on Phuket with its 40 luxury pavilions set in a coconut plantation above the beach. Amanpuri translates to place of peace, which this certainly is. Incredible service with many more employees than guests. The Aman Spa is one of the best in Thailand and offers everything from basic massages to holistic therapies, facials and scrubs. There are also salas for meditation and yoga. There is a choice of dining spots plus 24-hour room service. The pavilions cost from $675 a night for one set in the gardens to $1,550 for an ocean view. There are also homes available. The largest, with five bedrooms, costs $7,350 a night. Imagine taking it that for three weeks. Those prices do not include service and taxes, which amount to almost 20%. The tsunami caused minor damage to the beach equipment but flooding destroyed the gym. The resort was operating normally a few days after the tidal wave hit.

Banyan Tree Phuket, 33 Moo 4 Srisoonthorn Road, Cherngtalay, ☎ 07632 4374, fax 07632 4375, www.banyantree.phuket.com, $$$$. We love this place. Your own Thai villa, many with a private pool, set in lush landscaping. Transport around the resort provided by golf buggies that arrive at your door within minutes of a call to reception. Each villa has a large outdoor bath. Pleasant-smelling oils and lotion are provided. Word of warning: It takes a while for the bath to fill, because of its size. Ample time to enjoy a cocktail in your private end of the garden sala before you dive in. To experience the best dining anywhere in the Laguna Beach area you need to be staying in one of the villas here. During our stay we ordered a barbecue by our own private pool. And that was a meal we will never forget. A pair of chefs arrived and gently barbecued fish and chicken while we snacked on crunchy salads and starters. As we enjoyed the main course they vanished leaving us a plate of assorted deserts and fresh fruit. That is the way to barbecue. No coals to light, no dirty hands and no cleanup. Fortunately the tsunami had caused only minor damage and the resort operated normally through the remaining part of the Christmas holidays.

> *Every day a different local fruit is delivered to your Banyan Tree villa, with a card that tells you everything about the tropical item.*

Mom Tri's Villa Royale Hotel & Spa. This is a combination of two of Phuket's leading boutique resorts – the **Villa Royale**, $$$$, and **The Boathouse**, $$$. After the tsunami the owner of the properties, ML Tri Devakul, decided to merge the two, giving clients the benefit of using facilities at either one. The Villa Royale, at 12 Katanoi Road, Tambon Karon, ☎ 07633 3568, fax 07633 3001, www.villaroyalephuket.com, is the more exclusive, elegant and expensive of the two and it is at the southern end of Kata Noi Beach. Accommodation is limited to 26 luxury suites or studios in their own hillside gardens with stunning views over the Andaman Sea. The cliffs fall to a rocky shoreline and there are steps down to Kata Noi beach. There is a choice of three swimming pools, one of them sea water. The delightfully decorated accommodation is the perfect place for a honeymoon or for the rich and famous to hideaway. For us the big plus is the privacy and the magnificent views from the balconies. General Manager of both properties is Adisak Pitukrojananont who insists that the Villa Royale uses all organic and natural products in both the restaurant and the resort's spa, everything from rice to soap. High-season rate for the top suite with its own pool is 26,000 Baht per night excluding taxes, service charge and breakfast. NTD.

Less expensive and our favorite place to stay is **The Boathouse**, 182 Koke Tanod Road, Kata Beach, ☎ 07633 0015-7, fax 07633 0561, www.boathousephuket.com. This too is small – just 36 rooms around a marvelous restaurant – and we are loathe to recommend it for fear there will be no space for us. The owner, talented Thai architect Tri Devakul, designed it as a hotel for people who prefer not to stay in hotels. He was also the architect for the nearby Club Med complex. The Boathouse is right on a delightful beach and has very comfortable rooms and three extra nice suites.

The hotel has a magnetic pull. More than a third of its guests are return visitors thanks to a very loyal and friendly staff. The tsunami caused extensive damage to the ground floor of the resort forcing to close temporarily. The restaurant has now been redesigned, ground-floor rooms renovated and the resort is operating as normal.

Ice-cold towels and tidbits of tropical fruits on wooden spits are served to guests sitting on the beach or around the pool.

The Chedi Phuket, Cherngtalay Road, Pansea Beach, ☎ 07632 4017, fax 07632 4252, $$$$. One of the first luxury resorts on the island, The Chedi has 108 elegantly furnished, thatched cottages set amidst coconut palms above a quiet beach. A separate swimming pool for younger visitors. Beachfront cottages, the deluxe cottages and beach restaurant were damaged by the tsunami but the resort did not close its doors as guests were accommodated in other categories. Renovations are expected to several months.

Dusit Laguna Beach Resort, 390 Srisoonthorn Road, Thalang, ☎ 07632 4324, fax 07632 4061, www.lagunaphuket.com, $$$. Member of the *Leading Hotels of the World*, the Dusit is one of the grand Laguna resorts and has bargain prices in the off-season at a fraction of their high-season rack rate. The Bang Tao Bay beach is great but lush gardens with freshwater lagoons are a major attraction. Tsunami damage was limited to one restaurant and a swimming pool and the resort was able to operate throughout the period.

A free courtesy bus links all the major Laguna resorts and the Canal Village shopping complex.

TwinPalms, 106/46 Moo 3, Surin Beach, ☎ 07631 6555, fax 07631 6599, www.twinpalms-phuket.com, $$$. An elegant, modern boutique hotel with only 76 luxury rooms and suites surrounded by palm trees and cleverly arranged around large swimming pools. Fifteen of the rooms have direct entry to the lagoon pool and all the rooms have special mattresses that can be turned to provide firm support for Asian guests to a softer level for Europeans. This is something we have not seen elsewhere. The resort only came into full operation in 2005 and has an excellent spa with nine treatment rooms plus a larger room ideal families or groups, gym, wellness center, well-stocked library and has free Internet access in every room, something the Marriott charges 650 Baht a day for. The beach is 175 meters away and the hotel plans to have a shuttle operating in high season. There is a reserved area on the beach for hotel guests and there's no extra charge for sun beds on a very pleasant beach. The hotel's Alba Wellness Center combines western and eastern therapies under the supervision of a resident Swedish physician. The center is aligned with the Bangkok Phuket Hospital to deliver a range of medical treatments including physiotherapy treatments, health check-ups and other light healthcare services. Airy welcoming lobby surrounded by water shows off its modern Thai design. For information about the resort's excellent Oriental Spoon Restaurant & Oyster Bar, look in the *Where to Eat* section, page 238. NTD.

TwinPalms offers underground parking for guests, perfect for keeping the rental car cool.

Sawasdee Village, 65 Kate Kwan Road, Kata Beach, ☎ 07633 0979, fax 07633 0905, www.phuketsawasdee.com, $$$. This is a true Thai gem of a resort not in the best of locations but just full of Thai art and décor. Internet rate for a double runs 4,900 Baht but they do have a program for long stays, which brings the per-night cost down. Only 44 delightful double rooms – plus two triples – that look like they posed for an interior design magazine. Good gardens, nice pool and spa make up for the fact that you've got to ride the courtesy bus if you want to go to the beach. There is a sister property down the street – cheap and chic (their words not mine) – where you can get a room for 7600 Baht a night. NTD.

Crowne Plaza Karon Beach Phuket, 509 Patak Road, Karon Beach, ☎ 07639 6139, fax 07639 6122, www.crowneplaza.com, $$$. This is the former Karon Villas and Royal Wing that recently got a $20 million face lift to make it a top contender for the convention and business market. It also improved its facilities for family vacations. There are now three restaurants, an upmarket spa with 12 treatment rooms as well as one of the largest Kids' Clubs on the island with three separate categories for children between one and 16. The resort is within walking distance of Karon shops and is directly across from the beach. This is the first Crowne Plaza to open in Thailand. A second, Crowne Plaza Sukhumvit Bangkok, is scheduled to open in January 2006. The Phuket resort, with 150 villas and 210 rooms, has one of the largest meeting facilities available in Phuket with seven meeting and boardrooms as well as a ballroom capable of seating 750. The resort was still being renovated when the tsunami hit.

The Evason Phuket, 100 Viset Road, Rawai, ☎ 07638 1286, 0768 1018, www.six-senses.com, $$$. Luxury resort on the south of the island set in 64 acres of lush gardens. Perfect spot for honeymooners or families. The resort has a private island that is a 10-minute boat ride away. Sister resort to the ones at Samui and Hua Hin. Diving club, three pools and a kids' club. Our only complaint:

There are a lot of stairs to climb. Tsunami damage was limited to the resort's pier and its dive shop. Like many Phuket resorts the occupancy rate plummeted to single-digit numbers after the New Year.

Kata Thani Beach Resort, 3/24 Kata Noi Beach, ☎ 07633 0124-6, fax 07633 0127, www.phuket.com/katathani, $$$. Large resort, 433 rooms, it claims to have the largest beachfront of any hotel in Phuket. A package deal here to include a junior suite, breakfast and dinner would cost around $160 per night. The tsunami damage was limited to some ground-floor rooms, gardens, swimming pools and a restaurant in the Thani wing. Guests were accommodated in other rooms. The Bhuri wing was not affected.

Amari Coral Beach Resort, Patong Beach, ☎ 07634 0106, fax 07634 0115, www.amari.com, $$$. The address says Patong but this luxury resort sits on a headland at the southern end of the beach and enjoys spectacular views away from the nearby concrete clutter. The 200 rooms are all to the highest standard all newly renovated. The best rate we saw here for high season was $155 a night. Choice of pools and highly rated restaurants, plus longtail boats nearby to take you to a beach other than Patong. The resort suffered severe damage and was closed immediately after the tsunami hit, but renovations have been ongoing and the resort is open.

Pearl Village Hotel, Nai Yang Beach and National Park, Thalang, ☎ 07632 7006, fax 07632 7388, www.phuket.com/pearlvillage, $$$. Near the airport, but off the flight path this 243-room resort adjoins the national park and has easy access to Nai Yang Beach. Two separate restaurants. One offers award winning western dishes, the other Thai cuisine. Normal price for a suite is $165 a night, excluding breakfast. The tsunami caused minor damage and the hotel was operating normally soon after the tidal wave hit.

Hilton Phuket Arcadia, 78/2 Patak Road, Karon Bay, ☎ 07639 6038, fax 07639 6136, www.phuketarcadia.com, $$$. Three spectacular swimming pools with a waterfall complement this five-star resort, which became a Hilton late in 2004 with a major new look for its 685 rooms. The resort was given a more modern look in many of its public areas, with new furnishings and tile flooring in meeting rooms and reception areas, and a spa added in a new building beside the property's central lagoon. Tiles in the guest rooms were replaced with varnished wood floors and modern Thai furnishings and wall hangings added. Large deluxe rooms (44 square meters) have bathrooms that allow sea views while you bathe. High-season packages available from $150 per night. The resort covers a large area and there's plenty of space to take long walks. NTD.

Le Royal Meridien Phuket Yacht Club, 23/3 Viset Road , Nai Harn Beach, ☎ 07638 0200, fax 07638 0280, www.lemeridien.com, $$$. First five-star resort to be built on the south end of the island. Many repeat clients because of great food and service. There is an excellent beach but not exclusive to the hotel and it is an uphill walk back to the hotel. The resort reported some minor damage on its lower floors but operated as normal.

Andaman White Beach Resort, 28/8 Moo 4, Sakoo, ☎ 07631 6300, fax 07631 6 399 www.andamanwhitebeach.com, $$$. First impressions count: The doorman here is the happiest person around. Neat boutique resort close to the airport, but away from the flight path, and on Nai Thon Beach, which never seems to get busy even in high season. Choice of beachfront or sea-view villas with good Internet pricing and specials, which include spa visits. In addition to the dining room there's the Coconut Bar and Terrace a short walk from the beach with a daily barbecue. It's open from 10am until the last guest leaves. For directions to get here look under Nai Thon Beach listing in the *Things to See* section of this chapter, page 194. The tsunami caused minor damage to the beach but had no effect on the resort itself.

You can rent a laptop computer to use during your stay at the Andaman White Beach Resort.

The Mangosteen Resort & Spa, 99/4 Moo 7, Soi Mangosteen, ☎ 07628 9399, fax 07628 9389, www.mangosteen-phuket.com, $$$.The fantastic views from the high ground on which this new luxury resort sits are just one of the attractions of this 40-room complex set inland from the Chalong to Rawai road. Each of the suites has garden bathrooms and a private Jacuzzi. There's a stunning swimming pool featuring a water curtain with 14 waterfalls, a swimming channel with powerful stream jets, a built-in Jacuzzi and an infinity edge. It's worth checking on the Internet for package deals that include excursions, well-priced considering the luxury offered. From the expensive and extensive restaurant you get views of several bays and similar vistas from the highly ranked spa. Nai Harn beach is a five-minute drive away. One minor snag: Because of the high terrain it is a healthy climb from the guest parking to the resort lobby. NTD.

All the terraces at The Mangosteen come with a comfy hammock to further enhance the views.

Club Mediterranean, 7/3 Patak Road, Kata Beach, ☎ 07633 0455, 07633 0461, $$$. This all-inclusive resort is almost on the beach. You just have to step across a quiet road to enjoy the vast expanse of Kata Beach. One of the first resorts to open in the area and very popular for family vacations. The tsunami caused damage to some of the rooms, the restaurants, swimming pool and mini-golf course. The resort was forced to close for a short period.

Thavorn Palm Beach Resort, 128/10 Moo 3, Tambon Karon, Karon Bay, ☎ 07639 6090, fax 07639 6555, $$$. Ideal family hotel with 210 rooms and suites across from the beach with five swimming pools. Be aware that is not directly on the beach. High-season rates can be as low as $150 a night including full American breakfast. There is a sister hotel in Phuket City that may be ideal for businessmen but not well suited for a vacation. Its saving grace is the fantastic view you get from the top floor of the building. NTD.

The Aspasia Phuket, 1/3 Laem Sai Road, Kata Beach, ☎ 07633 3033, fax 07633 3035, www.aspasia.com, $$$. Unusually designed and decorated resort in a wonderful location overlooking Kata Beach. It's quite a clamber to the beach but that's the price you pay for getting such stunning views. The décor is an intriguing mix of chromium plated art deco and Mexican Mayan. A mix of 48 rooms and suites all with large bathrooms. When we stayed there the resort was not completed so it was hard to judge all the in-room facilities. There are two swimming pools, a well-equipped gym and a great spa where we spent a wonderful 90 minutes being revitalized. The all-day **Melina's** restaurant has a varied menu and at lunch time there is a special Issan menu featuring dishes from Northeast Thailand. Try the *miang kharm*, served with little dishes of onion, ginger, chilies, cashew nuts, dried shrimp, coconut and sweet and sour sauce to build your own appetizer in an edible leaf. The helpful waiters or waitresses will build the first one for you and then you're on your own. The shops and attractions of Karon Beach are in reasonable walking distance. NTD.

Karon Beach Resort, 120/5 Moo 4, Patak Road, Karon Beach, ☎ 07633 0006, fax 07633 0529, www.katagroup.com, $$$. The only Karon hotel that is actually on the beach. All 80 rooms are well equipped and although not spacious they all face the sea and overlook the swimming pool, gardens and beach. Fine dining at the **On The Beach Restaurant** with a good selection of Thai and international dishes. Poolside bar and café keeps you at sea level for the entire day. High-season rate just goes over $100 for the room and $6.50 for breakfast. There is a 1,300 Baht a night surcharge for stays over the Christmas Holidays. One facet we enjoyed was a street full of shops, bars and restaurants right outside the resort.

The tsunami caused severe damage to 24 ground-floor rooms. The resort was forced to close for four months for repairs to be made.

Rydges Beach Resort, 322 Moo 2, Srisoontorn Road, Bang Tao Beach, ☎ 07632 4021, fax 07632 4243, $$. Unassuming three-story resort with 255 rooms in the Laguna area. Plus here is that a number water sports on Bang Tao beach are free – sail boats, canoes and snorkeling equipment. Try for a room in the new royal wing. Expect to pay $130 a night with breakfast included and leave the $$ level. The resort only suffered minor tsunami damage and was fully operation within days of the disaster.

Cape Panwa Hotel, 27 Moo 8 Sakdidet Road, Phanwa Cape, ☎ 07639 1123-5, fax 07639 1177, www.capepanwa.com, $$. Away from the crowds and beach vendors, this hotel is situated on a hill above a beach at the southern tip of Phuket. Thanks to its protected location, swimming and water sports are available year-round. Choice of rooms or suites. NTD.

Kata Delight Villas, 3/1 Patak Road, Kata Beach, ☎ 07633 0636, 07633 0342, fax 07633 0481, www.kata-beach.com/delight, $$. Great location perched over Kata Beach. Only 16 rooms, all with sea view. Reasonably priced at $100 a night. NTD.

Kata Delight has an infinity pool with great views while you swim.

Holiday Inn Resort, 52 Thaweewong Road, Patong Beach, ☎ 07634 0608, fax 07634 0435, www.phuket.com/holidayinn $$. Excellent place to stay. The new **Busakorn Wing**, with 140 extra-large rooms and suites, is well worth the additional charge. Quality spa at reasonable prices. Severe tsunami damage to the ground floor, affecting restaurants, swimming pool and the lobby. The hotel was closed and renovations were expected to be completed before the high season.

Mini-bars at the Holiday Inn Resort come empty; there are two mini-markets in the hotel complex where you can buy a variety of drinks and snacks at supermarket prices.

Le Meridien Phuket, 8/5 Tambon Karon Noi, Karon Bay, ☎ 07634 0480-5, fax 07634 0479, www.lemeridien.com, $$. Large, lavish resort with its own pristine beach. Look for the baby elephant patrolling the lobby. Well priced considering all the amenities available. Nice boutiques and good restaurants. The resort was badly damaged by the tsunami and at the time of writing it was not known when the resort would be able to reopen.

Central Karon Village, 8/21 Moo 1 Tambon Karon, Karon Bay, ☎ 07628 6300-9, fax 07628 6316, www.centralhotelsresorts.com,

The charm of traditional Siamese dancing

Above: Southern Thailand, noted for its beaches

Below: Dining beside the Mekong River
Courtesy of Tohsang Resort

Above: Swimming pool at TwinPalms, Surin Beach, Phuket
Courtesy of TwinPalms Resort

Below: The warmth of a Thai greeting
Courtesy of Marriott Hotels

Above: The beach at Lanta Sand Resort, Ko Lanta
Courtesy of Lanta Sand Resort

Below: Sunset at Nai Harn Beach, Phuket
Courtesy of Mangosteen Resort

Above: Swimming pool at the Mangosteen Resort, Phuket
Courtesy of Mangosteen Resort

Below: The spa at the Pimalai Resort, Ko Lanta
Courtesy of Pimalai Resort

Above: The Pimalai Resort, Ko Lanta

Below: Ban Kan Tiang Beach, Pimalai Resort, Ko Lanta
Both photos courtesy of Pimalai Resort

Above: In Bangkok, they call this an express train

Below: Siamese dancers entertain passengers
Courtesy of the Eastern & Oriental Express

Lotus pond at the Legend Resort in Chiang Rai

$$. Great jungle setting in the hills overlooking Karon Bay. All 72 villas, decorated with Thai fabrics have sea views and large balconies. NTD.

Kata Beach Resort, 5/2 Patak Road, Kata Beach, ☎ 07633 0530-4, fax 07633 0128, www.katagroup.com, $$. Plenty of activity at this 267-room, and expanding, resort right on Kata Beach. The large open lobby gets a little noisy at night with buffet dinner and shows. Great high-season value at $100 a night. You'll pay extra for rooms with sea view. Popular spot for a late afternoon massage on the beach. Popular spot for a late afternoon massage on the beach. The resort suffered minor tsunami damage to eight ground-floor rooms and was fully operational for the New Year celebrations.

Layan Beach Resort & Spa Village, 62 Moo 6, Layan Village, Cherngtalay, ☎ 07631 3412, fax 07631 3415, www.layanphuket.com, $$. Small and inexpensive hotel. The 60 rooms all have sea views and there is a spa and attractive pool on the premises. Internet rates have been as low as $60 per night for the high season. The tsunami damaged facilities near the beach and the spa but the resort was operating normally within a few days.

Duangjitt Resort, 18 Prachanukroh Road, Patong Beach, ☎ 076 34 0303, fax 07634 0288, www.duangjittresort-spa.com, $$. We have deliberately not listed many Patong hotels but it was the 36 acres of tropical gardens here that warranted a mention. It's a large resort with 324 rooms and 57 bungalows with three spectacular swimming pools, which is just as well since the resort is not on the beach. The tsunami damaged many room bungalows but the resort was able to operate with while the damage accommodation was repaired.

Kata Sun Beach, 188 Koktanod Road, Kata Beach, ☎ 07628 4265 $. Small, spotless hotel with large airy rooms, good location and excellent rates. They range from low-season/mountain-view 750 Baht (€17.50) to high-season/sea-view 1,700 Baht (€35.00). The prices include an American breakfast. For longer stays the rates are negotiable. It is only a few yards from the beach and it adjoins an excellent massage parlor, The Tum Rub Thai Massage. And only yards from the Boathouse complex. NTD.

Computers with Internet connections available in the Kata Sun Beach lobby. We found the rates to be the lowest in the area.

Patong Grand Ville, 19 Sirirat Road, Patong Beach, ☎ 07629 4500, fax 07629 4504, www.patonggrandville.com $. Eighteen inexpensive rooms around a swimming pool on a hill just south of

Patong. Each of the large rooms has sliding windows that open onto the pool. NTD.

The Patong Grand Villa has a small refrigerator in each room for snacks and drinks.

Pearl, 42 Montri Road, Phuket, ☎ 07621 1044 $. If you want to be in Phuket City this 212-room resort is close to the main business centers of Phuket and downtown shopping. Surprising quality for a low price. NTD.

South Sea Resort, 36/12 Moo 1, Patak Road, Karon Bay, ☎ 07639 6611-5, fax 07639 6618, $. All 100 rooms are set in lush tropical landscaping and face Karon Beach. Great rates include breakfast. The tsunami caused some damage in the lobby but the resort was able to continue its operations without interruption.

Royal Phuket City Hotel, 154 Phang Nga Road, Phuket City, $, ☎ 07623 3333, fax 07623 3335, www.royalphuketcity.com Very acceptable inexpensive hotel right in the center of Phuket City with an enormous spa that occupies the entire third floor and as is part of a chain of fitness clubs operating throughout Southeast Asia. Internet rates for a double are 2,000 Baht a night including service, taxes, buffet breakfast, welcome drink and fruit basket and a round-trip airport if you stay more than two nights. Even the best suite is well priced at 7,000 Baht. If you want to take a break from walking around Phuket City, the friendly lobby bar serves excellent tea and coffee at a reasonable price. NTD.

■ Accommodation in the Bay of Phang Nga

The Racha, PO Box 213, Muang, Phuket, ☎ 07635 5465, fax 07635 5240, www.theracha.com, $$$$. This is now one of the premier resorts of the world, having opened all its facilities in 2005. It's an all-new millionaire's eco-friendly piece of paradise set on island that has the whitest sand and the most modern accommodation and spa that money can buy. Its stark minimalist décor blends incredibly well with the natural beauty of the island that it dominates. The 69 villas are fully equipped – 24-hour Internet connections, outdoor showers in a small garden, big bathrooms, and entertainment center are all standard features – but there is not one curtain in the entire development, as washing those takes valuable water and damaging detergent. Instead, wooden slats and blinds keep out the light and give a more natural feel. Everything was done in creating this special haven to protect the environment. Only seven trees were cut down (and they were replaced by fourteen) and holes were made in roofs or in walkways to accommodate the existing trees. The most expensive villa has everything a hideaway seeker could want – a private infinity pool overlooking the beach and beyond, a bath that could house a football team and its own espresso machine. There are some negatives about staying in on this fantasy island. Getting here involves a 12-mile crossing of Phang Nga Bay, which can get rough. We had delightful crossing both there and back and made the journey on the resort's speedy launch in 30 minutes. But there are times when it can take twice that long. There are normally three crossings in each direction a day and additional ones are made to accommodate arriving and departing guests or you can hire one of the launches for a personal trip. Not a place for families with youngsters or older travelers with walking difficulties. And you are cut off from the rest of the world – to those who come here, that is why they pay so much. During the high season dozens of boats from Phuket bring visitors to enjoy the beach. Fortunately they leave in the afternoon, bringing back the peace and tranquility for which The Racha will become famous.

The tsunami caused considerable damage to the interior of the main building. Four villas close to the beach were completely destroyed and others sustained heavy damage. The front office building, the spa and fitness center were also damaged. Rebuilding and repairs were quickly underway and the resort was open for clients in early summer. Despite its size the resort offers a choice of dining spots and live entertainment.

Koyao Island Resort, Ko Yao Noi, island in the bay of Phang Nga, $$. If you want peace and quiet, but not be totally cut off from the world, this is the place. It is a remote island but your room will have a direct dial phone, television, minibar and air conditioning. There are just 15 rooms at the resort, which is on an island that is surrounded by beaches and uninhabited islands and close to a rain forest. The resort has a restaurant and bar. To find out more about the area look in *Things To Do* section, page 209. Ten rooms were damaged by the tsunami but the resort continued operations with its remaining rooms while repairs were made.

The Paradise Ko Yao, Ko Yao Noi, $$. A little larger than the previous entry with 50 rooms and you have a choice of private villas or studios, all single story and in true Thai style. Prices for a double start at 4,000 Baht a night. The resort's **Seafood Grill**, on the beach between shady trees, offers local fish dishes and prides itself on contemporary Mediterranean cuisine. There's a swimming pool, tropical outdoor spa and massages are given in a sala set into the hillside overlooking Phang Nga Bay. If you feel guilty about relaxing too much there is a business center and the hotel arranges airports transfers.

Baan Mai Cottages & Restaurant, 35/1 Moo 3, Lone Island, ☎ 07622 3095, fax 07622 5096, www.baanmai.com, $$. Ten cottages and one three-bedroom villa make up this small resort that is nestled between the island hill tops and a secluded beach. Just 10 kilometers across the bay to Phuket the complex has great views of Chalong Bay. You have a choice of sea front or garden cottage with prices starting at $75 for a double. There is a nature lodge here as well as a swimming pool and the restaurant offers cosmopolitan cuisine. Around the clock boat service to Phuket. The tsunami caused damage to the garden area and forced the resort to close for a short period.

Where to Eat

Phuket has thousands of restaurants so it is impossible to eat at all of them, more is the pity. But it is fun trying. The ones we list here are ones that we have tried and liked. The few – and there are very few – we did not like are not listed. We have also listed restaurants that have been frequented by friends whose advice we trust.

DINING PRICE SCALE	
Per person, based on a two-course dinner (a main course with either a starter or dessert), with a glass of wine and coffee. Wine is expensive and will affect the bill accordingly.	
$	Under $10
$$	$11 to $20
$$$	$21 to $30
$$$$	Over $30

Seafood restaurants along Chalong Bay, $. There are three seafood restaurants along the beach that we feel offer the best value and food on the island. The most southerly is **Friendship Number One** (*Kan Eang I*, 44/1 Visiet Road, ☎ 07638 1212) and then comes **Friendship Number Two** (*Kan Eang II*, 9/3 Chafoa Road, ☎ 07638 1323) and finally **The Fisherman**, (*Tangkae*) 36

Moo 3 Sol Palal, Chaola Road, ☎ 07628 2341. It is hard to say which one is the best. If you ask a Thai his or her response will probably be based on a friend or relative who works at one of the trio rather than the food or service. Since most visitors to the island eat dinner in or near their hotels these restaurants never really get crowded in the evening. At lunch time several of the tours stop here but we never had a problem finding a table. All three have wonderful views overlooking Phang Nga Bay and be sure and take a look at the tanks where they store the live fish and seafood.

We have eaten numerous times at all three and even when we have been extravagant and selected the largest lobster and a whole fish we have never spent as much as $8 a head, provided we were in a group and sharing the more expensive items. Imported wine is expensive when you dine out in Thailand but we did find an acceptable French red at Friendship One for 650 Baht. If you dine less expensively – our favorite dishes are the curried crab, tamarind shrimp or sweet and sour fish – expect change from $10 for two. There is little English spoken but there are menus in English. If you decide on a whole fish, or lobster, it is just a question of pointing at the creature swimming around and then pointing at the menu for the cooking possibilities, barbecued with garlic or basted in a sweet and sour sauce.

Do not expect swish European service. Do expect lots of smiles and superb food.

The day we were finishing this section of the guide we discovered another little seafood restaurant that is worth a visit. It is located on the approach road to the Royal Meriden Yacht Club at **Nai Harn Beach**. It is the last restaurant on the right before you enter the resort. We had a whole steamed fish with a plum sauce that was excellent, and it only cost 190 Baht. Little English is spoken but the food is good and the only setback is the difficult trek to the bathrooms.

The Boathouse Wine & Grill, 182 Koke Tanod Road, Kata Beach, ☎ 07633 0015-7, 07633 0561, www.boathousephuket.com, $$$$. Without doubt our favorite dining spot in Phuket. The Boathouse claims to be a hotel but it is really a restaurant with rooms. The meals would win awards in any country in the world and the ambience of dining on the beach with the Andaman Sea gently lapping below you is unbeatable.

Every day executive chef Tummanoon Punchun and his army of helpers add a couple of specials to the already spectacular menu. The prices are high as is the quality, so do not look for bargains.

Expect dinner to cost around $40 a head provided you stay away from some of the really expensive wines. The Boathouse boasts on having the largest wine cellar in Thailand, and probably the largest in Southeast Asia.

One of the best meals we have enjoyed at The Boathouse was in the company of the then-general manager Louis Bronner, a savvy French hotelier whose dedication to perfection does not go unnoticed. Mr. Bronner later became the personal representative of owner ML Tri Devakul.

The first course is always preceded by a small complimentary dish that is different each night. Tonight it was a zesty Thai split pea soup. Then came a selection of seafood in a light sauce all encased in puff pastry. The garnish was a half-dozen spears of asparagus that looked identical (someone had gone to a great deal of trouble selecting the spears) and were poached to perfection. To help that slide down was a dry Sauvignon Blanc from New Zealand, Giesen Marlborough 2002. Our main dish was a small rack of Australian lamb served with tiny mounds of scrumptious accompaniments that included peppers and onions. A side order of scalloped potatoes completed that portion of the meal. The wine, as expected, was from France – a Château Beausite 1996. Somehow we managed a dessert of ice cream and local fruits. For a fine meal like this expect to pay $100 a couple.

Saffron, 33 Moo 4, Srisoonthorn Road, Cherngtalay, ☎ 07632 4374, fax 07632 4356. This elegant and peaceful restaurant is part of the Banyan Tree resort and the ideal spot to enjoy the top Thai and Southeast Asian cuisine at top prices. Top marks for service, décor and the food. Favorite dishes are the Phuket lobster in red curry sauce, seafood and banana flower salad and the coriander tuna. Expect your bill to be around $40 a person. Open daily for lunch from 11:30am until 2:30pm and for dinner from 5:30pm until 1am.

The Oriental Spoon, part of the TwinPalms resort, 106/46 Moo 3, Surin Beach, ☎ 07631 6555, fax 07631 6599, www.twinpalms-phuket.com, $$$. Sensible pricing and excellent cuisine are attracting a lot of the Surin ex-patriot community to the tables of this new restaurant with has a clever mix of Asian and European cuisine. Many resorts either price themselves out of the local market or have staid menus that are aimed at the traveler. Not so here. Several of the seafood dishes come in portions where you can adjust the size to how much you can eat or share. The seafood platter – oysters, black and blue crab, prawns, mussels, clams and cockles – comes in two sizes. The larger, at 900 Baht, is an ideal dish to share and comes with an assortment of dips. Non-seafood lovers are well cared for with pork, beef and lamb dishes and particularly appealing is the Northeastern Thai dish grilled chicken with sticky rice at 190 Baht. There are also weekly specials to attract the locals. The day we were there one of those was an enormous mixed grill with a rib eye steak, pork chop, lamb chop, bacon and sausage topped off with grilled tomatoes and sautéed potatoes at 890 Baht, enough to last you a week. Sunday morning the restaurant takes on a different look when the serving area and bar is covered with a medley of treats for a Sunday brunch. We especially enjoyed perfectly cooked roast beef and some magnificent mashed potatoes. The cheese board was one of the best we have enjoyed in Phuket. Leave some room for one of the excellent desserts, and try the fountain of hot chocolate, great coating for the strawberries. The brunch costs 750++ Baht.

Mom Tri's Kitchen, 12 Katanoi Road, Kata Beach, ☎ 07633 3568, fax 07633 3001, www.villaroyalephuket.com, $$$$. The superb location sitting high over the Andaman Sea provides the perfect setting for an elegant meal and that is what you'll get. It's an extensive and expensive menu so take your time selecting. We have always gone for the seafood items but others who have eaten here say the Australian beef and lamb dishes are good too. Our favorites are the sea bass dishes (there's a choice of five ways of preparation) and anything that contains the word lobster. Another plus is that the restaurant has all-day dining from 7am to 11pm. We enjoy a late lunch, which gives us plenty of light to enjoy the views and plenty of time to savor the meal. The service is so good you don't even notice it. The prices are high, but so are the location and quality. Gets busy in the high season so call for a reservation.

Baan Rim Pa, 223 Prabaramee Road, Patong, ☎ 07634 0789, www.baanrimpa.com, $$$$. Probably the most advertised and photographed eating spot in Phuket on a cliffside with spectacular views of Patong Bay. Favorite dishes are red duck curry, lobster with black pepper and curried tiger prawns. Excellent wine cellar and they do offer many of their wines by the glass, which gives you the chance of trying several varieties with your meal. A variety of live entertainment makes this expensive restaurant a place you can spend an entire evening.

Columns Restaurant, inside the Aspasia Phuket, 1/3 Laem Sai Road, Kata Beach, ☎ 07633 3033, fax 07633 3035, $$. We dined here with friends shortly after the opening and were the only diners, which must have been disappointing for the enthusiastic and efficient staff, but that didn't deter them for providing us with an enjoyable evening. Good, varied menu of Thai and European dishes with something for everyone. My beef curry was bordering on the hot side but still very tasty. The pasta dishes went down well as did the fish and chicken selections. The desserts were different and nicely presented. Well-priced and very drinkable Australian house wines.

Phuket Abalone Farm & Restaurant, 35/4 Moo 1 Thepphratan Road, Sirey Island, ☎ 07625 2944, fax 07625 2798, www.phuketabalone.com, $$. We had to decide whether to include this as a place to visit or a place to eat. We opted for eating since it took more time for that adventure than seeing how abalone is produced. It's worth watching the seven-minute presentation on how abalone is reared before seeing the tanks where the shellfish grow. As to be expected the restaurant features abalone on its menu, fried, grilled or boiled. Expensive at 400 Baht per 100 grams compared to lobster at 240 Baht for the same weight. The lengthy process warrants the price. A relatively new venture for Phuket and one that is expanding rapidly with export markets of the shellfish going to other parts of Asia. Sirey Island is off to the east side of Phuket City and connected by a small bridge.

La Gaetana, 352 Phuket Road, Phuket City, ☎ 07625 0523, $$. Odd place to find a truly authentic Italian restaurant, downtown Phuket close to Robinsons department store. Daily specials appear in English on a blackboard and favorite dishes include smoked salmon tagliatelle and carpaccio of smoked duck, beef and salmon. Intimate, cozy restaurant with limited space so call to insure a table. Open for dinner from 6pm to 10pm, closed on Wednesdays. Lunch available on Mondays, Tuesdays and Fridays from noon to 2pm.

> *A meal at La Gaetana includes a complimentary sorbet between courses.*

Angus O'Tool's Irish Pub & Restaurant, 516/20 Patak Road, Karon Beach, ☎ 07639 8262, www.otools-phuket, $$. Tired of Thai? This little eatery across from the Islandia Hotel in Karon may fill the bill. Open all day from breakfast – the full Irish breakfast is a bargain at 170 Baht until dinner where a steak Dianne will cost you 360 Baht or the all time favorite of bangers and mash goes for 180 Baht. They also have 15 nice rooms, which cost from 500 Baht for a standard room in low season to 1,500 Baht for the penthouse in high season.

> *There are no hidden extras added to the room prices at Angus O'Tool's, and in-room coffee or tea is free.*

Baan Had Rawai, 57/5 Rawai Beach Road, Rawai, ☎ 07638 3838, $. Fresh seafood gathered by neighboring fishermen makes this restaurant on the beach a popular place to dine if you're at the southern end of Phuket. Open every day from 10am to 10pm. We have dined here a lot and never had a disappointing meal. There was five of us on our last visit. We had steamed fish in a coconut and ginger sauce, a sea shell soup, a plate of mixed vegetables and a shrimp dish. The bill for five was 618 Baht.

Someone always comes to greet you when you arrive at the car park at the Baan Had Rawai.

Don's Café, 48/5 Sai Yuan Rood, Moo 7, Rawai, ☎ 07628 9314, fax 07628 9319, www.phuket.dons.com, $, is a major meeting spot for Phuket ex-pats, and every manner of holiday is celebrated here, be it a mammoth Thanksgiving Dinner or a Christmas party. The café is open all day every day with a very large selection of reasonably priced Thai and Western dishes (see *From Rockets to Rawai*, page 218).

The Natural Restaurant, 62/5 Soi Phuton, Bangkok Road, Phuket City, ☎ 07622 4287, $. This is the most unusual restaurant we have ever dined in. The place is rickety, rustic and looks entirely run down. Natural is aptly named; the restaurant is a series of floor boards nailed around trees and linked together by wobbly bridges. We ascended to the third floor, the highest point of the establishment, and were afforded a great view upwards of the heavens and below through cracks in the floor, of fellow diners. On our first visit we were a party of seven, and we got to try a wide variety of delicious Thai items from soups to a medley of local ice creams. A splendid place to visit and I sneaked a look at the bill – it was under 1,000 Baht. A must-see place. It's the sort of place you really want to go back to. Food quality high, the service friendly.

Two Chefs Bar & Grill, 5/6 Moo 2, Patak Road, Kata Beach, ☎ 07628 4155, fax 07628 4156, www.twochefs-phuket.com, $$. Two Scandinavians culinary experts gave their name to this great value small eatery where you sit overlooking the busy traffic. We've dined here a lot and never spent as much as 1,000 Baht on an enjoyable meal for two including an acceptable carafe of wine. The friendly staff never changes, which is a good sign, and their European daily specials provide a pleasant break from the excellent Thai cuisine.

At Two Chefs, there is always a small complementary starter, which changes every day. Another good value is the bungalows the two chefs operate, which are perched above the restaurant on the hillside. They're light and airy, and the rooms offer great views over the nearby

Andaman Sea. One snag: to get that high there are a lot of stairs to climb.

Banana Corner, 43/47 Saiyuan Road, Rawai, ☎ 07628 9045, www.bananacorner.com, $. Pleasant restaurant on the road from Kata to Rawai Beach offering incredible value for money. It may be close to the road but the gardens and with a small fountain and lily pond provide a relaxed dinner setting. We dined well for a total 240 Baht – less than $5. Two Sang Som, the local rum with Coke, 30 Baht each, gung makham, the shrimp in tamarind sauce 90 Baht, gai pad king, pork in a tangy ginger sauce 70 Baht and two plates of steamed rice at 10 Baht each. On Friday nights they offer an all you can eat barbecue for 100 Baht. That doesn't operate in high season. Bargains abound in the area. Just down the street Bruno's bakery has a complete American breakfast for 100 Baht. And they sell excellent bread, too.

Kata Kitchen: Across the road from the Kata Beach Resort (see page 233), take the alleyway between the Internet café and the optical store, which leads to this restaurant's terrace; $. We discovered this litle oasis after overhearing some swimmers talking earlier in the day. They were saying it was a bargain, and they were right. It's a delightful little bistro with good food, both Thai and European, at reasonable prices with pleasant service. I had prawns in a tamarind sauce and Lindsey had chicken in a Thai soy sauce. We had a large carafe of wine. A piece of very garlicky bread (served as an appetizer) and a pineapple for dessert were added as complements of the house. Total was 680 Baht, of which 350 Baht was the wine. Newly upgraded massage parlor alongside, and the Internet café you passed on the way in produces good-quality coffees.

Lobster & Prawn No View But Taste: Yes, that is the name outside this eatery across from the Kata Beach Resort. 7/7 Patak Road, Kata Beach, ☎ 07633 3178, $$. Some of the best shrimp we have eaten. I opted for those in tamarind sauce while Lindsey took hers in a pineapple baked with cheese. We came away with change from 800 Baht. Worth a return visit and the price included a salad bar. We drank Cokes, which helped keep the price down. Friends report excellent steaks and lobster but they paid a little more than we did.

Naithon Beach Resort, directly across from Nai Thon Beach (for directions look at the Nai Thon Beach listing, page 194), ☎ 07680 5379, fax 07620 5381, $. Quiet pleasant eatery just steps from the beach with a good menu both Thai and Western. We came away with change from 800 Baht after a substantial Thai lunch for four hungry people. They also rent out clean, adequate bungalows.

They looked a little dark and drab after our earlier visit to the mega expensive Trisara (see the *Where To Stay* section) but they are well priced from 1,000 to 2,000 Baht a night depending on whether you want TV and air conditioning. Just a few steps across a minor road to a wonderful quiet beach.

The Green Man, 82/15 Moo 4, Patak Road, ☎ 07628 0757, fax 07628 1453, www.the-green-man.net, $$. A Tudor-style English pub set in the middle of a tropical island looks as out of place like a snowman in the Sahara Desert. However it serves as a convivial meeting spot for the Brits who have set up home on the island and provides a break from Thai cuisine for visitors. The food is excellent thanks to the culinary skills of Sandeep Pande who has been chef de cuisine since the inn opened. The service is a little slow, which is great because it gives you time to enjoy reading the out-of-the-ordinary extensive menu, which is the work of pub owner Howard Digby Johns. Sunday is a great day to visit. The British Sunday lunches are authentic, truly spiffing, with loads of fresh vegetables all grown in Thailand. The roast beef comes with traditional Yorkshire puddings and I smothered my succulent roast lamb with lashings of mint sauce. Sunday is family day and the garden is the ideal place for younger ones to play. Other items worth a mention are the English sausages, locally made but as good as any English butcher can produce, and served with tasty home-made baked beans and proper mashed potatoes. No wonder British TV chef Keith Floyd was among the diners when we visited. If you're around over the Christmas period the pub offers an extensive Yuletide program with everything from roast goose to a Boxing Day pantomime. (If you don't know what that is look back in this section for the piece about the Simon Cabaret.) Prices are a little higher than elsewhere, but the portions are large, and you would pay a great deal more for similar meals in the UK. Good value for money.

Sea Breeze Café: This is the main dining area at the Holiday Inn in Patong. Every night they have a buffet with a different theme. We were there for a surf and turf barbecue and were most impressed. In addition to the steaks, shrimp and lobsters there were dozens of dishes, both Western and Thai on a huge buffet. The total food cost was $10 a person, which was reasonable for the food available. It does get busy so make a reservation and try for a table away from the heat of the barbecue area. The Holiday Inn also has an upmarket restaurant (flip-flops forbidden), **Sam's Steak House**, which is air conditioned and without views but with excellent US and Australian steaks. Nothing too Thai about that or at the nearby **Pizzeria** where they bake their pizza in wood-fired ovens.

Jasmine, Kata Beach: Truly Thai and truly pleasant, just south of the Kata Sun hotel. On our first visit lunch for the two of us was 260 Baht ($5.20). Lindsey enjoyed noodles with chicken and I made short work of shrimp in tamarind sauce. The price included steamed rice, Coke and a Sprite. The waitress had limited English. Her parting words were, "Papa you will come back." How right she was. We became regular visitors. There are excellent dinner specials that change every night and all at good prices. Breakfast is a bargain too. A full American breakfast with bacon and ham and sausage costs 150 Baht. The coffee is robust, to put it politely.

La Chaumiere, 50/7 Moo, 7 Thanon Siayaun, on the road to Rawai Beach, ☎ 01272 0074, $. Neat little French-Thai bistro on the side of the road. Strays into the $$ slot if you stay on the French part of the menu. We had a great beef bourgeon and fresh fish filets in garlic and spent 900 Baht. A snooker table provides the ambience.

Salaloy Seafood, 52/2 Rawai Beach, ☎ 07618 9003, $. Choice of where to sit at this very inexpensive seafood restaurant. There are mats where you sit on the beach or across the road in the restaurant itself. Five of us had an ample lunch including a whole steamed grouped in ginger sauce with mushrooms for 700 Baht. And that included a small bottle of Sang Som rum. They don't serve cocktails but will gladly sell a bottle of liquor and the mixers. Sort of brown-bagging Thai style. Entertainment is watching the waiters crossing the busy road to serve those sitting on the beach.

Mimmi's, 43/48 Saiyuan Road, Rawai. (At the junction with the road from Kata Beach).An upmarket restaurant with attractive décor and the prices are still very reasonable. The whole operation is well organized. Good combination of Thai and western food, fine service and the sort of spot you want to visit again. We haven't been disappointed with anything we have eaten here.

The Orchid Coffee Garden, about 500 meters from Mimmi's mentioned above heading towards Nai Harn Beach, ☎ 07628 8941. Very pleasant spot for coffee or a quiet drink and a place we have used many times for breakfast. For just 100 Baht you get a very complete English repast – orange juice, eggs, sausage, grilled tomatoes, a piece of liver, baked beans toast and coffee. Open from 8am to 10pm serving snacks, ice creams and a good hamburger. Relaxing place with very attractive girls to serve you.

Nightlife

So many hotels provide good in house entertainment in the evenings that many tourists don't venture far after dinner unless it is to visit the FantaSea show or the Simon Cabaret.

In every section of the island there are the street markets and neighborhood bars. At the time of writing laws have come into effect to close the bars at 1am but everyone thinks that is a temporary measure and will eventually be change.

One place that always attracts the crowds is Patong with its hundreds of neon-lit bars, clubs, pubs and girly joints. Prices are normally low and the noise high. A couple of places do warrant mention.

Safari Disco, 28 Thanon Sirirat, on the same side of the road as the Simon Cabaret but farther south. Great jungle décor complete with waterfall. The younger crowd stays away since the music is mostly from the 1980s. The place doesn't get going until 10pm and closes promptly at 3am. Expect to pay a little more here for drinks than the bars in Patong proper. Gets busy, particularly during the King's Cup regatta when the sailing fraternity tacks in.

Banana Pub & Disco, 124 Thanon Thaveewong. In the center of the main beachfront street, close to the large Patong Seafood Restaurant. Very popular spot with a mix of young Thais, farangs who live in the area, and tourists. There's a bar downstairs and disco upstairs. Live music nightly from 9pm to 2am. Interesting games of skill played in the bar area.

Molly Malone's, a block south of the Banana Club, claims to be the first authentic Irish bar on the Island. It's open all day from 11am until 2am serving Guinness on tap and Irish beers. There's an Irish band playing every night and if you don't like the bar food there is a Kentucky Fried Chicken outlet next door.

Beyond Phuket

Introduction

IN THIS CHAPTER

The change is quite dramatic when you leave Phuket after a few days on this holiday island, which was called *Jungceylon* by the Greek geographer Ptolemy back in the year 157 AD. As you travel north across the **Sarisin Bridge** linking Phuket with the Thai mainland it feels like you're leaving behind a haven of vacations and heading for the true Thailand where farming, and not farangs, are the main means of support.

That holds true for 50 kilometers as you pass through the lush countryside, where women on the roadside offer pineapples for five Baht apiece. The shops in towns like **Khok Kloi** sell everyday goods, not beach gear or souvenirs. Towards the coast, fishing and shrimp farming thrive and, inland, rubber trees stand ready to produce the latex that is a major earner for the local population.

Before departing Phuket, first-time drivers leaving the island will be faced with the daunting sight of large signs proclaiming "checkpoint ahead." In the median of the four-lane highway is a large tent housing a dozen policemen. There are road bumps to slow you down as the lane is brought to single file and you pass the check point. We have passed this point in both directions dozens of time and never once have we been stopped – or seen anyone else apprehended. The only time it is an inconvenience is if one is staying at the Marriott and wants to travel south into town: As you enter the four-lane you have to turn north and pass the checkpoint, make a U-turn and pass through it in the other direction.

In all fairness, Highway 402 is the only road on or off of the island and it probably offers good security if needed for checking dubious vehicles coming or going. On the way to the bridge there is a nice beach visible from the road, which would make an ideal picnic spot.

History

Phang Nga was first inhabited by people who built small communities on the banks of the Phang-nga River in a district called *Kraphu Nga*. The district expanded in the reign of King Rama II (1809-1824) when Burmese troops invaded southern Thailand. Large numbers of Thais fled from the towns of Takuapa, Takua Thung, and Thalang (then the capital of Phuket), which were held by the Burmese, and settled in Kraphu Nga. When the Burmese were expelled many of the families remained here. In the reign of King Rama III (1824-1851) Kraphu Nga village became a town named Phang Nga and was elevated to a province in 1933. The present population is estimated at 250,000 – 83% Thai-Buddhist and 17% Muslim.

North from Phuket

Crossing the bridge puts us in the province of **Phang Nga**. (The main city, which we will visit later, has the same name). The province borders on **Ranong** and **Surat Thani** in the north, **Phuket** and the **Andaman Sea** in the south, **Surat Thani** and **Krabi** in the east and the **Andaman Sea** in the west. The eight counties in the province are **Amphoe Muang**, **Kuraburi**, **Thap Put**, **Takua Thung**, **Takuapa**, **Thai Muang**, and **Ko Yao**. The terrain of the province is mostly mountains and forests combined with rubber plantations. The province has two major rivers, the Phang Nga and the Takuapa. There are 105 small islands in the Andaman Sea which belong to this province, most of them in the northwest.

Khok Kloi

The first town you reach after leaving Phuket is Khok Kloi, where Highway 4, the Phetchakasem Highway, splits. In one direction, it heads north to Bangkok; the right turn will take you around towards Krabi. Today we are heading north. Once clear of the town we leave the main highway, take a left turn and head towards the sea and the northern beaches of Thai Muang, which are undeveloped except for a couple of luxury homes and the 56-room **Hot Spring Beach Resort & Spa**, 79 Moo 8 Na Toey, Thai Muang, ☎ 07742 5532, fax 07742 5376, a hotel that is totally cut off from the outside world. Rooms here go for $70 a night during the low season and double that in the high season (from November to April). Main attraction has to be the hot-spring outdoor pool. It certainly is not for the surrounding attractions, of which there are none. The tsunami caused some damage to several rooms, the restaurant and beachfront area, forcing the resort to close for three months.

There is however one small restaurant on the main road leading out of Khok Kloi that is well worth a visit. It's called **Reun Mai Kaen**, 43/2 Moo 3 Reun Mai Kaen, ☎ 07658 1554. It's very Thai; they do have an English menu but you have to point at what you want, not just say it. Specials of the day feature all kinds of delicious game and poultry, including the very popular venison. A group of us ate there and concentrated on fish dishes, and lots of them. When we split the bill it was under 150 Baht per person. There's a coffee shop next door that sells all kinds of local cookies and cakes; get some to snack on as you travel.

Our 20-minute diversion gave us a quick look at fish farming, a rapidly growing industry throughout southern Thailand. Ironically the fish produced is not so popular with the locals. Several of the small roadside restaurants state on their menus that their fish does not come from the farms. One restaurant owner explained to us that the farm fish was fine for the farangs in the fancy hotels, but the local people wanted their fish from the sea.

Thai Muang

Back on Highway 4 we head for Thai Muang. We leave the road there to visit the town's northern beaches and stop off at the **Thai Muang Golf Course**. The course and clubhouse look in good shape but the chalets looked a little drab and lonely. Perhaps our love of luxury is beginning to show.

The beaches to the north are attractive and the promenade, before you reach the **Khao Lampi-Thai Muang National Park**, is undergoing a facelift. You get the feeling that it will not be long before this area starts developing.

Thai Muang Beach stretches for 13 kilometers parallel to the road. The water is clear, and good for swimming. From November to February sea turtles come on to the beach to lay their eggs. Locals venture down to the shoreline at night to watch the egg-laying and after the hatching period there is a turtle releasing festival similar to the one held in Phuket. When development comes, as it surely will, hopefully the national park service will be able to protect the turtle breeding areas.

The greatest surprise on this outing was just ahead. We had passed by the area a couple of years earlier and noted that there was a handful of bungalows available for rent; nothing lavish or luxurious. The accommodation was mainly for those interested in exploring the natural delights and wonders of the nearby mountains and national parks. On this trip, we saw that the 20-kilometer stretch of road from Khaolak Beach to Takuapa had been totally transformed into a new Riviera. But it would be short lived; the forthcoming tsunami saw to that.

Khaolak Beach to Takuapa

When we originally wrote this piece, new buildings were sprouting up everywhere. Some were luxury resorts, others were the old bungalows retuned for the new millennium looking shabby alongside their new neighbors. We were stunned by the rapid development, and many people were concerned that this stretch of coastline would become the Patong or Pattaya of tomorrow. Just a few weeks after we visit the tsunami charged the area for ever.

The dozens of new shops had either disappeared completely or were left as piles of rubble. Many of them were the "where you from?" tailor shops that dominate so many tourist areas (we gave the tailor shops this name since the opening line of the touts that parade outside the stores is, "Where you from?")

■ Things to See & Do

One thing the tsunami did not affect were the forests and mountains that lie to the east of Highway 4 and are part of the **Khao Lak-Lamru National Park**. The park spreads over the four counties of Thai Muang, Kapong, Takuapa and Muang and covers an area of some 150 square kilometers. It has deep virgin forests and a number of waterfalls, and its abundant flora and fauna make it the perfect area for trekking. For divers, the Similan Islands are more easily reached from the coast here than from Phuket.

There are several waterfalls that can be reached from Highway 4. They are well signposted. Other falls are best visited by entering the park from **Takuapa** in the north or from **Phang Nga Town** in the south.

Eco Khaolak Adventure, 47/7 Moo 9, Bangnaisee, ☎ 07642 0224 was closed for business because of the tsunami. Hopefully they will open up again. They operated a variety of tours in the area. One is a full-day safari, which includes elephant trekking in the jungle, swimming at a waterfall and bamboo rafting. Price, including a barbecue seafood lunch, was 1,950 Baht.

■ Where to Stay

This area was the worst hit of anywhere in Thailand. All the resorts we had earlier visited were completely destroyed or severely damaged, at the time of writing it was uncertain if any of the resorts would rebuild and reopen. We have left telephone numbers and Website addresses in the hope that some will open again. It's not only the resorts that were devastated but much of the local infrastructure was destroyed. The small shopping centers, little bars and cafés were all victims of the tsunami.

ACCOMMODATIONS PRICE SCALE	
Indicates rates charged per night during high-season for a double room, including breakfast and all service charges. Prices vary according to the exchange rate between the US dollar and Thai Baht. Most hotels offer discounts from their published rack rates during low season. All those listed accept major credit cards; rooms have direct-dial telephones and private bathrooms.	
$	Under $50
$$	$51 to $100
$$$	$101 to $175
$$$$	Over $175

Khaolak Merlin Resort, 7/7 Petchkasem Road, Lumkaen, ☎ 07642 8300, fax 07644 200, www.merlinphuket.com, $$$. The tsunami caused major damage to the resort; when we last visited repairs were underway but no date was given as to when it might reopen. We were here just a few weeks before the tidal wave, and admired the four swimming pools on the tiered hillside down to the beach level, the impressive focus of this luxury resort. Over 200 rooms and suites, some with direct access into a pool, and a choice of restaurants made this a favorite for German package tourists. When it reopens it will be worth spending 500 Baht a night to upgrade to the pool-access rooms. There were 12 private villas with their own outdoor Jacuzzi pools that went for as much as 30,000 Baht per night in high season. Tennis courts, fitness center and spa. Despite its size this was a tasteful and tranquil place to stay.

We liked our visit so well we decided to take lunch here. After so many inexpensive meals it was time to splurge. Lindsey selected the mixed seafood satay and I chose the lobster thermidor. Both dishes were delicious. The service was superb and the bill, including drinks and coffee a reasonable 1,350 Baht considering what we had, but it was very expensive by Thai standards.

Later in the day we got caught in a major rainstorm and pulled into a roadside café rather than drive through the weather. We ordered a plate of fried pineapple and a plate of fried banana; both were cooked in a tempura-style batter and served with local honey. We had a coffee and Coke to drink and the bill for that was 90 Baht. Once we entered the cover of the restaurant the rain stopped. It remained that way until we departed. Then the heavens opened up again.

Mukdara Beach Villa & Spa, 26/14 Moo7, T. Khuk Khak, ☎ 07642 9999, fax 07642 0098, www.mukdarabeach.com, $$$$. This was a lavish resort set on fifteen acres along Bang Niang and Khao Lak beaches before the tsunami devastated it. The place had everything from a small golf course to three swimming pools including the honeymoon pool with its own waterfall. When we visited before the tsunami there were 64 garden villas completed and a lot more were under construction. All were flattened. It was a great-looking resort in a once-great location. Whether it will be rebuilt remains to be decided.

Sofitel Magic Lagoon, 41 / 12 Moo 3, Khuk Khak, ☎ 07642 9300, fax 07642 0030, www.sofitel.com, $$$. This resort took a mighty hit from the tsunami. Many of the employees and guests died here, either taken out to see or trapped in their rooms. It was the ideal family hotel with 319 rooms and suites, an enormous 14,000-square-meter lagoon-style swimming pool, tennis court and well-run Kids Club. The resort's big plus was that it was right on the beach, the tragic reason it suffered so severely. Sofitel hotels are partners with Delta Airlines, in their frequent flyer program. Shortly before the tsunami frequent flyer members were offered generous discounts to stay here. The offer also extended to the **Sofitel Raja Orchid Hotel** in Khon Kaen, a fantastic hotel that we stayed in. You can learn more about that property and Khon Kaen on page 345 in the *Tour of the Northeast* chapter. At the time of this writing there was no word on whether the resort would be rebuilt.

Theptharo Lagoon Beach Resort & Spa, PO Box 5, Takuapa, ☎ 07642 0154, fax 07643 0152, www.theptharo.com, $$. This resort was a little older and its wonderful waterfront location made it vulnerable to the killer tsunami. Most of its 70 chalet-style bungalows faced the sea or the lagoon and were destroyed. They had been positioned to give spectacular sunsets over the Andaman Sea. Once again there is no news about rebuilding.

The Khao Lak Sunset Resort, 26/7 Khuk Khak, ☎ 07642 0075, fax 07642 0147, $$. Another victim of the tsunami, this unpretentious resort with 63 rooms and junior suites all enjoyed sea views. The property was near, not on, the beach and had beautiful gardens and a more than satisfactory swimming pool. Official word: "Badly damaged. Closed until further notice."

Le Meridien Khao Lak Beach & Spa Resort, 9/9 Moo 1. Kuk Kak, ☎ 07642 7500, fax 07642 7501, www.khaolak.lemeridien.com, $$$$. Probably the leading resort in Khao Lak and severely damaged by the tsunami, with the loss of many lives. The future of Khao Lak is uncertain if this resort is not rebuilt. Before the giant waves dealt their death blow this hotel had all the luxury you would expect from a five-star Le Meridien. It was a mega-new project, with 243 bedrooms, suites and villas. There were ballrooms, conference rooms, a spa. It employed hundreds. There was a scuba center, and a water-sports center for windsurfing, sailing, kayaking, and snorkeling. There was a Penguin kids club with special water sports area. There were two freeform pools with waterslides, fountains and Jacuzzis set in a tropical garden and two floodlit tennis courts. There was even a 25-meter pool in the spa area with its own bar. The low end of the accommodation, the deluxe rooms, had a sitting area, broadband data port, and 29-inch flat screen TV, bathroom with separate bathtub and rainfall shower. Top accommodation was the two-bedroom presidential villa, which had a vast living area with a 42-inch plasma TV, separate dining area including a kitchenette. Adjoining was a study – with wireless broadband data port and international telephone lines – that opened onto a private garden patio with secluded dining area. Each bedroom had its own lounge area with plasma TV and broadband data port and the bathrooms had a king-size Jacuzzi, separate rainfall shower and a secluded outside tropical shower area. The terrace had a 32-square-meter swimming pool surrounded by an exclusive private garden overlooking the beach. All of this spectacular luxury was wrecked in a matter of a few minutes.

Takuapa

This provincial capital, a pleasant, spacious market town, became even busier as a center for much of the after-tsunami activity. The town was spared any damage but it became the site for mortuaries and a center for identifying victims. When plans were announced to move all the unidentified remains to Phuket for DNA testing the villagers protested, saying they wanted the bodies of Thai victims to remain in Phang Nga province. We watched the peaceful demonstration and saw the sadness on the faces of the protestors who had lost relatives or friends to the tsunami. The officials listened and agreed to their request. Only the remains of the foreigners were moved to a new mortuary set up near Phuket Airport, which made it easier for repatriation once identities were confirmed.

East from Phuket

Krabi

Once you leave the island of Phuket, it is a pleasant and relatively easy two-hour drive to Krabi with spectacular scenery and fascinating towns and villages along the way to help pass the time. It's a four-lane highway all the way from the Sarisin Bridge to the town of Phang Nga. Then it's two lanes as you enter the province of Krabi and continue onto Krabi Town.

It is on these two-lane roads that the true quality of Thai driving comes into its worst. Many drivers assume there is a center lane for passing, which there is not, and dangerously head down the center of the road in the hope that the oncoming driver will move over and the vehicle being passed will do the same. Most times it works thanks to a lot of luck, good brakes and the use of the narrow strip on either side of the road that is reserved for motorcycles. Many times the two-wheeled vehicles are forced into grass verges. Traffic deaths in Thailand are tragically very high and most times it is the motorcyclist who becomes the innocent victim. New laws were introduced to make crash-helmet wearing mandatory. You see most drivers in the heavily policed areas wearing them, but rarely do you see the pillion passenger (or passengers) with one. Once you get into the rural areas crash helmets are as rare as a Thai town without a temple.

Several things have changed since we last made this trip years ago. The road is far better and there are now ample gas stations and an abundance of large green "U-Turn – Keep Right" signs, which appear with unpleasant regularity telling those who want to go back from where they came to use the right lane and not suddenly cut across the traffic to make the maneuver.

And there are those items that fortunately have not changed. As you get closer to the province of Krabi, more and more of those giant tree-covered limestone cliffs, called karsts, push out of the ground like giant fingers pointing to the sky. Then there are the tiny farms with the odd cow tethered by its nose at the side of the road, ignoring the traffic that roars by just a few feet away. Geese strut alongside young pineapples, and behind the tiny farmhouse is the constant background of rubber trees, still an important industry in Phang Nga province. Two hamlets flash by that look like Western towns with Japanese pickup trucks parked in front of wooden store fronts.

■ Getting Here

By Air

Krabi Airport, ☎ 07563 6541, fax 07563 6549, has direct services to Bangkok, Ko Samui and Singapore. **Thai Airways**, ☎ 07563 6541 (airport office), 07562 2439 (town office), has several daily flights from Bangkok, as does **Phuket Air**, ☎ 07563 6934. **Bangkok Airways**, ☎ 07569 2484, has daily services from Bangkok and also has flights to the island of Samui. **Silk Air**, ☎ 07562 3370, has three services a week linking Krabi with Singapore. The no-frills carrier **One-Two-GO** operates daily services from Bangkok to Krabi using either a 444-seat Boeing B747 or a 216-seat B757 depending on demand. Flights depart from Bangkok at 5pm daily except Thursday, when departure time is 8:20am. Return flights leave Krabi at 6:45pm. One-way fare is 1,650 Baht, www.fly12go.com/en/main.

By Car

We drove from Phuket. The distance to Krabi Town from Phuket City is 185 kilometers. From Bangkok there are two routes. If you take Highway 4 all the way the distance is 946 kilometers. There is a shortcut, although the road is not so good, if you leave Highway 4 at Chumphorn and take Route 41 and then Route 4035 until it rejoins Highway 4. That route is 814 kilometers and is the route taken by the buses from Bangkok.

If you're headed to the beaches you need to make a right turn before Highway 4 takes you into Krabi Town.

By Train

There is no direct train link to Krabi. You can take the train from Bangkok to one of several stations and then take a bus. For more information look in the Chapter Trains of Thailand or contact the **State Railway of Thailand**, ☎ 02223 7010.

By Bus

VIP and air conditioned buses leaves Bangkok's southern bus terminal in the late afternoon and take at least 12 hours for the trip. Local number for bus information, ☎ 07621 1480.

■ Things to Do

Beaches

The beaches of Krabi are, in our opinion, not the best that Thailand has to offer. And the water of Nga Phang bay along the coastal regions is not as crystal-clear as much of the promotional material will tell you. The best of the beaches and the crystal clear water is found in the numerous islands that are so easy to reach from the Krabi shoreline (see page 256). There, too, are the spectacular dive sites where the simple snorkel mask will reveal the underwater wonders of coral and multi colored tropical fish. For those who dive deeper with the aid of scuba, the wonders are even more magnificent (see page 257).

The first beach west of Krabi is known as **Shell Fossil Beach**, with an amazing number of huge blocks of compressed shell fossils said to be 75 million years old, although they could pass as odd shaped chunks of concrete. If you want to avoid the drive to the shell cemetery, the blocks are visible from the longtail boats that ply between Krabi Town and the spectacular Phra Nang peninsula.

Parks

Krabi Town is a bustling place and fishing port and a major transit point for those visiting the islands and beaches that can't be reached by road. Its crowning glory is **Thara Park**, an idyllic oasis at the southern tip of the peninsula where all the things you want in a park are here for all to enjoy. Its gardens are ideal for strolling through, there are places to sit and watch the world and boats go by, sturdy playgrounds for the young and several inexpensive bars and cafés where parents can watch the young ones play.

With its wonderful limestone cliffs and giants caves along the beaches it is easy to see why Krabi attracts so many rock climbers. Main centers for the activity are along the beaches of Railay and Nam Mao. What pleased us most about the rock climbers is the safety and organization that surrounds the activity. Numerous routes, over 600, are well planned and all graded depending upon the climbers' abilities. There are courses designed for novices up to challenging climbs for the most experienced.

If you want to learn more about climbing the cliffs and caves here are some companies that handle all levels of the sport: **Krabi Rock Climbing**, ☎ 01676 0642; **Krabi Cliff Man**, ☎ 07562 1768; **King Climbers**, ☎ 07562 2581; and **Pra Nang Rock Design Hot Rocks**, ☎ 07561 1509.

Scuba Diving

Diving is a major attraction for visitors to Krabi. Many of the major diving sites can also be reached from Phuket; those are listed in the previous chapter (page 209). Other sites in the province are at **Ko Lanta** and **Phi Phi Islands**, which appear later in this chapter (see pages 262 and 266).

PADI Centers

Ao Nang Divers, 143 Moo 2, Ao Nang, ☎ 07563 7242, fax 07563 7246, www.aonang-divers.com. **Aqua Vision Dive Center**, 137 Moo 2, Ao Nang, ☎ 07563 7415, www.aqua-vision.net. **Kon Tiki Co Ltd.**, 39/1 Moo 2 Ao Nang, ☎ 07563 7675, fax 07563 7676, www.kontiki-krabi.com. **Poseidon Dive Center**, 23 /1 Moo 2, Ao Nang, ☎ 07563 7263, fax 07563 7264, www.poseidon-krabi.com.

Phra Nang Peninsula

The peninsula is home to three beaches: **Railay West**, **Railay East** (also known as *Nam Mao*) and **Phra Nang** (also known as the Phra Nang Cave beach). The cave, *Tham Phra Nang Nok*, is named for a fertility goddess and contains large phallic symbols.

Local fishermen leave offerings here in the hope of improved prosperity and potency.

The peninsula is cut off from the mainland by the jungle valleys and the limestone cliffs. Three of the beaches, the two Railays and Phra Nang are connected by narrow pathways that wind around the base of the cliffs. The two best beaches are Phra Nang and West Railay. East Railay fails as a swimming site because of the dense mangrove growth and a tide that goes out, and out.

There are lots of places to stay on the peninsula but only one that we would consider and that is the Rayavadee, listed a little later. Much of the accommodation here is not inexpensive but it lacks some of the luxuries that we have come to expect. The peninsula gets busy in the high season but prices and the number of people drop considerably in the low season from May to October when the whole area is not at its best.

Getting Here

This is relatively easy. Longtail boats from **Chao Fa Pier** in Krabi Town leave as soon as they have a handful of travelers. The journey takes 45 minutes and the charge is 70 Baht. Longtail boats from **Ao Nang**, the next beach west, only take ten minutes to West Railey and charge 50 Baht.

A great way to enjoy the true beauty of Krabi is to rent a longtail boat from Ao Nang and visit some of the nearby islands like Chicken Island (Ko Gai) or Ko Poda. You can also hire boats from the waterfront in Krabi City to explore some of the mangrove canals, or visit Krabi's most famous karst, ***Khao Kanab Nam***, which is over 100 meters high and has caves that contain prehistoric paintings as well as stalactites and stalagmites.

Ao Nang is a typical seafront resort where the road passes along the coast. The beach isn't great but it a good place to rent a boat or stroll along the promenade. It has its fair share of tailor shops and massage parlors with many of the resorts staggered behind the main street. After Ao Nang the roads passes inland and winds around to Klong Muang Beach. The road finally dead-ends just beyond the **Tubkaak Resort**. There is a lot of construction in the area as new resorts are built and the roads may be closed off for limited periods of time.

On our return drive we thought we would explore the town of Phang Nga. The province is so scenic and varied we wondered what treasures the town might hold. The answer was precious little. We wandered north and south of Highway 4 and learned the town of Phang Nga was neither quaint nor cute, and contained little in the way of quality.

■ Where to Stay

For price scale see page 251

Krabi

The Nakamanda Resort & Spa, Khlong Moung Beach, Nongthale, ☎ 07652 8200, fax 07564 4390, www.nakamanda.com, $$$$. Friendly, small boutique resort with only 39 rooms and suites where a lot is included in the room price. Top price in high season for a very special villa is 45,000 Baht and a luxury room costs 9,000 Baht. The price includes transfers from Krabi airport, a daily English high tea served in the drawing room, breakfast either in the restaurant or in your villas, daily newspaper, butler served tea or coffee in your villa and a choice of foot-massage or body scrub at the resort's spa. Youthful staff whose lack of experience is adequately compensated by their enthusiasm and friendliness. Spectacular pool makes up for the limited beach, which does offer a walkway to an island at low water. The tsunami caused minor damage to the swimming pool, which was fixed in a couple of days.

Sheraton Krabi Beach Resort, 155 Moo 2, Nongthale, ☎ 07562 8000, fax 07562 8028, www.sheraton.com/krabi, $$$$. Stunning new expensive resort on Khlong Moung Bay with 246 rooms including 30 club floor rooms and six executive suites. Cheapest low-season rate is $220 plus service taxes rising to $588 a night for an executive suite in high season. Best swimming beach in the area and 30 minutes from Krabi airport. Large lavish grounds and swimming pool, spa, fitness center and tennis courts. Good selection of eating spots within the resort but cheaper and very acceptable local restaurants are close by the entrance gates. The tsunami had no effect on the operation.

Rayavadee Premier Resort, 214 Moo 2, Ao Nang, ☎ 07562 0740-3, fax 07562 0630, www.rayavadee.com, $$$$. With the cheapest pavilions at $500 a night this is the most expensive places to stay in Krabi. The resort is on the Phra Nang headland and accessible only by boat, a 15-minute ride from Krabi Town. The 100 fully equipped pavilions are nestled in a coconut grove surrounded by limestone hills and three beaches. The pavilions are grouped in "villages" named after the nearest beach. **Phra Nang** village: Located near one of Krabi's best beaches, the pavilions are more isolated with lots of trees and set between two cliffs. **Railay** village: Pavilions here are closer to each other and near the resort's excellent swimming pool. **Nam Mao** village: At the center of the resort and ideal for those who don't enjoy a lot of walking. Fortunately there was no loss of life here as a result of tsunami. There was minor damage to the property and some of the gardens near the shore had to be replanted. The resort closed for a few weeks to take care of the repairs.

Pavilion Queen's Bay, 56/3 Moo 3, Ao Nang Beach, ☎ 07563 7611, fax 07563 7609, www.pavilionhotels.com, $$$$. This luxury 108-room resort is set high on a hill overlooking Ao Nang Beach. The resort with all the facilities you could want also enjoys great views of the surrounding jungle. It suffered no ill effects from the tsunami. Rooms are extra large and prices including taxes and service range from 8,000 Baht for a standard room (66 square meters) to 14,000 Baht for the suites (98 square meters). There are numerous places to eat at the resort, all with reasonable prices for set meals, and you're just 17 kilometers away from Krabi town. Other Thailand Pavilion hotels and resorts are in Phuket, Kanchanaburi and Songkhla.

The Tubkaak, 123 Moo 3, Tubkaak Beach, Nongthale, ☎ 07562 8400, fax 07562 8499, www.tubkaakresort.com, $$$. Small, exquisite resort with only 44 rooms and suites at the end of a winding road (this road is under construction and likely to be that way until 2006, as development moves in this direction). Fabulous rooms are complimented by fabulous views across the bay. There was no damage caused by the tsunami. Cheapest of the accommodation is the superior room with a low-season rate of 5,500 Baht per night rising to 45,000 Baht in high season for an elaborate two-story suite with its own infinity pool.

> *Each guest at the Tubkaak gets a 600-Baht daily credit for food and drinks, which can be accumulated during your stay. The hotel's lobby sits above a library that serves as business center and bar.*

Krabi La Playa Resort, 143 Moo 3, Ao Nang, ☎ 07563 7015, fax 07569 5497, www.krabilaplaya.com, $$$. Oddly named since La Playa is Spanish for beach and this luxury resort is 150 meters away from Noppharat Thara and Ao Nang beaches. However the unusual, spectacular swimming pool with individual whirlpools and poolside salas, and the two acres of tropical gardens make up for that. Its position also assured that the hotel suffered no ill effects from the tsunami. The resort has 79 rooms split between three wings – a four-story building and two five-story building. There are elevators for all buildings. Rates for the rooms start at

4,700 Baht but the hotel's Website has good value last-minute packages, which brings that figure down substantially.

A Spanish touch: At La Playa, tapas are served at the swim-up pool bar from 10am until 10pm.

Andaman Sunset Resort, 31 Moo 2, Ao Nang Beach, ☎ 07563 7484, fax 07563 7322, $. Adequate and convenient complex of 33 rooms set around two small swimming pools, the smaller for youngsters, just across the street from the beach. The adjoining Wanna's Place restaurant serves a good combination of Thai and Swiss dishes and there are nice views across the bay. Room rates start at 1,460 Baht a night and the restaurant prices are just as attractive. The tsunami had little effect here. A few pieces of the furniture on the beach were washed away.

Best Western Ao Nang Bay Resort & Spa, 211 Moo 2, Ao Nang, ☎ 07563 7071-4, fax 07563 7070, $. This low rise, low cost resort, is nestled in dense tropical gardens in a hillside overlooking Noppharat Thara Beach and 200 meters from the sea. Prices for one of the 71 rooms start at 1,200 Baht. Facilities include a large swimming pool with Jacuzzi, a children's pool and a health club with an exercise room and steam and sauna rooms. The tsunami had no effect on the resort's operations.

Andaman Holiday Resort, Klong Muang Beach, ☎ 07564 4321, fax 07564 4320, $. This 79-room resort stands on a former rubber plantation and has retained some of the original coconut and rubber trees as part of its landscaping. The rooms are light and spacious and prices start at 1,900 Baht. Expect to pay more for the superior rooms and villas, which have individual roof top terraces to enjoy views over the sea. The resort is on a secluded one-kilometer stretch of Klong Muang Beach, north of the more developed areas of Had Noppharat Thara, Ao Nang and Railey Beach. There is a choice of restaurants and bars. Krabi Town is 20 kilometers away, Ao Nang Beach 15, and Krabi airport 26.

The Phi Phi Islands

We have mentioned these islands briefly in the Phuket chapter, but since they officially lie in the province of Krabi we give more details here.

Before the tsunami these once-peaceful and lonely islands of Phi Phi, set midway between Phuket and Krabi, were becoming over-visited and covered in litter. The tsunami changed that in a hurry. Much of the cheap basic bungalow accommodation on Phi

Phi Don, the larger of the islands, was destroyed. The beaches got a sudden deep cleansing. The daily arrival of thousands of trippers abruptly stopped and the islands returned to their former quieter state. How long that will last is not known, though most of the tour operators are now finding alternate destinations for their vessels. The islands are stunningly beautiful; fortunately, Phi Phi Leh remains undeveloped.

Sadly, the tsunami had a devastating effect on the islands. Hundreds died here. If you have ever visited **Phi Phi Don**, as we have done on several occasions, you will have stood at the narrow point where you can see the sea in both directions. It was at this point that the tsunami hit from both sides. People near here had no chance of survival.

The main gathering place on the islands is at the pier on **Tonsai Bay**, which got a severe battering. It was not the loveliest spot on Phi Phi but it was certainly the liveliest. The islands were a haven for backpackers as well as upmarket visitors. There were over 50 places to stay, the majority of them beach bungalows, which vanished in the tsunami. Miraculously, some of the quality resorts were unharmed. Some stayed open and continued to welcome guests, but very few came.

The true beauty of the area still remains on the nearby beaches and offshore islands, which are a wonderland for serious scuba divers and perfect for the timid swimmer who can enjoy the undersea vistas with the aid of a mask and snorkel. There were several scuba divers underwater at the time of the tsunami who knew nothing about the treacherous waves until they surfaced after their diving expedition, although others were not so fortunate.

Phi Phi Leh, to the south, is not inhabited, but attracts a lot of visitors. The island is all limestone cliffs, caves and small coves ideal for snorkeling. **Viking Cave** on the northeast side is special for two reasons. It houses some prehistoric paintings and it is where the sea gypsies (you can read more about them in the *Phuket* chapter, page 182) gather birds' nests, that delicacy needed in Chinese cooking. Harvesting takes place between February and May. The teams of gatherers have to balance on rickety bamboo scaffolding high into the cave to reach the nests. It is a lucrative, if dangerous, occupation, with the nests fetching $1,000 a kilo.

■ Getting Here

From Phuket

Most Phuket tour operators did have programs for day-trips here, with departures from various points along the eastern shoreline. Some include sightseeing while you're here, with visits to **Phi Phi Leh** and the **Viking Cave**. Although these were curtailed after the tsunami they are expected to resume when the Phi Phi Don is fully operational. Costs will vary depending on the speed of your crossing. Speedboats cost considerably more than the public ferry, which operates twice a day from the fishery authority port on Sirey Island just outside Phuket City. The ferry leaves at 8:30am and 1:30pm and there are two return trips. If you are staying at one of the resorts we have listed we suggest you organize your transfers when you book your room. Some of the hotels operate their own services, which can save you the unpleasant business of changing boats at Tonsai Bay. The **Holiday Inn** offers a round-trip transfer service from any Phuket hotel or the airport for 1,250 Baht.

The **Phi Phi Island Village Resort** operates its own speedboat from November 1 to April 30, which can carry up to 18 passengers. It operates twice daily from the Boat Lagoon Marina and goes directly to the resort's private beach area, which eliminates the stop and transfer at Tonsai Pier. The rest of the year it's all-change at Tonsai.

From Krabi

Ferries leave Chao Fa Pier in Krabi Town at 10am and 2:30pm. The two-and-a-half-hour trip costs 150 Baht per person. Return journeys leave Tonsai Pier at 9am and 1pm. There is also a speedboat service from Ao Nang that departs at 9am, ☎ 07563 7152.

From Ko Lanta

There is a daily service that only operates between November and April. Departure times are 8am and 1pm.

In addition to all the above, we've found a couple of ways to get to the Phi Phi Islands that are a little different from the norm. The first is on the executive yacht *Phi Phi Cruiser*, ☎ 07621 1253, fax 07624 8062, www.phiphicruiser.com, which operates a daily trip. The 1,500 Baht price (850 Baht for children) includes a 7:15am hotel pick-up, swimming and snorkeling at **Maya Bay**, sightseeing around the Phi Phi Islands and lunch on Phi Phi Don. The vessel, which can carry as many as 300 passengers, leaves Ton Sai Bay at 3pm and gets back to Phuket at 5pm. If you want to get there quicker, fly there with **Blue Water Air Co. Ltd.**, 39/18 Moo 5, Vichitsongkram Road, Kathu, ☎ 01895 1839, fax 07635 1439, www.bluewaterair.com. Their 8,900-Baht package (7,500 Baht for children) includes hotel pick-up and a flight on a Cessna seaplane from Phuket International Airport, which gives you sightseeing over Phang Nga Bay before landing on the sea at Phi Phi. There's a boat to meet you for more sightseeing, time for swimming and lunch ashore before the flight back. The aircraft also does regular transfers to the islands and is available for charters.

■ Where to Stay

There were more than 50 places to stay on Phi Phi Don, most of them basic bamboo bungalows or shacks where the fans outnumbered air conditioning units by an uncomfortable majority. That majority did not make to the list that follows. One piece of advice: Limit the luggage you bring to a bare minimum – this is not a place that requires any kind of dressing-up, and you will appreciate having packed light when moving your luggage from ferry to longtail boat and along uneven paths.

Holiday Inn Resort, Laem Tong Beach, ☎ 07562 1334, www.krabi-hotels.com/holidayinnpp, $$$. This resort was not affected by the tsunami. It is an intimate boutique-style complex of 80 beachfront bungalows, all 24 square meters, where its beautiful isolated location rather than luxury is the great appeal. This was formerly the Phi Phi Palm Beach Travel Lodge. The bungalows, set amid 20 acres of tropical gardens, all have air conditioning, private bathrooms with showers, polished wooden floors and a private terrace. Unless you come on an all-inclusive package, meals are extra but not expensive: Breakfast 290 Baht, lunch 325 Baht and dinner 520 Baht. High-season room rates, excluding service and taxes start at 5,000 Baht a night. Low-season rates start at 3,300 Baht. Windsurfers, canoes and snorkeling equipment are available at no charge. The resort received an award from the Architectural Society of Thailand for its unique design. Ton Sai Village is four kilometers away and Maya Bay, which was the location of the movie *The Beach*, is five kilometers away.

Phi Phi Island Village Beach Resort & Spa, Loh Bakao Beach, ☎ 07561 2915, fax 07561 2916, $$$. Closest thing to luxury on the island this resort has its own 800-meter beach and its 80 Thai-style villas set on stilts are well set out on 70 acres of land

and have many items that others here don't – 110 square meters of living space, a separate living room, a tub in its bathroom, TV in the room together with DVD and CD players, telephone with Internet access outlet and a refrigerator. Look for special offers during low season when the resorts offers a two-night stay here for under 4,000 Baht with the option of upgrading to a better room for 1,000 Baht. The package includes the land transfer and some meals and discounts at its Wana spa. The resort did suffer some minor damage but continued to operate.

The Phi Phi Island Village Resort & Spa offers restaurant delivery service to your villa from 6am to 1am.

The Sofitel Phi Phi Villa & Spa, www.sofitel.com, $$$. This resort opened for business in 2005 after the tsunami had dealt its death blow. There are 147 individual villas set on a hillside. Each has 59 square meters of living spaces and great views of the Krabi coastline. There is a kids' club, two swimming pools, tennis course and a business center.

Phi Phi Natural Resort, Laem Thong Beach, ☎ 07561 3010, fax 07561 3000, www.krabi-hotels.com/ppnatural, $$. This is the most northerly resort on Phi Phi and is close to Cape Laem Thong. It suffered no ill effects from the tsunami. There is a small private beach for the resort but the longer Laem Thong Beach is close by. A total of 70 rooms available in five kinds of accommodation from cottages with garden views to more expensive cottages with sea views, family cottages, multi-bed cottages and standard rooms with in townhouse-style buildings. All rooms are well furnished, air conditioned and have TVs and telephones. High-season Internet rate is 2,800 Baht plus taxes and service without meals, which will cost about 1,250 Baht a day. Lots of water sports and boat trips for snorkeling and sightseeing available directly from the hotel.

PP Princess Resort, Loh Dalam Beach, ☎ 07562 2079, fax 07561 2188, www.ppprincess.com, $$$. Sadly, this resort, which offered some of the best accommodation available on the island, was totally washed away. Thirty-six employees and 100 foreign guests were lost. There were 100 bungalows in the complex all well equipped. The hotel said in its promotions that its clientele gained the most enjoyment from the diving offshore and the resort's spa. The good news is the resort is being rebuilt and is expected to open in 2006.

Ko Lanta

■ Introduction

To us this island was just a tiny blob on the map of Krabi province, a little area stuck out in the middle of the Andaman Sea. The sort of place you'd could easily miss. Are we glad that we didn't. This is an island – in fact two, **Ko Lanta Yai**, the large island and **Ko Lanta Noi** the smaller – that is just waiting to boom. This is how we imagine Phuket must have been 20 years ago.

But this is not a deserted island by any means. Some 20,000 people live here, and there is a road of sorts that runs from north to south along most of the island's 27 kilometers length. It's cemented in part; crazy-paved in others, dirt track for most of the way and has some of the world's biggest potholes. When it's dry dust fills the air, and when it rains the mud overfloweth. It has an abundance of road signs that mostly tell you that anywhere you're going is straight ahead.

It's not the easiest place to get to, which many people find one of its major appeals, but once you see the island up close with its verdant mountainous jungle spine peppered with sandy coves and beaches you know this is a place that will be a bustling tourist resort within a decade.

The main island is almost entirely Muslim, with a small enclave of Buddhists in the oldest part of the island, **Lanta Town**, which used to be Lanta's capital. This explains the noticeable absence of temples but where the people come temples are sure to follow, along with tailors shops, ladies of the evening and vast rows of neon signs. Right now the biggest invasion is that of the bulldozers and building equipment. At the time of writing there were no McDonalds or Burger Kings but as I type the golden arches are probably being prepared and the Colonel is possibly pressing his white suit for yet another Thai franchise opening.

On Ko Lanta there seems to be a genuine desire to make the development as controlled as possible. The residents are anxious to preserve the special harmony that has existed between the Thai-Muslims, Thai-Chinese and the original inhabitants, the sea gypsies, for hundreds of years. And everyone is united in preventing sex tourism from becoming part of life on the island.

The Gypsy Life

Ko Lanta has two sea-gypsy settlements (see page 181), one at **Sang-Ga-U** on the south east tip of the island, the second just south of **Saladan Village**. The sea gypsies here preserve many of their ancient ceremonies and customs, including setting boats adrift to bring good luck.

■ Getting Here

By Ferry

There is a car ferry from the Krabi mainland that normally operates from 7am to midnight. The jetty for the ferry is a 50-minute drive south from Krabi Airport. You drive south on Highway 4 to Highway 4206 where you make a right turn and head for the **Baan Hua Hin Pier**. The ferry crosses the short link to Ko Lanta Noi and the pier at **Baan Klong Mak**. Then you drive for 10 minutes across that island to the car ferry at **Baan Lang Sog**. Another short boat trip takes you to Saladan on Ko Lanta Yai. Total cost for the two ferries is 110 Baht. There is normally little time to wait for the ferries since they continually ply between the two very basic piers. It's interesting to watch the speed they load and unload. As soon as the ferry – it might be a converted old rice barge, or an open transport vessel with a side awning to provide shade for the foot-passengers – touches land the vehicles start moving off. There's no tying up. The boat keeps powering slowly ahead to keep in touch with the pier; once the last vehicle leaves the boat reloads, and within in minutes sets off across the narrow channel.

All of the hotels we list will arrange transportation from Krabi Airport, Krabi Town, Trang Airport or Phuket Airport. Prices vary but expect to pay 1,300 Baht per person for one-way transfer from Krabi and 2,400 Baht per person from Phuket Airport. We drove here from the southern part of Phuket. The total distance was 250 kilometers. We left at 6:30am, early enough to avoid the Phuket traffic, and arrived at the ferry point at 10am. The **Pimalai Resort** has its own jetty with a very pleasant welcome station, complete with bathrooms and sitting areas. They operate powerful high-speed diesel powered cruisers that take you directly to their jetty on the resort's beach. Cost of that trip is 1,500 Baht per person each way that includes a pick-up from Krabi Airport in their mini bus. The 50-minute boat ride is a pleasant experience and a great improvement on some of the rides we have taken in small speedboats elsewhere in Phang Nga bay, where the pounding against the waves can induce jaw-ache and white-knuckle pain from gripping on too tightly.

There are also regular passenger ferries from Krabi Town, Phuket, Phi Phi Island and Ao Nang and Railay on the Krabi mainland.

■ Things to Do

It's possible to drive around the island in a couple of hours and visit the villages of **Saladan** in the north and **Khlong Toah** and **Khlong Khong** in the center of the western shore. Other things to do on the island are elephant trekking and hiking. From the pictures we saw it appears you get to do a little elephant rafting as well, since the trek takes you into mountain streams.

As interesting as the drive around the island was, with an assortment of shops and art galleries in the various towns, the main beauty of the area is out at sea. We spent some time cruising around the eastern side of Ko Lanta; its tiny deserted offshore islands with weird rock formations and sandy inlets are extravagant in their lonely beauty. If you can hire a boat for a few hours it is a trip well worth taking. And if you are lucky, as we were, you might be joined by dolphins diving around your boat. After the busy waters around Phi Phi and Phuket it is a wonderful contrast with just an occasional fishing boat to see.

If you can't stay relaxed around the pool or on the beach there is a cooking school on the island. **Time for Lime**, at the south end of Klong Dao Beach (☎ 09967 5017, www.timeforlime.net), offers creative Thai cooking workshops.

■ Festivals & Events

December

In addition to celebrating the typical Thai festivals, Ko Lanta has one of its own. Every year from December 7- 9, after the King's Birthday celebrations, the **Laanta Lanta Festival** takes place on Long Beach (*Phra Ae*). This three-day celebration gives the islanders a chance to show off their culinary talents, as well as their cultural history, when more than 50 stalls offer every kind of Thai edible delight.

■ Where to Stay

There are numerous places to stay but most of them are for the backpackers and those who can handle being very close to nature and its creatures. Some of the basic accommodation lacks a few of the modern-day amenities that we require while traveling around. One young Thai was quick to point out that his bungalows had warm water, which is a dubious benefit; considering that this is southern Thailand where it is always hot, the chances of finding cold water rushing from a faucet are slim indeed. Our prices here are the same as previous listings. We have not included the cost of transfers to and from the island.

For price scale see page 251

The Pimalai Resort & Spa, Lanta Yai Island, ☎ 07560 7999, fax 07560 7998, www.pimalai.com, $$$$. For the first time in our listings we begin this one with a description of the spa, by far the most spectacular we have seen or enjoyed. The seven thatched-roofed treatment rooms are set in jungle, linked by wooden bridges. Wherever you sit or lie there is the sound of water trickling through streams and pools. The sense of relaxation before the treatments begin is truly enchanting. Considering the location, the hour-long treatments are well priced starting at 1,700 Baht. The resort itself is spread over 100 acres most of it hidden amid lush gardens and jungle dipping down to the 900-meter powdery white beach of Ban Kan Tiang. The "standard" rooms, of which there are 64, are large, with private balconies, and completely equipped right down to bedroom slippers, beach shoes and bathrobes. The more expensive "deluxe" rooms have views over the Andaman Sea and are considerably larger with 70 square meters of living space and large verandahs. High-season rack rate 14,500 Baht ++. There are also several two- and three-bedroom villas available complete with private pools and elegant outdoor living rooms with kitchen facilities. The villas are well spread out and the sloping walks between rooms, three fine restaurants, the large infinity swimming pool, and the beach are short enough to be enjoyable even in the tropical heat. Pimalai is a favorite spot for holidaying Brits who make up the majority of clients. This explains the baked beans lurking on the mammoth breakfast buffet along with a couple of hundred other items.

The resort also has a dive center for those wanting to explore the numerous offshore islands and reefs. The library provides Internet access as well as books in various European and Asian languages. Tsunami damaged was limited to some villas near the beach and the beach restaurant. The resort was able to operate as usual.

> *General manager Franck de Lestapis, who has been at the Pimalai from its beginning in 2001, personally greets every arriving guest. His enthusiasm and friendliness is contagious and spreads through the large team of smiling service staff.*

Layana Resort & Spa, 272 Moo 3, Saladan, ☎ 07560 7100, fax 07560 7199, www.layanaresort.com, $$$$. A lavish new luxury resort with 50 rooms – 44 garden pavilions, three beach suites and three ocean view suites that are built over two floors with the upstairs a lounge area, which comes with a writing desk in case you want to send a few postcards to friends at home about tough island living. The Tides seafront restaurant is the resort's main dining area but snacks are available in The Lounge. The fully equipped spa is aptly named Linger Longer. Superb infinity swimming pool and wireless Internet connections are available anywhere in the resort, provided you can find a dark enough spot to view your laptop screen. Luxury doesn't come cheap: High reason rates start at $223 +++ a night and low season at $163. You have to add the transfers from Krabi Airport, which cost $30 per person each way via a minivan and private speed boat. Watch the resort's Websites for packages that include some meals and a massage. The tsunami caused some damaged to the guests and particularly the three beach suites. The restaurant, bar and lounge were closed for a short time while repairs and renovations were completed.

Sri Lanta Resort & Spa, 111 Moo 6 Klongnin Beach, Ko Lanta, ☎ 07569 7288, fax 07569 7289, www.srilanta.com, $$$. The resort built on a hillside is, according to its Website inspired by its unspoiled natural surroundings and the accommodation is 49 thatched villas, minimalist in style with pure natural furnishings. Its location assured it of no damage from the tsunami. Rates run from 3,000 Baht to 5,100 Baht per night plus the cost of transfers. We did see an Internet special for less than 12,000 Baht for three days, two nights, which said for Thai residents only. We saw this at another hotel and when we called to see if we qualified we were told that since were in Thailand we did. The special here included cottage accommodation, American breakfast, a set dinner for two at the resort's Surya Chandra restaurant, one-hour spa treatment, and use of a kayak and a choice of an excursion by speedboat or ferry. The package also included transfers from Krabi airport as well as the usual welcome drink and fruit basket and Sri Lanta souvenir.

Lanta Sand Resort & Spa, 279 Moo 3, Saladan, Ko Lanta Yai, ☎ 07568 4633, fax 07568 4636, www.lantasand.com, $$$. The location and its gardens make this 48-room resort a pleasant place to unwind. The resort attracts a lot of Scandinavians who obviously appreciate the reasonable prices. During our visit we were offered a net rate of 3,000 Baht a night including breakfast. The rooms are set around a swimming pool and lotus lagoon. Most rooms come with a pleasant outdoor bath and shower in a small private garden. If you want to shower or take a dip in the evening maids will pre-spray to keep the mosquitoes away. The airy restaurant overlooks the beach, which is just steps away. The resort organizes diving and snorkeling excursions to the nearby islands of Ko Rok, Phi Phi, Ko Has, Hin Daeng, Hin Maung, Ko Ngai and Ko Mook Chueh. Damage caused by the tsunami was limited to the beach area.

Royal Lanta Resort, Klong Dao Beach, ☎ 07568 4361, fax 07568 4362, www.royallanta.com, $. Budget prices for a resort that is on the beach, has a swimming and a choice of places to dine, and a playground for children. Internet rates for a double room in low season start at 1,500 Baht including breakfast. High-season price for the executive rooms is 4,000 Baht. The resort said that damage affected 25% of its operations but it was still able to accommodate guests. Main areas hit were the restaurant and swimming pool.

Andaman Lanta Resort, 142 Moo 3, Klong Dao Beach, ☎ 07568 4200, fax 07568 4203, www.andamanlanta.com, $$. Reasonably priced resort – prices range from 1,600 Baht to 2,700 Baht including breakfast – with a choice of accommodation. Standard and deluxe rooms are in a two-story building with either mountain or sea views. The more expensive bungalows are on the beach and can be connected for family use. All accommodation comes with showers and no bathtubs. Nice swimming pool and the lower prices make it a favorite for families looking for a good price rather than top of the line luxury. The resort suffered some damage from the tsunami. Two of its suites needed repairs as did the swimming pool. Within a few weeks everything was operating as normal.

Lanta Palace Resort & Beach Club, 29 Moo 8, Ko Lanta Yai, ☎ 07569 7123, fax 0 7569 7124, www.lantapalace.com, $. Here there are 35 air conditioned bungalows in rows. Expect to pay more for those in front with a sea view, about 2,000 Baht a night, and less as you move inland and see less of the sea. Each has a small patio and they are well spaced out to give a sense of privacy. The gym is atop the restaurant for views while you exercise. Sun beds provided around the pool or on the beach where there's a beach bar. Enjoyable and economical. The resort was able to operate normally after the tsunami despite damage to seven ground-floor rooms, the bar and restaurant.

Ko Lanta fishermen leave daily from the beach in longtail boats, and part of what they catch that day is available in the Lanta Palace Resort's restaurant that evening. You can't get fresher than that.

Ko Samui

■ Introduction

In the 20th century this idyllic tropical island did little more than grow millions of coconuts and welcome the occasional backpacker to its palm-fringed shores. Today all that has changed and Samui with its wonderful sweeping white sand beaches is a very sought after location for the world's non-budget minded tourist.

It's a different breed of backpackers who visit these days. Fortunately they only use Samui as a gateway and pass through to the nearby islands. Unfortunately they are not the environmentally friendly travelers of yesteryear but litter louts who are having an unpleasant effect on these islands, where they fail to clean up after their visit.

Tourism

You still get the feeling that tourism on Samui is less aggressive and more orderly than at some of the other popular destinations. It's not just the absence of the big buildings; there is less hassle and jostling on the streets. Taxis are easy to spot; they're all painted yellow and red like a Spanish flag and they are metered. We never saw a pirate taxi or people jumping out of store fronts trying to get us to ride in the rickety family sedan.

Government statistics insist that the major industry of this small isle – it's more or less square and measures 25 kilometers from north to south and 21 kilometers east to west – is sending two million coconuts to Bangkok every month. That's a lot of coconuts but it's going to be peanuts compared to the cash that the tourist industry will generate in future years. We've noted that several European tour operators have dropped Pattaya from their glossy brochures and replaced it with the quality resorts of Samui.

Ko Samui is the third-largest island in Thailand; only Phuket and Ko Chang are bigger. It is 700 kilometers south of Bangkok and

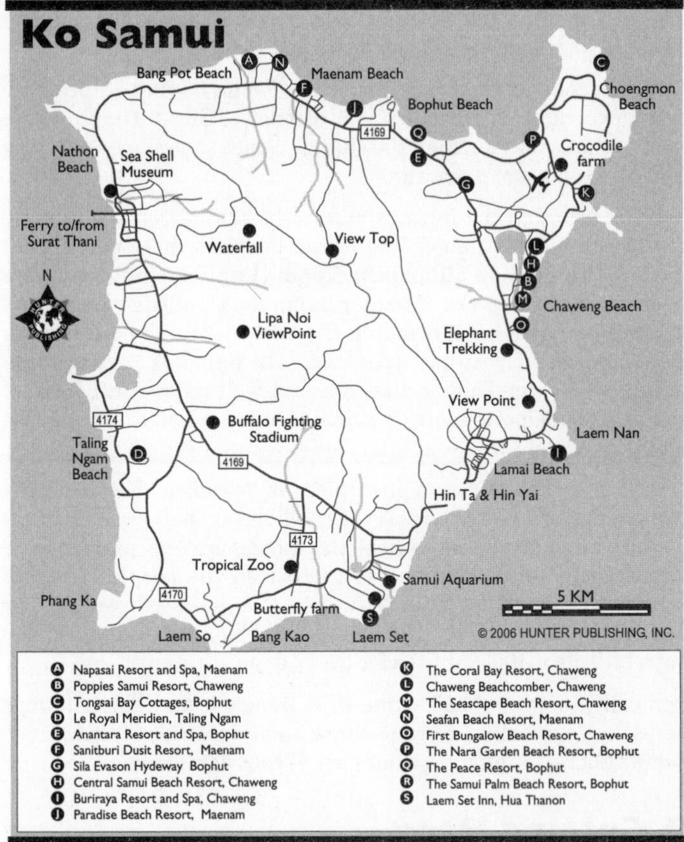

the permanent population is estimated at 40,000. But that is changing.

Samui gained from the tsunami, which hit other parts of Thailand. Many tourists destined for places like Phuket, Krabi and Khao Lak switched their bookings to this island. In January and February, after the tsunami, most hotels were fully occupied.

Development

Samui is buzzing with expectations as more resorts come to its shores and the farangs are building homes at an alarming rate. It's relatively orderly progress, with a few exceptions, the quality of the homes is high and there are no high-rises damaging the landscape. The roads are atrocious. We could have used some seasickness pills after 10 minutes of bouncing across the concrete patchworks they claim as carriageways.

That will change, the locals say, when Samui becomes a province in its own right. Right now it's a district of Surat Thani, where most of the taxes go. When the change comes that money will stay here and roads are a priority.

What is bringing the farangs here to build and settle or simply invest in a holiday home? The island now has those things that matter. There is now a Bangkok Samui Hospital, similar to those in other major centers. Another campus of Dulwich College is opening its doors here, bringing the best in British education to the island. Transport has improved with Bangkok Airways providing good inter-Thailand services as well as operating direct flights to Singapore, a major supplier of top-quality tourists and potential investors.

This is Bangkok Airways' own piece of paradise. The company owns and operates the airport – a good one at that – and no other carriers have been able to beat the monopoly. And provided the services and prices continue to get better, the people of Samui aren't about to assist Thai Airways – the national carrier – or other airlines to step in. The only downside is that Bangkok Airways collects a 400-Baht fee for every domestic departure.

Ironically, the day that I wrote this, Bangkok and Thai Airways signed an agreement to code-share some internal flights. However, flights to Samui were not part of that agreement.

■ Getting Here

By Air

Bangkok Airways has several flights daily between Bangkok and Ko Samui using a turbo-prop Franco-Italian ATR-72. There's an early morning flight that connects with many incoming European flights. It leaves at 7:40am and arrives at the island's **Don Sak** airport at 9:10am. There's another at 2pm that arrives at 3:30pm. Return flights begin at 10am and the last flight leaves around 8pm. The airline has two services a day, with a Boeing 717 jet aircraft that cuts the flying time to 50 minutes. A one-way ticket costs 3,550 Baht. Bangkok Airways also has flights from **Phuket** (1,720 Baht), **Pattaya** (2,155 Baht), **Hua Hin** (2,400 Baht) and **Singapore** (4,590 Baht). Presently there are two daily from Pattaya. The first one leaves at 9:55am and arrives at 10:45am. Bangkok Airways has a four-times a week Boeing

717-200 service from Singapore offering two-night land and air packages from $275.

We flew here from Phuket and were very impressed with the service. For the first time in our lives we arrived at an airport without tickets or reservations. We couldn't make a booking on the Internet. Either their Website was down or our computer was playing up.

We were able to buy two of the few remaining seats on their 9:20am service. Check-in was swift and we were shown to a Bangkok Airways lounge where there was a variety of coffees, juices and pastries provided at no charge. Also free was the use of the Internet. It was better treatment that you get in some US lounges where you pay for the privilege. The flight left a few minutes ahead of schedule and during the 35-minute flight the two cabin attendants served everyone aboard the ATR-72 a small breakfast box.

AUTHOR'S NOTE: *On arrival at the airport you'll find drivers meeting flights who will tell you your hotel is too expensive or that it is closed, and they will offer alternate accommodation. Most hotels will send transportation to meet you if they have advance warning. If you take a taxi, be sure to negotiate a price before you enter the cab.*

Thai International Airways has service from Bangkok to Surat Thani, on the mainland, with a bus-and-ferry transfer to Ko Samui. Price for one-way ticket is 2,800 Baht plus 150 Baht for the bus and ferry. Some times it is possible to purchase a combined ticket from a travel agent and save a little money. The flight takes just under an hour and the bus and ferry ride about three hours (the bus travels on the ferry). Once on the island the first stop is the ferry pier, and then Nathon pier. Again, hotels will arrange pick-up.

By Train

An overnight train from Bangkok to Surat Thani takes 10 hours, and then you have a similar bus-and-ferry transfer to Ko Samui as mentioned in the previous paragraph.

By Bus

An air conditioned bus to Ko Samui takes 12 hours and costs 750 Baht. Most comfortable service is the VIP bus that leaves Bangkok's Southern Bus Terminal, **Sai Tai Mai**, on Boromratchchonnani Road, ☎ 02435 1200. According to the regulations a VIP bus is air conditioned, has no more than 24 reclining seats, provides food and drink service, has a hostess onboard and has a toilet.

By Car

There are two ferry services from **Don Sak** on the mainland to Ko Samui. The **Raja** ferry leaves every hour from 5am to 7pm. Return journeys operate at the same times. If you are headed to Ko Phangan, the Raja ferry leaves four times a day at 7am, 10am, 2pm and 5:30pm. Return journeys operate at the same times. The **Seatran** ferry operates at similar times to Ko Samui but two of its services – at 9:30am and 4:30pm – continue on to Ko Phangan.

■ Rum from Samui

The dream of moving to Samui and having a small business eventually came true for Elisa and Michel Gabriel. The French couple now has a small distillery, **Magic Alambic**, at the south end of the island that is producing high quality rum that is slowly finding its way to bars and restaurants throughout Thailand.

But achieving their goal of semi retirement in this tropical island was not easy. They fell in love with Samui on vacations and decided to move here and set up a business to supplement their small pension. Initially they wanted to sell ice creams. But when the time came for their move several of the big companies had beaten them to it.

Because of their fruit-farming background they knew a little about distilling and making liquor so they decided on rum.

Thailand is noted for its rules and regulations and getting all the necessary licenses and permissions took a lot of effort. There are certain restrictions on what the Samui distillery can do – for example, the labels have to be in Thai and not English, and the strength can never exceed 40 proof.

Sitting in the tasting bar on their small estate, Elisa proudly explains their product. "It is the finest agricultural rum available," she says. They use the finest sugar cane, which is grown in southern Thailand and then brought to Samui for crushing. Other distillers use the cane that is left over after sugar refining. "Our rum is pure," she says, "and won't leave you with a hangover."

You can enjoy tasting the rums – it comes in orange, lemon, pineapple, coconut and just plain rum – at the tasting bar at the distillery, 41/5 Moo 3, Namuang, ☎ 07741 9023, on Route 417 at the south eastern end of the island near the turn off for the Laem Set Inn. The pineapples are brought in from Phuket and it's obvious where the coconuts come from.

For the tastings, Elisa has created her own mixer made from lemons, brown sugar, vanilla and cinnamon. The mix is becoming so popular she is thinking of marketing that, too.

Bottles can be bought in different sizes and in gift packs. The small bottles cost 300 Baht and the fifths cost 500 Baht. An ideal gift to take home – assuming you don't drink it all up before you leave the kingdom.

■ Things to See & Do

Marine Park

This is a must-visit attraction. Thirty kilometers northwest of Samui is the **Angthong Marine National Park**, consisting of 40 islands, which are a nature lover's paradise. These islands have it all. Dolphins swim in the waters, orchids grow in the cliffs, there are caves and grottos – some adorned with stalactites and stalagmites – 40 bird species, fine beaches for swimming and coral reefs for snorkeling.

The islands come under the control of the National Parks Department; they have an office on the largest of the islands, **Ko Wua Talab** (Sleeping Cow Island), which has a 430-meter peak that is worth the steep climb for fantastic views back to Samui.

There are numerous excursions to the park. The most popular are the day-long adventures that leave Samui at 8:30am, returning at 5:30pm. The cost is 550 Baht and includes lunch on board your boat and admission to the park. Most of the boats spend a couple of hours at Ko Wua Talab, allowing time to explore there. There's also time for swimming and snorkeling; most of the vessels have masks for rent. Tickets for these trips are available all over the island. If there's a group of you can charter a boat to cruise the islands. For anyone interested in spending the night on Ko Wua Talab you can rent a campsite for 50 Baht and if you didn't bring a tent you can hire one for 100 Baht. Big enough, we were told, to sleep two comfortably. We will never know. The National Parks

Department has some basic cabins that it rents out. Fishermen who live in the park and will happily take you on a tour on one of their small motorboats for a reasonable fee.

Water Sports

Samui is the perfect place for water skiing, windsurfing, sailing, scuba diving and snorkeling. There are several schools on the island where you can learn to dive. Fishing is another favorite pastime and boats go out from all parts of the island for short or long trips.

Golf

Samui is home to one of the most scenic golf courses in southeast Asia, the **Santiburi Samui Country Club**, ☎ 07742 1700, fax 07742 1790, www.santiburi.com.

What makes this challenging course so attractive is that from every tee there is an amazing view of the Gulf of Thailand and the tees are low as 20 meters above sea level going up to 200 meters. The course is part of the Santiburi group, which has two resorts in Samui as well as golf courses in Hua and Chiang Mai. If you go to their Website with a slow Internet connection be prepared to watch a shuddering golf cart while the information downloads.

Exploring the Interior

This island may be small but there is still a lot see away from the beaches. Of course there are millions of coconut palms, but the mountainous interior also has rubber and coffee plantations, two impressive waterfalls and a lot of virgin jungle.

The most impressive landmark is the **Big Buddha**, a huge golden image set on a rocky peninsula jutting into the sea.

If we haven't found something you like there is always a visit to the snake farm, and you can watch monkeys harvesting coconuts. The island also boasts a crocodile farm and a butterfly garden. If all else fails there is elephant trekking or, for the more athletic, a few hours of traveling on a mountain bike. And there is a large, modern Tesco Lotus bulging with bargains.

■ Where to Stay

For price scale see page 251

Despite being relatively small, the island has several areas with different appeal. **Chaweng Beach** on the northeast of the island is the main tourist center, with a seven-kilometer-long white sandy beach, the longest on Samui. Accommodation ranges from basic bungalows to luxury-laden resorts. The area, with a full array of discos, bars and shops, gets busy in the high season, which here runs from January to April. There is also a peak season over the Christmas holidays.

Unlike many other holiday areas in Thailand, the resorts here are all right on the beach. When you drive along Chaweng there is no chance of seeing beach or sea because of the buildings along its narrow, crowded streets.

Second in size and popularity is **Lamai**, 10 kilometers south of Chaweng, a little quieter but still providing a good locale for swimming and nightlife. The best of the beach is at the southern end.

If you want something less populated – and less expensive – **Choengmon Beach** on the northeast corner of the island may be your piece of paradise; west of that are **Maenam Beach**, **Bo Phut Beach** and **Bang Po Beach**. On the west coast, the least popular with tourists, are **Hua Thanon** and, south of that, **Ban Thong Tanote**.

Ko Samui's little brother to the north is **Ko Pha-Ngan**, less developed and normally very quiet and peaceful, though **Hat Rin**, on the south of the island, has become the "in" place to be, with its full-moon parties, when ravers from around the world party with a variety of substances – with predictable results. Apart from that the island has some excellent coral for divers to explore. There are no major resorts here, just a few inexpensive bungalows and guesthouses. And those around Hat Rin get overcrowded when the full moon approaches. Should you wish to visit, there are numerous ferries from Samui, travel time 30 minutes, as well as services from the mainland.

Best time to visit either of the islands is between December and June. The heaviest rains fall between September and November. Hotel rates reflect those times. There is a peak rate over the Christmas and New Year period and the hotels get fully booked at this time despite the higher prices.

Napasai Resort & Spa, 65/10 Ban Tai, Maenam, ☎ 07742 9200, fax 07742 9201, www.pansea.com, $$$$. You awake to the distant deep throbbing of longtail boats as fishermen cross the bay in front of this new 55-cottage luxury resort, on the north coast of the island on Maenam Beach. This is truly a laid-back hideaway, separated from the road by a large coconut plantation and the resort's two tennis courts. The lobby sits high above the complex of cottages, which are set up above the beach and all have large verandahs with terrific views of the nearby islands. The modern Thai-style cottages are fully equipped, and have a wonderful sense of comfort and privacy. The beach is not one of Thailand's best but the large infinity pool more than compensates for that.

Similar resorts claim gourmet dining but don't quite reach that level; here they do. Two chefs – one French, the other Thai – put together a very impressive array of diverse dishes. We began our experience with a platter of Thai appetizers that was delicious, with every Thai spice adding just the right amount of zest. The duck curry with grapes was brilliant, as was the red snapper on a bed of leeks with a coconut curry sauce that Lindsey ordered. Fairly priced considering the location and quality and, with Thai wine available by the glass, two can dine well for 2,000 Baht. The following night, after a hard day of sightseeing, we decided on a night in our cottage watching a DVD – good selection available at no extra charge. Our room-service meal – an excellent hamburger properly prepared, and crabmeat on a baguette all beautifully served – cost 835 Baht. Light entertainment is planned for evenings and we got to peek at the Christmas program, which looked very exciting. There are also 14 luxury villas within the complex which are being sold for around $1 million each. They offer the owners the benefit of living within the resort or when they're not there having them rented out by the hotel. Don't be put off by the high rack rates. Many times there are Internet specials particularly in the low season. We stayed here in mid-November, which is low season here and enjoyed perfect weather. In Phuket, where it was high season, the weather was not so good with several thunderstorms.

This resort is the fifth boutique property in Southeast Asia owned and operated by **Pansea Orient-Express Hotels**. The company's other properties are the **Pansea Angkor** in Cambodia, **Pansea Luang Prabang** in Laos, **Pansea Yangon** in Myanmar and **Pansea Puri Bali** in Indonesia. Their newest property, the **Ubud Hanging Gardens** in Bali, opened in 2005, is one of the great wonders of the resort world.

Poppies Samui Resort, on the southern end of Chaweng beach, ☎ 07742 2419, fax 07742 2420, www.poppiessamui.com, $$$$. This is one of those small boutique resorts where you get smoth-

The Grand Palace in Bangkok

Above: Pattaya by night

Below: An alfresco cultural presentation

Above: Children's pool, JW Marriott Resort, Phuket
Courtesy of Marriott Hotels

Below: An inviting tropical swimming pool

Above: Bangkok skyline at night

Below: Dinner cruise on the River of Kings

Above: Enjoy a massage by the shore

Below: Massage at the Mangosteen Resort, Phuket
Courtesy of the Mangosteen Resort

Above: Bangkok by night

Below: Candlelight dining

Above: Double-decker sightseeing bus, Bangkok

Below: The Grand Palace, Bangkok

Demon Guardian at Wat Phra Kaeo, Bangkok

ered in service and want to return as quickly as possible. Just 24 luxury cottages teeming with teak and Thai silks and cottons set amid superb tropical gardens that have ponds, bridges and a waterfall. The resort is at the south end of Chaweng, and does give you the benefit of being able to step outside and enjoy the island's main tourist hub. The fully equipped cottages all have a separate living area, fancy marble sunken tub bathrooms and a small private garden. The hotel rents out jeeps for those who want to discover the island or can arrange a driver to take you around. There is an excellent restaurant, which attracts a lot of the ex-pat community where the high quality and services are matched by high prices. You have the choice of dining in Ayutthaya-style teak pavilion beside the pool or under the stars overlooking the beach. If you don't want to splurge every night there are numerous eating spots along the busy street outside.

Tongsai Bay Cottages and Hotel, 84 Moo 5, Bophut, ☎ 07724 5489, fax 07742 5482, www.tongsaibay.co.th, $$$$. Until the new boutique resorts arrived this was very much the only quality place to be on the island. Fortunately it hasn't changed and still has 83 luxury suites with wonderful views of its private cove and beach. The hotel was the brainchild of Thai tycoon Akorn Hoontrakul who was chairman of the Imperial Hotels group that owned 10 hotels in Thailand and several Thai restaurants in Europe, including the first one in London, Akorn's in Knightsbridge. He opened the Tongsai resort in 1987 and seven years later sold out his empire, keeping just the Samui resort and moved to the island from Bangkok. Since then numerous improvements and additions have been made but it still remains the quality low-key resort that he built. He died several years and the operation is now run by his wife and son. There are three categories of accommodation: Beachfront suites, cottage suites, and the Tonsai Grand Villas. Rates began at 11,000 Baht ++. There is an excellent spa, fitness center with all the latest equipment and popular bars and restaurants.

Le Royal Meridien, Baan Taling Ngam, 295 Moo 3, Taling Ngam, ☎ 07742 9100, fax 7742, www.kohsamui.lemeridien.com, $$$$. Another stunning new expensive resort with 72 rooms and villas set on a cliff top amid 16 acres of tropical gardens. The accommodation sits on the hillside that leads down to a to a 2.5-kilometer beach. All rooms and villas are large and some of the more expensive have a shared private pool and some come with a kitchenette. Baan Taling Ngam Spa is one of the finest on the island and it is worth checking the Internet for packages that include treatments here. There are numerous places to wine and dine in the complex but it is not the easiest to get around. The hotel does point out that the resort is not suited for wheelchairs and there are no elevators.

Anantara Resort & Spa, 101/3 Bophut Bay, ☎ 07742 8300, fax 07742 8310, www.ananara.com, $$$$. Newest in this luxury chain's expensive resorts with 106 rooms and 24 suites on three floors with room prices starting at $235 and the suites at $740. All the rooms were designed to reflect the colors of the surrounding tropical gardens and each has a deep terrazzo bath big enough for two people and will either have a private terrace or balcony. Focal point of the resort is the 3,000-square-meter spa with its six bamboo-and-glass-walled rooms, which allow you spectacular views while enjoying a treatment. Italian cuisine and Thai specialties are served on the elevated terrace above the infinity-edge pool. The resort also has a cookery school.

Sanitburi Dusit Resort, 12 Moo 1 Tambon, Maenam, ☎ 07742 5031, fax 07742 5040, $$$$. Located on Maenam beach on the north of the island, the resort has 77 villas set in 23 acres of lush tropical gardens. Villa equipment includes video and CD player. There are bars, restaurants, and a beauty salon on the site as well a swimming pool, gymnasium, sauna, tennis and squash courts. The best beachfront villas, comprised of a bedroom, a living room, separate bath and shower and private terrace, cost $500 a night. And that does not include breakfast. All kinds of water sports are available on the beach.

Sila Evason Hydeway Samui, 9/10 Moo 5 Baan Plai laem, Borphut, ☎ 07724 5678, fax 07724 5671, www.sixsenses.com/hideaway-samui, $$$$. Sister resort to the one in Phuket but even more luxurious. Opened in 2004, the resort has 66 villas – 14 hideaway villas, 41 pool villas, 10 pool villa suites and one presidential suite. Each has its own private garden with shower. There are two pools, one a natural one set among rocks, a water sports center, library and restaurants and bars. The resort is on the north of the island and six miles from the airport.

Central Samui Beach Resort, 38/2 Moo 3 Chaweng Beach Road, ☎ 07723 0500, fax 07742 2385, www.centralhotelsresorts.com, $$$$. A prime location on Samui's finest beach this luxury resort set in stunning gardens has 208 fully equipped rooms all facing the sea. Dining and drinking takes place beachside, poolside and inside with a range of eateries catering to Thai and European tastes. Special Internet rates off-season as low as $85 but expect to pay more in high season and a lot more for the large suites.

Buriraya Resort & Spa, 208 Moo 4T, Maret, ☎ 07742 9300, $$$. There are 66 fully equipped rooms at this resort, which opened in 2003. Located on Chaweng Beach, the resort has two pools, one is Olympic size, and the other adjoins the beach. There is a gift shop, fitness center and cooking classes are available.

Paradise Beach Resort, 18/8 Maenam Beach, ☎ 07724 7227, fax 07742 5290, $$$. All 105 rooms and suites or bungalows at this luxury resort along the beachfront in the central part of Maenam are spacious and well equipped and either have a private balcony or terrace. Best accommodation are the suites, which cost 5,000 Baht in the low season and 9,000 Baht in the high season. The cozy bungalows are cheaper. The resort is surrounded by tropical gardens and there are great views from the restaurant.

The Coral Bay Resort, 9 Moo 2, Chaweng Beach, ☎ 07742 2223, fax 07742 2392, $$. This fine resort with 52 thatched-roofed wooden bungalows is at Yai Noi Bay, in the north east of Samui. Across from the resort is Ko Matlang, a small island that is accessible by a short boat trip or by wading across at low tide. The resort is set amid 10 acres of gardens and is only a few kilometers away from the main shopping and nightlife of Chaweng. The standard bungalows covering 50 square meters cost 3,300 Baht a night during the high season. The larger deluxe version with 65 square meters has a separate living room and sells for 4,600 Baht. Both versions feature king size four-poster beds and a day-bed for a third person or child. The resort has a large pool, small gift shop, restaurant with great views and is just 10 minutes from the airport.

Chaweng Beachcomber, 3/5 Moo 2, Chaweng Beach, ☎ 07742 2041, fax 07742 2388, $$$. In the center of Chaweng beach this resort has a combination of rooms and villas. The rooms are in the main three-story part of the hotel and the villas have a separate sitting area and are closer to the beach. Impressive gardens and within walking distance of the shopping and entertainment areas. In high season expect to pay 4,000 Baht for a room and 6,500 Baht for one of the villas.

The Seascape Beach Resort, 28/14 Moo 3, Boput, Chaweng Beach, ☎ 07742 2681, fax 07742 2685, $$. Not dissimilar to the Beachcomber with rooms in the main hotel building and bungalows set in the gardens. All accommodation has a private balcony or terrace with garden or sea views. The resort is on the south end of Chaweng beach and close to the markets, shops and nightlife. The somewhat limited luxury is reflected in the lower rates. In high season the rooms sell for 2,000 Baht a night and the bungalows for 2,300 Baht. There also family suites in the main building, which have two interconnecting bedrooms.

Seafan Beach Resort, Maenam Beach, ☎ 07742 5204, fax 07742 5350, $$. If you're seeking something unpretentious, quiet and inexpensive then this resort with a swimming pool, coconut groves and tropical gardens on the north side of the island might fit the bill and the pocket book. During high season expect to get change from 3,000 Baht for a night's stay. Like everywhere else on the island it will cost more over the Christmas holidays. The 40 modest wooden cottages are sparsely furnished.

First Bungalow Beach Resort, 4/6 Moo 3, Chaweng Beach, ☎ 07742 2327, fax 07742 2243, $$. There are 139 units here split between deluxe rooms (set amid gardens, a few steps away from the swimming pool and a few minutes from the beach, most with two single beds) and slightly more expensive bungalows set around the large swimming pool and Jacuzzi area with double beds and sea views. There's a pleasant restaurant where you can dine outdoors in the shade of trees. Rates go from under 2,000 Baht for a room in low season to over 3,000 Baht for a bungalow in high season. Those prices include taxes and breakfast.

The Nara Garden Beach Resort, 81 Moo 4, Bophut, ☎ 07742 5532, fax 07742 5376, $. Reasonably priced resort with 43 simply furnished rooms all with private terraces overlooking a pleasing courtyard. Nice pool and tropical gardens. Located on Big Buddha beach, a 20-minute drive to Chaweng beach and 10 minutes from the airport. The resort leaves the $ category over the Christmas and New Year holiday when rates jump to over $100, still a good price for the peak season.

The Peace Resort, 178 Moo 1, Bophut, ☎ 07742 5357, fax 07742 5342, $. This quiet resort with 104 spacious, modern bungalows is right on the beach and good value for the facilities the accommodation offers. Prices for garden-view bungalows start at 1,500 Baht a night including breakfast and go up to 2,900 Baht for sea facing bungalows in the high season, which is from January until April 30 and takes it from our $ to the $$ category.

The Samui Palm Beach Resort, 175/3 Thaveerat-Pakdee Road, Bophut, ☎ 07742 5494, fax 07742 5358, $. This resort in the center of Bophut beach has 76 modern Thai-style villas and enjoys panoramic views of the sea and nearby Phangan Island. At certain times of the year the resort has special deals where you stay for five nights and only pay for four or stay for eight nights and only pay for six. The only additional charge is 330 Baht per person, plus tax and service charges, for breakfast.

Laem Set Inn, 100 Moo 2, Hua Thanon, ☎ 07742 4393, fax 07742 4394, www.leamset.com. We have left this resort to the last of the listings since it's hard to put a price on staying here. This is an eccentric gathering of accommodation, which ranges from some very basic bamboo beach cottages that sell for the same low 1,200 Baht a night in any season, low or peak to large villas that sell for as much as 21,600 Baht. The resort explains, "An integral part of the philosophy of Laem See Inn is to create an interesting gathering of people from all walks of life, not excluding younger persons and not becoming an elitist establishment. These basic bungalows enable us to offer the experience of Laem Set Inn to persons who appreciate style and quality but who might find the other styles inaccessible." The Inn is in a wonderful location on the south end of the island and is well worth the drive just to enjoy the fantastic view from the restaurant. We had an excellent, inexpensive lunch here and were particularly pleased to see the facilities available for families with young children.

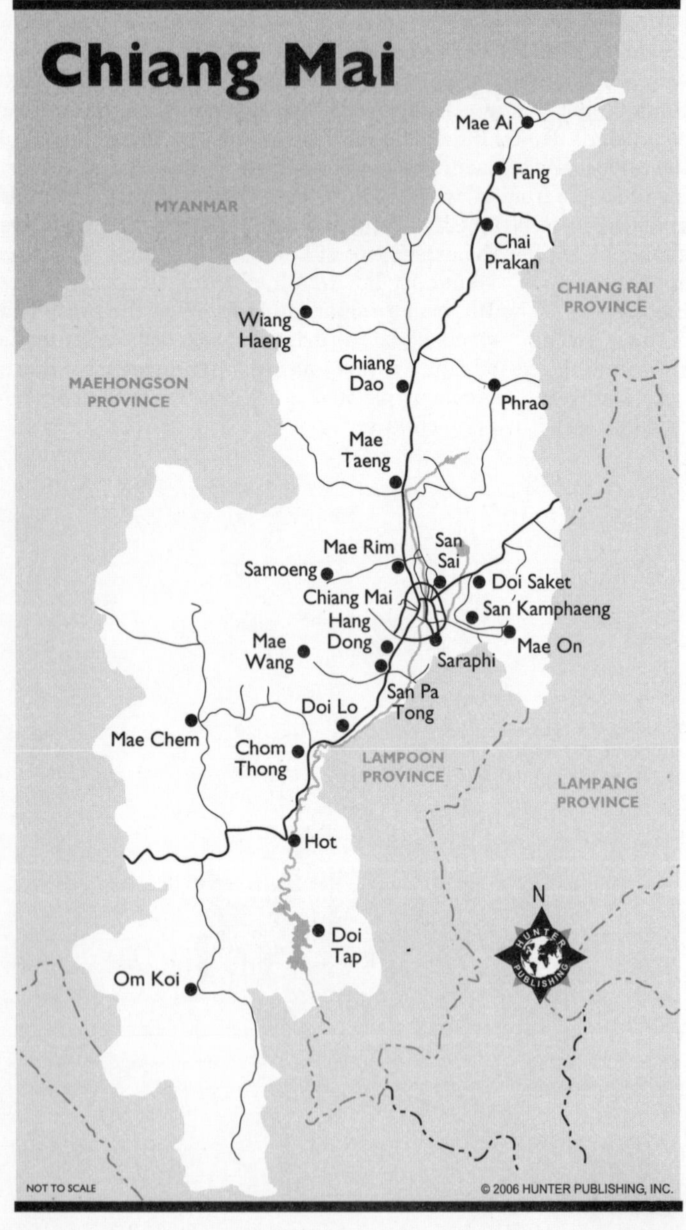
Chiang Mai
MYANMAR
Mae Ai
Fang
Chai Prakan
CHIANG RAI PROVINCE
Wiang Haeng
Chiang Dao
MAEHONGSON PROVINCE
Phrao
Mae Taeng
Mae Rim
San Sai
Samoeng
Doi Saket
Chiang Mai
San Kamphaeng
Hang Dong
Mae Wang
Mae On
Saraphi
San Pa Tong
Doi Lo
Mae Chem
Chom Thong
LAMPOON PROVINCE
LAMPANG PROVINCE
Hot
N
Doi Tap
HUNTER PUBLISHING
Om Koi
NOT TO SCALE
© 2006 HUNTER PUBLISHING, INC.

Chiang Mai & the North

Introduction

The north of Thailand – **Chiang Mai**, **Chiang Rai** and the surrounding areas – is becoming a more popular tourist destination for both foreign and domestic travelers. The attractions are magnificent scenery, cooler temperatures and less congestion. The entire area got an expected surge in tourism when the killer waves of the tsunami hit the Andaman coastline on December 26, 2004. Many who had booked flights to Thailand decided to switch their final destination from the beaches of the south to the countryside of the north. Those we spoke to who had done this were so impressed that they planned to return to the north on future visits to Thailand.

IN THIS CHAPTER

Chiang Mai

This is the main city in the region, known as the "rose of the north." Most that come here do so after spending a few days in Bangkok. And the contrast is incredible. From the buzz and bustle of the capital there is a gentler lifestyle with more greenery, less people, and on a clear day a wondrous mountain backdrop. There is lots of traffic and pollution but you can breather a lot more easily here. The nights are cooler. We find this a city with charm and character. Those items seem to have vanished from Bangkok with the construction of too many giant buildings between the old spires.

And the people here in Thailand's second city are more laid back. There seems to be more time to enjoy the sights and sounds. It seems totally removed from the kingdom's capital 700 kilometers to the south.

Its tourist attractions are more focused on tradition and things cultural, and away from the sordid nightlife that is a major part of the capital. There are myriad natural sights awaiting the visitor. There is a river that is not so busy and there are temples, hundreds of them, where the monks take time to talk to inquisitive tourists. There is quality shopping and the endless bargains at the very popular night-market. Somehow things appear to be more organized, and not just one street market emptying onto another.

Size may have something to do with it. Only a fraction of the size of Bangkok, Chiang Mai is growing rapidly as a tourist destination but it remains a major commercial center. Its international airport has direct links to **Rangoon**, the capital of Myanmar, and there are also flights to **Kunming** and **Yunan** in China and **Luang Prabang** in Laos; the latest addition is direct flights to **Singapore**. The airport handles more than two million passengers a year, 10 times the population of Chiang Mai.

The city is skirted by the Superhighway – a ring road something akin to London's M25 or Atlanta's I-285 – which makes getting around a lot easier and safer despite the numerous intersections. Once you are well outside it you enter incredible countryside.

Much of the modernization of the area goes on beyond the city itself where new homes and suburbs are being created to provide homes for the wealthy who want to escape the hot summers in Bangkok and chill out in the colder higher climes.

Nearby the hill tribes dwell in conditions that haven't changed in centuries. The hill tribe inhabitants now account for over 13% of the province's population. They venture down to the city to sell their wares while tourists dare to venture into the jungles to experience the back to nature living of the tribes. Unfortunately much of the jungle is not what it was. Many of the tall trees have been felled and in their place bamboos and underbrush still provide a rough enough terrain to challenge the intrepid trekker.

The city caters to the rich with lavish hotels and spas and to the budget back packers with cheerful guesthouses. There is an adequate supply of luxury rooms at affordable prices and more recently new resorts offer some of the finest and more expensive accommodation in Thailand.

The old city retains its charm and is still surrounded by an ancient moat that was restored in the 19th century, and there are remnants of the original city walls, which were built in a perfect square. Several of the gates have been restored.

From the old city the roads fan out in all directions. To the east the road heads to the **Ping River** passing the main shopping and business area and the night-market. Farther out is the post office and railway station.

The sacred 5,500-foot mountain of **Doi Suthep** to the west of town looks down on the Ping River as it flows though the Chiang Mai Valley. Adorning the mountain is north Thailand's most sacred shrine, the 600-year-old **Wat Phra Doi Suthep**.

Chiang Mai province is mainly mountainous and covers 20,000 square kilometers; parts of it are within national parks that are crammed with flora and fauna. The north border of Chiang Mai is the Myanmar state of **Chiang Tung**. The other borders are with the Thai provinces of **Lamphun** and **Tak** in the south, **Mae Hong Son** in the west, and **Chiang Rai** and **Lamphang** in the east.

Chiang Mai is noted for its trekking. And that comes in a variety of forms. You can walk, drive, be driven, take a boat, and go on horseback or climb aboard an elephant. The rewards for such excursions can be extremely satisfying, provided you play by the rules, which you'll find farther along in this chapter under *Trekking*. Chiang Mai is an adventure whichever way you turn.

USEFUL TELEPHONE NUMBER

Tourism Authority of Thailand (TAT) . . . ☎ 05324 8604

History

Chiang Mai was founded in 1296 by King Mengrai the Great after he defeated the city's original settlers, the Mons. Mengrai was the 25th king of the Lawa Dynasty and ruler of **Nakhon Hiran Hgoen Yang**, an ancient town on the Mekong River, near Chiang Saen. He founded Chiang Rai in 1262 and then merged the cities into the first Thai state, Lanna Thao, with its capital at Chiang Mai. Lanna Thao translates to "Kingdom of a million rice fields."

The king died in 1317. He is remembered with a statue in Chiang Rai.

Chiang Mai became an important cultural and religious center for the Thais, who had migrated here from southern China, but was constantly under attack from the Burmese, who eventually took control of the city in 1556. It remained part of Burma until 1775, when King Taksin (1767-1782) recaptured it and forced the Burmese back to an area close to the present border. It is hardly surprising that with so many years of Burmese occupation much of that heritage remains today. It shows itself in the architecture, culture, religion and cuisine.

During the Ayutthaya attack (see page 111), members of the old royal family had either been killed or captured by the Burmese. At the time Taksin was a general but he wasted no time in taking on the Burmese and setting himself up as king. He was the king who built the new Thai capital in Thonburi, across the river from Bangkok. Taksin put local princes in control of the city, but under the watchful eyes of the throne in Bangkok. In 1874 King Chulalongkorn (Rama V), who was partly educated by Anna Leonowens of *Anna and the King* fame, sent a commission to Chiang Mai to insure the Lanna kingdom remained firmly under the control of the Bangkok government. The king feared that the British, who controlled Burma at the time, would try to make inroads into northern Thailand because of its rich teak forests. Taksin became king after the Burmese destroyed Ayutthaya, the former Thai capital.

Chiang Mai became a major center for trade as the crossroads between China, Laos and Myanmar, and in 1933 the city was formally and fully integrated into the kingdom of Thailand.

Getting Here

■ By Air

Lots of services from Bangkok. **Thai Airways** has 10 direct flights a day. **Bangkok Airways** has a daily flight that makes one stop in Sukhothai. It also operates a twice-a-week direct service on Tuesday and Saturdays. Flying time is an hour and 10 minutes. Costs vary widely but expect to pay 2,500 Baht for a one-way ticket. **Tiger Airways** operates flights from Singapore on Mondays, Wednesdays, Fridays and Sundays with an Airbus A320 configured with 180 single-class seats. The flight leaves Singapore at 3:30pm and arrives at 5:30pm. The returning flight departs at 6:05pm and arrives in Singapore at 8:05pm.

If you arrive in Bangkok from a foreign destination and transfer directly to a Chiang Mai flight you will not clear customs and immigration in Bangkok but here, since Chiang Mai is an international airport. If your baggage was checked to Chiang Mai you do not have to claim it in Bangkok. There are several banks in the airport, as well as a post office and numerous places to make overseas calls. Taxis are readily available outside the arrivals area and it will cost you around 120 Baht for the short journey to downtown.

■ By Train

There are numerous trains from Bangkok and you can read more details about costs and the different classes of service in the *Trains of Thailand* chapter. For local train information, ☎ 053 245 363.

■ By Car

There are several ways to make the journey. Allow yourself 10 hours for the 700-kilometer trip from Bangkok although others tell us they did it nine hours. Simplest way is take the **Asia Route**, Highway No. 1, from Bangkok to Nakorn Sawan. There you pick up Highway 106, which goes direct to Chiang Mai.

■ By Bus

Air conditioned buses run throughout the day from Bangkok. Traveling time is between 10 and 11 hours. Most leave from the Northern Bus Terminal near the Chatuchak Weekend Market, ☎ 02272 5761. Most comfortable are the VIP buses with reclining seats that cost 470 Baht for the trip. Beware of a scam by some bus operators, who drop their clients off on the Superhighway that rings Chiang Mai. There you are confronted with touts selling accommodation. Check before you leave to insure you are taken to one of the city's two bus stations, either the **Arcade Bus Station** on Kaeo Nawarat Road, three kilometers northeast of the Tha Pae Gate, or the **Chang Puak Station** on Chotana Road.

Things to See

■ Temples in the Old City

There are three important temples within the city walls – **Wat Chedi Luang**, **Wat Phra Singh**, and **Wat Chiang Man**. Wat Chedi Luang is on Pokklao Road and is where the city pillar shrine is located. (See the City Pillar festival, page 301). This temple, built in the 14th century is famous for its massive chedi, or pagoda, which is 282 feet high and 144 feet wide at its base. Its spire collapsed during an earthquake in 1545. The pair of staircases at the front porch is a major feature of the temple.

Wat Phra Singh, on Samlan Road, was built in 1345 and is home to the North's most revered Buddha statue, **Phra Phuttha Sihing**. Every year on Songkran Day, the Thai New Year on April 13, local residents sprinkle scented on the statue as it is paraded on the streets of Chiang Mai.

Wat Chiang Man, off Ratchapakhinai Road in the northeast corner of the old city, is the oldest temple in Chiang Mai. It was built in 1296 by King Mengrai, the founder of the city. The temple is noted for its Lanna-style chedi supported by rows of elephant-shaped buttresses.

■ Temples Outside the City

The most notable of these is the famed **Wat Phra Doi Suthep** (see page 291), which is well worth the journey. Others include **Wat Suan Dok** on Suthep Road, which has a 500-year-old bronze Buddha, one of Thailand's largest metal images. The temple was built in 1370 during the reign of Lanna ruler King Kuena. **Wat U-Mong**, also on Suthep Road, was built in 1296 by the city's founder King Mengrai. The temple is noted its unusual tunnel-like construction.

■ Chiang Mai Zoo

On Huay Kaew Road, outside the Superhighway on the road to the Doi Suthep Mountain. Something we didn't expect to find in Chiang Mai was this well-stocked and well-run zoo. Within this 40-acre park, which attracts 700,000 visitors a year, they've got an endless number of things to do and see. There are 7,000 animals, 5,000 birds, 1,200 fish and 218 reptiles. There is a children's zoo where they encourage group visits of youngsters to play with a variety of pets and enjoy animal shows; call them at ☎ 05322 1179 if you want to arrange special treatment for a younger group. There is an island where gibbons live and breed freely without cages or enclosures. Another area is dedicated to the Humboldt penguins, which seem to have adapted well to Thai living. For those who care to sleep under canvas there is a camping ground used mostly by day-trippers for picnics. Animal feeding times are posted by the entrance gate where you also find an assortment of dining spots for human visitors. The zoo is open from 8am-6pm – come early to avoid the heat – and the entrance fee is 60 Baht. Thai civil servants and teachers pay only 10 Baht.

Things to Do

■ Trekking

Trekking is a major business in Chiang Mai, which you'll quickly discover as you explore the sights of the city. There are strings of offices and hordes of guides ready to take you into the jungle to see the lost tribes, their strange habitats and odd customs. Since you've journey this far north you need to do something. The amount you do depends not so much on your pocketbook but on your personal stamina.

Perhaps the perfect way to say you've done it is to take the special day-trip that you'll find offered in most places, including your hotel. After breakfast you are picked up from your hotel and taken by jeep into the jungle. You get to visit a couple of villages, exchange pleasantries with folk in fancy costumes, do a short elephant trek, some soft-water rafting and all being well you're back safe and sound at your hotel by the cocktail hour. Cost of a trip like this will set you back about 2,000 Baht, a few scratches (and possibly a bad back from the elephant ride). You will probably have some good pictures and some local handicrafts to show the neighbors on your return.

For those more intent on learning a little more about the hill tribes, and spending more time in their domain, we suggest a visit to the **Tribal Museum** in Ratchamangkla Park on Chotana Road, ☎ 05322 1933. This used to be Chiang Mai University's Tribal Research Institute. The exhibits and information you gather here will give you a better insight into the lives of the hilltribe people. The museum is open on weekdays from 9am-4pm.

If you are intent on serious trekking it is important to go by the rules set down by TAT (The Tourism Authority of Thailand) and the tourist police. They advise against going it on your own – although a lot of people do – and hiring a properly licensed and registered guide. All of the regulated trekking companies have a variety of programs ranging from a couple of days to a week. Prices vary widely, so shop around. Chances are the longer the trek the more likely you us to visit villages that are more remote and away from the normal tourist circuit. Many of the longer tours involve a great deal of time walking. Make sure you have the stamina and the right shoes. Best time to go is from November to Easter, during the cooler, dryer season.

A couple of pointers: Beware of getting involved in any demonstrations involving drugs or narcotics and be sure to leave valuables in safe custody before you set out. Most of the better hotels have safety deposit boxes. Be sure you know what services are going to be provided on your trek. Where will you sleep? What meals are included? To get the most from your trek try to encompass different modes of transport. There should be some rafting and either riding on horseback or by elephant. And the more you ride in a jeep the less you'll have to walk.

Do not take photographs of the tribespeople or their homes without getting permission. Be respectful of their religious symbols and rituals. Don't be surprised by some of the things you'll see. Amid the poverty young children wear valuable jewelry and many smoke cigarettes.

Remember this is a remote part of the world – the area covered is vast – and it is impossible for the government to provide total security. There are not going to be convenience stores on the way so be sure to have sufficient film and batteries for your cameras. It's better to buy the odd handicraft than hand out money.

■ Cycling

A new attraction for visitors to Chiang Mai is a 10-day cycle tour to Bangkok organized by tour operator **Spice Roads**. Company general manager Struan Robertson assures us the tour is designed for the "moderately fit," who should be prepared to pedal for five hours a day to cover the 950-kilometer trip. The company provides road/hybrid bikes, English-speaking guides, and quality hotels on the journey, which will avoid main highways and visit several historical destinations including Lampang, Sukothai, Kampang Phet, Nakorn Sawan and Ayutthaya. Cost of the package is $950. The company, based in Bangkok, offers cycles tours throughout Thailand. Its varied programs are described fully on its Website, www.spiceroads.com.

■ Golf

Gymkhana Club Golf Course, Ratuthit Road. This is the only nine-hole course we have included in the guide simply because of its history. To read a little more of its history read *Cricket in Thailand* at the start of the Chiang Mai chapter. The club was founded in 1898 and claimed to be the oldest course in the kingdom. It's right in Chiang Mai, only five minutes from the night-bazaar. It's historical past, large oak and monkey pod trees make it a pleasant place to visit even if its 2,953 par 36 course is not in the best shape.

Chiangmai Green Valley Country Club, 183/2 Chotana Road, Mae Sa Mae Rim, ☎ 05329 8222, fax 05329 7386. This is a long par 72 course – 7,205 yards – with not too much shade because of the wide fairways. Lots of water hazards and most holes are well protected by bunkers. Opened in 1990, weekend visitors' green fees are 2,000 Baht.

Chiangmai-Lamphun Golf Club, Sankumpang-banti Road, Sankumpang, Lamphun, ☎ 05388 0880, fax 05388 0888. Website: www.chiangmaigolf.com. This 6,808-yard course lies in a natural valley surrounded by majestic rolling hills. This challenging course with lots of water hazards and well-placed bunkers was designed by Dr. Sukhum Sukapanpotharam and opened in 1990. Weekend green fees for visitors are 1,800 Baht.

Lanna Golf Club, 183/2 Chotana Road, Changpheug, ☎ 05322 1911, fax 05322 1749. This tough 27-hole course offers the best value for money. Green fees for a weekend visitor are only 800 Baht. Lots of trees along the fairways give welcome shade and there are superb views of Doi Suthep Mountain and its famed temple from every hole.

Royal Chiang Mai Golf Resort, 169 Moo 5, Chiangmai-Prao Road, Km. 26, Mae Fak, Sansai, ☎ 05384 9301, fax 05384 9310, www.royalchiangmai.com. Challenging course where accuracy is more important than hitting long shots. This 18-hole par 72 course was designed by Peter Thomson and opened in 1996. Weekend green fees for a visitor are 1,400 Baht.

■ Cricket

The typically British game of cricket has been played in Northern Thailand for over 100 years, thanks in part to Louis T. Leonowens, the son of English teacher Anna Leonowens ("Mrs. Anna," of *The King and I*). Louis was one of 14 residents of Chiang Mai who purchased the grounds of the **Chiang Mai Gymkhana Club** in 1898.

Initially they wanted a venue for horse racing and their first meet was held over the Christmas holidays in 1898. The cricket competition, the **Chiang Mai International Cricket Sixes Tournament**, was started in the 1980s and takes place at Easter. It has grown in stature each year, attracting both amateur clubs and professional players from around the world.

The early days of the club were far different when the farangs had control. The foundation rules set forth that the club be run by a committee of five Europeans. Over the years that changed to the present day when Thais control the operation. The club still maintains high standards and still operates in the same location. It has the oldest golf course in Thailand. If you're interested in playing. see page 295 in the golf section in this chapter. The horse racing has long since stopped but it is an excellent club for tennis and squash.

Louis Leonowens was a childhood friend of King Chulalongkorn, King Mongkut's son, so it was no surprise that the king visited the club in 1905, which enhanced its prestige. Another important visitor in the '20s was British author W. Somerset Maugham.

When Louis's mother went to the US at the end of her five-year stay in Thailand he went with her. He had a varied career and then moved to Australia before returning to Thailand and founding the L.T. Leonowens Company, a corporation that still exists today. Like his mother he was a controversial person and the Gymkhana Club records show instances where fellow committee members quit because they found working with him impossible. He eventually moved back to England, where he died in 1919.

And Anna? She left Thailand in 1867, the year before King Mongkut died, and moved to the US. The first of her books was published in 1870, the second two years later. She lived in Halifax, Nova Scotia from 1876 to 1897 where she founded the Victoria School of Art, known today as the Nova Scotia College of Art and Design. She died in Montreal in 1915. She was 85 years old.

The Hill Tribes

There are probably a million people living in the hills and mountains of Northern Thailand who are grouped together as the Hill Tribes. There are a dozen different tribes. They have little in common except where they live. They do not share the same life styles, or the same language. They practice different religions. Some are Buddhists, others are animistic and some Christian. In many cases the easiest way to distinguish one tribe from another is from their traditional attire. Many have adapted their lifestyle because of the invasion of the tourists who come trekking into their domain. Others carry on, unaware that the rest of the world has entered the 21st century.

They do share one thing in common and that is they are hospitable people and welcome visitors to their villages. Some have changed their lifestyles now that some, if not all, of their income is derived from the tourist invasion.

Most of them migrated from China, Laos, Myanmar or Tibet within the last 200 years. The major clash they have had with the Thai government is with their agricultural slash and burn techniques and the growing of opium. The campaigns against these items have met with mixed success. Switching from opium growing to less profitable crops meant more land was required, which meant farmers hacked down more of the dwindling forests. And the need for pesticides left much of the area streams polluted.

Five of the main tribal groups are the **Karen** (called Gariang in Thai), the most populous tribe, the **Akha**, (Egaw in Thai), the **Lahu** (Musay in Thai), **Hmong** (Meo in Thai) and **Lisu** (Lisaw in Thai).

■ Karen

By far the largest hill tribe, numbers vary from 200,000 to half million. Their migration began in the 18th century and most of their villages are in the foothills below the mountains of Mae Hong Son province and the western areas of Chiang Mai, Chiang Rai and Phayao along the border with Myanmar. Dress: Single girls wear white V-necked long blouses, adorned with decorative beads while married women normally wear bold red or blue blouses with similar colored skirts. Baggy blue trousers are the choice for the men with a masculine version of the married women's tops. Karens live in bamboo homes that are built on stilts, allowing them space below to keep their animals: pigs, chickens and even buffalo. Many families keep elephants. They were traditionally used to help with forest work but now spend more time helping tourists trek around. Karens are famous for their skill as elephant trainers, or *mahouts*, and you'll find them sitting atop elephants all over Southeast Asia. Originally the tribe was animistic and practiced ancestor worship but in recent years many have been converted to Christianity by the influx of western missionaries.

Karens are good farmers with proper crop rotation and have nothing to do with opium. They have high moral standards and there was a time when adultery was punished by death. They are probably the most peaceful and accommodating of the tribes but they do give border guards a problem, since they do not recognize any border and wander when and where they want to.

■ Akha

The most retiring, as in timid, the Akha tribe has been the least affected by tourism and missionaries. Dress: The women's headgear is heavily decorated with an assortment of beads and silver jewelry and topped with curls of red fabric. Their oversized jackets are equally ornate, with boldly embroidered edges.

The Akhas began their migration to Thailand from Southern China in the early 1900s and there are thought to be 40,000 of them now in remote village along the mountain ridges of both Chiang Mai and Chiang Rai provinces. They originated in Mongolia.

Ancestor worship – most tribal members can recite 65 generations of family – ancestors and animism are a very important part of their life. Every August each village has a celebration around a large swing when offerings are made to spirits and ancestors are remembered.

■ Lahu

There are about twice the number of Lahu as Akhas in Thailand, most of them living in villages close to the Burmese border. Originally hunters, the tribe has adapted to farming and has replaced its opium operations with a wide range of items, including orchids and coffee. Dress: Many of the tribe now wear normal Thai clothes but you occasionally see woman in their traditional black cloaks with white stripes. The tribe originated in Tibet and then to southern China before moving on to Myanmar and Thailand. There has been a large conversion to Christianity but the unconverted still believe in spirits and worship in village temples.

■ Hmong

They say it takes all sorts. These people are totally different from the Karens. Most of them arrived in the 1950s and 1960s to escape the civil war in Laos. Thais refer to them as *Meo*, meaning barbarian. They have different moral standards from the Karen, allowing premarital sex and trial marriages. Brides' dowries are not paid until after the trial period. Dress: There are two major divisions and numerous clans within the tribes. The **Blue Hmong** mainly dwell west of Chiang Rai and Chiang Mai. These women wear their hair in large buns and don vivid blue pleated costumes. Again it is baggy black pants for the men, with embroidered jackets that fasten with a button on the left shoulder. The **White Hmong** keep themselves to the east of Chiang Mai and Chiang Rai. These women wear home-made hemp skirts and plain jackets with frilly blouses. The men dress much as their fellow tribesmen, often adding a colorful sash around the waist. The tribe believes that silver is good for the spirits and the women wear chunky jewelry every day, including wide neck bands, which they claim keep the good spirits inside.

The Hmong live in extended families. They originated in the cold regions of Mongolia and Tibet and then moved on to China, Laos, Vietnam and Thailand. Tradition was that the men, who were mostly slash-and burn-farmers, did all the income-producing work, but with the cutting back of that style of agriculture and the outlawing of the opium crop, many have stopped working and rely on their women to provide income from the sale of handicrafts. Their hemp fabric is produced with an attractive sheen and then dyed, and is sold at many markets. There is a high rate of opium addiction among the men.

■ Lisu

Originally from eastern Tibet, the Lisu migrated through Myanmar into Thailand during the 1920s. Dress: Both men and women dress colorfully. Men wear baggy pants in an assortment of colors with blue jackets, and the women have multi-colored long tunics with a broad black belts and blue or green pants. The tribe is animistic rather than Buddhist; sacrifices of cockerels are part of their religious practice. Witch doctors heal their sick and they have a great belief in fortune telling. Funerals differ, according to how you died. If it was a natural death then burial takes place in the family burial field. If the death was caused by a bad spirit then the body is cremated so that the spirit will not be passed along to future generations. Unlike Thais, the Lisu do not believe in keeping spirit houses outside their homes, which have long sloping roofs that reach close to ground level.

Festivals

January

The village of Bo Sang lies eight kilometers east of the town center, beyond the railway station, and is renowned for its delicately painted umbrellas. The village and its cottage industry is worth visiting anytime but in mid-January they hold a celebration fair, the **Bo Sang Umbrella Festival**, which makes it more appealing. The festival headquarters is the Bo Sang Handicraft Center. In addition to learning about the manufacture of umbrellas there are parades, cultural shows and a Miss Bo Sang beauty pageant. The Thai women are all dressed in traditional costume and perform art wonders on paper, silk and cotton. If you leave without buying a painted parasol it will be an odd occurrence.

The **Ban Thawai Wood Carving Fair** is another fair held outside the city, this one at Ban Thawai Village in Hang Dong District. The event, held at annually at the end of January, highlights the talents of northern Thai woodcarving artisans and features demonstrations on wood carving and local handicrafts. There is a street parade, numerous contests and lots of folk performances.

February

Thailand is not all orchids as the annual **Flower Festival** will prove. The event begins on the first Friday of February each year when the areas wide variety of blooms is at their best. Highlight of the three-day event is on the Saturday morning when a parade of floral floats, normally there are at least 30, and marching bands makes its way from the railway station, crosses the Nawarat Bridge and ends at Nong Buak Hat Park. The festival was started in 1977 to promote the growing of flowers and ornamental plants in the province. The floral work on the floats shows exceptional talent with designs relating to Buddhism, Hindu gods and scenes from the Ramayana. Adorning the floats are local lassies who vie for the title of Miss Flower Festival. The festival also provides another opportunity for the display and sale of local handicrafts.

April

Songkran, the Thai New Year, is celebrated in mid-April throughout the nation but friends tell us that they travel here each year because they have more fun. In Chiang Mai on Great Songkran day the Phra Phutthasihing Buddha image parade takes place around the city. In addition to the water-splashing, a great deal of efforts goes into making sand pagodas. Word of warning: Trains and planes get booked up early for the holiday.

May

On the night of Visakha Bucha Day, worshippers gather to light candles and make the seven-kilometer **Doi Suthep Pilgrimage** from Chiang Mai up to the temple on Doi Suthep Mountain. The pilgrimage is held on the first full-moon day of the sixth lunar month, which normally falls in May.

June

The **City Pillar (*Inthakin*) Festival** is an annual event to ask for peace, happiness and the rain to fall at the right time, and to bring prosperity for the city and its residents. Buddha images are paraded around the city. It is held at **Wat Chedi Luang** for seven days and seven nights in the seventh lunar month (which normally falls in June). This temple holds the city pillar, which traditionally marks the center of a town.

October

The **Northern Lantern Festival & Loy Krathong** is a national festival but they add a little extra to it in Chiang Mai. This is the day at the end of October, full moon day, when Thais launch traditional floats (krathongs) into the water to take all their cares – and bad spirits – away. Here they set off Lanna-style hot air balloons, which some locals claim does a better job of ridding problems. They launch the floats as well all along the Ping River. The starting point for the day of festivities is the Chiang Mai Municipality Office. Numerous other events take place including launching lanterns into the sky to worship the gods, a beauty pageant and fireworks.

December

Northern Thai food is the focus of the **Chiang Mai Food Festival**, an annual event held in the middle of December at Tha Phae Gate. In addition to demonstrations of fruit and vegetable carving there are several cultural performances.

Where to Stay

ACCOMMODATIONS PRICE SCALE	
Indicates rates charged per night during high-season for a double room, including breakfast and all service charges. Prices vary according to the exchange rate between the US dollar and Thai Baht. Most hotels offer discounts from their published rack rates during low season. All those listed accept major credit cards; rooms have direct-dial telephones and private bathrooms.	
$	Under $50
$$	$51 to $100
$$$	$101 to $175
$$$$	Over $175

Mandarin Oriental Dhara Dhevi, 51/4 Chiang Mai-Sankampaeng Road, ☎ 05388 8888 $$$$$. This incredible resort complex only went into full operation early in 2005 and already challenges the Four Seasons as *the* place to stay in Northern Thailand. Nightly cost for one of the 142 lavish, luxury suites – claimed to be the best resort accommodation in the world – starts at $500 per night. A sister operation to the renowned Oriental Hotel in Bangkok, the management promises "the retreat will provide a holistic approach to the rejuvenation of body, mind and spirit."

The resort is spread over 52 acres of natural landscaping and incorporates rice paddies, tropical hardwoods and exotic plantations. Each of the suites, handcrafted in keeping with traditional Lanna architecture, has its own museum-quality artifacts and antiques. And some have their own plunge pool. You get a choice of two swimming pools, neatly landscaped between formal gardens and expansive lawns, and four separate restaurants. And if you haven't seen enough of them there is a traditional Lanna temple, complete with hand carvings and religious artifacts on site. And there is a vast spa modeled on the ancient palaces of Mandalay, a Thai cooking school and an amphitheatre. We forgot to mention the health club, two tennis courts, two air conditioned squash courts, boutiques and a traditional Lanna building, which houses a ballroom that can entertain 600 people with the latest in sound-and-light technology. All of this is just 10 minutes from downtown or the airport. Please do not remove the antiques from the room.

The Buddhist-inspired design of the Mandarin Oriental did create problems before the hotel opened, when local monks complained that use of religious architecture in a commercial building degraded Buddhism. A hotel spokesman said the hotel did not wish to offend Buddhists but wanted to bring local culture to an international audience. The resort was intended to be a living museum, built in a traditional method by local craftsmen, where cultural performances and lectures would be held.

Four Seasons Chiang Mai Resort & Spa (formerly The Regent), Mai Rim-Samoeng Old Road, Mae Rim, ☎ 05329 8181 $$$$$. Out of town and out of this world. This is the most luxury you'll find in Northern Thailand. Or it was until the Oriental set up shop. Minimum size of suites is 750 square feet and they are elegantly decorated with traditional Thai fabrics and art. Each room has teak floors, an adjoining private sala, large bathroom with oversize sunken tub and separate shower overlooking a secluded garden. The resort has sixteen clusters of Lanna-style pavilions, each housing four suites. Luxury comes with a price. Expect to pay $500 a night, without breakfast. There are specials to be had. For $1,100 there is a two-night package, which includes your own full-time housekeeper, breakfast prepared and served in your own suite, a special dinner and airport transfers. The resort is a 20-minute drive north from the city set in 20 acres of landscaped grounds with lakes, lily ponds and terraced rice paddies. Some of the suites have their own private plunge pool and others have adjoining children's bedrooms. There is a 10,000-square-foot spa, two swimming pools, two flood lit tennis courts and superb restaurants. There are only 77 rooms but every one is a winner.

Sheraton Chiangmai (formerly The Westin Chiangmai), 318 Chiangmai-Mamphun Road, ☎ 05327 5300, fax 05327 5299, www.starwoodhotels.com/cheraton, $$$$. One of the best places to stay in Chiang Mai without breaking the bank, south of the city and on the east bank of the Ping River. All 528 spacious rooms with teak furnishings have great views over the river or to the sacred Doi Suthep Mountain. Watch for Internet specials (the best rooms can go for 4,000 Baht in the high season). Three excellent restaurants, each with a different cuisine. Even if you're not staying here the River Terrance Restaurant is worth visiting at lunchtime when there is an enormous buffet at a very reasonable price. There's a business and fitness center, swimming pool, beauty salon and the relaxing Vienna Lounge to collapse after a day of sightseeing.

Duangtawan Hotel, 132 Loykroh Road, ☎ 05390 5000, fax 05327 9100, www.dtwhotel.com, $$. New 24-story hotel has 504 rooms at reasonable prices starting as low as $43 ++ including breakfast. Impressive executive suites sell for $148. The opening here marked the northern debut for the DTW hotel chain, which operates hotels in Bangkok, Pattaya, Phuket and Samui. Well located near the night-markets and a 15-minute drive from the airport. The hotel has numerous restaurants and bars including the Malibu Lounge, which features live bands nightly. There is a wine and cigar boutique, spa, swimming pool, fitness center, shopping center and business center. Large meeting rooms, one big enough to seat 350 theater-style.

Royal Princess Chiangmai, 112 Chan Klan Road, ☎ 05328 1033, fax 05328 1044 $$. Quality hotel in the center of the city, easy walking distance to the night-market, with 198 fully equipped rooms. A good restaurant, cafeteria, gymnasium, sauna and swimming pool complete the picture.

Chiang Mai Plaza, 92 Strindonchai Road, ☎ 05327 0050, fax 05327 9547 $$. Another town center hotel but larger than the Princess with 242 rooms and similar facilities. The hotel prides itself on a tropical garden, something to enjoy in the center of town.

Mae Rim Lagoon Hotel, 65/1 Moo6, Mae Rim-Samoeng Old Road, ☎ 05329 7288 $$. Pleasantly away from town amid mountains this resort looks like something between a small castle and a grand mansion set on a private lake. They offer special programs where you become more Thai by dabbling in rice paddies and helping in the kitchen. Luxury rooms all with stunning views. Lots of gardens to stroll in and two fine spots to eat, the **Bussababan Dining Room** or the **Lanrumpeay Garden Restaurant**. Enjoy a mountain bike ride, play some snooker or sing along in the karaoke lounge. All room rates are include the transportation to and from airport, railway station and from any hotel in Chiangmai City The reasonable 3,500 Baht per-night rate includes a transfer from the airport, railway station or any hotel in the city, a welcome drink and a massage or other body treatment. For every two days you stay you get a free dinner or lunch and a choice of massage or special sauna treatment.

Amari Rincome Hotel, 1 Nimmanahaeminda Road, ☎ 05389 4884, fax 05322 1195, www.amari.com $$. Out of town in a quiet area but only 500 meters away from **Kad Suan Kaew**, the largest shopping center in Northern Thailand. This 158-room hotel in a garden setting combines interior décor of Thai antiques and handicrafts with a modern exterior. More popular with tourists than businessmen this hotel is noted for its fine swimming pool and offers great value for money. Huge grounds, swimming pools and tennis, variety of restaurants. Rooms all with balcony. Rates from US$

Empress Hotel, 199 Chang Klan Road, ☎ 05327 0240, fax 05327 2467, www.empresshotels.com, $. Great value for a quality hotel on the banks of the Ping River and only a 10-minute walk from the night-market. We have seen low-season rates on the Internet for under $30 for a double, including breakfast. The hotel has 375 rooms, a discotheque, shopping arcade, swimming pool, 24-hour coffee shop and two good restaurants, **Panda Palace** Chinese restaurant and **The Beefeater Grill** for European cuisine.

Felix City Inn, 154 Ratmankha Road, ☎ 05327 0710 $. well-priced hotel within the old city and walking distance to temples and just one kilometer to the night-market. If that's too far to walk the hotel does offer a shuttle service. Helpful for the return journey if you buy a lot. All 134 rooms have tubs and showers, a refrigerator and mini-bar. Free in-house movies. The hotel also has a shuttle service to the airport.

Hmong Hilltribe Lodge, 301/8 Soi Sbun-Nga, Nimman Hae Min Road, ☎ 05321 6780, fax 05321 5072 $. This is a great way to get close to the hilltribes in relative comfort. The lodge has a total of 40 rooms and is an hour's drive northwest from the city center, set on a hillside between rice paddies and forest. The lodges were built from the material gathered from the surrounding jungles and each has a balcony. Every evening there is a buffet dinner of local delicacies and a cultural demonstration by members of the Hmong tribe. A double room with full board costs less than 3,000 Baht. There are packages for longer stays that include adventures into the jungle featuring white-water rafting and elephant treks. The lodge provides transportation between Chiang Mai city hotels and the airport for an additional charge.

Imperial Mae Ping, 153 Sridonchai Road, ☎ 05327 0160, fax 05327 0181, $. Large, bargain priced 15-story hotel with 371 rooms and great views of the city and Doi Suthep Mountain. The daily buffet brunch is a favorite with hotel guests and outsiders. Central location near the night-market and look for the unusual elevator.

Lotus Hotel Pang Suan Kaew, 99 Huay Kaew Road, ☎ 05322 4333, fax 05322 4493, $. A big hotel with 690 rooms, located in the

Kad Suan Kaew shopping center (see previous page). The prices are low but service is better than average. Good views of city and mountains, and live music most of the day in the 24-hour coffee shop. The hotel has a selection of restaurants and is a 10-minute drive from the airport. There is a swimming pool, but this is not as luxurious as others in the area.

Novotel Chiang Mai, 183 Chang Puak Road, ☎ 05322 5500, fax 05322 5505, $. Good combination of services for the business traveler or tourist. The 159-room hotel on five floors is inexpensive and only five minutes from the city center. Built in 1995, the hotel has a business center, beauty salon and nice pool. And you get a free newspaper every day.

Banana Bonbon Resort, 28-28/1 Moo 8, Baan Pong, ☎ 05336 5440, fax 05336 5460 $. This 20-room retreat with superb mountain scenery is set in gardens in the village of Mae Ha, 500 meters above sea level and a 30-minute drive from downtown Chiang Mai and equidistance from the airport. All rooms are decorated with teak and have antique furniture. It is a 10-minute drive to the **Krisada Doi Gardens** and 25 minutes to **Wat Doi Kham**. The small pool features a waterfall. Expect to pay 1,700 Baht for a double including breakfast.

Belle Villa Resort, 135 Moo 5, Baan Pong, ☎ 05336 5318, fax 05336 5222 $. New, small boutique resort with all the frills you'd find at a large hotel. Far enough into the mountains to warrant fireplaces in the two-bedroom house suites. All rooms have a private balcony or terrace and enjoy incredible views. A total of 30 rooms and 15 two-bedroom suites at the 19-kilometer marker on the Hangdong to Samoeng Road, just 25 minutes drive from downtown and the airport. Expect to pay 2,000 Baht for a room, more for the suites.

The Imperial Chiang Mai Resort, Spa & Sport Club, 284 Moo 3 Donkeaw, Maerim, ☎ 05329 8326, fax 05329 7297, $. This is an unusual combination of sports club and small hotel in parkland on the banks of the Ping River, just 20 minutes north of the city off the Mae Rim Road. Favorite spot for sportsmen and nature lovers, with a wide range of sport facilities that includes an Olympic size pool and a polo club. There is also a jogging track in a shaded lychee orchard and a horse-riding trail by the river. It is a 15 minutes drive north from the city center off Mae Rim Road, an area that has its own attractions. Just 45 rooms and additional facilities include children's pool and playground, tennis, badminton and squash courts and a fitness center.

Suriwongse Hotel, 110 Chang Khlan Road, ☎ 05327 0051, fax 05327 0063, $. Centrally located in Chiang Mai and within walking distance of the night-market. The hotel has 120 spacious and well-furnished rooms and suites. Maybe worth paying a little more in enjoy spectacular views of Doi Suthep Mountain. Facilities include swimming pool, pleasing restaurant and 24-hour room service. Expect change back from 2,000 Baht for a deluxe room.

Amity Green Hills Hotel, 24 Super Highway Chiangmai-Lampang Road, ☎ 05322 0 100, fax 05322 1602 $. The hotel is on the outskirts of the city, a few minutes' drive from the city walls and within walking distance of Chiang Mai's financial, shopping and entertainment centers. Hotel facilities include restaurants, swimming pool and fitness center. The hotel has 200 spacious rooms and a double deluxe here with breakfast and a mountain view should be under 2,000 Baht. Free shuttle bus to the night-market.

Chiang Mai Plaza Hotel, 92 Si Don Chai Road, ☎ 05390 3161, fax 05327 2230 $. Within walking distance of the night-market, Chiang Mai Plaza has 444 rooms with classic Lanna décor. Best rooms for spectacular mountain views of Doi Suthep are the deluxe rooms from the third floor to the 12th floor. Expect to pay 2,000 Baht for those, and up to 10,000 Baht for a large junior suite. There is a snooker room in addition to the normal trio of pool, fitness center and sauna.

Chiangmai Hills 2000, 18 Huay Kaew Road, ☎ 05321 0030, fax 05321 0035 $. A 15-minute drive from the city center, this hotel has 281 spacious rooms all well decorated in traditional northern Thai style. Reasonably priced at 1,400 Baht including breakfast. Choice of restaurants, fitness center and swimming pool.

Baantai Hotel, 41/10 Sri Ping Muang Road, ☎ 05327 5938, fax 05320 2946 $. We have added this small and friendly downtown hotel to our list because they have extremely good rates for people who would like to linger a while in Chiang Mai. They offer the following long-stay rates: one month, 7,000 Baht; two months 6,500 Baht; and three months for 6,000 Baht. That's less than $2 per day! All 39 rooms have private bath, are air conditioned, have a small refrigerator and television. Normal daily rate for a room with breakfast is 800 Baht.

Chiang Mai Gate Hotel, 11 Suriwong Road, ☎ 05320 3895 $. We have left the best deal to last. Book direct with the hotel on the Internet and pay only 650 Baht a night for a standard room in the Chatree Wing or pay 800 Baht for a deluxe room in the Chiang Mai wing. The price includes a full American breakfast. A good location, 100 meters from the Chiang Mai Gate and the heart of the old city, and a 10-minute drive to the night-market. The hotel is close to the entertainment district on Moon Muang Road and has 160 rooms, a swimming pool, 24-hour room service and a beauty salon.

NEW HOTEL PLANNED

Meritus Hotels & Resorts plans to open a five-star, 150-room resort in Chiang Mai on the banks of the Ping River. Resort owner, Chiang Mai lord mayor Boonlert Buranupakorn, is also the owner of a major teak factory, which will supply materials for the eighteenth-century Lanna-style property. In keeping with traditional building techniques, no nails or concrete will be used.

Where to Eat

The wide variety of food and restaurants in Chiang Mai is just another reason why Thailand's second city continues to grow as a tourist destination. It rivals Bangkok for quality, choice and price. And you don't have to spend half the evening stuck in a traffic jam while your appetite is appeased by noxious fumes.

Much of the local food, like the architecture and culture, has a strong Burmese influence. But if you want to stray away from Thai there is every possible alternative within a few blocks. As you will see from the restaurants we list you can have everything from American steaks and hamburgers to Mexican burritos or Italian pastas.

The true local meal is known as *khantok*, served with several dishes of assorted meats and vegetables along with sticky rice, the north-Thailand staple. Many of the hotels provide this meal and accompany it with folk dancing and northern music.

We have deliberately been a little vague about pricing meals. So much depends on what you drink. Wine is expensive, like everywhere else in Thailand, and can often cost more than the food. Western meals are considerably more expensive than Thai, the more you stick to rice and noodles you more you'll save. If you find a bottle of good wine under 1,000 Baht you'll be doing well.

A great place to sample some of the typical spicy northern delicacies is at the night-market. If you find something you don't like there is no great financial loss. But if you find something you do enjoy, as we did, with pork in a tamarind sauce, you have something to ask for when you dine in a restaurant.

DINING PRICE SCALE	
Per person, based on a two-course dinner (a main course with either a starter or dessert), with a glass of wine and coffee. Wine is expensive and will affect the bill accordingly.	
$	Under $10
$$	$11 to $20
$$$	$21 to $30
$$$$	Over $30

El Toro Mexican Restaurant & Cantina, 24/5 Loi Kroh Road, ☎ 05327 3574, $. Seems strange to find quality Mexican food this far from south of the border but Chiang Mai is full of surprises. In addition to the Mexican favorites they serve Thai dishes, salads, vegetarian specialties and sandwiches. Excellent frozen margaritas, cheaper if you buy the jug! Easy to spot, the restaurant is just east of the moat on Loi Kroh Road.

The Fillmore East Bar & Grill, 15/7 Loi Kroh Road, ☎ 05390 4016, $$. Their slogan is when you are tired of rice and noodles come to the Fillmore East for the food you miss the most. Known for serving prime-USDA beef, this eatery is open from noon until 2am. In addition to the steaks, the menu boasts the best in barbecued pork ribs and chops, happy hour every day from 4pm to 7pm. One of the few places we know that invites customers to bring their own CDs.

Nightlife

Chiang Mai Simon Cabaret: Next to the Novotel Hotel, Chang Phuak Road, ☎ 05341 0321. Lovely laddies looking like gorgeous gals provided a fun evening of music, dance and comedy with stunning sets and striking costumes. Sister show to those in other Thai cities. If you've seen one you may not need to see another. Two shows every night at 7:30pm and 9:30pm.

Charlie's Place Bar & Massage: 105 Kampaengdin Road, www.charliesplace-chiangmai.com, ☎ 05320 8254. This is one of those places that falls into so many categories. It hardly rates as nightlife since they open at 11am but they do stay open until late. You can have a home cooked meal, a bar snack or enjoy a traditional Thai massage from properly trained operators who call themselves Charlie's Angels. Caters to everyone serving afternoon tea or full bar service watching UK football in the air conditioned lounge. Charlie's also operates a hotel delivery service. You can have a meal or massage served in any nearby hotel. Across from the Mae Ping Hotel's Beer Garden on Kampaengdin Road.

Chiang Rai

History

This is Thailand's most northerly city, the gateway to the **golden triangle**, which is anxious to swap its opium-growing image of days gone by for that of an up-and-coming tourist town. Slowly it moves in that direction with some newer and more luxurious hotels, but it remains a typical provincial capital that tends to get more day-trippers from Chiang Mai than people intent on spending a lot of time here.

Chiang Rai was once the capital of the Lanna Kingdom and was founded in 1262 by King Mengrai. His statue is in town at the intersection with the road that goes to Mae Chan. Mengrai (1238-1317) is considered to be on of Thailand's greatest kings. He was a descendant of a King Lawa Changkaraj of the Thai Yuan Tribe. He built the town of Chiang Mai, and established it as the center of government of the Lanna kingdom. A total of 18 kings of the Mengrai Dynasty ruled the Lanna until 1558 when it was conquered by Burma.

The Golden Triangle

Several years ago we toured Israel, which included a visit to the Sea of Galilee. I'm not sure what we expected to find there but it was certainly not the very modern Holiday Inn and the nearby Joseph's Fish and Chip Shop that greeted us. It's a similar disappointment that most tourists feel when they arrive at **Sop Ruak**, the small town that is at the center of the golden triangle. There are several placards and an impressive arch saying you're at the golden triangle but little else. There is the odd hill-tribe dweller

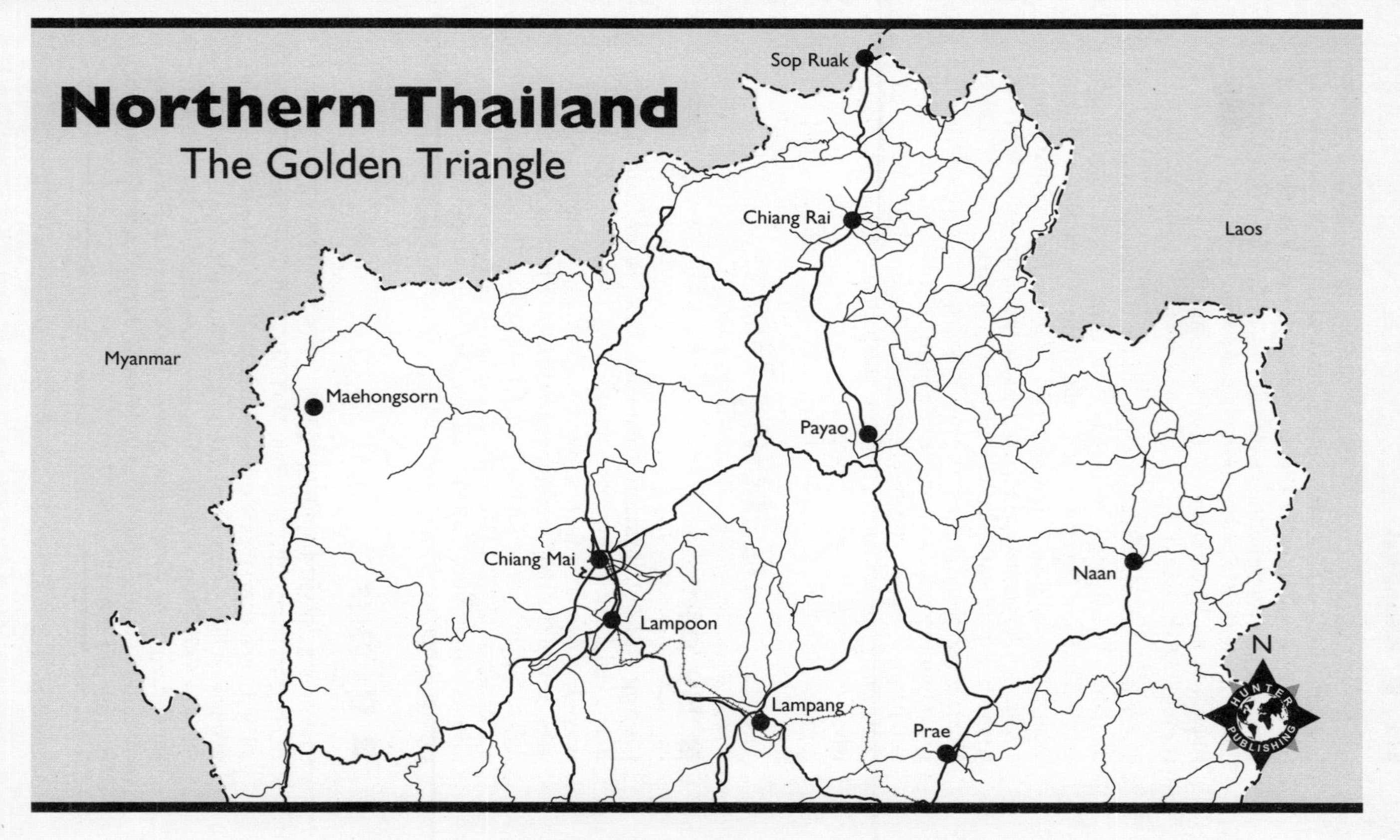
Northern Thailand
The Golden Triangle
Sop Ruak
Chiang Rai
Laos
Myanmar
Maehongsorn
Payao
Chiang Mai
Naan
Lampoon
N
Lampang
Prae
HUNTER PUBLISHING

available for a cash-earning photo opportunity. The views across the river are spectacular and there are some good restaurants; at most you can combine the vistas with good Thai food. The nearby opium museum is worth a short visit and there is an abundance of souvenir stalls catering to the tour buses, which stop here throughout the day.

There is no definitive explanation of how the golden triangle got its name. The triangle is obviously the three countries that abut here – Thailand, Myanmar and Laos. It was within this area that most of the world's opium was grown. Supposedly the opium dealers earned large amounts from the sale of the drug and that was where the gold came in. Sop Ruak sits at the junction of the Mekong and Sop Ruak rivers some 25 kilometers north of Chiang Rai. Opium production has been illegal in Thailand since 1959 and its production today has been virtually eliminated. We're told that across the border in Myanmar the poppies continue to flourish.

Getting Here

■ By Air

Chiang Rai International Airport (CEI) is on Phaholyothin Road, eight kilometers from downtown Chiang Rai. **Thai Airways** has five daily flights from Bangkok. Flying time is 80 minutes, ☎ 07621 1195, www.thaiairways.com. **Phuket Air** has two daily shuttle service flights from Chiang Mai. Flying time is 40 minutes, ☎ 05392 2118, www.phuketairlines.com. Annually the airport handles over 500,000 passengers, 3,900 flights and 2,700 tons of cargo.

■ By Bus

The nine-hour journey from Bangkok can be made on air conditioned coaches originating from Mo Chit 2 Bus Terminal, ☎ 02936 3659. Coach operators include **Bor Kho Sor's** 24-seat VIP coach ☎ 02936 2963; **Siam First Tour**, ☎ 02936 2492; or **Indra Tour**, 02936 2495. From Chiang Mai, air conditioned buses leave 12 times daily from Chiang Mai Arcade Bus Terminal. Some services continue to Mae Sai and Chiang Saen. Chiang Mai ☎ 05324 6503, Chiang Rai ☎ 05371 1154.

■ By Road

Getting here by road from Chiang Mai is a three-hour scenic pleasure. It is 190 kilometers on Highway 118, a good, fast road passing through the villages of Mae Khachan, Wiang Pa Pao and Mae Suai before joining Highway 1 just south of Chiang Rai. The more adventurous can travel here by raft along the Kok River, which flows gently through the city.

Getting Around

The 130-kilometer river is noted as one of the most scenic rivers in the kingdom as it passes through dense jungle and mountains. Trips can be arranged in either direction with stops at some of the hill tribe villages. The journey by raft takes three days. Shorter two- and three-hour excursions on longtail boats can be taken from the city.

USEFUL TELEPHONE NUMBER

Tourism Authority of Thailand (TAT) . . . ☎ 05371 7433

Things to See

■ Temples

Wat Phra Sing, on Singhakhlai Road near the town hall was home to a major Buddha statue, the Phra Buddha-Sihing, which is now enshrined in Chiang Mai. A special feature is the Lanna-style *ubosot*, the hall where new monks are ordained and other important ceremonies take place, and the wooden door panels carved by contemporary Chiang Rai craftsmen.

Wat Phra Kaew on Trairat Road was home of the Emerald Buddha, which is now enshrined in Bangkok's Wat Phra Kaew. The temple also houses a 700-year-old bronze statue, *Phra Chao Lan Thong*, which is in the Chiang Saen-style *ubosot*.

Wat Phra That Doi Chom Thong, on Doi Chom Thong, on the bank of the Kok River, contains an ancient holy relic pre-dating the time when King Mengrai built Chiang Rai.

■ Nam Tok Khun Kon Forest Park

This is the home of Chiang Rai's highest and most scenic waterfall, the *Khun Kon*, which cascades from a height of more than 70 meters. To get there, take Highway 1, the Chiang Rai, to Phayao road, for 15 kilometers and turn right at the park sign for another 17 kilometers. Then there is a 30-minute walk, which has several pleasant spots to rest.

■ Oub Kham Museum

Located near *Den Ha* market, one kilometer from the town center of town, the museum houses many items used by the Lanna royal courts. This includes numerous items of jewelry and lacquer ware from northern Thailand, northeast Myanmar, southwest China and Vietnam. Open daily from 9am to 6 pm. Admission 100 Baht, ☎ 05371 3349.

■ Ho Watthanatham Nithat

Located at the former town hall, Ho Watthanatham Nithat is a museum exhibiting ancient artifacts and written records on history and literature as well as exhibits on royal activities by the late Princess Mother. Open to the public Wednesday-Sunday from 8:30am until 3:30pm.

Festivals

■ January

The city remembers its founder every year at the **King Mengrai Festival**, held between January 26 and February 1 with a full program of competitions, cultural performances and colorful parades.

■ April

Songkran, The Thai New Year, April 16-18, is celebrated throughout the province but the most activity takes place at Chiang Saen, where the highlight is the boat races on the Mekong River. Beauty contests add glamour to the festivities.

■ May

Chiang Rai is said to produce the best lychees. Every May the province celebrates by holding a **Lychee Fair** with agricultural and local handicraft displays. Once again local lassies compete in a beauty contest.

Where to Stay

ACCOMMODATIONS PRICE SCALE	
Indicates rates charged per night during high-season for a double room, including breakfast and all service charges. Prices vary according to the exchange rate between the US dollar and Thai Baht. Most hotels offer discounts from their published rack rates during low season. All those listed accept major credit cards; rooms have direct-dial telephones and private bathrooms.	
$	Under $50
$$	$51 to $100
$$$	$101 to $175
$$$$	Over $175

Most hotels have Internet specials, which we did not take into account when assessing their $ rating.

Dusit Island Resort, 1129 Kraisorasit Road, ☎ 05371 5777, fax 05371 5801, www.chiangrai.dusit.com, $$$. Situated on an island in the Mae Kok River that flows through central Chiang Rai, the resort has 176 rooms and suites, with a choice of six places to eat, be it a snack in the lobby lounge or a fine steak in The Peak, a steak house with great views of the river. The hotel caters to both business and holiday clients with a wide range of activities available. There's a swimming pool, tennis courts, fitness and health club, yogi and Thai massage center as well as a jogging track, snooker and games room. It's just over one kilometer from the city center. Check the hotel Website for good value two-night packages that include dinner, round-trip airport transfers for $150 +++.

Anantara Resort & Spa Golden Triangle, Chiang Saen, ☎ 05378 4084, www.anantara.com, $$$$. We have seen rooms for this lavish, Lanna-style resort on the Internet for as low as $87. Great location perched on a ridge overlooking the hills of Laos and Myanmar. There's a choice of swimming pools, one indoor and one outdoor (remember, it can get chilly in the north). The deluxe rooms have bigger bathtubs and larger balconies. All rooms have a contemporary Thai finish; the décor relies heavily on teak for its luxury look. Full range of amenities including tennis and squash courts. There are indoor and outdoor terraced restaurants serving Thai and International cuisine, as well as the **Elephant** bar, offering traditional Thai music in the evenings.

The Legend Chiang Rai, 124/15 Kohloy Road, ☎ 05391 0400, fax 05371 9650, www.thelegend-chiangrai.com, $$$. This quality boutique resort on the banks of the Mae Kok River is within walking distance of the city center. The area around the resort is still undeveloped despite its proximity to the city, and there are spectacular views of the nearby mountains. Pleasant swimming and excellent spa, with treatments starting as low as 500 Baht for a 20-minute foot massage and climbing to 2,000 Baht for the 90-minute Royal Siamese body massage. For a high-priced resort the dining charges within the hotel are reasonable; room rates include a full American breakfast. In low season, May to October, a superior studio costs 3,400 Baht and a villa with private pool costs 7,600 Baht. That rises to 8,200 for the remainder of the year. Prices increase over the Christmas holiday. Least expensive accommodation runs 6,800 Baht a night and the most expensive 11,000 Baht.

Imperial Golden Triangle, 222 Golden Triangle, Chiang Saen, ☎ 05378 4001, fax, 05378 4006, www.imperialhotels.com, $$. Another attractive rustic resort in Chiang Saen, slightly smaller than Anantara, with 73 nicely equipped rooms including 10 river-view deluxe rooms, the one-bedroom Chiangsean Suite and a two-bedroom presidential suite. All rooms have balconies and traditional teak furniture. Décor features local handicrafts. A deluxe room in high season, from November to February, costs $75 including breakfast. At other times of the year the same room sells for $55.

Wiang Inn, 893 Phaholyothin Road, ☎ 05371 1533, fax 05371 1877, www.wianginn.com, $$. A reasonably priced quality hotel with Internet rates starting at $34 for a double. All 260 fully equipped modern rooms, with a Northern Thai motif, enjoy panoramic views of the city. The hotel is equipped to handle business groups but also caters to individual tourists. There's a pleasant pool terrace, where barbecue dishes are served and the large **Golden Teak** dining room features an international buffet.

Tour of the Northeast

This is the journal of a 16-day, 4,500-kilometer adventure we undertook to discover some of the least-known areas of Thailand. We were a little apprehensive about leaving the tourist towns and venturing into what was, to us, the unknown. Each day was an exciting new challenge. We had no idea what the roads would be like or what wonders waited around the next bend.

IN THIS CHAPTER

Climate

Rainy season: May to the middle of October, with heavy rains from August to October.

Cold season: December and January, with record low temperatures in December at 16.7°C.

Hot season: February to May, with highs near 40°C in April.

Average annual temperature: 33°C.

Travel Advisory

Driving Skills

We knew something of the perils of driving in Thailand after experiences in the busy urban areas of Bangkok and the major tourist destinations. We knew that lane discipline did not exist except on the Bangkok expressway, and that could change when the roads

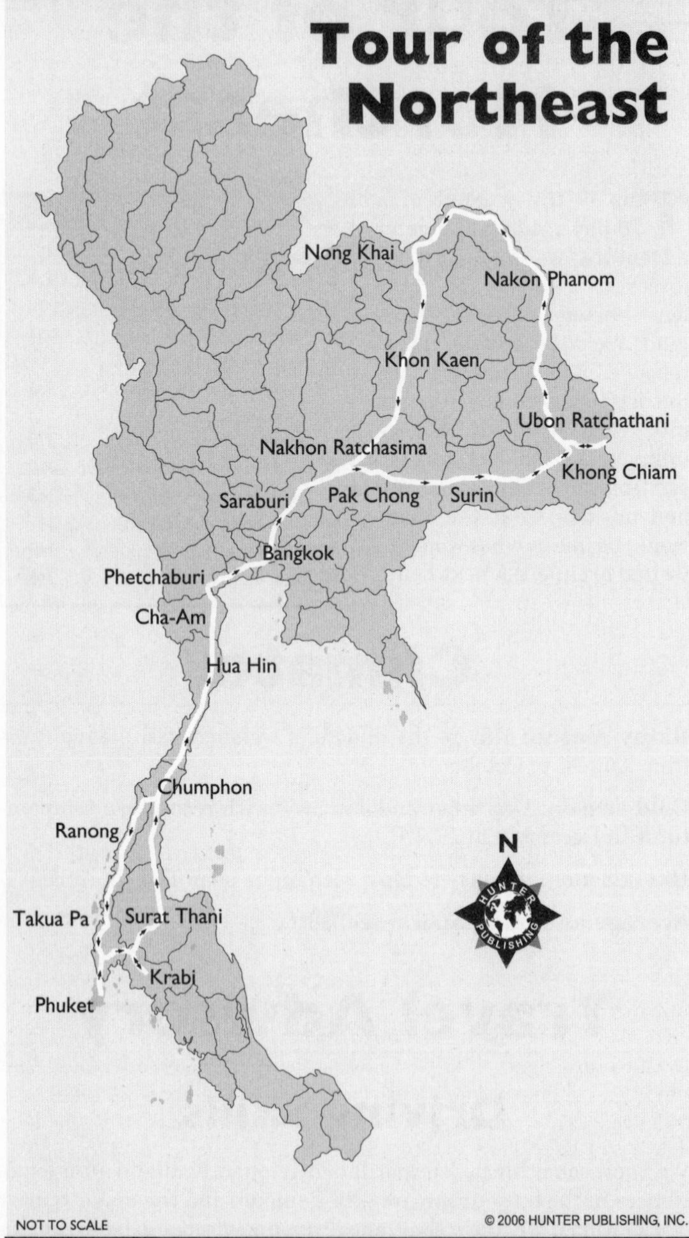
Tour of the Northeast
Nong Khai
Nakon Phanom
Khon Kaen
Ubon Ratchathani
Nakhon Ratchasima
Khong Chiam
Saraburi
Pak Chong
Surin
Bangkok
Phetchaburi
Cha-Am
Hua Hin
Chumphon
Ranong
N
HUNTER PUBLISHING
Takua Pa
Surat Thani
Krabi
Phuket
NOT TO SCALE
© 2006 HUNTER PUBLISHING, INC.

became clogged. We knew only too well that passing on blind curves and into oncoming traffic was common practice. We saw at least one traffic accident daily and marveled that there were not more. Defensive driving is essential; you have to forget about relaxing and assume that every other road user is about to do the unexpected. On the other hand, the roads were better than we expected, and on the major highways there were good road signs in English.

Road Signs

It is incredible how many road signs are in the English alphabet. However, many times we found that the destination we were looking for was not shown. If you are heading for Bangkok, for example, look at a map and get the names of the towns that are on the way to Bangkok. You may be quite close to Bangkok before that city name is shown. Another problem we encountered is that the compass points are rarely shown. A road sign will tell you are on Highway 4, but not say whether it is north or south. If you turn off the road to do some exploring and then return to the main highway you can easily go quite a distance in the wrong direction before you realize it. The kilometer markers on the sides of the roads can be a great help telling you distances to and from the closest towns. We had a problem however with these on the way back from Bangkok. Some of the markers had recently been repainted in white, and obliterated the numbers. We assume the painters will return with the black paint shortly.

Gas Stations

There are plenty of those on the major highways but we were never certain when they might appear. Every night we filled up with gas before quitting for the day knowing we had sufficient fuel for the following day's trip. We found it more convenient to use the major gas stations. They mostly had good coffee shops attached and acceptable toilets. We heard complaints that some of the smaller stations sold gasoline that was not always up to the best standards.

Road Conditions

Most of Thailand's roads are in good condition. The main highways do have poor patches and when work is being carried out you get very little advance warning. It's not uncommon to come around a bend and find part of the highway ahead of you closed for maintenance.

Caution

We took the advice of the Tourism Authority of Thailand (TAT) and did not drive at night when, according to that organization, there are more accidents, many of them alcohol related. The TAT promised numerous guesthouses or inns available while traveling, which we did not find. Fortunately we had pre-booked most of our accommodation and tried to limit our driving to five hours a day. We also filled up with fuel each evening to avoid finding fuel stops between towns.

We had been warned by friends of some of the possible dangers of travel here. Always watch the vehicle while it is being refueled to insure that nothing is attached to it while you are stopped, and never tell strangers where you are going. Our fears that the trip might prove dangerous or difficult were groundless. The only error we made was not taking more time. This is a country with an unlimited wealth of treasures to explore. We are already planning a return journey to undercover more of the wonders that Thailand has to offer.

Self-defense

Driving in Thailand is never relaxing. If you're expecting the comfort of a US Interstate, sipping coffee with the cruise control engaged, forget it. You need to be totally concentrated all the times. Vehicles come at you from all directions, create lanes where lanes should not be, and carry incredible loads. Do not be surprised to see a family of four with the family dog and a week's groceries all jammed on a small motorcycle.

Never make assumptions: Just because the colorful bus ahead of you is signaling to turn right and is in the right lane, don't assume that he will turn right. Chances are he will stop, turn left or, worse still, start backing up.

Proper Planning

We are so pleased we took the time to plan our stops ahead of time. Without that the trip would have been a disaster. Thailand is not blessed with the endless motels of the US or the roadside inns of Europe. Most major towns do have hotels but once you are away from those there is little accommodation to be had except for the odd guesthouse, which may lack modern facilities. We had pre-booked everything except for a couple of nights and they proved to be more expensive since we didn't always get the best rates.

The Journey

Phuket to Surat Thani

The events following the tsunami in southern Thailand changed our itinerary. We decided to drive from Phuket for the northeastern tour instead of starting farther north. It gave us the opportunity to see what damage, if any, had occurred around Phang Nga, the capital of Phang Nga province. We drove around towards Krabi and found the road and its surroundings virtually untouched by the devastating waves that brought so much death and destruction in other parts of the province, particularly in the coastal regions of Khao Lak.

With some feeling of relief we left the coast and took the new northbound Highway 44 from Krabi to Surat Thani. The heavy traffic we had endured from Phuket and around Phang Nga bay happily vanished and for the first time driving in Thailand became a speedy, pleasurable event. We traveled 100 kilometers in 45 minutes. One minor problem: Many Thai drivers do not fully understand the use of four lanes being separated by a very wide median. If you're traveling north do not be surprised to find someone heading towards you on the hard shoulder. This is a favorite shortcut for motorcyclists but cars and small pickup trucks also do it.

Surat Thani is a small city on the banks of the Tapi River that is noted as a stopping-off point for Ko Samui and other offshore islands. It's not a tourist town, few signs are in English, and there was a pleasant lack of the tourist stalls. The center of town is small but it is still easy to get lost as we discovered when we drove the wrong way into the bus station. Fortunately smiling faces greeted us, stopped the traffic and got us headed in the right direction. The area is a transportation hub. Its railway station is the closest to Phuket and Krabi and travelers who elect to travel by land face a six-hour bus journey to reach the resort areas to the south. Its airport north of town services a wide area and everywhere colorful buses provide transportation to the dozens of nearby hamlets and more distant towns.

Surat Thani translates to "city of the good people," and was at one time the capital of the Srivijaya Empire that flourished between the 7th and 13th centuries. The city is 650 kilometers south of Bangkok and the province is bordered by the Gulf of Thailand on its north and east. Thailand's largest oysters are collected from the estuary of the Tapi River and the province is noted for several kinds of textiles including silver-brocaded silk and printed batik.

■ Festivals in Surat Thani

August

Surat Thani has two of its own festivals. In August the city remembers the fact that the first rambutan tree was planted here in 1926. Today the province is a major supplier of the fruit. The **Rambutan Fair** highlights this fruit along with other agricultural products in a parade of fruit-adorned floats. There are also exhibitions of the province's plants and other products as well as cultural shows and demonstrations by trained monkeys who retrieve and split coconuts.

September-October

The second festival is **Chak Phra Festival** held at the end of the Buddhist Lent, which is at the start of the eleventh lunar month normally at the end of September or beginning of October. Buddha images are pulled along the Tapi River by tugboats and ornately decorated carriages perform a similar function on land.

■ Things to See & Do in Surat Thani

As we said earlier, Surat Thani is not a tourist town, but it does have a couple of attractions that appeal to visitors. One is the monkey-training center (see next page) and the second is **Wat Suan Mokkha**, a forest monastery in Chaiya and renowned Buddhist retreat for Thais and farangs. It is one of the few temples in Thailand that offers meditation studies in English.

Ironically, there is a connection between these two attractions. The founder of the monkey-training center, Somporn Saekow, was anxious to teach monkeys to collect coconuts without the use of force. As a child he had seen his parents and other coconut farmers mistreat monkeys when trying to teach them. Somporn's Buddhist teacher, Phra Buddhadasa from Wat Suan Mokkha, encouraged him to teach monkeys in a positive way by encouraging them rather than hurting them. He began his monkey college in 1957 and several others, following his methods, have opened since then. The most suitable monkeys are the pig-tailed macaques; once trained they can pick up to 800 coconuts a day and are able to select the ripe fruit from the rotten. Somporn died in 2002 but his family continues the college. The **Monkey Training College**, 24 Moo 4, Tambon Thungthong, ☎ 07722 7351 about a 30-minute drive east on Talad Mai Road. There are shows all day, the first one at 9am. Admission is 300 Baht.

■ Where to Stay in Surat Thani

There is limited accommodation here. We spent the night at the **Saowaluk Thani Hotel**, 99/99 Thanon Surat-Kanchanadit, ☎ 07721 3700, fax 07721 3735, just east of the town center, considered the best hotel in town, where a sixth-floor suite cost only 1,500 Baht including a buffet dinner and breakfast. The buffets were entirely Thai and there were no English-speaking chefs to tell us what the different dishes were. It gave us the chance to sample everything in small amounts to discover true Thai food, not prepared for European palates. There was a menu in English that did provide a limited amount of Western fare for lunch and dinner. Very limited English spoken either at the front desk or by the dining-room staff. For less money we could have stayed at the **Wang Tai Hotel**, 1 Thanon Taladmai, ☎ 07728 3020, fax 07728 1007. The 240 rooms here are spacious but basic.

> *You'll enjoy a pleasant view of the Tapi River from the Saowaluk Thani hotel's dining area.*

BJ Hotel, 17/1 Donnok Road, ☎ 07721 7410, fax 07721 7414. Centrally located near the bus station where we made the wrong turn, the hotel offers good value at 500 Baht a night for its 72 rooms; they are small but each has a shower.

> *Today we traveled 339 kilometers and spent 750 Baht for gasoline.*

Surat Thani to Hua Hin

A pleasant and easy drive. We listened to the bellhop's advice at the hotel and took the by-pass road that skirted the city center. We joined the main highway northwest of town. Once we passed Surat Thani airport traffic thinned out and we managed to keep a speed of 120 kph whenever the road surface allowed. The speed limit on most Thai roads is 90 kph but motorists ignore that. We learned that in many places the outside lane gives a smoother ride. Long-distance bus drivers know this too. If you want to pass you'll have to do so on the inside lane and suffer a few moments of road shudders. Once past you can return to the right hand lane, remembering that Thais drive on the left side of the road, or at least most of them do. With people shunning the southern resorts because of the tsunami disaster Hua Hin was crowded. There were few rooms to be had and fortunately we had reserved a room at the Marriott. To learn more about Hua Hin, check out that section in the *Beyond Bangkok* Chapter, page 122.

Today we drove 460 kilometers and spent 840 Baht on fuel.

Hua Hin to Pak Chong

An enjoyable early morning drive north from Hua Hin past the airport and through Cha-am turns into a bumper to bumper expedition as we join the trucks and buses on Highway 4 all headed north towards the kingdom's capital. The flow moves well but there's nothing noteworthy as we pass through towns and villages that come closer together and get more congested as our journey continues. We make a brief stop in Petchaburi, an historic town with more than its fair share of older temples. The town is divided by the River Phet and is a popular day-trip from Bangkok. The hills outside the town have become a popular spot for paragliding and are the closest area to Bangkok for practicing the sport.

There are two inexpensive places to stay in town: **The Royal Diamond Hotel**, on Highway 4, ☎ 03241 1060, has rooms for 800 Baht a night; the **Petchakasem Hotel**, behind the Royal Diamond, ☎ 03241 0973, has rooms available for as little as 200 Baht a night. For something a little different, and more expensive, there is **Rabiang Rua Resort**, 80/1-5 Moo 1, Anamai Road, Chao Samran Beach, ☎ 02967 1911, 02967 1913. The resort is 23 kilometers north of Cha-am. Turn off Highway 4 at the Nissan car gallery and head towards the beach. The accommodation is split between boathouses and small villas; rooms cost 2,300 Baht a night on weekdays and 2,900 Baht at weekends. Rates include breakfast.

Our dreaded crossing of Bangkok is just as bad as we had expected. We take the eastern ring road – an error, since we planned to take the western road – and speed along merrily in very light traffic thinking we have got the cross-city nightmare beaten. All too soon the expressway ends and we are on a crowded street somewhere south of Bangkok. As the traffic inches forwards we see the entrance to the city's expressway system and squeeze our way onto it. It takes several minutes for the traffic to pick up speed and our patient wait is well rewarded. The road rises ahead of us onto a high bridge over the Chao Phraya, the river of kings, and we are afforded a memorable view of the city ahead and the river below. That expressway ends and we join another out towards Don Muang airport.

SOUR NOTE

As we pass through an unmanned toll booth at the end of the expressway we are pulled over by a traffic cop who wants to see my driving license. He speaks limited English – just enough to tell us that he will keep the license until we pay the fine for speeding. Where do we pay? He tells us we will have to go back to Bangkok to pay it. His eyes brighten when I ask if I can pay on the spot. He tells me the cost will be 3,000 Baht. I part with the three notes and they vanish as quickly as does his receipt book. His stern look is replaced with a happy grin and he wishes us a happy holiday.

The vistas do not improve as we head through the suburbs of north Bangkok. The road surfaces are good, however, and we make good speed. It is not until we pass through the town of Saraburi and its huge, ugly cement factories that we are repaid with wonderful scenery. This is the welcome to the Northeast of Thailand that we had expected, and we were not disappointed.

It was reminiscent of some of the mountain scenery of the Carolinas, rich in colors but still hot and tropical. The temperature outside our air conditioned car was still a balmy 31 degrees Celsius – over 90 degrees Fahrenheit. Saraburi is said to have been founded in 1548 during the reign of King Maha Chakkraphat. The province has two major shrines. *Phra Phutthabat*, which means the Buddha's Footprint, was discovered here in 1622 and now draws

Thai pilgrims twice a year for festivals. The second shrine is *Phra Phutthachai*, the Buddha's Shadow, which is four kilometers off the Bangkok to Saraburi Road at kilometer marker 102. The attraction is the shadow of a Buddha image seen on a cliff wall.

The northeast of Thailand is known as *Isaan*, also spelled *Isan*, *Issan* or *Esarn*. The area is located on the *Korat* – also spelled *Khorat* – Plateau, which is bordered by the Mekong River to the north and east and by Cambodia to the south. To the west it is separated from northern and central Thailand by the Phetchabun Mountains.

■ Where to Stay in Pak Chong

Our overnight stop in Pak Chong is at the **Sak Phu Duen Resort**, 119 Moo 6, Sak Phu Duen Road, Nongnamdaeng, ☎ 04426 5384, fax 02439 1536, www.sakphuduen.com. This resort truly lives up to our theme of luxury at an affordable price. The suite we have is large, elegantly furnished and the countryside views we enjoy in all directions are dramatic. We are amazed that such serenity and scenery is only two hours away from the noise, clamor and pollution haze of Bangkok.

And the prices are incredibly low considering the quality of the accommodation. The royal suite is the most expensive room and costs $100 a night and the least expensive room costs $60. The resort has a large swimming pool, snooker club and fitness center and for those so inclined, there is a special karaoke room that stays open until 2am. There's a children's playground and the resort has facilities to handle large banquets and conventions, none of which are taking place right now.

The hotel mainly caters to vacationing Thais but extends a warm welcome to farangs who venture here. Dinner at the resort's restaurant was an inexpensive pleasure and although we opted for a Thai meal there was a good selection of western dishes. The morning breakfast buffet catered both for Thai and European tastes and we enjoyed eggs and bacon while our dining companions filled plates with rice and noodle dishes.

We didn't expect to find a high quality restaurant out here in the countryside – but we did, just a few kilometers away from the Sak Phu Duen. The **Fabb Fashion Café**, 219 Moo 4 Thanarat Road, Pak Chong, ☎ 04429 7533, www.fabbcafe.com. provided us with a fine Italian lunch that would be hard to better anywhere. The place is not cheap by Thai standards but the quality merits the prices. Our bill for lunch including drinks and tips was 900 Baht.

There's an extensive menu including steaks, ribs and several fish dishes and even an ostrich steak. It's the first restaurant in Thailand that we've visited that did not have a single Thai dish on the menu. How does a restaurant of this caliber operate in such a remote place? Our waitress said they get a lot of European tourists as well as Bangkok families who spend vacations in the area. We later discovered by checking the Website that the restaurant is the brainchild of Luv Kamonsawedkun, who operates several successful restaurants in Bangkok.

Today we traveled 506 kilometers and spent 800 Baht on gasoline.

■ Exploring Pak Chong

It was a delightful early morning experience to open wide the sliding doors of our suite and let in the fresh mountain air. The major attraction in the area is the vast **Khao Yai National Park**, which is just 10 kilometers away. The road that leads from the town of Pak Chong to the national park passes close to the Sak Phu Duen Hotel and many other upmarket resorts. We spotted areas where new homes are being constructed.

The park is Thailand's oldest, having been established in 1962, and also the kingdom's most popular. Thais flock here at weekends and during the cool season, from November to February things get very crowded, which explains the need for the numerous roadside stands and restaurants that surround the park's main entrance and approach road. We visited during the week and it was pleasantly quiet. The park, the third-largest in Thailand, covers more than 2,160 square kilometers. It is one of the few in the country that is still home to wild elephants and tigers. We didn't get to see any but were told that the best time is at night when specially led safaris watch near salt-licks where the animals visit. It's easy to spend a day touring the area with its numerous nature trails and several spectacular waterfalls. These are at their best in the rainy season between May and October when the flora is at its brightest green. The trails are designed for short journeys looking at plants and trees, special paths for birders who want to watch some of the 300 plus species recorded in the park and for the truly serious hikers there are lengthy trails that involve one to three days trekking and camping. Other mammals in the park include the Asian jackal, Asiatic black bear, Malayan sun bear, leopard, several species of deer, golden cat and a variety of monkeys, which were friendly enough to come close to our car.

It's possible to camp in the park and there simply furnished bungalows available for rent. Normal entrance fee to a National Park for foreigners is 200 Baht plus 50 Baht for the car. More info: Khao Yai National Park, ☎ 03731 9002, www.dnp.go.th.

Not far from the resort we stayed at is the **Juldis Khao Yai Resort & Spa**, at kilometer marker 17 on the Thanarat Road, ☎ 04429 7297, www.khaoyai.com. A variety of accommodation is offered at this 107-room resort, ranging from luxury suites to cozy bungalows. Prices are as low as 1,000 Baht a night. There's a choice of cuisine too. Eat Thai in the **Chommanade Restaurant** or European in the **Steak House**. Lots of outdoor activities: In addition to the pool, there is cycling, canoeing, horse riding and tennis. We noticed more farangs here than at our resort but again it is mainly Thais who visit here.

Best accommodation we saw in the town was the **Pakchong Landmark Hotel**, 151/1 Mittraphap Road, Pak Chong, ☎ 02673 0966. The Landmark offers nicely decorated rooms at 950 Baht and suites from 1,600 Baht. The hotel has 140 rooms, good restaurant, popular karaoke bar, snooker, and business center. There is a golf course and shopping center close by. Hopefully you won't need it, but the local hospital is across the street.

Pak Chong is a little prettier than your typical Thai town with attractive planting stretching through the central median. We saw few signs in English except for the car galleries and repair shops that are a common site marking the entrance or exit to most town limits.

> *We drove 180 kilometers today, touring Pak Chong and visiting the state park.*

■ Exploring Korat

The first major town east of Pak Chong is Korat. This is the short name for **Nakhon Ratchasima**, the official gateway city to Thailand's northeastern region. The area is far enough north that you do notice a slight climate change from Bangkok, some 260 kilometers to the south. Helping provide a little cooler air is the fact that the area sits on a vast plateau with elevations between 130 and 300 meters above sea level. As a result the surrounding area is popular for camping and golf. The city is well served by public transport. There are more than 140 daily buses from Bangkok. They operate around the clock from Bangkok's Northeastern Bus Terminal on Phaholyothin Road and arrive here at the bus terminal of Burin Lane. During rush hour a bus departs every 15 minutes. It is a major rail junction and as a result there are 26 round-trip services to Bangkok daily. Korat makes an ideal center for touring around. Among the bustle of city life you'll find a trace of American influence since many GIs who served in Vietnam have retired and set up home in the area. The village of Dan Kwian famous in Thailand for its unusual pottery is just 15 miles south. The prehistoric archaeological site at Ban Prasat is 42 kilometers northeast heading up Highway 2. And if you want to get up-to-date on local and national events get at copy of *The Korat Post*, the local newspaper in English.

■ Festivals in Korat

March-April

The annual **Thao Suranaree Victory Celebration Fair** is held from March 23 to April 2 to commemorate the victory of Thao Suranaree, better known as Khun Ying Mo, a local heroine who rallied the local people to fight off Laotian invaders who threatened to seize Nakhon Ratchasima at the time when King Rama III was on the throne. He reigned from 1824 to 1851 at the time when Zachary Taylor was president of the United States. The fair includes events for children as well as exhibitions, cultural displays and lots of fireworks.

May

The **Yasothon Bangfai Rocket Festival** takes place each year in May, when huge rockets are launched into the air. The festival also includes presentations of art and culture, and parades.

November

The **Phimai Boat Races & Phimai Festival** take place on the Mun River near the old Khmer city of Phimai during the second week of November. In addition to the regatta there is a boat-decorating contest where the competitors recreate the famous old royal barges. (If you want to learn more about the royal barges look in the *Bangkok* chapter under the Royal Barge Museum, page 68.) The festival coincides with the races and is based at the Phimai Historical Park. Plenty of entertainment including a sound and light show, stalls selling local produce and handicrafts and exhibitions on items Buddhist, historical and cultural.

■ Things to See in Korat

The Village of Dan Kwian

A tribe of Mons stopped off here on their way from Burma in the 18th century and discovered that the clay from the nearby Mun River was ideal for their ceramic work. Some 20 families continue the work today and it is highly thought of it because of its unusual unglazed metallic finish. There are shops lining both sides of the road selling the pottery in addition to other items in wood and bronze. Recently an open air mall was constructed giving even more space for the villagers to demonstrate their crafts and sell their wares.

Dan Kwian means "a stopping place for oxen carts," the transportation that brought the original settlers here. There are a number of them displayed at the entrance to the village along with agricultural antiques. They may look old but most of the implements are still used today. Pottery prices are low – $4 will buy you a fine vase – but bargaining is expected. You can find this pottery elsewhere in Thailand but it will be a lot more expensive. If you want to visit by bus there is a service every 20 minutes from Korat. It takes 30 minutes to get here at a cost of 6 Baht. If you're driving, as we were, you take Highway 224 southeast from Korat.

Nakhon Ratchasima Zoo

This is the fifth-largest zoo in Thailand, and one of the most modern. It is 13 kilometers from the town center on Nakhon Ratchasima-Pak Thong Chai road (Highway 304). There is a full range of animals, snakes and birds and the zoo is particularly proud of its peacocks, which hail from India and Thailand. There is a mini-train to take you around, a petting zoo for younger ones and exhibitions about penguins and seals. Open daily from 8am to 4:30pm and admission is free.

Wat Sala Loi

This temple is on the banks of the Lam Takhong River, on a side-road northeast of the town. It's hard to miss since it is constructed in the shape of a Chinese junk. The main chapel has received several architectural awards because of its design as a modern religious monument.

Maha Weerwong National Museum

After Bangkok, this seems a little tame. There are several sand stone Buddha images from the Khmer and Ayutthaya periods along with wood carvings and ceramic pieces from ancient monasteries. Located across from the city hall and open from 9am to 4pm. Closed on Mondays, Tuesday and public holidays.

The Statue of Khun Ying Mo

The much-revered heroine mentioned a few paragraphs earlier is remembered with her statue, which was erected in 1934 at the western gate of the old city walls. Khun Ying Mo was the wife of the Deputy Governor of Korat and her deed of heroism is not dissimilar to the three heroines who are remembered in Phuket.

Archaeological Site at Ban Prasat

There was little to attract tourists to Ban Prasat, a pretty Thai village with typical stilt houses alongside the Tan Prasat River until the early 1990s, when archaeologists discovered burial sites dating back 3,000 years. The site is well signposted from the village. The village is 42 kilometers north of Korat on the road to Khon Kaen. There are two excavation sites, each with three pits. The artifacts that have been unearthed are well marked in Thai and English. The site is thought to have been inhabited in 1000 BC by rice farmers. There are items from that time to the present. There are ancient and relatively modern weapons, skeletal remains, gold jewelry from the Dvaravati period, and glazed pottery from Khmer times. There is a small museum and information center on the site but they have no set hours.

Meanwhile back in the village there are numerous local handicrafts to enjoy. You can learn all about silk, its story from mulberry leaves to finished fabric from one family, or how to make mats from bulrushes from another.

■ Where to Stay in Korat

All the hotels listed here have double rooms under $50, including breakfast and taxes. You may pay more if you opt for a superior room, suite or bungalow. There are several hotels, or guesthouses, in the downtown area, which are even cheaper. Some come with a choice of air conditioning or fan.

Royal Princess Korat, 1137 Suranarai Road, ☎ 04425 6629. Quality hotel, part of the Royal Princess chain, noted to have the best swimming pool and Chinese restaurant in town. North of the city, away from the noise, 186 rooms and suites with prices starting at under $40 for a double. Gift shops, business center and a library all set in pleasant gardens. Twice a day mini bus to the airport. Hotel rents out cars with drivers if you want to visit some of the surrounding attractions.

Sima Thani Hotel, 2112/2 Mittraphap Road, ☎ 04421 3100. Larger than the Princess with 265 rooms and suites. Expect to pay less unless you opt for one of their plush suites. Surprisingly quiet since it is on the main road on the western side of the town. The five-story atrium lounge is an airy indoor rest area. All the rooms are decorated with Khmer-style art and have attractive granite-faced bathrooms. The hotel has a pool, fitness center, two restaurants and a pub.

Chomsurang Hotel, 547 Mahatthai Road, ☎ 04425 7088. The other hotels we mention are a little out of town. This one is in the old town and close to the night-market. Expect to pay under $30 a night for one their 119 rooms. It is one kilometer to the railway station and within walking distance of the Khun Ying Mo statue. This is an older property, has a small swimming pool, and a good inexpensive restaurant. Cars and drivers available and same-day laundry service.

Hermitage Resort & Spa, 725 Thao Sura Road, ☎ 04424 7444. Gracious resort with 139 rooms, which includes 12 executive suites. Close by is **Wat Sala Loi** for temple visiting and, farther along, **Tesco Lotus** for bargain shopping. The hotel is just past the southeastern corner of the old city moat, on the road to Dan Kwian and Buriram. With rooms available at $35 it is great value.

■ Where to Eat in Korat

There are dozens of small eateries in the downtown area and all of the hotels we list have good restaurants. You'll also find plenty of food stall near the night-market. If you do have a yen for something different there is a Pizza Hut at 754 Ratchadamnoen Road, ☎ 04426 0576. Or if you want more of a US feeling visit the VFW (Veterans of Foreign Wars) meeting spot on Thanon Pho Klang, where you'll find steak and French fries prominent on the menu. Low prices and an ample supply of ketchup.

Thaweephan, Sueb Siri Road, ☎ 04425 7775. A typical inexpensive Thai restaurant close to the tourist office. The large menu also includes Chinese dishes and the most expensive plates are under 200 Baht. Little English is spoken here. The restaurant is open from noon to 11pm, the tourist office from 8:30am to 4pm. More English is spoken at the tourist office, where you can get a free city map plus more brochures about things you ought to have seen but didn't seem to have the time for.

Cabbages & Condoms: If you've read the Bangkok eating section you'll remember the name. Hard to forget! This is a similar operation to Bangkok with the profits going to the Population and Community Development Association of Thailand (PDA). The restaurant is at 86 Serbsiri Road, ☎ 04425 8100. You will find some different regional dishes here that are not on the Bangkok menu. We were told that, should you wish to give a taxi driver instruction on how to get to Cabbages & Condoms, you say, "*Sukhumwit soi sip sawng*." We have not tried that. One other thing you should know: The complimentary items in the bowls as you leave the restaurant are not after-dinner mints.

Pak Chong to Surin

Our 300-kilometer trip to Surin today gave us a better insight into why the northeast is able to provide so much of the fine food that finds its way to Thai tables and many more across the world. The roadside fields were abundant in rice, corn and sugar cane. Trucks loaded with cane and rice trundled along with mighty loads that looked like they would tumble.

We left Pak Chong on Highway 2 and then joined Highway 226 on the eastern side of Korat. Our overnight stop was at the **Thong Tarin Hotel**, 60 Siriat Road, Surin, ☎ 04451 4281, fax 04451 1580, www.thongtarin.com.th. It was billed as the best Surin has to offer with the motto: *Your satisfaction is our pride*. It was the most disappointing stop on our journey so far and it was a great relief we only spent one night here. The messages pasted in our junior suite give you an idea of the place:

"*Ironing in the room is not allowed. Please contact the room maid on your floor to laundry service. Damage from ironing on the carpet will be charged 1,500 Baht per one spot. Best regard the management. In case of fire do not use elevator.*"

"*Honored guests: As this time of year it is a holiday in Surin. Many tourists come to large hotels. Thieves have been known to come into hotels . . . and steal belongings of guests. So International police are informing guests to lock their doors and keep all belongings in a safe place. The hotel will not be responsible for lost / stolen items. Safety boxes are available at the front cashier's office.*"

The lack of smiles on our arrival was untypical Thai and we thought it was perhaps an anti-farang sentiment. We watched Thais and other Asians check-in and realized it was standard hotel procedure. We thought the 1,800 Baht a night for a junior suite to be a reasonable price, but it was expensive for this hotel. Whatever the price, it was too much. The swimming pool was a characterless concrete rectangle and the restaurant with its plastic-covered chairs had the ambience of a bus station in the middle of the night.

There is one other large hotel in Surin, **The Phetkasem**, 104 Chit Bamrung Road, ☎ 04451 1274, fax, 04451 4041. Its brochure says it is "the hotel of a perfect happiness." There are 162 rooms and it is in the town center. Rates for a superior double room with breakfast are normally 1,200 Baht a night but climb to 3,300 Baht during the elephant festival.

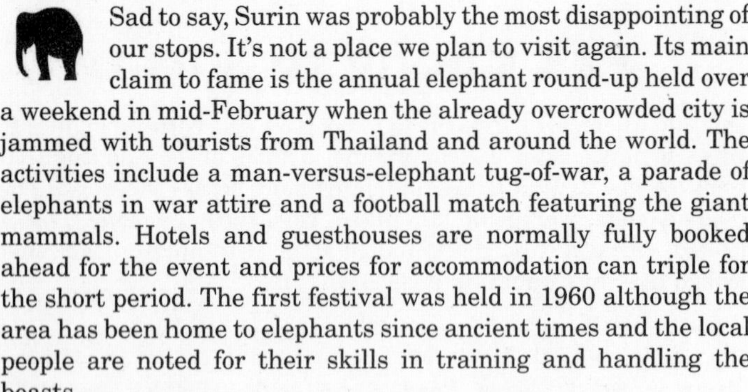

Sad to say, Surin was probably the most disappointing of our stops. It's not a place we plan to visit again. Its main claim to fame is the annual elephant round-up held over a weekend in mid-February when the already overcrowded city is jammed with tourists from Thailand and around the world. The activities include a man-versus-elephant tug-of-war, a parade of elephants in war attire and a football match featuring the giant mammals. Hotels and guesthouses are normally fully booked ahead for the event and prices for accommodation can triple for the short period. The first festival was held in 1960 although the area has been home to elephants since ancient times and the local people are noted for their skills in training and handling the beasts.

The **Banthat Mountains** separate the province of Surin from Cambodia. During the terror reign of the Khmer Rouge in the 1970s, thousands of Cambodians crossed into Surin and many have stayed. The province is also home to a large number of Laotians. There are several villages near Surin noted for handicrafts and souvenirs. **Ban Buthom** at Tambon Muang Thi on the Surin to Si Khoraphum Road is noted for basketry. The villages of **Ban Khawao Sinnarin**, **Ban Chok** and **Ban Sado** are noted for silverware and silk products. These villages are close together, four kilometers off Highway 213, the Surin to Chom Phra Road.

Today we drove 307 kilometers and spent 900 Baht on gasoline.

Surin to Khong Chiam

Highlight of the day was discovering the Tohsang Khongjiam, 68 Moo 7, Baan Huay-Mak-Tai, ☎ 04535 1174, fax 04535 1162, www.tohsang.com. This is a truly splendid small resort set in over 14 acres of grounds overlooking the **Mekong River** with views of neighboring Laos that epitomizes our theme of affordable luxury. We looked at the selection of rooms and opted for a spacious bungalow that was wonderfully furnished, had its own private garden with water features and magnificent views of the river and the hills of Laos beyond. We paid 3,500 Baht a night and that included an enormous breakfast buffet, which had a wide variety of dishes to satisfy the hungriest Westerner or Asian. There are a total of 40 rooms, eight suites, and seven bungalows. There are rooms available, with river views, from 2,000 Baht and there are packages available on their Website.

We enjoyed the large swimming pool, although the water temperature was a little cooler than we had been used to farther south. A good restaurant with reasonable prices and young, cheerful staff makes it a place you want to visit again.

Somehow we imagined the **Mekong** to be mightier than it was. This great river that flows from China through Myanmar, Thailand, Laos, Cambodia and Viet Nam was slow and low. Locals told us that the Chinese were to blame because of dams they built at the start of the river – a charge that China denies, pointing out that every country along the river takes water in increasing amounts for irrigation projects. We saw now, and later, how fertile the areas close to the river were. Away from the river, and its tributaries and canals, much of the land was barren and dry. Despite the irrigation projects that turned much of the northeast from a near-desert into productive, usable agricultural land we never saw the deep greens that color so many other parts of Thailand. When we made our tour the area was in the depths of a deep drought.

Our drive from Surin was a simple one on Highway 226, paralleling the rail line that terminates in Ubon Ratchathani. It was truly a rural excursion, flat with fields of grain and more livestock grazing, but all tethered. The tiny hamlets we passed were colorful and obviously depended on farming for their livelihood. There were plenty of gas stations, wats and most communities supported a soccer field. We bypassed Ubon to the south and took Highway 217 from Warin Chamrap to Phibun Mangsahan, where we saw the sign for the **Tohsang Khongjiam Resort & Spa**, where we stayed. From here we took Highway 222 east to Khong Chiam.

To get to the resort go to the end of Highway 222 and turn right into Khong Chiam. After you pass through the village you'll cross the Mun River on an impressive new bridge. Take the first left turn at the foot of the bridge and drive 2.4 kilometers and the resort is on your left; Tohsang Khongjiam, 66 Mu 7 Baan Huay-Mak-Tay, Khongjiam, Ubon Ratchathani, ☎ 04535 1174, www.tohsang.com.

The village of **Khong Chiam** is worth a visit with its attractive waterfront, public park and assorted roadside stalls. A place you can enjoy a quiet stroll even if you are the only person who speaks English.

■ Things to See in Khong Chiam

The Border Market: There's a daily street market at Chong Mek, the border town with Laos. The stalls and shops are open from 8am until 5pm. Unbelievably low prices on everything from clothes to cases. Even though the prices are low – nice quality cotton tops and shirts starting at 50 Baht – you are still expected to bargain. Big plus is you don't get pestered the same way you do at the tourist markets. We felt safe and comfortable wandering around the stalls.

Without your own transport you are trapped at the resort – a very pleasant experience – but there are numerous tours that you can take. Here are a couple of examples: A half-day trip to **Patem National Park**, **Soy Sawan Waterfall**, **Kangtana National Park** and the **Pak Mun Dam** costs 3,200 Baht for two people and includes transportation costs, admission charges to the park, the services of a guide and drinking water. A full-day tour, including all of the previous stops plus a visit to the Thai-Laos border market at **Chong Mek** costs 4,300 Baht for two people and includes a lunch box. There's also a full-day cultural tour including the Khmer palaces – **Prasat Sri-Kornraphum**, **Wat Sa Kampang Lek**, and **Wat Sa Kampang Yai**, all in the Khmer ruins district in Surin Province – and the **Ubon National Museum**. This tour cost 5,600 Baht for two including a lunch and admissions. You can also take a cruise down the river for 500 Baht a person and if you time it right you can be one of the first people in Thailand to see the sun set, because this is the most easterly point in Thailand.

The cruise on a longtail boat takes you to the village of **Woenbuk**, past **Kangtana National Park** and the bi-colored river.

This is the first place we have stayed in Thailand where we have not switched on the air conditioning at night. It was cool enough to sleep well and in the morning there was the slightest bite of cool as we sipped coffee on our terrace. Below us on the river bank a small herd of cattle, their cow bells softly clanking, trudged by as a light mist on the Laotian hills burned away in the morning sun.

The resort has a large swimming pool, spa and a restaurant serving a good selection of western dishes as well as an extensive Thai menu. Added bonus at dinner was a show staged by local musicians and dancers who performed traditional Isaan music and dances. The group had been hired for the evening as part of a wedding celebration that was being held at the hotel.

The hotel offers a transfer service to Ubon airport or railway station, 1,250 Baht one-way per person and also trips to the border market at Chong Mek for 900 Baht round-trip.

Today we traveled 290 kilometers.

■ Exploring Ubon

Ubon Ratchathani, the Lotus City, is one of the biggest cities in Isaan, the fifth-largest in Thailand, and is the capital of the province with the same name. The city is a major trading center for the area's agricultural products of rice, sugarcane, cattle, timber, pigs and cotton. It is steeped in history and full of temples, places of higher learning and abuzz with day and night street markets and traffic. The best of the province is outside of the city and we mentioned some of the favorite tours above. It is definitely worth visiting the **Ubon National Museum** on Thanon Khuenthani, open daily, except Monday and Tuesday, from 8:30am to 4:30pm, as it is one of the best museums in Thailand. There is a vast range of exhibits and a major plus is that most have good English descriptions. A couple of hours spent here and you'll have a good idea about the province's history as well as learning about the traditional handicrafts that are a very important part of the local economy. Some of the strange musical instruments we had seen being played the previous evening were among the exhibits. The blue and gray single-story building that houses the museum was built in 1873 and was originally the Governor's office.

In the center of the city there is a vast open space known as **Thung Sri Muang**, which was once used by governors for special ceremonies. King Rama V changed that when he came to reign and ordered that the land be given to the people of Ubon for a recreation area where they could holds festivals. And that is how it remains today.

The city is well known for its annual **Candle Festival**, which is held at the City Hall Stadium in July at the beginning of Buddhist Lent, a three month period during the rainy season when monks remain in their temples. Wonderfully carved candles, some of them several meters tall, are exhibited in colorful parades before being presented to local temples. The festival attracts visitors from all parts of Thailand, as well as foreign tourists, to watch the parades, beauty contests and musical performances.

■ Getting Here

The city, referred to locally as just Ubon, has good transportation links. In addition to the scores of buses that come here there are numerous services by train and Thai Airways has regular services from Bangkok to Ubon airport, which is north of the city.

■ Where to Stay in Ubon

There are almost 20 hotels in the city. We have selected three of the best.

Tohsang Khongjiam Resort, 251 Palochai Road, ☎ 04524 5531, www.tohsang.com. Sister hotel to the delightful resort we stayed in at Khong Chiam (page 336). This top-quality hotel is in the middle of a calm residential area of the city, within easy reach of all local attractions including the **Indochina Market** (see page 341), which is only a few minutes walk. Internet rates range from 1,050 Baht for a room to 3,000 Baht a night for a suite including breakfast.

Ubonburi Hotel & Resort, 1 Srimongkol Road, ☎ 04526 6777. Resort is just a few minutes drive from Ubon Ratchathani International Airport. Reasonably priced business hotel that has the capability of handling a formal party for 1,200 guests. Impressive lobby and a choice of dining locations. Internet rates range from 1,600 Baht a night for a cottage to 2,500 a night for an executive suite.

Laithong Hotel, 50 Pichit Rangsan Road, ☎ 04526 4271. This hotel is slightly cheaper than the previous two, but each of the 124 rooms is well equipped and well decorated in the classic *Isaan* style.

Khong Chiam to Nakhon Phanom

Reluctantly we left the Tohsang Khongjiam resort and headed north. Unfortunately our eager desire to cut across country and join a major northbound road failed miserably. Our maps showed that Highway 2134 would take us from Kong Chiam to Highway 212. It started off well but somewhere near the village of Phana we were suddenly on a mud road. All the signs in English had vanished and those in Thai were hand-painted on cardboard. After several attempts at trying to retrace our steps, which took us through farmyards, up to someone's back porch and through a schoolyard, we spotted the words *Police Station* in English. A plus about driving in Thailand is that every town that has a temple has a police station; there are lots of them, and they all have flags in front and the words "Police Station" in big readable letters boldly displayed. The officers on duty proved to be a great help. One spoke limited English but they all tried to give directions pointing this way and that. Eventually they had us point in what they decided was the right direction and told us to just keep going until we hit the good road. We set off across the mud once again feeling heartened that we were not completely lost, despite the fact that the policemen had been unable to pinpoint where we were on any of our maps.

On our drive thus far, we had seen economically poor areas. Now as we bumped over the mud we saw true poverty. There were no motorcycles, the occasional push bike and lots of hand carts. We assumed the buildings lying at odd angles at the side of the road were homes, but they lacked any modern fittings like windows, water or power.

At last we came to a paved road and heaved a sigh of relief. Just minutes later we were back on mud again. The police had said to keep going. So we did. The houses got even more flimsy and the tethered cattle looked thinner as we bounced along. Thirty minutes and two stretches of concrete and mud later we arrived on a main road..

At last we were on the main northbound Highway 212 and we picked up speed on a wide four-land road that offered great promise. Unfortunately the highway was under construction. After a few minutes we were back on mud and shunted from one side of the highway to another as the giant earth moving equipment battled on to complete the road construction. Where the highway is complete it is superb, where it isn't complete it's extremely perilous. Oncoming drivers who have failed to heed the signs appear directly in front of you, or the road suddenly drops off several feet without warning. Future drivers will enjoy a good ride all the way from Ubon Ratchathani to Nakhon Phanom. The route is well marked and there is a good bypass already operating around the towns of Mukdahan and That Phanom.

The town of **Mukdahan**, directly on the banks of the Mekong, is noted for its markets selling cheap goods from Laos and Vietnam. The province is said to produce the sweetest tamarinds in Thailand. The impressive market gardens that you glimpse along the banks of the Mekong River are proof of the fertility of the areas that are served by this river and its tributaries. **That Phanom** is considered an important sacred site because shrines here were visited by Buddha. The temple complex of That Phanom is also considered sacred because, legend has it, the site was visited by Kakusandha, Konagamana, and Kassapa, the Buddhas of the three previous ages.

We spent the night at the **Nakhon Phanom River View Hotel**, 9 Nakhon Phanom-That Phanom Road, ☎ 04252 2333, fax 04252 2780, www.northwest.com, a high-quality hotel at a very low price. We had an acceptable room with a wonderful view over the Mekong River for 900 Baht, including an excellent breakfast buffet. We also had a good hour-long massage for 300 Baht, another bargain, and the low rates are year-round. Only exception is in October when the city has its annual illuminated boat processions held during the Buddhist Lent (more information about this later on). This is the kind of hotel we could visit again and not have to worry about the cost. The staff was efficient, friendly and most spoke acceptable English.

For something even cheaper, and closer to town, **The Mekong Grand View**, 527 Sunthon Wichit Road, ☎ 04251 3564, also fronts the Mekong River. We dined at the restaurant north of the hotel and enjoyed Mekong River catfish from the river. An inexpensive and enjoyable meal helped by super views.

Today we traveled 343 kilometers and spent 900 Baht on fuel.

■ Exploring Nakhon Phanom

We awake to a brisk wind and a chilly 18° Celsius, the coldest temperature we have ever experienced in Thailand, and realize that we have no sweaters or jackets. First stop is the Tesco Superstore in the center of this pleasant and spacious town. No luck. Plenty of swim suits and lightweight tops but nothing warm. On the main street we are spoiled for choice of where to shop with numerous shophouses and roadside stalls. We try on a variety of windbreaker-style jackets, many bearing fake designer labels, and eventually find two that provide warmth. They are ill fitting but the low price – 800 Baht for the two – offsets the garish colors and ugly fashion statement. The town is a pleasant place to stroll around and the large market area has abundant displays of flowers, fruits and meat. For once we are able to admire the quality of the meats without the unpleasant smells we have encountered in other market towns. Maybe the lower temperatures help. This is one of the few Thai towns where you feel relaxed. It could be the lengthy promenade along the banks of the river, nicely paved and landscaped, or the lack of traffic, which doesn't seem to hurry. The town is small enough to get around easily and we take time to gaze at the wonderful buildings, ancient and modern, which adorn the wide streets. There is a blend of cultures here because of its closeness to the Laos – the settlement of **Tha Teak** is easily visible across the river – and the area is home to numerous immigrants from Viet Nam. They are responsible for two of the city's landmarks. The **Clock Tower** on Sunthon Wichit Road was built by Vietnamese expatriates in 1960 before they returned to their homeland. **St. Ann's Catholic Church**, farther north on the same road, was built by the Vietnamese community in 1926 and is just one of many fine buildings on that stretch of waterfront. Among them is the Tourism Authority of Thailand (TAT) office, the nicest of all the TAT buildings we've seen (184/1 Sunthon Wichit Road, ☎ 04251 3490, fax 04251 3492).

We only covered 129 kilometers around the area and filled up our fuel tanks for 600 Baht.

■ Things to See in Nakhon Phanom

There are three main temples in the city. **Wat Okat**, on the banks of the Mekong, next to the **Indochina Market** on Sunthon Wichit Road, houses two ancient Buddha images as well as some beautiful murals. The pagoda **Phra That Nakhon**, also on Sunthon Wichit Road, was constructed in 1922 to resemble the larger Phra That Phanom (more details about that in the next paragraph) to house disciples' relics and golden Buddha images. **Wat Srithep Pradit Tharam** on Srithep Road is noted for its attractive ordination hall, murals and a Buddha image of Phra Saeng.

■ Festivals in Nakhon Phanom

February

The **Phra That Phanom Festival** takes place during the full moon period of the third lunar month – which normally falls at the end of February – in That Phanom district, 52 kilometers south of Nakhon Phanom on Highway 212. The week-long festival attracts pilgrims from northeast Thailand and Laos for religious merit making. Native bazaars as well as folk entertainment take place near the Phra That shrine with its 53-meter high square-shaped pagoda believed to date back more than 12 centuries.

October

The **Annual Illuminated Boat Festival** attracts a lot of spectators from all parts of Thailand, as well as overseas, and hotels get fully booked way ahead of the event, which takes place in October at the end of the Buddhist Lent. Major feature is the parade of colorfully lit boats on the Mekong River together with the dragon-boat races between teams from Thailand and neighboring Laos.

Nakhon Phanom to Nong Khai

Today's 320-kilometer drive was the most pleasant and interesting of the trip to date. Our fears that the smaller road, Highway 212 around the north eastern tip of Thailand, would be more difficult proved groundless. Road surface and conditions were both good as we passed attractive small villages including **Tha Uthen**, **Ban Phang**, **Bueng Kan** and **Phon Phisai**. It was early in the morning and there were scores of school buses taking the young ones to their lessons. Everywhere we drove on our trip we were impressed with the standard of school buildings, be they elementary or places of higher learning. It was an encouraging sign to see so many youngsters clad in smart, neat uniforms, smiling as they started their day at school. Education in Thailand has improved tremendously in the last decade. It may of course prove a problem for future generations. Will these better-educated youngsters want to follow in their parents' footsteps as farmers or handicraft makers?

As we approach Nong Khai, an incredible display of topiary appeared. Roadside trees had been fashioned into amazing designs of animals and people. On one side of the road an elephant trunk juts out while farther along an amazing foliage sculpture of warriors greeted us.

Nong Khai is a large sprawling town that is also tranquil and tasteful. Its greatest asset is the delightful four-kilometer stretch of shoreline along the Mekong, with wide roads that are scarily quiet unlike so many Thai towns. The main street is Thanon Meechai, with the post office in the center. To the west is the **Chaiyaporn night-market**, and the **Po Chai day-market** is by the bus station. Dining out along the river front restaurants is pleasant, inexpensive and truly Thai. Most of the menus had no English but somehow we managed to be well fed at very low prices.

Nong Khai to Khon Kaen

■ Laotian Interlude

It was a strange and stressful day, as our first job was to leave Thailand, get visas for Laos, enter Laos and then return to Thailand. Our allowed time in Thailand had expired and first we had to pay the fine for exceeding our 30-days visas. That was painless but cost us 200 Baht a day each for every day we had overstayed. Then we got to cross the **Friendship Bridge** that spans the Mekong River – an impressive structure that keeps the two countries apart. We were warned it could take hours to get the Laos visa. It took minutes and cost us $20 each plus an additional 20 Baht since we didn't have new passport photos. They copied our old passport pictures; problem solved. Then we entered Laos and had to pay a 20 Baht entry fee.

Since we were in Laos we decided to splurge 300 Baht and take the 24-kilometer ride into **Vientiane**, the Laotian capital. After a quick whirl downtown – been-there-done-that – we returned to the bridge and officially left Laos, made a brief stop at the duty-free shop before crossing back and entering Thailand where we got another 30 days' visa. The whole episode, which we had been dreading, took less than three hours, and we were again headed south. Once we cleared Nong Khai, the vast expanse of land on both sides of the road, and the highway itself, reminded us of those long stretches of the Floridas Turnpike from Kissimmee south, where there is no sign of life. The difference here was the acres of sugar cane. Occasionally we would sight a lone man cutting the sugar filled fibers, dwarfed by the very high canes. Trucks overloaded with cut cane chugged slowly along towards the refineries that appear from time to time along with the small hamlets.

■ Exploring Khon Kaen

Khon Kaen was a surprise. It's a big, prosperous city and has to be the most rapidly developing region in the northeast.

When you look at Khon Kaen today, with its quality hotels and bustling streets and stores, it is hard to believe that this is the capital of what was one of Thailand's poorest provinces. One of the major factors that has helped this area blossom is its trade agreement with China. The province is able to produce low-cost clothing and household goods, which are much in demand in southern China. Vast quantities are shipped by truck every day to the port area in Chang Rai province. Chinese cargo vessels, bringing a variety of manufactured food items to Thailand, return with the products of Khon Kaen province. We questioned businessmen here about being able to compete with Chinese manufactured goods. They told us that road transport within China, particularly to certain southern areas, was difficult, which made the Thai products price competitive.

The city and province are steeped in history. The first dinosaur fossils in Thailand were discovered here. The city, surrounded by superb countryside, is a major center of commerce, and is the home of one of Thailand's largest the public universities.

A must-see while in the city is the **Khon Kaen National Museum**, Lang Sun Ratchakan Road, open daily except public holidays from 9am to 4pm, which has exhibits on the ancient civilizations and artifacts found in the Northeast. There are numerous items from the prehistoric civilization of *Ban Chiang*.

■ Where to Stay in Nong Khai and Khon Kaen

Our overnight stop in Nong Khai was at the **Royal Mekong Nongkhai Hotel**, 222 Panungchonprathan Road, ☎ 04242 0056, fax 04242 1280, an imposing typical Thai business hotel, which towers nine stories high on the banks of the Mekong River and stands just a few hundred yards from the **Friendship Bridge** that links the Kingdom of Thailand to Democratic People's Republic of Laos. Accommodation is adequate, though not luxurious; our junior suite on the corner of the seventh floor had lots of space and a bathroom you'd expect to find in an older Holiday Inn in small-town USA. Our suite cost 1,800 Baht including an acceptable buffet breakfast, and rates for a regular room start at under 1,000 Baht. The hotel has one royal suite, 14 suites and 140 rooms, a large swimming pool, health club and a large lobby with numerous local product stalls scattered around. There is another hotel in town, **Nong Khai Grand Hotel**, 589 Nong Khai-Poanpisai Road. This is a little cheaper, has 130 rooms, no signs outside in English and lacks the views of the Mekong River that the Royal Mekong enjoys.

We were stunned when we arrived at our hotel in Khon Kaen. The **Sofitel Raja Orchid Khon Kaen**, 9/9 Prachasumran Road, ☎ 04332 2155, fax 04332 1575, is one of the finest hotels we have seen not only in Thailand but anywhere. This is a large hotel – 293 rooms and 80 suites – with eight restaurants and seven bars. If you're a karaoke lover, which we are not, there are 10 private karaoke rooms. The hotel also boasts that it has the first mini brewery in a hotel in Thailand. The Kronen Brauhaus uses vintage wood paneling to create a German beer house where you can enjoy the brew made on the premises.

We had booked a junior suite for 2,200 Baht. The large room on the corner of the seventh floor was well equipped and pleasantly furnished. The price included an impressive breakfast buffet that had all the European favorites in addition to an even larger display of Asian delights. We liked the place so well that we asked to stay a second night. The only room available was an executive suite on the eighth floor at 4,000 Baht. We accepted that and got to stay in the largest hotel room we have ever occupied. The living area had a dining table with six chairs, and full suite of furniture. The bedroom was vast too, as was the bathroom and wardrobe area. There were three TVs – the third being in the bathroom, something we have never seen before. The price included a high-speed Internet connection, which we had paid for separately the previous day. Even though the hotel was full it never appeared crowded. This is a very well-managed property with professional staff, and everyone we spoke to had a good command of English.

One evening we decided to have dinner in our suite. We ordered a Caesar salad with shrimp as a starter. Lindsey had a beautifully baked lasagna and I had an excellent cheeseburger with mushrooms, salad and fries. The meal was delivered, served on our dining-room table where a vase of fresh orchids was placed. Crisp fresh linens, a basket of assorted breads and glasses of iced water and an assortment of condiments completed the setting. The total bill including taxes and service: 460 Baht. It was a five-star repast at youth-hostel prices!

The high-rise **Charoen Thani Princess**, 260 Sri Chan Road, ☎ 04322 0400, fax 04322 0438, www.royalprincess.com, is close to the Sofitel, with slightly lower rates for its 320 rooms and suites. Choice of restaurants, good swimming pool with popular poolside bar. Internet rates available at 1,000 Baht a night including breakfast.

Kosa Hotel, 250-252 Sri Chan Road, ☎ 04322 5014, fax 04322 5013. For over two decades this was the best place to stay in Khon Kaen. The 17-story building, with a helicopter pad on top, has 120 rooms and suites. The hotel's convention hall can accommodate up to 1,000 people. Great views from the sky lounge on the sixteenth floor. Rates from 1,400 Baht a night.

Kaen Inn Hotel, 56 Klang Muang Road, ☎ 04324 5420, fax 04323 9457. Most economical of the hotels we list where 900 Baht will buy you one of their 160 rooms, all well equipped considering the price.

The Bussarakam Hotel, 04243 3666, fax 04324 2222. Good value – all rooms under 1,000 Baht a night – and new hotel aimed at the MICE market. (For those not in the know that stands for meetings, incentives, conventions and exhibitions.) The 157-room, seven-story hotel is 15 minutes from Khon Kaen International Airport and five minutes from the Khon Kaen Golden Jubilee Convention Hall. Among the hotel's features is a conference room, which can handle 75 people classroom-style or 140 people theatre-style. It also has two restaurants including an all-day dining restaurant with Thai and international cuisine.

■ Festivals

April

The **Dok Khun Siang Khaen Festival** is held from April 13-15 every year at Bung Kaen Nakhon, a 600-acre park and lake area surrounded by restaurants. At the northern end of the lake is the **Chao Phia Mueang Phaen monument** that was built to honor Khon Kaen's founder. The religious part of the three-day festival involves pouring holy water on Buddha images. Aside from that there is a procession of floral carts, contests involving northeastern food, boat races, performances of local dramatic arts and stalls selling local products.

November

The annual **Silk and Phuk Sieo Festival** is held between November 29 and December 10 in front of the Khon Kaen town hall. The main events center on silk making. There are contests as well as displays. The Phuk Sieo part of the festival is an old Isaan tradition that involves making new friends.

Khon Kaen to Cha-am

We didn't plan to drive quite so far today but as we had an easy time driving around Bangkok on Highway 9 West (the outer ring road) we kept going and eventually arrived in Cha-am. We spent the night at the **Dusit Resort & Polo Club**, 1349 Petchkasem Road, Cha-am, ☎ 03252 0009, fax 03252 0296, www.huahin.dusit.com. (More about the resort in the *Hua Hin* section of *Beyond Bangkok*, page 122). Since we had not planned ahead we had to pay the full price of 6,000 Baht for a room. We were fortunate to even get a good room in the area. We had called several resorts and they were all full. The Dusit is a quality hotel with lots of space and even though the occupancy rate was high we never felt crowded. That was in stark contrast to our earlier stay in the area at the Marriott in Hua Hin, where we couldn't even get two chairs at either the beach or the swimming pool.

Today we drove 645 kilometers and spent 640 Baht on fuel.

Cha-am to Rayong

After our long drive yesterday we planned a shorter trip today. We headed south on Highway 4 and noted how the landscape slowly became more verdant and lush. At Chumphon we stayed on Highway 4 as it cut west across Thailand and brushed the side of Myanmar. The quickest way to Phuket from Chumphon is to take Highway 41 but we wanted to see something new. The road across was slow and winding and the occasional convoy of trucks kept the driver occupied while the passenger admired the exotic flora that colorfully adorned the roadsides. We were gaining height but there were no views as we passed within 100 meters of the border with Myanmar. The drive was longer than we imagined and we covered a lot of ground before we reached Ranong and our overnight stop at **The Royal Princess Hotel**, 41/144 Tamuang Road, ☎ 07783 5240, fax 07783 5238, www.royalprincess.com. A perfectly adequate hotel but nothing like the luxury we had enjoyed on our previous two stops. But what can you expect for 1,300 for the night, including breakfast? Sadly, there were few people staying at the resort and the evening's entertainment only provided amusement for the hotel employees. We enjoyed a very professional 90-minute massage for a bargain 400 Baht and the hotel does have a good fitness center and pleasant swimming pool.

Ranong is a small town but we got horribly lost before finding the hotel, probably the largest building in the area. Weaving our way between the market and the main streets showed us that this was one Thai town that we didn't need to linger in for too long. The only cheerful feature about the place was the happy cacophony of young voices coming from the school.

Today we drove 384 kilometers and spent 680 Baht on fuel.

Return to Phuket

The final day of our adventure was to be the slowest day of our trip and the most depressing as we headed south towards the grim ruins of Khao Lak, the area hardest hit by the tsunami.

It was shortly after 7am on a Saturday morning when we left Rayong – with no plans to return – and as it was a weekend we were spared the traffic generated by children going to school.

Highway 4 started off as a fast four-lane but before we had reached Rayong Airport it became two lanes, twisting and turning through beautiful scenery. There were numerous blue tourist information signs indicating waterfalls in the area. We encountered these blue signs, in English, throughout the trip; they are a great aid if there is a particular beauty spot, temple or national park you'd like to visit.

The first major settlement was encountered was **Ratchakrut**, where a street market was throbbing with activity despite the early hour. The road on to **Kapoe** and **Khura Buri** was just as scenic and winding as we dipped up and down still high above the coast but rarely a chance to see the sea. There were more mosques and fewer Buddhist temples, showing we were passing through Muslim-dominated areas, their villages more somber than the Buddhist ones. Several times there were military road-checks where we were greeted with smiles and polite waves with no need for us to stop.

One of those little gems of places to stay appeared as we approached Kuraburi. **The Greenview Resort**, 125 Moo 5, Bangwan, ☎ 07640 1401, fax 07640 1400, www.kuraburigreenview.com is a rustic retreat of bungalows and cabins set alongside a lake. Year-round rates, including breakfast, are either 1,800 or 2,000 Baht a night depending on the accommodation and a place we would consider staying on a future occasion. It is set in spectacular scenery, has a large pool and is surrounded by hiking trails and national parks. For those wanting to be on the sea, the resort can organize trips to the **Surin Marine National Park**, which lies below the resort. The marine park is home to sea gypsies and has some of the finest coral, which can be easily viewed with a mask and snorkel.

Large crowds and a strong police presence greeted us as we drove into **Takua Pa**, a spacious provincial capital. We learned later that this was a protest meeting by villagers hit by the tsunami, who were demanding that the bodies presently being stored in Phang Nga be identified there and not moved to Phuket. As we eyed the protesters we had nothing but sympathy for them. Not only had many of them lost family members or friends but also most were now without a home. It was depressing to say the least. And we followed that by the dismal drive through **Khao Lak**, cruelly destroyed by the unbelievable force of water. We decided then that we had to something to help the people of these small communities that once were dotted along the coast. Only an occasional tree, the remains of a road or the barest skeleton of a building gave an indication that these had been villages. We would return and give some help, however limited. You can read about our small relief effort in *The Tsunami* chapter.

A few minutes later we were across the Sarisin Bridge and were back on the island of Phuket. We breathed a huge sigh or relief. The saddest part of our adventure had come at the end. That night we collapsed into a bigger than king-size bed at the luxurious Villa Royale resort on Kata Noi. (There's more about this wonderful place to stay in the *Phuket* chapter, page 226). We were engulfed in luxury while just a few miles away the villagers of Khao Lak were not.

> *Today we covered 368 kilometers and spent 650 Baht on fuel.*

The Verdict

Our trip was complete, and for once we slept with no plans to go anywhere in the morning. We had traveled over 4,500 kilometers and seen some of the poorest and richest that Thailand had to offer. Would we do it again? Certainly. There are a couple of places we would skip, but there is a lot more we want to see. On this trip we didn't visit enough of the numerous villages where so much of Thailand's quality handicrafts are produced. Next time we want to learn more about the production of silk and the growing wine industry and visit some of the more remote islands. Although we covered almost 5,000 kilometers on this trip we only got a taste of what the kingdom has to offer. While we unpack, the maps will not be put away. We are already thinking of places to visit on our next expedition.

The Trains of Thailand

IN THIS CHAPTER

I have been fascinated by trains since I was old enough to hold a pencil and write down the numbers of steam locomotives that thundered their way between London and Scotland. I should point out that I am the male part of the writing team and I am enjoying looking at the trains of Thailand while "she indoors" is hard at work on the chapter on Thai food.

This love of trains has stayed with me from those boyhood days, through school when I worked out a program where I could travel on three different trains to get to school and an equal number to return. I was forced to curb my love of trains when I spent 11 years in the Bahamas where trains are as rare as falling snow.

History

We can thank King Chulalongkorn (Rama V) the son of King Mongkut for Thailand's rail system. He had traveled to Europe and Asia and saw for himself the benefits that a railway would bring. He was fearful of colonization of the kingdom. He knew that a railway would help unite his country and bring far reaching economic benefits.

Traveling around Thailand was incredibly slow. It could take weeks or even months to get from Bangkok to Chiang Mai. Land travel was by oxen carts or riding in a howdah strapped to the back of an elephant. Traveling along rivers was laborious, particularly if you had to paddle against the flow. He knew a railroad was the solution. Not only would it enable him to visit his subjects more easily but it would open up the country's natural resources of teak, rice, tin and rubber to the rest of the world. Today the railway carries over 100 million tons of cargo.

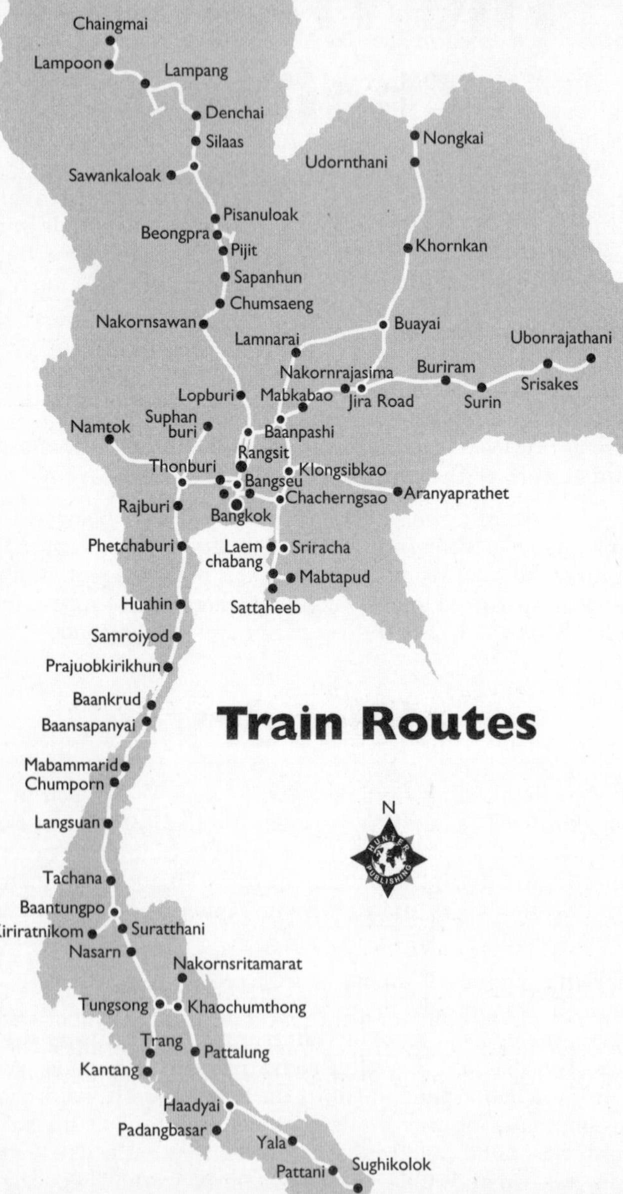
Train Routes
N
HUNTER PUBLISHING
Chaingmai
Lampoon
Lampang
Denchai
Silaas
Sawankaloak
Nongkai
Udornthani
Pisanuloak
Beongpra
Pijit
Sapanhun
Khornkan
Chumsaeng
Nakornsawan
Buayai
Lamnarai
Ubonrajathani
Nakornrajasima
Buriram
Srisakes
Lopburi
Mabkabao
Jira Road
Surin
Namtok
Suphan buri
Baanpashi
Rangsit
Thonburi
Klongsibkao
Bangseu
Aranyaprathet
Rajburi
Chacherngsao
Bangkok
Phetchaburi
Laem chabang
Sriracha
Mabtapud
Huahin
Sattaheeb
Samroiyod
Prajuobkirikhun
Baankrud
Baansapanyai
Mabammarid
Chumporn
Langsuan
Tachana
Baantungpo
Kiriratnikom
Suratthani
Nasarn
Nakornsritamarat
Tungsong
Khaochumthong
Trang
Pattalung
Kantang
Haadyai
Padangbasar
Yala
Pattani
Sughikolok

The first line planned would link Bangkok with Korat. He hired a British businessman, a Mr. G.M.Campbell, to oversee the project and the initial phase of 40 miles, linking Bangkok to Ayutthaya, opened for service on Monday March 26, 1894.

The **Royal State Railway of Siam** was first established in 1890 and was split in two, the Northern and Southern Railways. One problem was the two divisions operated on different gauges. In 1920 it was decided to adopt the 1.00-m gauge as the standard for Thailand. It took 10 years to have that standard available throughout the country, which also made it compatible with its neighbors in Burma, Cambodia and Malaysia. The bombings of World War II caused a great deal of damage to the railway. Bridges and tracks were destroyed along with locomotives and rolling stock. The only major construction was that of the notorious Thailand to Burma Death Railway, which the Japanese built between October 1942 and October 1943 at great cost – close to 200,000 people lost their lives during its construction. There is a lot more information on this later in this chapter.

In its earlier years all the trains were hauled by wood-burning steam locomotives. Now everything is powered by diesel locomotives or diesel cars. After the war the railway was quickly renovated and expanded to its present route system of 4,000 kilometers, and employs over 26,000 people.

Travel in Style

What's so special about the trains of Thailand? They can be very cheap; they are basically very clean; and the people who work for the rail lines are very professional and polite. Those three factors alone make them unique. And there are two other important plusses. Trains generally run on time – the exception is in some of the rural areas, where delays are part of the charm of rail travel – and most seats can be booked in advance.

Thai trains are not fast, despite the word "express" that is added to many services. If you want fast then go to Tokyo, or take the *Eurostar* to Paris. (In France the expressway parallels the London-to-Paris railway in several places. When the *Eurostar* goes past when you are driving close to 100 mph, you think you're standing still.)

If it is glamour or nostalgia you seek, then take the *Venice Simplon-Orient-Express* from Venice to Paris and dine in the authentic restaurant cars, where finely attired guests relive the journey of the 1920s.

Practicalities

Bus or Train?

Traveling by train in Thailand is more comfortable than going by bus, although in many cases it is a lot slower. And the trains don't go everywhere. If you want to go from Bangkok to Phuket, the train service stops six hours away and you still have a bus journey to reach your destination.

Two major features distinguish the Thai train system from its western counterparts, and they are the narrow-gauge track, which at first glance looks like an overgrown miniature railway, and the fact that much of the system is single-track. Having to wait for trains coming in the opposite direction is the main reason that travel times are longer than you would expect.

The country stations are, for the most part, beautifully maintained, with stunning gardens ablaze with color and sweet-smelling blooms. They appear to be a great meeting spot, not necessarily for rail travelers but for local people looking for a pleasant place to congregate.

TRAIN TRAGEDY

There's a varied assortment of crossings for vehicles needing to traverse the Thai rail lines. In cities there are elaborate automatic lights and arms systems similar to those in the US. In rural areas there are crossings where railway workers move barricades onto the road to stop traffic a few minutes before a train is due. In other areas there is just a warning sign. Accidents do happen; shortly before our first Thai train trip, three people were killed and 10 injured when a train collided with a pickup truck. All 13 were related and were traveling in the truck – vehicle loads like this are common in Thailand – after a family reunion. Police said the accident happened because the crossing was unmanned and thick trees on both sides of the crossing obscured the truck driver's view.

Way to Go

Thai trains have three classes. We strongly recommend not traveling in third class; the hard wooden seats get very uncomfortable in a very short space of time. There are, however, two good things about third-class travel. It is very cheap, and you don't have to reserve a space. The seats go on sale shortly before departure. The State Railway of Thailand carries over 100 million passengers a year and 97% of them travel third class. And that says a great deal for the staying power of the Thai people.

In addition to the three classes of accommodation there are different categories of trains. The slowest are the ordinary trains and normally only have third-class carriages. The long-distance trains have three categories – rapid, express, and special express. There is little to choose between them but the special express is the quickest, followed by the express and then the rapid. So the rapid is the slowest!

■ First Class

First class is only available on overnight trains. The sleeper carriages have modern air conditioned lockable two-berth compartments with a small wash basin and stowaway table. A toilet and shower, cold water only, is available at the end of each carriage. If you are traveling alone you will be expected to share the compartment with someone of the same sex unless you pay for two tickets. Cabin stewards provide clean sheets, a towel and soap and transform the seats into two bunk beds around 9pm. They return in the morning around 7am to transform the cabin to its daytime configuration.

■ Second Class

Second class comes in two varieties – with or without air conditioning. Needless to say the fan-cooled carriages tend to get a little hot at night. The second-class sleepers are not compartments but open plan. There are facing seats on each side of the carriage, which are pulled together to form the lower bed. The upper berth folds out from the wall of the carriage. Again you get fresh bedding and a mattress on each bunk. A curtain is hooked in front of each berth, which gives you some privacy but can be a little claustrophobic. The upper berth, which is slightly narrower and very close to the air conditioning vent, is cheaper.

Dinner in the Diner

Have no fear, you will not go hungry on a Thai train. All long-distance trains have good Thai meals, which are either served in the carriages or in the restaurant car. If you are in a first-class compartment the cabin steward will give you a menu, in English, to peruse. Whenever the train stops you can expect to find food vendors on the station platforms eager to sell their wares. And should you by chance be traveling in the cheap seats you can buy a complete meal in a plastic pack for the princely sum of 20 Baht.

Carry-on Luggage

There is supposedly a baggage weight allowance similar to that in operation on airlines. But when you see the boxes and cases being pushed aboard, it seems that this is one of those Thai regulations that gets ignored. It is wonderful to see a train pull into a station where the family awaits the return of a relative who has been shopping in the capital. Large cartons tied with string or mammoth plastic packages accompany the shopper who, upon arrival, unloads onto the station platform by pushing them out of the large carriage windows.

WHISTLE STOP PM

Taking a page out of US political campaigns, Thai Prime Minister Thaksin Shinawatra made a whistle-stop train tour of the Northeast during his 2005 election campaign. It was the first time the trains of Thailand had been used in such a manner. The PM made brief stops at numerous points wooing voters. His Thai Rak Thai party scored a landslide victory in the elections.

Fares & Reservations

Fares for children are pretty straightforward. Children under three go free, provided they are no taller than 100 centimeters and do not require a separate seat. Children over three and under 12 go at half-price, provided they are no taller than 150 centimeters.

Reservations are important, particularly around holiday times. You can reserve space 90 days in advance at any of the major stations. This can be a hassle and take time but there are several travel agencies in Bangkok who will do the work for you. If you go to Hualampong station to make reservation you take a number and wait your turn. An hour-long wait is not unknown. The reservation office is open from 8:30am to 6pm from Monday to Friday and from 8:30am until noon on weekends and holidays. There are charges for changing a reservation and refunds can be claimed but again fees are payable.

Plans for a rapid-rail link between Nakhon Ratchasima (better known as Korat) and Bangkok are continually being studied. The idea is to make the journey in one hour. Those in favor of the scheme say it will help businessmen and improve commercial development in the northeast. Those against say it will be too costly. One opponent commented, "Why would anyone want to get to Bangkok so quickly anyway?"

TRAIN TICKETS ON THE INTERNET

The State Railway of Thailand does not sell tickets on the Internet. However, the Asia Discovery travel agency does. Their Website, www.asia-discovery.com/train.htm, has a listing of all the major routes and fares. The prices they show include their 200-Baht charge for handling all the hassles of getting tickets in advance. They offer free delivery to downtown Bangkok hotels and will also forward tickets, at an additional charge, to overseas addresses.

■ Safety

Thai trains are safe, but use your common sense. Don't leave valuables lying around. Railway police patrol every train. In a first-class compartment you'll have your luggage with you. In second class, baggage is stowed at the sides of the seats and the aisles are illuminated throughout the night.

All Aboard!

The Thai Train system – like everything else in the country – is based in Bangkok. The main station is **Hualampong** on Rama IV Road. In an effort to ease congestion, long-distance services are being moved to **Bang Sue** station, seven kilometers north of Hualampong, with its connection to the new subway station. Hualampong will remain a major station for commuters traveling in from the suburbs and nearby provinces. There are also long-distance departures from Thonburi station, which is across the river and west of the city.

> *Budding basketball stars get penalized on Thai trains. To qualify for children's fares it is not your age that counts but how tall you are. There are measuring sticks at the stations to get the discounts. We wonder what happens if you buy a round-trip ticket and put on a couple of inches while you're gone!*

■ Main Lines

The Thai rail network heads out from Bangkok in all directions. There are four major routes: The Northeast, The North, The South and The East.

Northeastern

The Northeastern route splits at **Korat**. One section goes to **Nong Khai**, near the Laotian capital of Vientiane, while the other goes to **Ubonratthani**.

> *During the winter months Nong Khai can get chilly. Temperatures as low as 11°C have been recorded and may go even lower in the higher mountain areas.*

Ratchathani

Nong Khai is on the Mekong River, which marks the border between Thailand and Laos. Farangs are not normally allowed into Laos without the correct visas. If you want to cross over, there are several places in Nong Khai where the visits can be arranged. However, since regulations are continually changing it is best to check with the Laotian embassy in Bangkok before making the trip.

There are several rail services from Bangkok to Ratchathani. The overnight train, with first-class compartment, will cost you 1,200 Baht for the 624-kilometer journey. If you prefer a daytime trip, which will give you a chance to see the countryside, a second-class seat in air conditioning costs 658 Baht. Tough-duty seat in third class costs only 183 Baht.

The overnight train leaves Bangkok at 8:45pm and arrives the following morning at 8:55am. The day-train leaves at 8:40am and arrives at 5:30pm. On the return the express with first-class compartments leaves Nong Khai at 7:05pm and gets into Bangkok at

7:35am the next day. There is a daytime express that leaves at 7:30am and arrives in Bangkok 5:55pm.

The overnight service to Ubon Ratchathani leaves at 9pm and arrives the following day at 7:55am. A first-class compartment costs 1,080 Baht and prices slide down to 175 Baht for the third-class trip.

The northeastern line also serves the town of Surin where the elephant round-up takes place every November. Trains are always fully booked way ahead of time for this event. Many people travel up one night and back the next. There is an express service that makes the trip in seven hours or you can take the overnight train to Ubon Ratchathani and leave the train at 5:15am when it makes a brief stop in Surin. Other towns on the line include Ubonratthani and Korat.

Northern

The Northern Line serves **Chiang Mai**. Other important stops on the route are at Phitsanulok, Nakhon Lampang, Khun Tan, and Lam Phun. You have similar choices for Chiang Mai as on the northeastern line. There is an express daytime service that leaves Bangkok every day at 8:30am and arrives in Chiang Mai at 7:45pm. A second-class air conditioned seat will cost you 511 Baht. Manage with only a fan and pay 341 Baht. The overnight service leaves Bangkok at 6pm for the 750-kilometer trip and arrives the next day at 6:50am. Cost for the first-class compartment is 1,253 Baht per person. The trains leave at roughly the same time for the return journey. Want to know the third-class fare? 181 Baht.

Southern

The southern route splits at **Hat Yai Junction**. One fork heads north to Sungai Golok on the east coast and the south fork heads towards Malaysia and Singapore. The connection with Malaysia is at Padang Besar and at Sungai Kolok. There is a daily service from Bangkok to Butterworth, which is used by foreigners who spend long periods in Thailand without becoming residents. Every three months they have to leave the kingdom and re-enter with extended visas. The most convenient place to do this in the south of Thailand is Penang, which is opposite Butterworth. The unfortunate political unrest has deterred many from taking this route. Instead they travel to Ranong and cross into Myanmar to complete the formalities. It is possible to buy tickets from Bangkok to Singapore but the connections are not always good.

Eastern

The main part of the eastern line goes to the town of **Aranyaprathet** at the Cambodian border, an area we have not visited and of which we have heard no glowing reports. The main industry in the area seems to be on the Cambodian side, where two casinos attract Thais. Casino gambling is illegal for Thais in their own country, but not in neighboring Cambodia. Only the third-class non-air conditioned diesel cars make the 200-kilometer journey, which takes five hours and makes about a dozen stops on the way. The journey is a questionable bargain at 48 Baht. It is hoped at some point to establish the rail link into **Cambodia** and **Phnom Penh**, but right now it is a long way from where the Thai train stops and the Cambodia trains start.

The train station is about six kilometers from the border. A tuk-tuk will cost you more than the train fare from Bangkok. There is little problem getting a visa at the Cambodian border town of **Poipet**, provided you've got US $20 or 1,000 Baht and one passport picture. You'll probably be asked for money for additional forms that you don't need. Most foreigners leave a little extra money as a goodwill gesture. The immigration office is open every day from 7:30am to 5pm. If you are going to travel onwards by train, the first operating station is at **Sisophone**, 35 kilometers away. Getting there is a major problem. There will be lots of people giving you ideas; if possible, try to get with a group and share whatever transport is available; most likely it will be a pickup truck. Cambodia is noted for having some of the worst roads in Southeast Asia. If you are offered a trip to see a temple at **Seam Reap**, where **Angkor Wat** is located, it could take up to six hours if the weather is good, a lot longer if the weather is bad.

A shorter branch of the Eastern Line goes along the coast, passing by Pattaya and onto **Ban Plu Ta Luang**. The train is not convenient if you want to visit Pattaya since the station is a fair distance from the town; the best way to visit from Bangkok is by bus.

However, The State Railway of Thailand does organize special tourist trips and these normally include Pattaya. It is worth checking with a travel agent or at the Hualampong station, since the excursions are well done and offer good value. Other destinations they offer are Kanchanaburi for the River Kwai, and Ko Samed.

Hall of Railway Heritage

This train museum only opens on Sundays from 5am until noon in an exhibition hall on the western side of **Chatuchak Park** near the Northern Bus Terminal in Bangkok, where the infamous weekend market is held. The project is operated by members of the **Thai Rail Fan Club**. The exhibits include train models, a couple of old steam engines and paraphernalia about train systems throughout the world. The main theme is trains but there are also model cars, assorted paintings, artwork and some military vehicles. To contact the club, ☎ 02243 2037.

■ The Eastern & Oriental Express

Railway From Heaven

At the start of this guide we emphasized that the focus was to be luxury at an affordable price. Once in a while we admit to straying from the affordable to the expensive. When we took this 57-hour trip on the *Eastern & Oriental Express* we went off the rails big time.

This is one of those luxury adventures you take once in a lifetime. After it's all over you still feel exhilarated, even if you have to refinance your home or drastically cut the kids' allowance.

This express oozes decadent living to a degree that is almost indecent. This is a journey that demands to be enjoyed, and even the world's most fastidious traveler must be stunned by the train's exquisite interior. The food is fabulous. Chef Kevin Cape and his culinary crew provide five extraordinary meals. That alone is a great accomplishment. But to do it while the train shudders along Thailand's narrow gauge railway in two cramped kitchens is more the work of a master magician than that of an award-winning chef.

The Adventure Begins

We knew we were in good hands the moment we arrived at Bangkok's main railway station, **Hualampong**, a brute of a building on Rama IV Road in a particularly busy part of a busy city. Our chauffeur whirled around to the side of the station, away from the crowds in the main entrance, many sitting or lying on the floor waiting for trains or to buy tickets for future journeys. At the side entrance a small sign politely announced this was the place to check in for the *Eastern & Oriental Express*.

As we were ushered from the car, deft hands grabbed our cases and we were diverted into a small air conditioned lounge where our fellow travelers gazed upon each other with inquisitive looks wondering who would become friends or foes on our journey north.

Minutes later clutching small cards giving us our cabin number and our seat assignment for the first meal aboard we trooped across the station to find the 22 gleaming carriages that were to be our home for the next two nights and three days. The carriages are painted in British racing green and adorned with golden emblems and brass fittings. Their numbers didn't make any sense until it was explained to us that, thanks to Chinese beliefs, only combinations of the lucky numbers 2, 3, 6, 8 and 9 had been used.

> *The* Eastern & Oriental Express *operates several services most linking Singapore in the south with Chiang Mai, Thailand's most northern station. For those like us who were just interested in seeing as much of Thailand as possible the company introduced its Thailand Explorer. This is a journey that takes you north to Chiang Mai and then brings you back. Not a commuter service, we thought, until we learned that several wealthy Thai businessmen do travel on it regularly, just for the style and comfort.*

Settling In

Our stateroom/compartment was much larger than we had imagined. When we stepped inside our luggage was already there and the cabin was in its daytime trim with one of the beds stowed away to provide space for a comfortable sitting area. Our cabin steward appeared to tell us all we needed to know about lights and water. It seemed more like an ocean-going cabin and we expected to be told about lifeboat drill and how to wear life jackets.

En Route

At the appointed minute the train began to slide gently away from the platform. We made our way to the bar car to sip on champagne, and the lengthy express gathered a little speed as it left the nation's capital. The train moved out from under the halo of pollution that is as much a symbol of Bangkok as are its magnificent temple spires. We went to the rear of the train and out on the observation deck. Words failed us as we passed through the slums of northern Bangkok, its inhabitants eking out a living alongside polluted canals or streets strewn with garbage. Such a stark contrast as we geared up for hours of luxury living and those we passed, mostly smiling and happy, prepared for another night of heat with only a sheet of corrugated tin to keep off the predicted rain.

As we passed beyond the airport the vistas became green and lush, and our thoughts were distracted as the call for lunch was made and we stepped inside the air conditioned carriages to discover what culinary creations could be made in such confined kitchens. The meal was excellent, like all those that were to follow, and would have been greatly acclaimed in a restaurant that was firmly fixed to the ground and not swaying around.

Elegant Dining

Our first meal started with Asian-style fish and vegetable croquettes in a fragrant turmeric sauce. It was followed by pan fried medallions of halibut served with mushrooms and black bean puree in a red wine and star aniseed jus. To finish were tartlets of tropical fruits. While coffee was served the train waited patiently on a spur.

AUTHOR'S NOTE: *As we have mentioned before, one of the problems with traveling on Thai trains is that most of the system is single-track. So there is continual stopping and starting while other trains pass. Everyone waits their turn, be it the* Eastern & Oriental *or the third-class diesel cars with their hard wooden seats crammed with passengers carrying boxes, many of them bigger than the traveler.*

We were fortunate that the train was not running at a capacity crowd, and the dining was limited to only one seating. There was no rush to finish our coffee in the restaurant car and nobody asked that we vacate the table and have coffee elsewhere on the train. We were given assurances that even with a full train there was ample time for all diners to complete their meal at a leisurely pace. There was an elegant aura of a Victorian-era London club as we chatted with our table companions. For each meal you are assigned a different table giving one the opportunity to meet new people knowing that should you fail to enjoy someone's company you only have to endure it for a limited time.

Sightseeing

Our first meal completed, the train slowed into the station at Ayutthaya, the old capital of Siam, and it was time to take our first sightseeing excursion. (You can read more about Ayutthaya in

Beyond Bangkok, page 107). Like all the excursions that were to follow our visit was a brief one, giving sufficient time to get a taste of the area. The emphasis was placed on the quality of things to see rather than quantity.

After a temple visit – we were taken to see **Wat Phananchoeng**, the most revered and oldest of the city's shrines – it was all-aboard a converted rice barge for a trip down the Chao Phraya River with musical accompaniment. A Thai lady from the train's entertainment team kindly obliged at that Thai instrument that looks like a sawn-off xylophone and has the ability to produce a continual bonging of inconsequential chords. The instrument is a *khim,* something that appears with great regularity in fancy hotel lobbies and top-notch restaurants. The music was quiet and fitted in well as we headed downstream following the paths the Thais made when they moved their capital from here to an area across from Bangkok hundreds of years earlier.

We moored alongside one temple and were driven to yet another temple, this one the **Wat Phra Si Sanphet**, set amid a vast park where elephants toted Japanese tourists from one side to the other. The guide explained that the Japanese visitors to the city loved riding on the elephants. Looking around, there was nothing much else they could do apart from take pictures of the temple. Time up and it was back to the train and a very welcome afternoon tea was served in the compartment, all very English, with fine china and fruit cake. All that was missing were those cute little cucumber sandwiches with the crusts removed.

Sipping our cup of Boh tea from the Cameron Highlands we examined the delightful décor of the compartment, which was paneled with cherry wood and elm burr, with marquetry friezes and intricate design inlays. The delicate embroidery work on the pelmets was hand crafted in Malaysia and the carpet was hand-tufted in Thailand, a mega-project you would appreciate if you've every hand-hooked a small rug. Can you imagine taking on an entire train!

Unexpected Comfort

Preparing for dinner was a breeze. On an earlier trip on the *Venice Simplon-Orient-Express*, getting dressed in the cramped quarters was a challenge – one of us had to wait in the corridor while the other dressed. Today we had ample space, and there was the added luxury of having bathroom, something that did not exist on the other train. The bathroom worked well. There was an adequate shower and the luxurious touch of toiletries from the House of Bulgari.

There's something special about getting dressed for dinner. After a couple of weeks of wearing nothing but shorts and casual shirts at beachfront eateries, putting on some finery was a welcome change. Fellow travelers, too, donned suits and ties, and several of the ladies had long gowns; the occasional string of pearls looked very much at home as we sipped cocktails in the bar car before the call for dinner.

I won't embarrass myself by reciting every menu, suffice it to say there was not a disappointing one served. At dinner there was always a choice (tonight's decision was between medallions of beef or *penaeng kai*, a Thai chicken curry). The stories over dinner are worth repeating.

The Company You Keep

Tonight we heard from an American who was touring all of Asia in a handful of days. He had worked out that his state compartment on the train was costing him and his wife $79 for every hour of the 52-hour journey. "While we are eating like this," he told us, "it seems a reasonable price. But a good night's sleep is very expensive."

The wine cellar on board is elaborate, considering we are on a train. Prices are high. A basic Burgundy costs $37 a bottle and a bottle of Dom Perignon a heady $240. Again the American had a comment. "Wine improves with age," he told us. "The older I get the more I appreciate it."

The other story we enjoyed came from a young English couple who were heading for a rustic and rural retreat, bamboo and bungalows, in Viet Nam after the *Eastern & Oriental Express* experience. Were they in for a change in lifestyle?

They had taken an excursion on the *British Pullman*, a sister Orient-Express enterprise, where a steam locomotive pulls a luxury train through English countryside while afternoon tea is served. (I bet they got those cucumber sandwiches.) It's a very upmarket journey and they said they were treated like royalty. The excursion ended in London where they boarded the local train for the journey to their home in suburban Surrey. What a shock they had. The commuter departed late, there were no seats available so they had to stand, and the lavatories on the train had been vandalized and weren't operating.

had to stand, and the lavatories on the train had been vandalized and weren't operating.

Abed on Board

Back aboard the *Eastern & Oriental* we were hurtling our way north as we headed for bed. Our bunks looked inviting, with crisp white linens, and there was ABO. I should explain that when keeping notes while traveling one develops a shorthand for recurring items. The beautiful flower synonymous with Thailand is the orchid and it appears everywhere, in drinks, adorning table settings, in people's hair, strewn round your neck in a garland and in this case nestled on a pillow. So ABO is another blooming orchid. There are a couple more we use. So many of the young Thai women are beautiful that rather than waste time writing it out in full we developed the acronym ATB, another Thai beauty. Finally, no matter where you go sightseeing in the kingdom you are certain to see more than your fair share of temples. So ABT is another Buddhist temple.

And so to bed. We have to admit it was not the best night's sleep we ever had. The strange surroundings and the shuddering of the train with its stopping and starting made it a night of naps rather than continuous sleep. We wonder how people survive on the less luxurious trains, which lack the suspension system that we had below us on that narrow-gauge track. Hopefully we will not have to find out.

Breakfast at Chiang Mai

The steaming jug of coffee, Colombia's finest, and a pot of tea on the breakfast tray were a welcome sight as we closed in on Chiang Mai, Thailand's most northerly train station. Within seconds the compartment became a sitting room and, dressed in *Eastern & Oriental Express* robes (for sale at the train's boutique), we munched on freshly baked croissants and admire the mountain and jungle scenery that whirls past outside.

We gathered on the station with our fellow travelers, none boasting it was the best night's sleep they ever had, anxious to make the most of our few hours in this wonderful city, Thailand's second-biggest. (For more about Chiang Mai see page 287).

the most interesting of any temple visit we have ever made and gave us, and the others in the group, a better understanding of Buddhism and its place in Thai life.

The temple, **Wat Buak Krok Luang**, is east of Chiang Mai town on the way to Sankamphang, the silk cottage village and close to the new and very expensive **Mandarin Oriental Hotel**. The monks and their abbot were awaiting our arrival and we sat on the floor before them while our gifts were collected and placed before them. This is how we earned merit, by bringing gifts to the temple and to the monks. The monks began chanting in *Pali*, the Indian dialect of all Buddhism, and according to our guide we were given blessings and then each presented with a hand-made woven amulet to bring us good fortune. The whole ceremony probably didn't take 20 minutes but it was a very enlightening experience.

Why did we get such special treatment? My guess is that the temple's wall murals, dating from the early 19th century, are in need of restoration and inviting farangs into the temple will hopefully bring the additional funds.

A Princess at Home

Then we were off to meet a princess, not in a castle, but in a very attractive award-winning northern Thai home set in splendid grounds. This was not a show-piece tourist attraction but her actual home. **Princess Chao Surai Sukrachan** is a descendant of the Lanna kingdom's royal family, and although not connected to the present Thai royal family she obviously keeps in contact with them, as she was pleased to show us with numerous photographs of herself and her family with members of the Chakri Dynasty.

She was the most amiable of hostesses and chatted easily with members of our group asking about where they came from and what they had seen in Thailand. After touring her home we were faced with tables laden with Thai tidbits, all beautifully hand crafted and she invited several local women to give displays of local handicrafts. There was a presentation of fruit carving, examples of wooden sculptures and other women proudly showed their prowess with cloth and leather products.

The house was very much a lived-in home with books and magazines, many of them in English, dotted around. We were free to ples of wooden sculptures and other women proudly showed their prowess with cloth and leather products.

The house was very much a lived-in home with books and magazines, many of them in English, dotted around. We were free to look where we wanted and all too soon it was time to return to the train.

Why did the Princess open her home in this way? It certainly wasn't for money. Her husband is an important member of the Thai military and her two sons, both educated in England, are successful businessmen in Bangkok operating several restaurants. On the ride back to the railway station our guide told us it was her way of showing tourists something of true country life in Thailand. He said that too many people only saw the nightlife and tawdry side that the country had offered. It was her way of showing that there was a more normal way of living and she hoped that it would also promote the work of the local artisans. She only allowed a few small groups to visit and we were one of the first to be invited. Hopefully others will have the same opportunity as we did.

Soup to Mousse

We had been wondering if the train's chef, Kevin Cape, would attempt serving soup on a moving train. At lunch he did just that. Somehow the creamy Thai pumpkin and yellow-pepper soup stayed in the bowls as we headed south. It didn't remain in the bowls long, though – it was too tasty, as was the crispy duck that followed. To ensure we got an ample intake of calories in the middle of the day there was a passionfruit mouse with coconut cream in lime and lemongrass sauce to finish with.

As we enjoyed the splendor of the **Singapura** restaurant dining car, with its rosewood and decorative lacquered panels hand-painted with delicate flowers, small country stations sped past. Each of them is tended by a uniformed stationmaster who proudly waves his green flag as the lengthy express flashes through his domain. The stations were ablaze with colorful gardens. Blue painted barrels overflowed with jasmine. Jungle plants brightened up a concrete platform. Each deserved a prize for transforming a drab railway stop into a small oasis for passengers and passers-by to enjoy. It reminded us of the locks on the upper reaches of England's River Thames where lock keepers produce delightful garden settings for river travelers to enjoy.

only Thai town that still uses colorful horse-drawn carriages for everyday transport, and there is a school for training baby elephants. Our stop was too brief to sample either. We did however get the chance to walk across the narrow-gauge tracks as we ventured out from the railway station. As you step across the meager width you wonder how the mighty carriages of the *Eastern & Oriental Express* balance on such a slender base.

Carriage Trade

The carriages themselves have a little history. They were first built in Japan in 1972 by Nippon Sharyo and Hitachi and operated as the Silver Train in New Zealand. They were shipped to the Orient-Express workshops in Singapore, where the same crew that transformed the magnificent rolling stock for the *Venice Simplon-Orient-Express* began the laborious task of converting them into the exquisite carriages they are today. It wasn't just the luxury interiors that were created. Air conditioning systems had to be developed to cope with the tropical heat and humidity. Panoramic windows installed to allow passengers better views of the countryside. And they had to fit abeam the narrow rails of Southeast Asia.

It was time for tea served in our compartment. An assortment of dainty cakes adorned the silver tea service tray as we continued south. The vistas switched from dense jungle to wide fields where scarecrows, attired in those Thai lampshade hats, scared away seed-seeking birds. A golf course was under construction, and then a clump of new homes. And always there was light reflecting from the colorful spires of temples as the sun descended, reminding us it was time to prepare for cocktails and a pre-dinner display of Siamese dancing in the bar car.

Again there was a choice of the main entrée for dinner. We opted for the medallions of lamb served with a spicy sauce and a potato terrine wrapped in bacon. We could have had Nasi Goreng Istimewa, a traditional Malaysian fried rice served with grilled satay. A very rich chocolate and banana delice with sesame seeds completed the meal.

Tonight's Entertainment

We stopped for a brief listen to the pianist in the bar car before returning to the cool, crisp sheets of the compartment. Tonight we would sleep better, I believed, since we were now traveling in the opposite direction and would have our heads back towards the engine. We did sleep better but my theory of direction was shot

Tonight's Entertainment

We stopped for a brief listen to the pianist in the bar car before returning to the cool, crisp sheets of the compartment. Tonight we would sleep better, I believed, since we were now traveling in the opposite direction and would have our heads back towards the engine. We did sleep better but my theory of direction was shot when we raised the blinds to find we were now traveling in the opposite direction. Sometime during the night the train had stopped and a locomotive was placed at the other end of the carriages to pull us along the line to Kanchanaburi, our next port of call.

Kanchanaburi

Our stop here again was brief but we did get the chance to see the train cross the **Bridge Over the River Kwai** and we got to listen to *Colonel Bogey* played in the bar car. You can read more about Kanchanaburi in *Beyond Bangkok*, page 113.

A Chef's Story

After our final meal aboard the luxury express – soup again, this time a pork wonton dish followed by a butterfish steak – we chatted with chef Kevin Cape in the bar car as the train hurtled towards the suburbs of northern Bangkok. Looking a little weary from the hectic life he leads aboard the train, the chef, a confident Londoner, said he feels more like a football manager rather than a player. The culinary success of the journey is all in the planning. Once the train is underway you're committed. He modestly claims that the success of the dining experience is due to the team he has spent 10 years putting together. He loves the challenge each journey brings with clients from different parts of the world all anxious to sample the culinary delights that he has in store. He joined the Orient-Express team back in 1993 when the train made its debut.

We wondered where and when the multi-national train staff ate. He admitted that this had been a problem in the early days with each nationality wanting different food. After lots of discussion it was suggested that each crew member be paid pocket money to buy food along the way. The idea worked out wonderfully. It didn't take long for the workers to discover where the best stops were to disembark and purchase their favorite dishes.

adventure stood smartly alongside the train to say goodbye. Within minutes we were lost in the hustle and bustle of Bangkok. This may be the capital of Thailand, but is only a tiny part of the kingdom. The real treasures are just a train ride away.

Nuts & Bolts

Our **Thai Explorer** trip, which normally operates five times a year, cost $2,030 per person for a state compartment that included all meals and excursions. The larger presidential suite costs $2,780 per person and the smaller Pullman compartment costs $1,360 per person. The traditional Singapore-to-Bangkok (or vice versa) runs weekly throughout the year. This two-night, three-day itinerary (via Butterworth, Kuala Lumpur, Hua Hin and Kwai) costs $1,730 for a Pullman $2,570 for a state or $3,510 for a presidential suite. The full Singapore-to-Chiang Mai journey runs only when the Thai Explorer operates with a three-day stopover in Bangkok between itineraries. In the UK, ☎ 0845 077 2222; in the US the toll free number is 1-800-237-1236, or visit www.orient-express.com.

The Railway From Hell

Our chapter on the railways of Thailand would not be complete without mention of the **Death Railway**, the grim link that stretched 415 kilometers from Myanmar or Burma, as it was then, to Ratchaburi province in Thailand. (For the story of the Bridge over the River Kwai see the *Kanchanaburi* section, page 113).

The Japanese desperately needed a rail link across Thailand in the early 1940s to get supplies to their army, poised in Burma hoping to invade India. The alternative to the rail link was to move the cargo by sea, which they feared would leave them exposed to allied attack. Thailand had been unable to stop the Japanese occupation of its kingdom. The Prime Minister at the time, Field Marshal Phibun, had little choice but to sign an agreement in August 1942 allowing the construction of the rail link to go ahead. Planning engineers estimated it would take five years to complete such a project. But the Japanese military could not wait that long. The engineers said it would take thousands of additional laborers to reduce the five-year construction period.

And the military had those thousands of men, the prisoners of war, most of them in camps in Singapore. They ignored the Geneva Conventions and immediately started moving the men north. Work started in October 1942 and was completed in Decem-

1942 allowing the construction of the rail link to go ahead. Planning engineers estimated it would take five years to complete such a project. But the Japanese military could not wait that long. The engineers said it would take thousands of additional laborers to reduce the five-year construction period.

And the military had those thousands of men, the prisoners of war, most of them in camps in Singapore. They ignored the Geneva Conventions and immediately started moving the men north. Work started in October 1942 and was completed in December 1943 – just over a year – and in that short space of time more than 13,000 Commonwealth, Dutch and American prisoners of war lost their lives. At least 150,000 civilians also died in the course of the project, chiefly forced labor brought from Malaya and the Dutch East Indies, or conscripted in Burma and Thailand. Historians say that each sleeper along the track represents one death. Or that 38 prisoners of war died for every kilometer of construction.

■ Construction

Construction of the railway began at the two ends, **Thanbyuzayat** in Burma and **Nong Pladuk**, west of Bangkok. The lines were joined at **Konkoita** just south of Three Pagodas Pass. When completed, 306 kilometers of the track were in Thailand and 108 kilometers in Myanmar. The link into Myanmar has long been out of commission but the government has said that they are considering reestablishing the link as a tourist attraction.

The initial 50 kilometers of the Thailand construction was relatively easy because of the flat terrain. It was beyond Kanchanaburi, home of the Bridge over the River Kwai, that things became difficult and the prisoners named part of the area as Hellfire Pass. The prisoners were forced to work 16 hours a day on a diet of rice and salted vegetables. Most deaths were from malnutrition and exhaustion. Others succumbed to tropical diseases. Torturous punishments were handed out and there was little medical treatment available.

A tour of the museum alongside the Kanchanaburi cemetery will give you a grim idea of what equipment the medical teams had to contend with.

Bodies were buried alongside the camps where they died. Within six months so many prisoners had died that the Japanese were forced to bring in 200,000 Asian workers to keep construction

When the railway was complete the situation for the remaining prisoners of war got no better. They were housed in camps along the track, near bridges and marshalling yards that came under heavy attack from Allied bombers. Many more deaths were recorded.

■ After the War

At the end of the war the graves of those prisoners who died during the construction and maintenance of the Death Railway were moved to three cemeteries. Two are in Thailand, at Chungkai and Kanchanaburi and one is in Myanmar at Thanbyuzayat. The remains of the American prisoners were repatriated.

The **Thanbyuzayat War Cemetery** is some 65 kilometers south of Moulein in the foothills that separate Myanmar from Thailand. The total number of graves in Thanbyuzayat is 3,771 – 1,588 British, 1,335 Australian and 621 Dutch.

The **Chungkai War Cemetery** is situated on the banks of the Kwai Noi River, about five kilometers south of the center of Kanchanaburi and is the smaller of the two POW cemeteries in Thailand. There are 1,740 graves here. The cemetery is on the same spot that the Chungkai POW camp used during the construction of the death railway.

Largest and most visited of the cemeteries is **Kanchanaburi**, where 3,500 British, 1,400 Australians and 2,000 Dutch are buried. All three cemeteries are well maintained and a visit is one of those experiences that you will never forget.

There is an eerie sense of gratitude as you wander between the gravestones on the well-manicured grass. Gratitude to those who gave their lives and gratitude that they are well remembered for the job they did in serving so bravely under such barbaric conditions. There is a wonderful feeling of serenity as you enter and leave the cemetery. Normally where tourists gather the street vendors are hard at work selling their wares. Here things are different. If you want to buy a drink or some postcards you have to ask. Nobody will ask you.

Before we came here we had been told that we would be surprised at the number of young men buried here. That was not the case. Yes, we did see graves of some teenagers but many were older. Few would be alive today had they survived their ordeal. At least the families who lost men here know that their father, grandfather, uncle or distant cousin is remembered.

dors are hard at work selling their wares. Here things are different. If you want to buy a drink or some postcards you have to ask. Nobody will ask you.

Before we came here we had been told that we would be surprised at the number of young men buried here. That was not the case. Yes, we did see graves of some teenagers but many were older. Few would be alive today had they survived their ordeal. At least the families who lost men here know that their father, grandfather, uncle or distant cousin is remembered.

Shortly after our visit to Kanchanaburi we watched an informative *National Geographic* documentary on television. It emphasized the hardships the POWs and the Asian laborers endured. There were remarks by a number of surviving prisoners whose emotional comments were a painful reminder of the awful atrocities.

Rod Beattie, curator of the Thailand Burma Railway Center (see page 117), was featured in the documentary, exploring parts of the disused railway where conditions were far worse than at the River Kwai Bridge. At one immense embankment two kilometers long he estimated the prisoners would have made 12 million trips carrying 20 kilos of soil to build the bank to its necessary height. And many would have done this backbreaking labor in the slippery jungle terrain without shoes or boots. The only thing to spur them on was the brutal drive of their armed Japanese guards.

Rod had also discovered a cutting built by the Asian laborers where he estimated 5,000 Asian laborers, their wives and children died. And he added that to this day there are only three graves of Asian workers and those are marked as unknown.

Bangkok's Public Transportation

■ The SkyTrain

The capital's elevated rail system opened in 1999 and you can learn about costs and tourist routes in the *Bangkok* chapter. Here we'll explain some of the extensions and improvements that are planned. Three new sky bridges are being built that will link the capital's best shopping centers. On the **Silom Line** there will be a link to the Thaniya building and the Silom 64 building from the

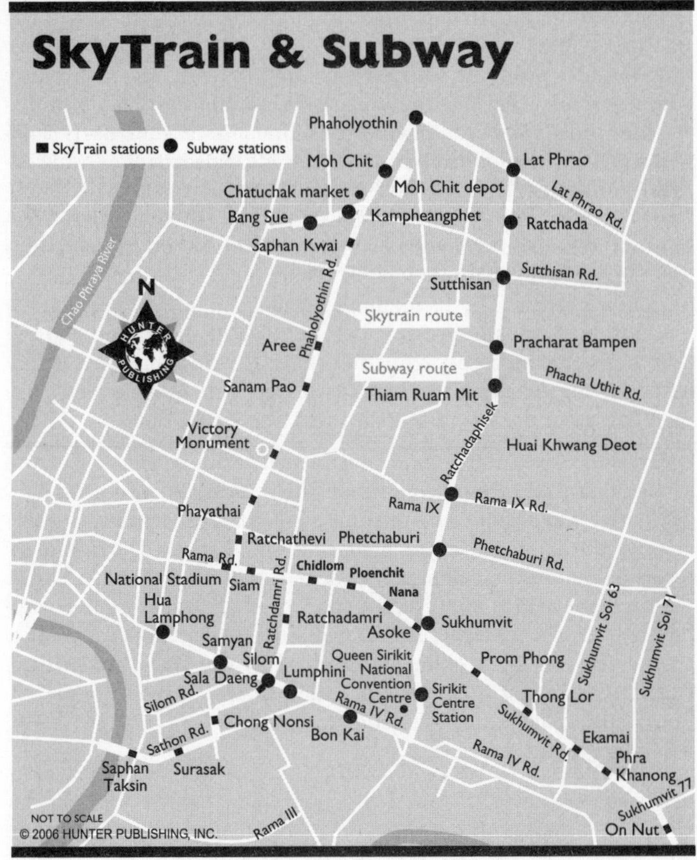

Sala Daeng Station. On the **Sukhumvit Line** a new bridge from the Chit Lom Station will link up Central World Plaza.

Both rail lines are to be extended. The Silom Line will continue from Taksin Road, extending 6.7 kilometers to Phetchkasem Road. At the west end of the line the tracks will be extended 6.8 kilometers to Phran Nok. The extensions for the Sukhumvit Line will be from Samrong out to Samut Prakan, a distance of 7.9 kilometers, and in the north the line will eventually continue for 12 kilometers, from Mo Chit out to Don Muang.

■ The Subway

Thailand's newest rail system, the subway in Bangkok, has not eliminated the traffic congestion in the country's capital despite proponents' claims that it has. There are more details about the existing system in the *Bangkok* chapter. Hours of operation are from 6am to midnight. During morning and evening rush hours trains operate every five minutes, and they run every ten minutes at other times. The system suffered a major setback in early 2005 when two trains collided and more than 200 people were injured. Prime Minister Thaksin Shinawatra blamed the crash on one "lousy" driver. The system was closed temporarily while an investigation was made and subway employees given additional training. The Prime Minister said, "Nothing is wrong with the computer system. The accident was caused by human error. I will make several trips to prove it is safe." The investigation showed that a driver of an empty train disengaged an automatic drive system allowing an empty carriage to roll back into a stationary train filled with commuters at the Cultural Center Station.

Fears that commuters would not return to the system after the accident proved groundless. When the subway was reopened 14 days after the accident more than 95,000 travelers used the service in the first 12 hours of operation, close to the numbers recorded before the collision. Several of those who traveled after the accident said they were not concerned about safety but were happy to travel underground to avoid the problems of congestion on the streets. The system is operated by the **Bangkok Metro Public Company Ltd.**, with its headquarters at the Administration Building on Rama IX Road, ☎ 02354 2900, fax 02354 2040, www.bangkokmetro.co.th.

Living in Thailand

Climate

If you have read the previous chapters you already know about Thailand's climate. It gets hot and sticky, and when it rains it rains a lot. Unless you elect to live in the far north of the country you can forget your winter clothes and concentrate on light cottons and silks.

Cuisine

The wonderful world of Thai cooking is an around-the-clock adventure. The abundance of ingredients in this fertile kingdom is just the start of the saga. In the north all manner of vegetables flourish in rich soil. Rice paddies in the center of the nation yield different varieties of the country's main staple and in the south tropical fruits cover the ground like weeds. The harvests from the seas that surround the country yield all manner of seafood and fish. Before the sun comes up, trucks laden with produce, chickens and pigs rumble along rough farm tracks and onto the roads that lead to the hundreds of markets throughout the kingdom. There is a daily market in every major town. Restaurant owners mingle with the chefs of top hotels and the general public to barter for the goods, and the produce is fresh – in this tropical heat things have to move quickly before they spoil.

The markets are bursting with piles of spices, mountains of lemon grass. Sweet and pungent smells mix with the odor of chickens. Fish markets are normally held in the afternoon when the fishermen return with their catches. Much of the shrimp comes from large coastal farms where the creatures are reared like plants.

When problems arose with export quotas of shrimp a glut hit the local market and prices plummeted. When the European community put a limit on the amount that could be imported some politicians wanted to cancel orders placed for the European Airbus and deal with the US to buy Boeing jets. Their plan was to trade prawns for planes. The idea seemed logical to the Thai minds, but it failed. One can imagine the reaction of a Boeing employee being handed a bag of shrimp instead of a paycheck.

Most tourists, when they arrive in Thailand, have little or no experience of Asian cooking. Perhaps their local Thai or Chinese restaurant or maybe a program on television is about the extent of it. However, nothing can prepare you for the sight of the real thing. I say sight because that is the first thing that hits you. Most of the incredible array of vegetables, fruits, pastes, spices, fish and meats is totally unrecognizable to the western eye. Wandering through a local market, even if you don't actually buy anything, is a fascinating experience. Do go early and do go with a strong stomach. The sight of pigs' heads all hanging up in a row at 6 o'clock in the morning can be a little challenging.

One of the easiest ways to understand the concepts of Thai cooking is to take a class at one of the hotel cookery schools. I went to **The Boathouse Culinary Workshop** for a weekend class under the direction of chef Tamanoon Pumchun. This excellent course gave me an understanding of ingredients and hands on practice of techniques. Step-by-step, he takes you through the blending of flavors, the use of herbs, the methods of chopping and pounding in a mortar, the preparation and presentation so important to Thai cooks. A definite side benefit is that you get to eat what you have prepared. Normally, within families, the food is all served in the center of the table and the whole family sitting down to eat together is still an important part of the day.

Thai meals, which feature lots of vegetables and fish, are normally very low in fat and the diet, while simple, is healthy and tasty. Tasty, of course, is a relative word. With the heavy addition of lemon grass, ginger, garlic and chili peppers, what is pleasantly spicy to them can be knock-your-head-off spicy to foreigners.

Street Vendors

Walking through city streets you experience a world of food unlike anywhere in Europe or the United States. From the street vendors with their barbeque pots or small gas rings to the glamorous hotels and top restaurants with their head chefs and exquisite table settings the food here is simply different. The Thais love to snack. Small, spicy tidbits wrapped in little packages of leaves or perhaps in small plastic bags tied at the top filled with soup or curry can be bought on most street corners or outside office buildings. Fish balls, grilled dry squid hanging on racks, tiny coconut puddings all sold from carts or maybe a motorcycle sidecar.

Sticky rice packed into bamboo canes or wrapped in banana leaves makes an easy takeaway for busy workers. Or in Chinatown *joak* porridge with fish, meat or egg is a favorite with the Chinese Thai. The carts may move from place to place or sometimes set up shop in the same location everyday but locals know what time to expect their favorite seller.

Thai food is internationally famous. Whether chili-hot or comparatively bland, balance is the guiding principle behind each dish. Thai cuisine is essentially a marriage of centuries-old Eastern and Western influences harmoniously combined into something uniquely Thai. The characteristics of Thai food depend on who cooks it, for whom it is cooked, for what occasion, and where it is cooked.

Originally, Thai cooking reflected the characteristics of a waterborne lifestyle. Aquatic animals, plants and herbs were major ingredients. With their Buddhist background, Thais shunned the use of the meat of large animals. However, later influences introduced more substantial use of meat, which is often shredded and laced with herbs and spices.

Traditional Thai cooking methods were stewing, baking and grilling. Chinese influences saw the introduction of frying, including stir-frying and deep-frying. Culinary influences from the 17th century onwards included Portuguese, Dutch, French and Japanese. Chilies were introduced to Thai cooking during the late 1600s by Portuguese missionaries who had acquired a taste for them while serving in South America.

Thais were very adept at Siamese-ing foreign cooking methods, and substituting ingredients. The *ghee* (clarified butter) used in Indian cooking was replaced by coconut oil, and coconut milk substituted for other dairy products. Overpoweringly pure spices were toned down and enhanced by fresh herbs such as lemon grass and galangal. Eventually, fewer spices were used in Thai curries, while the use of fresh herbs increased. It is generally acknowledged that Thai curries burn intensely, but briefly, whereas other curries, with strong spices, burn for longer periods.

Instead of serving dishes in courses, a Thai meal is served all at once, permitting dinners to enjoy complementary combinations of different tastes. A proper Thai meal should consist of a soup, a curry dish with condiments, a dip with accompanying fish and vegetables. A spiced salad may replace the curry dish. The soup can also be spicy, but the curry should be replaced by non-spiced items. There must be a harmony of tastes and textures within individual dishes and the entire meal.

Recipes

We invited two chefs, an Englishman and a Thai, to give us recipes that could be produced in Western kitchens but still give an authentic reminder of the culinary treats of Thailand.

■ From Two Chefs

The Brit was **Kevin Cape**, executive chef aboard the *Eastern & Oriental Express* (see page 363). Kevin has worked throughout the world and spent many years training under legendary Michel Bourdin, executive chef at London's Connaught Hotel. During his early days in London he became interested in Asian cuisine and spent his spare time working in London's Chinatown. In addition to several assignments in the UK, Kevin has worked in France and the US, and made visits to Asia as a guest chef at the Pan Pacific Hotel in Kuala Lumpur and the Mandarin Hotel in Singapore before joining the *Eastern & Oriental Express*. At his last post in Britain, Kevin was executive chef at the Tarnhouse Hotel in Cumbria, where he was awarded a three-star rosette by the Automobile Association, and the Salon Culinaire Gold Medal. He has his own Website: www.kevincape.freeservers.com. The first recipe is for a soup we enjoyed aboard the *Eastern & Oriental*. The recipe serves 10.

Thai Scented Pumpkin & Yellow-pepper Soup

Ingredients:

Two yellow peppers, diced
500 g of pumpkin, cleaned
200 grams of sweet potato, diced
One large potato, peeled and diced
One large white onion, peeled and diced
One leek, diced
50 g of garlic, coarsely chopped
50 g of galangal (*kha*), sliced
25 g of chopped *kaffir* lime leaf
500 ml coconut milk
Yellow curry paste to taste
3 liters of chicken stock

Preparation:

Simply sweat the vegetables in the herbs until you get the nice aroma. Add the chicken stock, allow to simmer very gently until all the vegetables are completely cooked. Allow to cool. Remove the hard herbs (lemon grass, galangal). The vegetables are then liquidized and passed through a medium sieve. Then reheat, add the coconut cream, this is placed in the soup cup, garnish with coconut milk and julienne of lime leaf. Baby corn muffins make a nice accompaniment.

Grilled Shrimp with Sweet & Sour Sauce.

For these recipes I thank **The Boathouse** executive chef **Tamanoon Pumchun**, a genial Thai with an international reputation. Chef Tamanoon has traveled extensively in Europe gaining knowledge of European cuisine as well as conducting seminars on Thai food. He has published *The Boathouse Cookbook* and the number of people taking his cooking classes is in the thousands.

Ingredients:

200g [7 oz] large shrimp, cleaned and de-veined
Pinch of salt and pepper
125ml (½ cup) sweet-and-sour sauce

Sweet and Sour Sauce:

1 tbs oil

3 or 4 small red chili peppers, finely chopped

2 tbs garlic, finely chopped

1 cup coriander or cilantro leaves, with roots if possible

175 ml (2/3 cup) vinegar

2 tbs sugar

2 tbs Thai fish sauce (*nam pla*)

2 tbs oyster sauce

250 ml (1 cup) chicken stock

Sauce Preparation:

Heat oil in a pan, add garlic, hot chilies and coriander root and cook until just tender.

Add the remaining ingredients; simmer for five minutes, stirring constantly.

Yields about 375ml (1½ cups) which may be stored in the fridge.

Shrimp Preparation:

Marinate the shrimp with salt and pepper (about five minutes) and grill on a charcoal grill or pan grill until cooked. Set them aside.

Warm the sweet-and-sour sauce and pour over the grilled shrimp. Serve decorated with more cilantro.

Herbed Coconut-milk Soup with Chicken or Seafood

Ingredients:

1.5 liters (6 cups) coconut milk

750 liters (3 cups) chicken stock

6 kaffir lime leaves, finely shredded

15 g (½ oz) galangal (*kha*), sliced

1 stalk of lemon grass, cut into pieces

8 whole birds-eye chilies (*prik kii noo*)

400g (2-½ cups) chicken or seafood, sliced into 4cm (1-½ inch) strips

16 small straw or button mushrooms

120ml (½ cup) lime juice

4 Tablespoon Thai fish sauce (*nam pla*)

Preparation:

Combine coconut milk and chicken stock in a pan and place over a medium heat. Add the kaffir lime leaves, galangal, lemon grass and chilies.

Stir in the chicken or seafood and mushrooms and cook until the soup begins to boil.

Remove from the heat and adjust seasoning to taste with fish sauce and/or lime juice. Serves six.

■ Top Thai Dishes

A world-wide survey of Thai restaurants was conducted discover the two most-requested dishes. And the winners were: *Tom Yum Kung*, the hot-and-sour shrimp soup, and *Kaeng Khiao Wan*, the green curry. And here are the recipes for those two.

Tom Yum Kung

Normally made with prawns but you can use chicken or fish. The dish is flavored with chilies and kaffir lime leaves and to be truly authentic Tom Yum is often cooked and served in a hot-charcoaled bowl.

Ingredients:

3 cups (24 fl oz/750ml) water or light chicken stock

8 oz (250 g) shrimp/prawns, shelled and divined

2 garlic cloves, minced

5 kaffir lime leaves (*bai-ma-krut*)

3 leaves of fresh or dried galangal (*kha*), thin sliced

¼ cup fish sauce *(nam pla)*

2 stalks lemon grass/citronella *(ta-krai),* lower 1/3 portion only, cut into 1-in (2.3 cm) lengths

5 hot green Thai peppers *(phrik khi nu),* optional

½ cup sliced straw mushrooms

¼ cup (2 fl oz/60ml) lime juice

1 tsp roasted chili paste *(nam phrik pao)*

1 tsp cilantro/coriander leaves *(bai phak chi)*, chopped

Preparation:

Bring the stock to a boil over medium heat. Add the garlic, lime leaves, galangal, fish sauce, lemon grass, and shallots, then the mushrooms and chili peppers, if using. Simmer for two minutes. Add the shrimp and reheat to boiling. Cook until the shrimp are pink, opaque, and firm but no longer than one minute. When the shrimp are cooked, place the lime juice and chili paste in a serving bowl. Pour the soup into the bowl, stir, and garnish with cilantro leaves.

Kaeng Khiao Wan

A green curry cooked with coconut milk, sweet basil and chilies. Coconut milk gives curry a mild, almost sweet flavor. Green chilies add more spice. *Kaeng khiao wan* can be eaten with rice noodles known as *Khanom jeen kaeng khiao wan.*

Ingredients

Green curry paste:

2 stalks lemon grass, bottom part only, cut into ½-in(1-cm) pieces

1 tablespoon galangal (*kha*) or fresh ginger, sliced

1 teaspoon cumin

½ cup fresh cilantro/coriander root (*rak phak chi*)

8 garlic cloves

10 green Thai chili pepppers (*phrik khi nu*)

10 jalapeño peppers (*phrik chi fa*)

1 teaspoon chopped shallot

¼ teaspoon minced kaffir lime skin *(phio ma krut)*

Other ingredients:

2 cups (16 fl oz/500 ml) coconut milk

1 lb (450g) beef or chicken, cut into ½-in x 2-in (1-cm x2.5-cm)

¼ cup (2 fl oz/60ml) chopped garlic

4 tablespoons fish sauce *(nam pla)*

3 tablespoons sugar

1 cup Thai eggplant *(ma-khuea phuang)* or tinned bamboo shoots

½ cup (4 fl oz/125 ml) coconut cream

6 fresh kaffir lime leaves (*bai ma-krut*)

4 or 5 sweet basil leaves (*bai horapha*)

Preparation:

Place all the green-curry-paste ingredients in an electric blender and process until smooth, or pound in a mortar. Pour the coconut milk and green curry paste into a large saucepan and heat to boiling. Add the beef or chicken, fish sauce, sugar, eggplant, coconut cream an garlic. Cook at a slow boil for 5 minutes. Add the kaffir lime leaves and basil leaves. Remove the contents to a serving bowl and garnish with red jalapeño pepper (*phrik chi fa daeng*).

Pad Thai

Another favourite dish is wok-fried rice noodles with prawns. This is a signature dish of the **White Elephant Restaurant** at the JW Marriott hotel in Bangkok, and we thank them for providing this recipe.

Ingredients:

100 g shrimp meat

30 ml cooking oil

20 g bean curd, diced

10 g dry shrimp

10 g pickle turnip, chopped

15 g shallot, sliced

100 g thin rice noodles

20 g bean sprouts

15 g Chinese flat onion leaves

1 lemon or lime wedge

1 tbs finely chopped peanuts

Pad Thai Sauce:

30 g tamarind juice

15 g fish sauce

20 g palm sugar sauce

10 g ketchup

Preparation:

Combine tamarind juice, fish sauce, palm sugar sauce and ketchup in a saucepan, bring to boil over a low heat until sugar dissolves and mixture thickens, put aside.

Place the frying pan on the heat, add a little oil. When its smoking, stir-fry the shrimp, bean curd, dry shrimp, pickle, turnip and sliced shallot. Stir them constantly and add one beaten egg. Mix in the rice noodles and add the Pad Thai sauce. When the noodles are light brown and soft, add the Chinese flat onion leaves and bean sprouts and mix well.

To serve, garnish with a lemon or lime wedge, Chinese onion, chili powder, ground roast nuts or banana blossom.

■ Regional Dishes

Most countries have their regional dishes. You'd have a hard time getting biscuits with country ham and gravy in New York or a platter of haggis in London. Thailand is much the same, and there are a few dishes that are special to the island of Phuket.

Khanom chin are Thai rice noodles; these are normally eaten with curried fish or shrimp. Though it is available in any part of Thailand, khanom chin of Phuket has a richer flavor and is served with a variety of fresh and preserved vegetables. It is a typical local breakfast, and it is also delicious when complemented by beef curry or chicken curry.

There are two styles of fried noodles that Phuket claims as its own. One is *mi hokkian* or *mi hun* (soba noodles), which are fried with fresh shrimp, pork, shellfish and green cabbage. The other, originating in Sapam Village, is *mi sapam* with seafood and gravy on top. *Ho Mok* is steamed curried fish (or other seafood, often crab) with vegetables, wrapped in a banana-leaf or foil container. It should be eaten with steamed rice. *Namphrik Kung Siap* is Phuket-style hot shrimp paste with sweetened crisp shrimp, eaten with fresh vegetables.

When talking about Thai curry, foreigners will probably think of chicken or beef curry only. If you are in Phuket, why not try Phuket's *kaeng luang* (sour curry with fish and vegetables), a popular southern curry with an unusual taste.

Cooking Classes

They are available all over in Thailand, and may be conducted in homes and guesthouses as well as at the top hotels. The course at the Oriental in Bangkok is world renowned, and the management hopes that similar success will come to their new super-resort in Chiang Mai.

For those in a hurry, the **Shangri-La Hotel** in Bangkok offers a different approach to Thai cooking classes. It's all done in a few hours and apart from the knowledge you gain you will have a diploma from one of the world's top hotels.

You start at 8:30am when the class is taken from the hotel in air conditioned comfort to the **Or-Tor-Kor** fruit and vegetable market, which isn't air conditioned or quite as comfortable. Here you'll learn your *kha* root from a *pomelo* (that's a very meaty oversized grapefruit). Then it's back to the hotel where the cooking class begins at 10:30am. You'll have 90 minutes of hands-on cooking learning simple favorite Thai dishes.

Then comes the best part: At noon everyone sits down to a fine meal at the **Salathip Restaurant**. At 1:30 you're free to leave, armed with a diploma and a souvenir apron, which will impress your neighbors on your return. It's a great experience, but don't expect to know it all in one busy morning.

Language

To Western ears the Thai language is a strange cacophony of noise that sounds like an early-morning battle in a barnyard. The written letters are just as confusing, with little symbols that make a printed page look like an overworked blotting pad.

We don't intend to try to teach you the language, just give you an insight to make life a little easier. The wonderful thing is that Thais don't mind if you make errors with their language. They'll smile and laugh perhaps, but they do appreciate that you have made an effort.

If you want to know more about speaking Thai, there are numerous phrase books on the market, and most tourist towns in the kingdom offer lessons. Better still, if you can avail yourself of a Thai girlfriend or boyfriend you can have the language mastered in a matter of weeks.

Thai is a phonetic language using five different tones – rising, falling high, low and mid-tone. The same word can have five meanings, it just depends which of the tones you use. The language was first developed over 700 years ago along with the alphabet and today is a complex mixture of Pali, Khmer, Malay, Sanskrit, Chinese and even some English, which you might find hard to believe.

First the very basic words important in any foreign country. It is important to know that politeness dictates that men and women end their sentences differently. Females end with *kaa* and males with the word *krap*. Many Thai males, especially younger people do not pronounce the "r" and simply say *kap*. The correct and more polite pronunciation is to say *krap*, preferably with trilled r's.

The Very Basics

Hello, good morning, afternoon,or just plain hi! ..... *Sawadee kaa/krap*

How are you? .... *Sa bai dee rheu kaa/krap*

I'm fine .... *Sa bai dee kaa/krap*

Thank you .... *Khop khun kaa/krap*

No thank you .... *Mai kaa / krap khop khun*
Yes .... *Chai kaa / krap*
No .... *Mai chai kaa / krup*
Goodbye .... *Laa gorn kaa / krup*
My name is (male speaker) .... *Phom cheu*
My name is (female speaker)...................... *Chan cheu*
Help! .... *Chuay duay!*
It's an emergency! .... *Chuk choen!*
Call the police!.................. *Chuay riak tam-ruat duay!*
Call a doctor!................... *Chuay taam maw hai duay!*
Do you know – ? .... *Khun rhoo jak...mai?*
Can you find a lawyer who speaks English?
Riak thanaaikhwaam thii phuut phaa-saa ankrit dai mai?
I'm sorry, or excuse me .... *Kho thod kaa / krup*
You're welcome, don't worry, no problem .... *Mai pen rai*

Place Names

These are terms you'll see on maps or street signs. In this instance we put the Thai word first followed by its English equivalent.

Amphur .... district
Ban .... village
Khoa .... mountain
Chedi .... pagoda
Had .... beach
Klong .... canal
Ko, Koh .... island (either spelling is correct)
Muang .... town or city
Namtok .... waterfall
Tham .... cave
Tambon .... sub district
Viharn .... image hall in a temple
Wat .... temple

"Ngoen" means money and "tang" also means money. Tang comes from "satang" – 100 satang equals one Baht.

Numbers

We found it was important, when we started learning Spanish, to get the numbers right first. So here are the Thai ones.

One . . . . *neung*
Two . . . . *saung*
Three . . . . *sahm*
Four . . . . *see*
Five. . . . . *hah*
Six. . . . . *hok*
Seven . . . . *jet*
Eight . . . . *padt*
Nine . . . . *gow*
Ten. . . . . *sib*
Eleven . . . . *sib-et*
Twelve . . . . *sib-saung*
Thirteen. . . . . *sib-sahm*
Fourteen . . . . *sib-see*
Fifteen . . . . *sib-hah*
Sixteen . . . . *sib-hok*
Seventeen . . . . *sib-jet*
Eighteen . . . . *sib-padt*
Nineteen . . . . *sib-gow*
Twenty. . . . . *yee-sib*
Twenty-one . . . . *yee-sib-et*
Twenty-two . . . . *yee-sib-saung*
Thirty. . . . . *sahm-sib*
Thirty-one . . . . *sahm-sib-et*
Thirty-two . . . . *sahm-sib-saung*
Forty . . . . *see-sib*
Forty-one . . . . *see-sib-et*
Forty-two . . . . *see-sib-saung*
Fifty . . . . *hah-sib*
Fifty-one. . . . . *hah-sib-et*
Sixty . . . . *hok-sib*
Sixty-one. . . . . *hok-sib-et*
Seventy. . . . . *jet-sib*
Seventy-one . . . . *jet-sib-et*
Eighty . . . . *pat-sib*
Eighty-one. . . . . *pat-sib-et*

Ninety . . . . *gow-sib*
Ninety-one . . . . *gow-sib-et*
One hundred . . . . *neung rhoy*
Two hundred . . . . *saung rhoy*
Three hundred . . . . *sahm rhoy*
Four hundred . . . . *see rhoy*
Five hundred . . . . *hah rhoy*
One thousand . . . . *neung phun*
Two thousand . . . . *saung phun*
Ten thousand . . . . *neung mheun*
One hundred thousand . . . . *neung saen*
One million . . . . *neung lhaan*

Useful Terms

Do you speak English?
Phood pasa ang-grid dai mai kaa / krup?
Where is the toilet? . . . . *Hong nam yoo nhai?*
Turn left . . . . *Leaw sai*
Turn right . . . . *Leaw khwa*
Stop . . . . *Yud*
Go . . . . *Pai*
Where is the nearest garage?
Oo sorm rot thee glai thee sud yoo thee-nai?
Can I change money here? . . . . *Laek ngoen thii nii dai mai?*
Can I use my credit card to get money?
Chai bat khrehdit laek tang dai mai?
Where is the post office?
Thii tham kaan praisanii yuu thii nai?
How much will it cost to send this to...?
Tha ja song khong nee pai ... raakhaa thao rai?
I'd like to send a postcard . . . . *Yaak song praisanii bat*
Police Station . . . . *Sa tha ni tam ruat*
Hotel . . . . *Rong-ram*
Embassy . . . . *Sathan toot*
Airport . . . . *Sa nam bin*
Bus Station . . . . *Sathani rot may*
Train station . . . . *Sathani rot fai*
Good luck . . . . *Chok dee*
Mr., Mrs. or Miss . . . . *Kuhn*
Beautiful . . . . *Suay*

At the Airport

Here's my baggage . . . . *Nii krapao doenthang khong phom*
You may open it . . . .*Shern perd duu dai*
I'd like two tickets . . . . . . *Phom/chan yaak dai tuah sawng bai*
I want to go to . . . .*Phom/chan yaak pai*
Excuse me, can you help me?
Khaw thot chuay phom /chan noi dai mai?

Eating & Shopping

Are you hungry? . . . . *Kun hiew kahw mai kaa/krup?*
I'm hungry . . . . *Chan hew*
Breakfast . . . . *Aa-han chow*
Lunch . . . .*Aa-han glaang wan*
Dinner . . . . *Aa-han yen*
How much is it? . . . . *Ra kha tao rai kaa/krup?*
Too expensive . . . . *Pang maak*
Where can I buy ...?. . . . .*Seu...dai thii nai?*
Do you have any ...? . . . .*Mii ... mai?*
How many Baht? . . . . *Kii Baht?*
Any discount?. . . . . *Lot ra kha dai mai?*
Please wrap it for me . . . .*Ho hai duai*
Is it far from here? . . . . *Yuu klai jaak thii nii mai?*
Can you show me the way? . . . . . . *Bawk thaang hai noi dai mai?*
Which street is this?. . . . .*Thii nii thanon a-rai?*
Can I try this on? . . . .*Long sai dai mai?*
Please bring me a fork. . . . .*Chuay yib sawm hai nauy*
I like eating Thai food . . . .*Chawp thaan aahaan Thai*
I don't like it hot and spicy . . . . *Mai chawp thaan ped*
I like it hot and spicy . . . .*Chawp ped ped*
Do you have a menu in English?
Mii menu pen phaasaa ankrit mai?
I eat only vegetarian food . . . .*Phom/chan kin jeh/pak*
Can I have the check? . . . .*Chek ngoen duay/kep tang duay?*
Or simply . . . .*Chek bill kaa/krup*
Excuse me (to get someone's attention)
Nong kaa/krup (for a younger person)
Pee kaa/krup (for an older person)

Days of the Week

Monday . . . . *Wan Chan*
Tuesday . . . . *Wan Angkaan*
Wednesday . . . . *Wan Pud*
Thursday . . . . *Wan Paruhat*
Friday . . . . *Wan Sook*
Saturday . . . . *Wan Sao*
Sunday . . . . *Wan Aa-thit*

Medical Terms

With thanks to the Bangkok Phuket Hospital

Aches . . . . *puad*
I have diarrhea . . . . *chan thong sia*
Headache . . . . *puad-hua*
I have constipation . . . . *chan thong phook*
Stomach ache . . . . *puad-thong*
I have a cold . . . . *chan pen wad*
Back ache . . . . *puad-lung*
Fever . . . . *khai*
Toothache . . . . *puad-fun*
Flu . . . . *khai wad yai*
Pains . . . . *jep, puad*
Dengue fever . . . . *khai luat auk*
Sore throat . . . . *jep-khaw*
Heart disease . . . . *rok-hua-jai*
My hand hurts . . . . *jep-meu*
Abscess/boil . . . . *fee*
My eye stings . . . . *seab ta*
Allergic/sensitive to . . . . *phae*
Broken bones . . . . *kra-duke-hak*
Can't breathe . . . . *hai-jai mai awk*
Broken leg . . . . *kha hak*
Dizzy . . . . *wian hua*
Cut/injuries . . . . *bat jep*
Faint . . . . *pen lom*
Cut/wound . . . . *phlae*
Itches . . . . *kun*
Infected . . . . *ak-sayp*

Shake/tremble . . . . *sun*
Swollen/inflamed . . . . *buam*
Unconscious . . . . *sa-lop / mot sa-tic*
Burns . . . . *mai*
Vomit . . . . *uak / a-jian*
Sunburn. . . . . *phiu mai / daet phao*
Weak . . . . *awn plea*
Illness . . . . *puay*
Drown. . . . . *jom nam*
I have a cough . . . . *chain ai*
Help . . . . *chuay duay*

Popular Thai Proverbs

Don't catch fish with both hands.

One rotten fish can make the whole catch smell bad.

Don't worry about being sick until the fever arrives.

Escape from a tiger's grasp into the jaws of a crocodile.

Politics

Thailand is different from Western countries both culturally and politically. Shortly before the 2005 elections the prime minister made incredible promises of jobs for everyone, free healthcare and schooling, land ownership for farmers and everyone would have more of everything if he was re-elected. Not even the most optimistic of Western politicians would make promises like that.

And in his book, *Thailand, a Short History*, David K. Wyatt writes, "Those who would rule Thailand face the challenge of placating and managing innumerable vested interests, legal and illegal. Some political groups are dominated by people who are deeply involved in activities that cover a broad range of illegality, from drugs and prostitution to gambling and smuggling." He added, "As ugly as that may be, there is much about Thailand that is good and even charming."

Tying the Knot

Valentine's Day is a popular day for Thais to marry. In Phuket, on that day in 2005, 321 couples registered their marriages. The *Gazette* had this quote from the Phuket chief administrator: "The atmosphere today was very happy, every couple was smiling. Some brides were pregnant, some couples brought their children with them, and some couples had just come from their wedding party."

Owning a Home

This is one section of the book where we are not going to be frivolous. Acquiring a home in Thailand can be an extremely expensive venture. We will stress throughout this section that it is vital that you get the best possible help, legal and financial, before you sign the first piece of paper.

We have heard too many horror stories of people thinking they have bought a home here to discover later, sometimes years later, that it is on land that is not theirs or, because of some legal loophole, the property is confiscated.

And these people aren't stupid. Many of them are well-to-do businessmen and women who have bought and sold property at home and who thought they were doing the right thing. What they did not consider is that they were doing business in Thailand, a country with its own way of handling matters, totally different from the land from which the buyer came.

One further hindrance to purchasing a home in Thailand is that under Thai law a foreigner, or farang, cannot own land in the kingdom. There are exceptions to that too, but only under certain circumstances and again you need the advice of a lawyer.

Legalities

There are two ways you can own a home here. The first is by forming a Thai company and the second by leasing the land.

■ Incorporation

Forming a company is relatively simple. Costs vary, but most people we have spoken to say it should cost less than 25,000 Baht. Our understanding is that the company has to have a minimum of seven stockholders, you and six Thais. At the time the company is formed you can only have a minority holding in the company and the Thais must have a minimum of 51%. At the same time, you get an undated share-transfer commitment from the Thais, which virtually gives you 100 percent control of the company. Again, we stress the need for proper professional advice. Just because you see our explanation here in black and white does not mean it is entirely correct.

There is a necessary annual maintenance fee for a public company, but to have this done and properly filed is inexpensive, about 1,500 Baht. At the present time there are no real estate taxes in Thailand, but, of course that can change. At one time there was no income tax in Britain, and people who live there know that changed.

■ Leasing

The second alternative is the long-term lease of land. Farangs can lease land on a 30-year contract with options for an additional 30 years, for a maximum of 90 years. These leases are recorded and registered at the Government Land Office, a national agency with regional offices. The law states that the landowner, and his or her heirs, has to honor the contract and that you, the lessee, can convey the lease to another party or deed it to your heirs.

The snag here is that the landowner could take legal action during the course of the lease to annul the contract. He or she would need to prove that you had done something to the property that made it less valuable than it was when you entered into the lease. An unlikely event perhaps, but something you should discuss with a professional.

■ Maintenance

Another point that many prospective buyers overlook is long-term maintenance. It is important to find out if you buy in a housing project what happens when the developer has sold all the land and homes. While the developer is selling you can be assured that landscaping and the public areas will be well maintained. Ask the question: What happens when you're gone? If the answer comes back that the local municipal authority will maintain the roads and street lights and pick up the garbage, beware.

If you are considering buying a condo, things work a little differently, and again, you need to arm yourself with good professional advice and guidance. If you want to learn more about living or buying in Thailand we have found two good Websites. The first, www.thaivisa.com, will give you a mountain of information on getting the right visas. You can learn about special visas for people over 50 who want to retire here and how that can be handled. The second site is www.thailawforum.com, which has numerous legal articles and also tells you how to find a lawyer, whether it be for civil matters like buying property or for criminal matters should you find yourself in trouble.

■ Household Help

Help around the home is easy to find most anywhere. And it comes at a low price. The minimum wage for laborers is 127 Baht a day and you can get a good housekeeper for about 6,000 Baht a month.

Despite what we have said about problems there are thousands of foreigners who have bought here without a hitch and those we have spoken to have never regretted their purchase. You only have to visit the food stores in the major cities to realize how many farangs live in Thailand either full-time or part-time; the shelves are packed with items from around the world. You'll find cake mixes from the US and salad dressings from the UK. And you know they are not being bought by the Thais.

If you can accept all of these issues, this kingdom is a wonderful place in which to live or spend more time. In most places it is safe, the people are charming, and the cost of living is very low.

Where to Buy?

We have limited ourselves to those areas where many foreigners already have established themselves – the southern islands of

Phuket and Samui; Pattaya and Hua Hin, both of which are within easy driving distance of Bangkok; and the northern city of Chiang Mai, a popular area with Thais who normally live in Bangkok and seek a cooler climate for their free time.

■ Phuket

At the start of 2005 there were over 150 housing projects in progress on this island. We have picked a few that we think give an idea of the range of homes and prices available.

Land & Houses, 80/15 Moo 7, Chaofa Road, Chalong, ☎ 07636 1150, fax 07638 1111, www.lhphuket.com. The Land & Houses company is Thailand's leading housing developer having built over 32,000 homes in the last 20 years. In addition to the project in Phuket they have properties elsewhere in the kingdom, in Bangkok, Chiang Mai, Khon Kaen, and Korat. We think this is a good place to begin looking for a home in Thailand since we feel the development offers the best value for money and it gives a varied range of properties and prices, which is helpful when you start looking elsewhere.

The concept here is that you can only buy a completed house. There are numerous different floor plans, but the company keeps its costs down by constructing many of the units identically. The homes were originally designed for the Thai market, but Ruksapong Khumkhuanjum, the general manager of L.H. Muang Mai Co. Ltd., told us that now more and more foreigners were buying.

The company only accepts freehold purchases, no lease options, so farangs would need to form a Thai company to buy here (see page 395). The big advantage is the fact that you are in a large, well-secured and established community. When complete this development will have over 500 homes in it.

The latest homes offered are situated around a lake and are the most expensive in the development, selling for as much as 12 million Baht. In other areas of the development new homes are available for as little as three million Baht. All are ready to move into. Since they are designed for the Thai market, prospective purchasers would have additional cost to pay if they want a Western-style kitchen.

Few of the homes come with their own swimming pool, but there is a large clubhouse complex that is extremely inexpensive to use and includes a pool, restaurant and indoor basketball court. Numerous activities take place here; during one visit ballet lessons were being offered. Our personal complaint is that it is a very big complex, although this does give you the advantage of lower per-home community fees, but we prefer something a little smaller. The development is centrally located, close to the Chalong roundabout, and adjoins Wat Chalong.

Nai Harn Baan-Bua, 24/28 Moo 1, Soi Naya, Rawai, ☎ 07638 8136, fax 07638 8103, www.phuketcasa.com. This is a delightful small project on the south end of Phuket, which has been a tremendous success for developer Akachai Koysombat. His initial projection was that his first phase would take five years to complete, and it was completed in three. The second phase is selling quickly. He has developed a superb environment that has attracted buyers from all parts of the world. Every house is custom-built to fit the particular lot. Kuhn Akachai has not built any spec houses but does have numerous designs which are customized to client's needs. Each home is different but they all share the same Thai-Balinese architecture.

Complete home prices here start at $300,000. As at Land & Houses, homes here can only be bought freehold, so foreigners need to form a Thai company (see page 395).

The development is a gated community with two entrances. The main one is attractively set between two low-lying fields where the water buffalo roam. The second one is a shortcut to Nai Harn beach, an area that has undergone a beautification project. The landscaping throughout the development is impressive and by maintaining control of the design and positioning of each home to suit the terrain the developer has created an ideal setting for those seeking a home just for holidays or for full-time living.

Villa Santi, 328 Prabaramee Road, Patong Beach, ☎ 07629 0324, fax 07634 4847, www.phuket-villa-santi.com. Upmarket luxury apartments and villas on a seven-acre hillside facing Patong Bay. Here you get the choice of three different homes that you can live in year-round or rent out when you're away from Phuket. Views from the complex are stunning. When complete the resort-cum-home complex will have 20 spa villas, 22 apartment suites and eight full-sized homes. Highlights of the landscaping are two natural pools and a waterfall. The complex will have its own swimming pool, a spa, gourmet restaurant, reception area, fitness center, tennis and squash courts and covered parking area.

Royal Phuket Marina, 68 Moo 2, Thepkassattri Road, Kohkaew, ☎ 07623 9762, fax 0623 9756, www.royalphuketmarina.com. This is a vast upmarket project on Phuket's eastern shore where 400 luxury villas and apartments are being built around a marina.

Apartment prices start at $300,000 and villas are being offered at $1,400,000. Many of the homes were bought before the first apartment was completed; early buyers were from Hong Kong seeking a holiday retreat. When it is complete the complex will have an elaborate shopping complex and a wide range of restaurants. Earlier developments in the area were not so attractive. In its early promotion the developer promised, "Royal Phuket Marina will be far more than just one of the world's best marinas. It will be a complete community, with more than half of the development devoted to leisure and shopping facilities amidst superbly landscaped parks and gardens."

Ban Prangthong, 10/2 Kwaang Road, Phuket, ☎ and fax 07626 3294, www.bangprangthong.com. This is an older, larger development midway between Chalong and Phuket City, which is getting a new lease on life with the introduction of new homes. Three different styles are offered. The least expensive, the **Villa Wichit** with 230 square meters of living space, is offered at 8.4 million Baht, and the largest, **Villa Piman** with 350 square meters, has a price of 11.9 million Baht. Biggest advantage here is that all services are already installed and the roads and entrances complete.

Here briefly are three other projects that were underway when we went looking: **L'Orchidée Residences**, 13/2, Soi 4, Prabaramee Road, Patong Beach, ☎ 07629 0404, fax 07634 1612, www.lorchidee-residences. Twenty-eight two-story modern Thai-style villas are planned for a site that should enjoy good views to Patong Bay. Floor plans look great but the approach road is not the easiest to navigate. **Kamala Orchid Estates**, 65/1, Moo 5, Kamala Beach, ☎ 01891 7499, fax: 07627 9530, www.kamala-orchid-estate.com. A neat private enclave on the quieter Kamala Beach area north of Patong, where just seven luxury villas, each with its own pool, are being constructed. One of the few developments we've seen where the developer will help you finance part of the construction costs with a Thai bank. **Phuket Forest Hill**, 120/24 Ratutit, 200 Pee Road., Patong Beach, ☎ 07634 1465, fax 07634 1466, www.phuketforesthill.com. A modest, less expensive development of 21 homes, all priced under $150,000 with a choice of three home styles. Biggest drawback here in our opinion is that the development is right below the hill that carries traffic out of Patong. At night the sound of trucks shifting gears to make the gradient may prove a little noisy.

■ Samui

In many ways the island of Samui provides a quieter and more relaxed way of living than the busy bustle of Phuket. Many farangs have already set up home here, either as a holiday haven or as a permanent place to live or retire. Two major essentials, health and education, were supplied when the Bangkok Hospital group opened the Bangkok Samui Hospital and Dulwich College opened up its doors. The mega-projects of Phuket don't appear here and the demand for waterfront property has sent prices soaring as there is only a limited amount of land available for home construction. A major attraction here is that planning rules seem to be adhered to and the high rises of Pattaya don't put a blot on the landscape.

Many of the new homes are being constructed away from the coast and you can expect to spend more on a home here than in many other parts of Thailand.

Villas at Napasai, www.pansea.com/samuires. These are the nicest ready-to-move-into villas we have seen anywhere in Thailand. The big advantage here is that the homes will be managed and maintained by Pansea Orient-Express Hotels. The disadvantage is the cost. By the time you're ready to move in expect to spend over a million dollars for one of the smaller two-bedroom villas. There are a total of 14 villas and they are linked to the Napasai resort (see page 279, *Beyond Phuket* chapter). It means you get to use all the resort facilities, and the resort will rent out your villa if you want the income when you're not in residence. Each of the villas is set high enjoying great sea views, has its own swimming pool and sala, and much of the furniture is built in. Despite the high prices, several of the homes were sold as soon as they were completed.

Royal Living Resident, 7/9-16 Moo 6, Bang Po, ☎ 07742 0670, fax 07732 0673, www.royalliving.de. This pleasant little development caught our eye because of its good beach location. The developer is retired German schoolteacher Heinz Woolenheil who has constructed nine villas around a pool and now manages the property for owners. There are still a couple of villas for sale – asking price over 16 million Baht – or you can rent one by the day, month or year. High-season rental rates are 7,700 Baht a night but the longer you stay the less you pay per night. There are no restaurant or spa facilities on the site but both are available across the street. Friendly atmosphere and fairly priced for Samui.

It comes as no surprise that real estate offices are appearing all over the island to handle the property boom that is taking place. One of the larger operations is **Samui Villas & Homes Co. Ltd.**, ☎ 07742 7648, fax 07742 7649, www.samuivillasandhomes.com. This international team can handle everything from finding a site, designing a home and arranging for construction. If you want income from your investment they handle rentals and if all else fails their sales department can find you a buyer.

■ Hua Hin

Foreigners are now learning what the Thai royal family discovered back in the 1920s: Hua Hin and its environs is a great place to set up a second home. There's a wide range of homes available, from small inexpensive two-bedroom chalets to large apartments in very high-rise buildings. Prices here seemed higher than Pattaya but lower than Samui or Phuket. There's a long stretch of coastline stretching from Pranburi in the south to Cha-am in the north where property is available.

We found the area to be more Thai than foreign but realtors told us that many Europeans are now looking at homes in the area. We were surprised when we visited the beach of north Cha-am that it was entirely Thai, with few signs in English, and we did not see a restaurant along the beachfront offering European food. It was interesting to note that the deck chairs were arranged in squares for family groups, and all of them very much in the shade. Thais come here for holidays, we were told, but the last thing they wanted was a suntan. Europeans seek tanned skin, but most Thais prefer pale skin.

Hua Hin Blue Lagoon Resort, Petchkasem Highway, three kilometers from Hua Hin town, ☎ 02650 5115 or 03244 2531. This is a planned development of condominiums, villas and a hotel and the complex will have a large lake as its centerpiece. Plans call for the Sheraton organization to operate the hotel, which is scheduled to be operational by early 2006. When complete the complex will have 108 condominiums, priced from 7 million Baht and 37 villas with a starting price of 11.5 million Baht. There is a model apartment available for viewing.

Hua Hin Sunset-Village, 11/48 Soi Mooban Samorprong, Hua Hin, ☎ 07006 4508, www.huahinsunset-village.com. This is a lower-cost development, with homes starting as low as 3.6 million Baht. All homes here are custom built and several are under construction. Top-of-the-line home here is a 255-square-meter house with pool with a price under 7 million Baht.

Santi Pura Boutique Resort Condominium, ☎ 03257 2191, www.santipura.com. This new eight-acre development currently under construction is a 12-minute drive from the center of Hua Hin on the beach close to the Pranburi National Park. A total of 77 units are planned in five low-rise buildings. Developer Songkran Grachangnetara says, "There are so many products out there catered to the mass-market – residential homes, high-rise condos – but virtually nothing for customers looking for something more personal – something that's tailored especially to suit their tastes."

Palm Hills Golf Resort & Country Club, ☎ 03252 0800, fax 03252 0820, www.palmhills-golf.com. This is a planned development of expensive and elegant villa homes set around a golf course in Cha-am.

Observer Property, The Observer Group Co., the company that publishes newspapers such as the monthly *Hua Hin Observer*, is also involved in property. It has model homes of Thai and European-style golfing villas in different locations in Hua Hin and Cha-am, ☎ 01944 9372, www.observergroup.net.

■ Pattaya

Of all the areas where we looked at property, Pattaya appeared to be the least expensive, with heavy emphasis on reasonably priced condos and apartments. The English-language newspaper, the *Pattaya Mail*, www.pattayamail.com, is filled with real estate advertising in every issue. Two realtors with Websites are **Pattaya Realty Company Ltd.**, 325/9 Pattayaland 2, ☎ 03841 2301, www.propertypattya.com and **Pat Properties & Services Co., Ltd.**, www.pat-properties.com.

Siam Royal View, 143/47-48, Moo 12, Thepprasit Soi 10, Thepprasit Road, Banglamung, ☎ 03832 2640, fax 03832 2644, www.siam-royal-view.com. This large housing development with several hundred homesites three kilometers inland from Jomtien Beach. Small two-bedroom villas are available for less than three million Baht plus the cost of the land. The elevation gives views across the Gulf and the developer promises a wide range of facilities, including a medical center, for homeowners. There are five different villa styles available, the largest being a four-bedroom home that sells for 10.4 million Baht plus the cost of the land.

Northshore Condominium, Pattaya Beach Road, north of the Hard Rock Hotel and south of the Dusit resort, ☎ 03872 3615, www.northshorepattaya.com. This high-rise twin-tower condo building is being planned as the number one apartment address in Pattaya. Buyers have a choice of one, two and three-bedroom units ranging in size from 64 to 268 square meters. Each floor on the south-facing tower is devoted to a single unit, with its residents enjoying spectacular views over Pattaya Bay, Jomtien and the Gulf of Thailand.

■ Chiang Mai

Chiang Mai has become a popular summer retreat for more affluent Thais. While most of Thailand has its hottest time during March, April and May, the Chiang Mai area is relatively cool. Many of the new homes are seasonal residences, not used during the winter months, since their owners return to Bangkok and other cities; not unlike Florida's snowbirds who travel south to avoid the winter cold, and northwards to avoid the summer heat.

Local Developers

Koolpunt Property Co. Ltd., 333 Moo 13 Chiangmai-Hangdong Road, Hangdong, ☎ 05343 1888, www.koolpuntville.com. This company has been in business for 15 years and not only sells homes but has also developed several residential areas in and around Chiang Mai. Their services include finding home sites and all phases of construction.

Satihoga-Tropical Homes Co. Ltd., 79/157 Moo 2, Chiang Mai-Doi Saket Road, Taladkhuan, ☎ 09266 2289, www.chiangmai-property.thailand-real-estate.info. This company's Website gives you a good idea of the properties and prices available in the area. It also proclaims, "We cannot assist you in financing property in Thailand." Saves any misunderstanding later.

■ Financing for Farangs

In late 2005 there was a move by some Thai banks offering financing to farangs for home buying, but on a very limited scale. Initially, loans are only available on condominiums, and the maximum amount that will be financed is 25% of the purchase price.

■ Home Building

We spent more than a month watching a home being constructed across from the house we were renting in Phuket. This provided an intriguing insight into Thai construction practices. Most amazing is the fact that almost all of the heavy humping and heaving is undertaken by women, most of them young and weighing less than the items they carry. They all wear Wellington boots, surely not the most cooling footwear in this tropical climate. Their bodies are covered in what appears to be heavy clothing, and their faces are smeared with light-colored mud, which we assume is for sun protection.

The pace of work is slow but continuous, and the results of a very high standard. Work begins before 8am and continues until dark. Occasionally floodlights are brought in and work continues for a few more hours. Men take on the more skilled crafts as masons, carpenters, plumbers and electricians. There are very few breaks, and work continues through the rain (it's scary to hear electric saws and drills while the skies pour down torrents of water). We have even seen a painter at work in the rain – his broad-brimmed hat kept the water away from the area he was painting.

Construction continues through weekends at the same steady pace. Laborers are entitled to one day off a week, but from what we see many work on, grateful for the double-time they receive for working on that seventh day. Minimum rate for construction workers is around 200 Baht a day ($4.50), and nobody seems unhappy, judging by their smiles and cheerful chattering.

Everything is put together on-site. Nothing comes preassembled. The only concrete that was not mixed on-site was for the driveway; a truck arrived and poured that. Otherwise, it's the girls mixing and carrying up to the masons. Where else in the world could you put so many women to work on a building site without distracting the men?

■ Real Estate Agents

The following area real estate agents have Websites and also have English-speaking staff.

Hua Hin Property Shop, 222 Petchkasem Road, Hua Hin (in front of the Grand Hotel) ☎ 03251 6485, fax 03251 6486, www.huahin-property-shop.com.

Manora Co. Ltd.,1/10 Sra Song Road, Hua Hin, ☎ 03253 0532, www.manoraproperty.com.

Skandi Real Estate Co. Ltd., 130/3 Chomsin Road, Hua Hin, ☎ 03251 3966, fax 03251 4238, www.skandiproperty.com.

Stone Head Company Ltd., Tanawit Plaza, 18/4 Soi Amnuaysin, Petchkasem Road, ☎ 03253 1038, www.Stone-Head.com.

■ Useful Websites

Real Estate Information Center, ☎ 02202 1760, www.reic.or.th

The Thai Real Estate Association, ☎ 02229 3188, www.thairealestate.org

Agency for Real Estate Affairs Co., ☎ 02295 2294, www.area.co.th

The Thai Valuers Association, ☎ 02260 3880, www.tva.or.th

The Real Estate Broker Association, ☎ 02986 5388, www.reba.or.th

The Association of Siamese Architects, ☎ 02319 4124, www.asa.or.th

The Thai Contractors Association, ☎ 02255 3991, www.tca.or.th

Medical Vacations

IN THIS CHAPTER

This is one of the fastest-growing sectors of tourism in Thailand, but the least explored by guidebooks or promoted by tourism authorities. Other countries in Asia have attempted to attract foreigners to their medical facilities, but none have been as successful as Thailand. Estimates suggest that around one million people visited Thailand in 2005 to take advantage of its wonderful, extensive and inexpensive medical services. There are now close to 500 private hospitals and clinics in the country most with extremely well-trained medical staff able to perform practically every modern medical procedure.

The idea of coming to Thailand for medical treatment is not new, but the current growth began in 1997. Bangkok's Bumrungrad Hospital, searching for new sources of income at the time of the Southeast Asian financial crisis, decided to look overseas to promote its procedures.

Since then, medical visits by Westerners have become the multi-million dollar business that we see today. Experts tell us that something close to 23 billion Baht will be injected into the Thai economy thanks to "medical vacations." Many hospitals and clinics report that more than 30% of their income is derived from foreigners. If that money were to diminish it would have a tremendous impact on the Thai medical service, forcing many institutions to either downsize or close.

The Thai government more recently saw the benefits of the medical vacation and decided to establish three areas in the country – Bangkok, Phuket and Chiang Mai – as the kingdom's medical centers. All three continue to attract patients from overseas, but the primary markets for North Americans and Europeans have been Bangkok and Phuket.

Health & Wellness

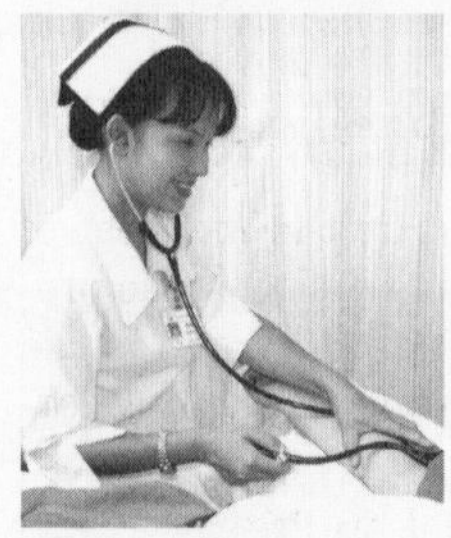

Phuket International Hospital has produced an elaborate coffee-table book, *Healthy Living in Phuket*, with over 100 pages of information about healthcare and living in Phuket and Thailand. It covers everything from snake bites to sexual encounters, and gives both the positive and negative aspects of life on this tropical island. If you're thinking of moving to Thailand or coming for any medical procedures the book is required reading. The hospital produced the work as a community project. It is supported by advertising, which explains the low cost of 450 Baht. For contact information see page 412.

Most visitors taking medical vacations are here for minor items, like general check-ups, or dental- and eye-care examinations. They take just a day out from their time touring or beachcombing to visit a hospital or clinic for an overall health check. Most hospitals don't even require appointments for these visits. You arrive early in the morning and a few hours later leave with a report giving you a breakdown of what's right and wrong.

If you choose one of the more expensive packages you can expect an in-depth examination, which will normally include a discussion with a specialist about how you can maintain or improve your health.

Others come for more elaborate procedures. Knee and hip replacements are common. And a great benefit here is that if you opt for a hospital in a tourist area you can enjoy all the benefits of a Thai resort for convalescence.

Call Me Mister

Surprisingly, perhaps, the number-one operation sought by foreigners is the sex-change procedure for which Thailand is noted as the world leader. Many of the country' top surgeons give symposiums sharing their knowledge with visiting physicians from different parts of the globe.

Thai doctors have developed expertise in the complex operation of turning females into males, which attract clients from around the globe but especially from Japan.

Practicalities

Cost

Potential patients from the US are attracted by the low cost of medical care in Thailand. Despite the weakened dollar, some procedures can cost as little as one-eighth of the price charged in the US. We were unable to get exact figures of how many North Americans visited Thailand for a medical vacation but some estimates put it as high as 50,000 a year. Considerably more Europeans, dissatisfied with the health systems in their home countries, welcome the rapid response that the Thai hospitals and doctors offer.

We met one woman who came to Thailand for a breast implant. She said she paid a total of $2,500 for the procedure. That price included all the doctors and nursing costs, medicine and an overnight stay in a very pleasant room. She was impressed with the attention she received, the fine food and most of all she was delighted with her new look. She told us that she would have paid $5,000 in the US for just the surgeon's fee.

One reason for the lower costs is lower payrolls. Many of the Thai doctors we met are qualified to practice in the US and other parts of the world but opt to work in their homeland. And the reason isn't money. Doctors' salaries in Thailand are significantly lower than that of their counterparts in the US, perhaps only a third. Another major area of saving is that Thai hospitals and doctors don't have to pay the extraordinary costs to protect themselves against horrendous malpractice claims.

What happens if something does go wrong? Unhappy patients can make a formal complaint to the Thai Medical Association, which investigates. On some occasions that organization has taken criminal proceedings against doctors and hospitals. It is also possible to sue doctors and hospitals. Most of these cases get settled out of court but don't expect the mega compensation payments that plague the US medical system.

Referrals

Although it is extremely unlikely that Western doctors would recommend or forward their patients to Thailand, we did talk to two US doctor friends and neither offered any negative comments about medicine in Thailand. One, in fact, had previously had dental work done in Bangkok and he was extremely complimentary about the work.

Insurance & Claims

Insurance companies, in business to make money, normally have no problems settling claims with Thai hospitals. Provided their client has coverage for a particular medical procedure, the lower the claim the better. One insurance agent did tell us, however, that the companies were now asking for more than one quote for elective surgery since there had been wide deviations in prices from Thai hospitals.

No figures are available about how much income the Thai hospitals derive from insurance over individuals paying directly but sources estimate it to be less than 50%.

Many visitors say that the amount they save on their bills with doctors and hospitals more than covers their airfare and hotel stay. There are those contemplating surgery who first visit for a medical check-up just to get an insight of the hospital's operations before committing to something more extensive.

Hospitals

Medical facilities catering to foreign visitors make an effort to train their staff in creating a friendly environment more like a hotel than a hospital. Gone is that cold antiseptic aura. Replacing it is pleasant music, delicate aromas from scented oil burners and quiet cafeterias.

If anyone doubts the efficiency of the hospitals, they should have been here after the tsunami struck southern Thailand on December 26, 2004. Phuket's hospitals were swamped with patients and throughout it all we never heard of one complaint, only praise for the treatment and help the hospitals gave. Not only did they handle the medical problems, the hospitals set up special multilingual teams to help foreigners who were searching for relatives and friends lost in the tragic event.

■ Bangkok & Phuket

We have selected four hospitals that have international sales departments to attract and help potential clients. All have elaborate Websites where you can get a very good idea of their capabilities. Rooms at all three are of a high quality and compare well to a three- or four-star hotel. We estimate that the hospitals we selected account for about 70% of the market.

Bumrungrad Hospital, 33 Sukhumvit 3, Wattana, Bangkok, ☎ 02667 1000, fax 02667 2525, www.bumrungrad.com. This is where the Thai medical vacations we see today became popular. This is a big hospital with centers for everything, and it has to be the number-one spot in Thailand, favored by farangs seeking medical help. The hospital sees 850,000 Thais and foreigners a year. Patients come from over 100 countries and the hospital's Website is available in 15 languages. You can select prices from a menu; for specialized needs they'll promptly send you a quote. Prices in Bangkok will tend to be higher than in Phuket simply because capital cities are always more expensive than other areas. Hospital charges start as low as 1,350 Baht for a basic check-up and, if you're prepared to share a room with three others, the nightly charge is only 800 Baht. A VIP suite costs 7,200 Baht a night. The hospital also operates the BH Residence, a 74-room serviced apartment complex that caters to the needs of patients, family and visitors to Bumrungrad Hospital. The Residence is connected by an air conditioned elevated walkway to the hospital and provides several kinds of accommodation at reasonable prices.

Bangkok Phuket Hospital, 2/1 Hongyok Utis Road, Phuket, ☎ 07625 4421, fax 07625 4430, www.phukethospital.com. We selected this hospital since it is part of the Bangkok Hospital group, the largest integrated hospital group in Southeast Asia. We spent an entire day here seeing the incredible range of services that are available. Most of the hospitals we list farther on have similar programs so it is worth shopping around.

Bangkok Phuket is designed rather like a shopping mall with its varied assortment of services. They include a heart center, manned by some of the top cardiac surgeons in Thailand (including the King's personal physician); the rejuvenation center, where Thailand's traditional medicines are combined with modern-day techniques to help alleviate stress-related illnesses; an aesthetic center devoted to all forms of cosmetic surgery including sex reassignment operations (a procedure in which Thailand leads the world); dental center that handles everything from laser cleaning to denture construction; eye center, where the latest laser technology is used to correct vision; cancer center offering a full range of treatments and support services; and a hyperbaric oxygen therapy center originally designed to help scuba divers in distress but also being used as therapy in treating a range of diseases. There are also centers for dialysis (6,500 Baht a session), hearing and rehabilitation.

For us, the main attraction of entire facility was that it was run more like a quiet resort. There were none of the antiseptic smells, just the pleasant fragrances of jasmine, lemon grass and lotus. In the central lobby, gentle Thai music was provided by a lady playing a *khim*, the Thai instrument that looks like a small xylophone. The hospital rooms were large, fully equipped with TV and refrigerator and enjoyed pleasant views. They cost a reasonable 3,000 Baht a night. The hospital has a total of 200 rooms. It is presently expanding with what assistant hospital director Dr. Sompoch Nipakanont describes as a "boutique hospital" that will enable them to handle up to 1,000 outpatients every day.

It is interesting to note that the hospital is managed by doctors, not by businessmen or accountants and the Bangkok hospital company was founded by a doctor.

The hospital employs 500 people, 60 of them doctors, and 55 of those are specialists. The hospital's travel center offers a complete range of packages for people who want to link a hospital visit with their vacation. Costs start as low as 1,500 Baht for a basic health check-up to 300,000 Baht for sex reassignment surgery. For a more comprehensive check-up expect to pay 10,000 Baht. At the end of that you get to discuss the results with a specialist physician. You leave with a booklet detailing the results of all the tests. The hospital retains the information too for comparison purposes should you return for a later examination.

Most of the packages include being met at the airport and a hotel stay after medical procedures. An eight-day breast augmentation package, which includes all the medical costs and a stay at a hotel after the procedure, costs around 100,000 Baht. A three-day tooth-whitening-by-laser package sells for around 20,000 Baht, depending on the resort you pick. And you can get a week-long stay in Phuket and have both your eyes adjusted with a Lasik treatment for as little as 85,500 Baht.

Dr. Adam Hickenbotham, a graduate of the University of California, director of international patient care for the Lasik eye center, says that prices for a similar treatment in the US or Europe would be more than double the prices offered in Phuket. Dr. Hickenbotham previously worked in the Lasik Center in Bangkok, which was the first such center to open in Asia. He came to Phuket when the center first opened at the end of 2004. Initially the center had two surgeons, both longtime laser operatives.

Demand was so great for the treatment that additional surgeons were recruited just weeks after the center opened.

The travel center can also arrange packages for knee and hip replacements with the added advantage you can recuperate on the beach.

The **Bangkok Hospital**, ☎ 02310 3101, fax 02310 3367, www.bangkokhospital.com, is the parent of the Bangkok Phuket hospital. The hospital, by far the largest of all the Bangkok hospital chain, offers all the services of the Bangkok Phuket Hospital, plus a few more. Since it is in the capital, prices tend to be a little higher than at the regional hospitals (see below).

Phuket International Hospital, 44 Chalemprakiat Ror 9 Road, Phuket, ☎ 07624 9400, fax 07621 0938, www.phuket-inter-hospital.co.th. A major competitor of the Bangkok Phuket Hospital, the Phuket International Hospital offers many similar services, some of which are at a lower price. The hospital, with 105 beds and more planned, is centrally located amid pleasant gardens across from the Tesco Lotus shopping center. In addition to modern-day medicine, the hospital has a large unit devoted to traditional Oriental remedies. Director of that center is Dr. Wang Pengyao, a graduate of China's Tianjin University. The center specializes in acupuncture, Chinese massage, cupping – using a partial vacuum in jars placed on the skin to draw out underlying tissue – and herbal medicines. These treatments are used for numerous problems including allergies, asthma, arthritis, stress, weight control, strains and sprains, and can assist in helping smokers quit. The hospital offers a basic health check-up for 2,100 Baht. A more in-depth check-up for women over 40 is available at 9,100 Baht. No appointments needed for the check-ups. Just be at the hospital at 9am, Monday thru Friday, and don't eat or drink anything for at least 10 hours before going to the hospital. Room rates are as low as 600 Baht a night, climbing to 2,000 Baht a night for an impressive private room. Those prices do include meals but not nursing fees.

The hospital was founded in 1982, the first private hospital to open in the area. It has over 50 full- and part-time physicians under the supervision of medical director Dr. Anuroj Tharasiriroj, who leads this professional and caring team of dedicated individuals. The hospital has an International Office with multi-lingual staff that assists international patients and referring physicians looking for a consultation, a second opinion or treatment for a complex illness or injury.

During the tsunami the hospital attracted worldwide attention when, with the aid of the local English-language newspaper *The Phuket Gazette*, it was able to find the family of a two-year-old Scandinavian boy who was found lost and alone in Khao Lak. The boy was brought to the hospital, which arranged for his photograph to appear on the *Gazette's* Website. An uncle in Finland recognized the lad. The youngster was eventually reunited with his father, who had been injured by the giant waves. Sadly, his mother was never found. The hospital's motto: Caring People, Curing People.

■ Chiang Mai

If your travel plans do not include Bangkok or Phuket, we have included two Chiang Mai hospitals that provide service for international clients.

Chiang Mai Ram Hospital, Boonleungrit Road, ☎ 05322 4851, fax 05322 4880, www.chiangmairam.com. This modern high-rise hospital is close to Chiang Mai's largest shopping center, Kad Saun Klaew. The facility can handle up to 1,000 outpatients a day with accommodation for 350 inpatients. There is a heart center, and clinics tackle infertility, pain and plastic surgery. There is a varicose vein clinic every Saturday morning.

Integrated Medical Clinic, 54/9 Singharat Road, Chiang Mai, ☎ 05340 0242, fax 05374 0337, www.dreddyclinic.com. Integrated medicine is, according to this clinic, the holistic wisdom of the past, the scientific knowledge of the present and the wave of the future, here today. The clinic combines Western medicine with complementary and alternative medicine and mind-body-spirit approaches to health and healing. Specialties include: Food and allergy management through the use of integrated medical therapy, chronic fatigue, autism, natural thyroid replacement, weight loss and lyme disease.

The following hospitals are related to the Bangkok hospital group and have Websites showing the services they offer.

■ Regional

Bangkok Pattaya Hospital, 301 Moo 6, Sukhumvit Road, Km. 143, Pattaya, ☎ 03842 7777, fax 03842 7777, www.bangkokpattayahospital.com.

Bangkok Rayong Hospital, 8 Moo 2 Soi Saeng Chan Neramit, Rayong, ☎ 03861 2999, fax 03861 0777, www.rayonghospital.com.

Bangkok Hat Yai Hospital, 54/113 Moo 3, Klongrean 1 Road, Hat Yai, ☎ 07436 5780, fax 07436 5790, www.bangkokhatyai.com.

Bangkok Samui Hospital, 57 Moo 3, Thaweerat Phakdee Road, Bophut, ☎ 07742 9500, fax 07742 9505, www.samuihospital.com.

Traditional Thai Medicine

A book on medical care in Thailand would be incomplete without some mention of its traditional medicine. Western medical practice is a feature in modern-day Thailand, but the three traditional methods of healing are still practiced throughout the nation, particularly in the rural areas. The first is herbal medicines, the second is massage, and the third is psycho-spiritual healing.

Herbal Medicine

The herbs are usually classified into their tastes and flavors to decide their best use. Bitter medicines cure jaundice and help with allergies. Salty medicines help used to work on ulcers and for skin infections, chili-hot medicines help with digestive problems, sweet medicines are used for helping with respiratory problems and good to alleviate physical exhaustion. Cool, menthol herbs are used for combating various poisons, and pungent herbs are used for fast-acting medicines.

Bangkok's **Chulalongkom University**, www.chula.ac.th (be sure to click on to the English version) has determined that there are 300 species of herbal plants in Thailand that have positive pharmaceutical applications. The major benefit of herbal medicines is that the ingredients are cheap and locally produced.

Massage

We have mentioned places and prices of Thai massage earlier in the book. Not only is it wonderfully relaxing, it has a major role as a medical therapy. Authentic Thai massage comes in three phases, the most familiar being the rubbing and kneading of **muscles**. At the next level is the chiropractic manipulation of **skeletal** parts. The last of the phases is acupressure, using deep and consistent pressure applied to specific **nerves**, **tendons** or **ligaments** in order to balance the functions of the body. Wat Pho in Bangkok has the official responsibility of maintaining the standards of Thai massage. You may arrange to have a massage at that temple or to take a course in Thai massage. There are more details about this on page 66.

Psycho-spiritual Healing

Meditation is another healing tradition that brings visitors to Thailand. This aspect of traditional Thai medicine, called *raksaa thaang nai,* translates to inner healing. The practice involves meditation on ones own or with the help of a qualified healer. This form of healing is normally for medical problems that have no apparent physical cause. In many ways it is similar to treatments by hypnosis and is often used as a last resort when other treatments have failed.

■ Meditation Centers

International Buddhist Meditation Center (IBMC), Mahachulalongkornrajvidyalaya University, Wat Mahathat, Tha Phrachan, Bangkok, ☎ 02623 6326. Meditation instruction given at the temple complex in English, as well as Thai, by monks from the university, which we won't spell out again. Lectures on insight meditation are held on the last Saturday of each month from 3pm to 5pm. Eight-day retreats are available in English.

Wat Mahathat, Section Five, Wat Mahathat, Tha Phrachan, Bangkok, ☎ 02623 5325, fax 02222 4981. English instruction can be arranged. Meditation times daily from 7am-10am, 1-4pm and 6-8pm. Dormitories are available.

World Fellowship of Buddhists, 616 Benjasiri Park, Sukhumvit Road, Bangkok, ☎ 02261 1284, fax 02661 0555, www.wfb_hq.org. There is a morning Dhamma talk on the first Sunday of every month. Sometimes help is available in English.

House of Dhamma (Vipassana) Insight Meditation Center, 26/9 Soi 15, Lat Phrao Road, Bangkok, ☎ 02511 0439, fax 02512 6083. One-day, weekend and eight-day retreats all conducted in English.

Vivek Asom Vipassana Meditation Center, Ban Suan, Chonburi, ☎ 03828 3766.

Sorn-Thawee Meditation Center, 80 Moo 3, Sanet Nua, Bang Khla, Chachoengsao, ☎ 03854 1405. Participants here are expected to practice up to 20 hours a day either in the meditation halls or the center's cottages.

The **Suan Mokkh Forest Monastery**, 68/1 Lamet, Surat Thani, ☎ 07743 1596, fax 07743 1597, www.suanmokkh.org. Ten-day meditation retreats in English are held at the start of every month. Participants are expected to pay 1,200 Baht for staying at the International Dharma Heritage.

Wat Khao Tham International Meditation Center, Wat Khao Tham, Ko Pha-nga, Surat Thani. Well known for its regular 10-day retreats but does offer longer stays for experienced meditators. Neither this center nor the following one have telephones, best way to contact is in advance by mail.

Wat Pah Nanachart, Ban Bung Wai, Ubon Ratchathani. This monastery can only accommodate a few participants but English is spoken.

Afterword

All books should have a happy ending so, rather than end with the medical vacation section – which may not be that happy if you are planning to have something replaced or removed – we will finish with a list of our favorite hotels. All of them are happy places.

This is a good place to ask you to forgive any errors or omissions in the book. We are two mortals capable of mistakes. If you would like to correct us on any items, or add comments of your own, we would be pleased to hear from you. Simplest way to contact us is by e-mail – cevans@readysoft.es – this will find us wherever we might be in the world. Hopefully we will be able to include your comments in future editions of this guide.

Now we come to the part where we say thanks to those who helped us compile this volume. We greatly appreciate the efforts of Khuns Alex, Anchalee, Bandhit, Bobby, Boonsong, Chaiwat, Dan, Don B., Fiona, Franck, Franz, Hugh, Janice, Jaruwan, JO, John B., Kathryn, Kenneth, Kevin C., Niti, Noot, Oithip, Peter C., Peter D., Prajuah, Rod, Ruksapong, Sanit, Sao, Sari, Sirinya, Siripun Sompoch and Thip. Finally we must make special mention of our dear friend Khun Jarinee whose support was invaluable. She spent endless hours helping us. This is a lady whose kindness and friendship we will always treasure.

Christopher and Lindsey Evans

Top 20 Hotels

We've picked 20 hotels that we like very well. They all have something special that we find attractive. We admit that we have not seen all the hotels in the kingdom; that would be almost impossible. Phuket alone has 540 hotels and that's just one island. Our list is based on personal knowledge.

Evason Hideaway & Six Senses Spa, Hua Hin: The latest in luxury retreats, small and exceptional. See page 134.

Holiday Inn, Patong, Phuket: Busakorn wing rooms provide inexpensive luxury in a town not noted for top quality. Page 232.

InterContinental Hotel, Bangkok: Large, lavish and close to super shopping. Page 95.

JW Marriot, Bangkok: Capital city quality at out-of-town prices. Page 95.

Mandarin Oriental Dhara Dhevi, Chiang Mai: Spectacular décor and decadence. Page 302.

Mom Tri's Villa Royale Hotel & Spa, Phuket: A double delight. Page 326.

Nakamanda Resort & Spa, Krabi: A great welcome is the extra touch. Page 259.

Napasai Resort & Spa, Ko Samui: Cottages over the sea are stunning. Page 280.

Oriental, Bangkok: A slice of Thai history. Page 94.

Pimalai Resort & Spa, Ko Lanta: Spa-tacular and relaxing. Page 269.

Poppies Samui Resort, Ko Samui: Cozy, comfortable amid lush gardens. Page 281.

Shangri-La Hotel, Bangkok: Swift, silent service is a specialty. Page 94.

Sofitel Central, Hua Hin: Elegant and graceful. Page 133.

Sofitel Raja Orchid, Khon Kaen: Truly affordable luxury inland. Page 344.

Sugar Hut Resort, Pattaya: A breath of fresh air in Pattaya. Page 157.

The Racha, Racha Island: Truly a resort away from it all. Page 234.

Tohsang Khongjiam, Khong Chiam: Blissful bungalows alongside the Mekong River. Page 335.

Trisara, Cherngtalay, Phuket: Finest in so many way. Page 224.

TwinPalms, Surin Beach, Phuket: Modern Thai with old world courtesy. Page 227.

Sak Phu Duen Resort, Pak Chong: A touch of class in the country. Page 326.

Index

T

U

V

W

Z